URBAN
REINVENTIONS

URBAN REINVENTIONS

San Francisco's Treasure Island

Edited by

Lynne Horiuchi and Tanu Sankalia

University of Hawai'i Press
Honolulu

This publication is made possible in part by the University of San Francisco, College of Arts and Sciences, Faculty Development Fund.

Printed in the United States of America

22 21 20 19 18 17   6 5 4 3 2 1

Library of Congress Cataloging-in-Publication Data
Names: Horiuchi, Lynne, editor. | Sankalia, Tanu, editor.
Title: Urban reinventions : San Francisco's Treasure Island / edited by
    Lynne Horiuchi and Tanu Sankalia.
Description: Honolulu : University of Hawai'i Press, [2017] | Includes index.
Identifiers: LCCN 2016058320 | ISBN 9780824866020 (cloth ; alk. paper)
Subjects: LCSH: Treasure Island (San Francisco, Calif.)—History.
Classification: LCC F869.S36 U73 2017 | DDC 979.4/61—dc23
LC record available at https://lccn.loc.gov/2016058320

Designed by Nord Compo

Jacket photo: View of San Francisco Bay, Treasure Island, and San Francisco from the Berkeley Hills. Courtesy of Sudhish Mohindroo.

Contents

Introduction

Part I

Treasure Island, an Airport, and the Golden Gate International Exposition

Part II

Naval Station Treasure Island and Military Occupation

Part III
The Treasure Island–Yerba Buena Island Development Project

Illustrations

Acknowledgments

The first iteration of this collection dates from a panel at the conference of the International Association for the Study of Traditional Environments (IASTE) held in Beirut in 2010. Later Greig Crysler suggested we organize a collection around the panel with a generous offer to contribute an essay. In the interim of converting a panel forum into a collection of essays, we have incurred many additional debts.

We thank Richard Walker, Andy Shanken, Diane Harris, David Moffatt, Gray Brechin, Michael Southworth, Elizabeth Deakin, and Mary Corbin Sies for working with us and cheering us on. Masako Ikeda, our editor at the University of Hawai'i Press, has been key to the development of the project as have been Nadine Little, Emma Ching, Debra Tang, and the design and production team led by Cheryl Loe. A special thanks to Helen Glenn Court for copyediting and Barbara Roos for the index. We are indebted to the assistance of Mimi Manning, vice president of the Treasure Island Museum Association Board, and the museum's staff. At the San Francisco History Center of the San Francisco Public Library, a special thanks to Jeff Thomas and Tami Suzuki. We express our gratitude to the staff at the Bancroft Library at the University of California, Berkeley, particularly Susan Snyder, Teresa Salazar, Jack von Euw, Crystal Miles, and Peter Hanff. We thank Sudhish Mohindroo for providing our cover photo and Treasure Island Community Development for access to images from the Treasure Island–Yerba Buena Island Development Project.

The University of San Francisco, College of Arts and Science Faculty Development Fund provided Tanu Sankalia with a generous subvention to defray publication costs, and the college also supported the research and writing for the collection. A residency sponsored by National Endowment of the Arts at MacDowell Colony provided Lynne Horiuchi with ideal writing conditions, and the Institute of Regional and Urban Development at the College of Environmental Design at the University of California at Berkeley sponsored her as a visiting fellow during a good portion of the work on the collection. We extend our gratitude to all the others who helped us along the way, especially Devyani Jain, Shiven Sankalia, Tracy Peters, and Chiyo Horiuchi. Last, we owe an even greater debt to our contributors for their marvelous essays. Working through the production of this book with good meals, garden chats, endless cups of tea, and the good cheer of our contributors has been a great pleasure. We hope this effort will reflect on the experience of reading the book.

Oakland, California

Abbreviations

BCDC	Bay Conservation and Development Commission
BRAC	Base Realignment and Closure
CAB	Treasure Island/Yerba Buena Island Citizens Advisory Board
CCI	Clinton Climate Initiative
CCSF	City and County of San Francisco
CMG	Conger Moss and Guillard
CRC	Citizens Reuse Committee
CSLC	California State Lands Commission
D4D	Design for Development
DOD	Department of Defense
EIR	Environmental impact report
GGIE	Golden Gate International Exposition
GGNRA	Golden Gate National Recreation Area
HRA	Historical radiological assessment
HRASTM	Historical Radiological Assessment, Supplemental Technical Memorandum
LEED	Leadership in Energy and Environmental Design
LRA	Local Reuse Authority
MINS	Mare Island Naval Shipyard
NAACP	National Association for the Advancement of Colored People
NCR	National Cash Register
NIMBY	[not in my back yard]
NRDL	Naval Radiological Defense Laboratory
NSTI	Naval Station Treasure Island
OMBC	Office of Military Base Conversion
ONI	Office of Naval Intelligence
POW	Prisoner of war
RFP	Request for proposals
RFQ	Request for qualifications
SF	San Francisco
SFBCDC	San Francisco Bay Conservation Development Commission
SFBOS	San Francisco Board of Supervisors
SFPL	San Francisco Public Library
SMWM	Simon Martin-Vegue Winkelstein and Morris
SOM	Skidmore Owings and Merrill
SPUR	San Francisco Planning and Urban Research
TI	Treasure Island
TICD	Treasure Island Community Development
TIDA	Treasure Island Development Authority
TIDP	Treasure Island–Yerba Buena Island Development Project
TIHDI	Treasure Island Homeless Development Initiative
TIMA	Treasure Island Museum Association
WPA	Works Progress Administration
YBI	Yerba Buena Island

INTRODUCTION

1. Urban Reinventions

LYNNE HORIUCHI AND TANU SANKALIA

Flat and rectangular, Treasure Island is a contained mass of landfill surrounded by water. It looks like a floating platform from which you can gaze out, 360 degrees, and take in spectacular views of the varied geography that forms the San Francisco Bay Area (Figure 1.1). The island is so low lying that it feels as though you can almost touch the cold waters that steadily lap its well-defined edges. On some days, the island is cloaked in fog and on others bathed in sun; yet you can always feel the brisk, chilling, ocean winds that unforgivingly sweep the island (Figure 1.2).

Set in the middle of the San Francisco Bay, Treasure Island is a man-made island of approximately four hundred acres. The island is suspended roughly midway

FIGURE 1.1 Treasure Island appears like a floating platform in this 2010 photograph taken from an airplane with Yerba Buena Island, the San Francisco–Oakland Bay Bridge, and the city of San Francisco in the distance. © Barrie Rokeach 2016. All Rights Reserved.

FIGURE 1.2   The western edge of the low-lying Treasure Island in 2012, with Yerba Buena Island and the
San Francisco–Oakland Bay Bridge in the background. Photo: Tanu Sankalia.

between the urban agglomerations of San Francisco to the west and the cities of
Oakland and Berkeley to the east. Vehicular access is limited to a narrow cause-
way from the adjacent natural Yerba Buena Island—the mid-span anchor of the
San Francisco–Oakland Bay Bridge—that serves as the island's only link to the Bay
Area's roadway systems. Although within the jurisdiction of the City and County of
San Francisco, Treasure Island resembles an edge condition, the discontiguous and
liminal space of an artificial island that seems as if it were not part of the city at all
(Figure 1.3). Its flat topography is tucked in peripheral vision as one drives past it on
the San Francisco–Oakland Bay Bridge and through the Yerba Buena Tunnel.

From the time of Treasure Island's creation to the present, local and federal
government agencies have vied for its control, contested its use, and shaped its
physical character. Treasure Island has thus been central to San Francisco's urban
ambitions, recurrently constituted as global projects through utopian planning, architecture, and war. The island's flat land surface has provided an ideal springboard
for development in repeated, grand urban reinventions driven by capital, property,
and government legal jurisdictions. Located in one of the most expensive real estate markets in the world, Treasure Island remains a highly coveted prime property
that the City of San Francisco and its developers have reclaimed as a new eco-city
for about nineteen thousand residents, the plan for which was approved by the City
and County of San Francisco Board of Supervisors in 2011.

FIGURE 1.3   Treasure Island in the middle of San Francisco Bay, looking north with the city of San Francisco to the west and the cities of Oakland and Berkeley to the east, circa 1939. San Francisco History Center, San Francisco Public Library.

With its material history serving as an illuminating backcloth, this collection of essays brings Treasure Island into focus just as plans for the new city are materializing. The volume coalesces around the phenomena we call *urban reinventions.* We envision urban reinventions as a concept associated with formidable state power over land and, paradoxically, with moments of vulnerability that permit state powers to reconfigure sites. Urban reinventions share with reclamation projects the common use of landfill—often over bodies of water or wetlands—to create property for development through state configured investment and without a significant stable constituency in private citizens or residents who have invested culturally, materially, or economically in sites. State control has enabled urban reinventions to use tabula rasa development that sweeps sites clean of most visually recognizable previous occupation or natural features. Unlike urban infill or redevelopment on previously settled land, urban reinventions incorporate entirely new and utopian futures conceived through the mobilization of capital in spaces exceptional to the norm. As part of regional and global boosterism, urban reinventions are often configured through the deployment of spectacular form with new technologies linked to the larger dynamics of commerce, governance, development, and transportation infrastructure. Even though urban reinventions attempt to erase the material archive of successive development histories, they never entirely succeed, because traces from the past tend to linger.

The concept of urban reinventions was tailored out of our work in editing this volume. Urban reinventions are not intended in aggregate to be a universal concept, but rather one that collectively reflects the multiple ways the authors in this volume interpret underresearched topics through Treasure Island's material conditions. In this sense, the volume contrasts with collections organized around a universal concept into which contributions about different case studies, often about specific sites or places, are folded. It also contrasts with predefined methodologies for case studies of places in the social sciences such as ethnographies. Instead, the volume offers a wide spectrum of critiques of race, imperialism, gendered orientalism, military land use, property capital exchange, new eco-cities, sustainability, and waste as a byproduct of development. We do, however, see urban reinventions as a useful analytical tool and Treasure Island as an example to look more deeply at other similar sites.

Tensions between Treasure Island's visionary developments and its historical uses connect the essays. They follow the material arc from the creation of Treasure Island as property through landfill for a regional airport, which then becomes the site of the Golden Gate International Exposition (GGIE)—an ephemeral world's fair dedicated to peace, commerce, and cooperation across the Pacific. The narratives of San Francisco and GGIE boosters turned toward the Pacific Rim without acknowledging the military aggression of the Axis powers in Europe and Asia. The arc of utopian building was broken by the US entry into World War II—one essay demonstrating the military's persistent racism in the San Francisco Bay Area. Essays on military base reuse and their toxic leftovers raise questions about the design of the new eco-city and the reconfiguration of property in the face of hazards associated with global warming, earthquakes, and nuclear waste.

The essays demonstrate how a single site may be interpreted in multiple ways through the critical analyses of successive urban reinventions. By drawing out narratives linking to larger historic and contemporary topics, the essays require the reader to adjust to different lenses and to think about the importance of local to global linkages. The essays also provide multiple models of robust and rich interdisciplinary work, in depth and breadth, available to the interpretation of one site. They will be of particular interest to teachers, scholars, and practitioners in the fields of geography, architecture, planning, urban design, history, environmental studies, American studies, Asian studies, and military history, among others. As a teaching tool, for instance, the volume may be used as an example to compare and contrast planning practices and urban form across time. Broadly, this collection will serve a growing audience in the San Francisco Bay Area and beyond interested in the reinvention of urban spaces.

The chronological order of three periods of Treasure Island's material history provides the organization for the collection: the making of Treasure Island, an airport, and the Golden Gate International Exposition (1931–1941); Naval Station Treasure Island and military occupation (1941–1993); and the Treasure Island–Yerba Buena Island Development Project (1993–2011). The following is a brief history of these periods that provides the context for Treasure Island's urban reinventions.

The Making of Treasure Island, an Airport, and the Golden Gate International Exposition

American cities produced six major international expositions within eight years during the 1930s, liberally funded by the New Deal. They were often envisioned as ways to improve infrastructure and counter the economic malaise of the Depression. In San Francisco, city boosters had already demonstrated remarkable skill in capturing federal funding for major transportation infrastructure improvements. Of these, the Golden Gate Bridge cost $35 million to build, the San Francisco–Oakland Bay Bridge cost $77 million, and the cost of construction of Treasure Island as a new regional airport was $4.7 million, all largely subsidized by

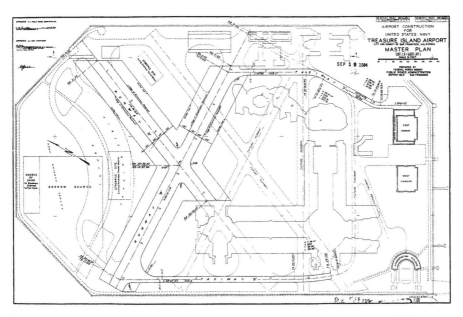

FIGURE 1.4   Master plan for Treasure Island Airport showing runways superimposed on the GGIE site plan, July 27, 1941. Mare Island Naval Shipyard 1996.

the federal government (Reinhardt 1973) (Figure 1.4). The GGIE incorporated the celebration of these major regional infrastructure projects into its theme of transportation and communication.

Between February 11, 1936, and August 24, 1937, the US Army Corps of Engineers simultaneously built a rectangular sea wall and discharged bay fill into it, anchoring the new island to the shallow northern shoals of Yerba Buena Island. The planned airfield thus formed an ideal flat plane for architects and designers of the GGIE on which to draw a vision of San Francisco as an important metropolis in the Pacific Rim. As Andrew Shanken notes, "Such visionary projects were often born of insecurity in an era when cities proposed momentous, sometimes radical, and even economically destabilizing interventions as ways of spurring growth and upstaging rival cities" (see Shanken, this volume). This visionary power created an island airport as the crowning piece of heroic construction and connectivity. For example, a 1939 GGIE promotional brochure describes Treasure Island as a "Tierra Nueva"—a phoenix-like invention of new land and property where none had existed—"rising clean and solid and fresh from the middle of the San Francisco Bay" (Associated Oil Company 1936) (Figure 1.5). Treasure Island's creation embodied the state-driven character of urban reinventions in the transformation of this small part of the San Francisco Bay for an ephemeral world's fair and an unlikely site for an airport.

Even though advances in aeronautics requiring long runways had ironically made the Treasure Island airport obsolete by the time the fair first opened in 1939, GGIE officials continued to advertise Pan American World Airways and their China Clipper airplanes as part of Treasure Island's development. San

FIGURE 1.5   "Tierra Nueva" under construction as it emerges from San Francisco Bay, 1936. The Bancroft Library, University of California, Berkeley.

FIGURE 1.6   Montage view of a design for the "Magic City"—the Golden Gate International Exposition—on Treasure Island, foregrounded by naval ships, circa 1935. The Bancroft Library, University of California, Berkeley.

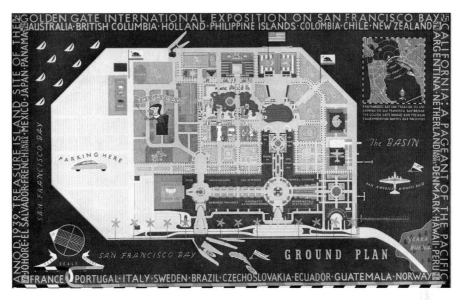

FIGURE 1.7   Site plan of the Golden Gate International Exposition with a list of countries showing international participation at the Exposition. Inset map shows the location of Treasure Island in the San Francisco Bay, 1939. San Francisco History Center, San Francisco Public Library.

Francisco and GGIE boosters proclaimed and romanticized the industrial revolution ideologies of progress, technology, and prosperity as part of the natural order of things on the unnatural and man-made island (Shanken 2014; see also Shanken, this volume).

The global utopian reach of San Francisco's urban ambitions was spectacularly represented in the GGIE with elaborate plans, landscape schemes, and exotic architecture (Figures 1.6 and 1.7). Before his death in 1936, George Kelham, chair of the GGIE Architectural Commission, designed a Beaux-Arts plan form literally as a key to San Francisco. Kelham's successor, Arthur Brown Jr., designed even more exotic, eclectic, and orientalized components for the fair, such as the placement of Roger Stackpole's eighty-foot statue *Pacifica* in front of a shimmering "Persian" metal curtain in the Court of Pacifica (Figure 1.8). With an ample budget of $1.8 million, Julius Girod and John McLaren, Golden Gate Park superintendent, directed the planting of five million shrubs, trees, and flowers (Reinhardt 1973, 45). The "Pageant of the Pacific" became an urban fantasy tour of the world, cloistered behind tall wind baffles. Illuminated in the evenings by a complex color palette of lights, the fair was visible all through the Bay Area, setting the island afloat like the proverbial bejeweled "Magic City" (Figure 1.9).

The GGIE opened on schedule on February 18, 1939, and remained open to the public through October 29, 1939, reopening for a second season on March 25, 1940, and running through September 29, 1940. With a focus on commerce in the Pacific, the fair's publicity proclaimed its message:

Here is a World's Fair that will lend impetus to the progress of the Western Hemisphere, will focus the attention of all the nations of the earth on America's great seaport on the Pacific Ocean, and lay the cornerstone of a new Pacific Empire, united in a common bond of social and commercial well-being. . . . There will be found a new spirit—truly Western and Pacific—that will lend inspiration to the lives of all who will come to this "Treasure Island" in 1939. (*Progress* 1937, 4)

World geography and the Pacific Rim played an important part at the western edge of the United States compared with other fairs of the 1930s (Figure 1.10). The GGIE's definitive break with American fairs between 1933 and 1939 was the articulation of the Pacific Rim as the fastest-growing region for US investment and an ideological extension of the American frontier toward the Pacific (see Schrenk, this volume). Because of the region's ties to Asia and South America, the GGIE's organizers felt that it was uniquely positioned to compete with the New York World's Fair, "All the World's Tomorrow," held contemporaneously at Flushing Meadows–Corona Park.

The GGIE's official architecture was a kind of arcadian magic encrusted with the high culture ambitions of peace, harmony, and commerce. The fair's official architecture resonates with Shanken's use of D. H. Lawrence's phrase "void Pacific" as a metaphor for California's architecture that expressed its special relationship to climate and left coast traditions of turning west toward Asia and Latin America

FIGURE 1.8 Cinematically lit, the eighty-foot statue *Pacifica* by Ralph Stackpole in the Court of Pacifica with the Fountain of Western Waters, at the Golden Gate International Exposition, 1939. The Bancroft Library, University of California Berkeley.

FIGURE 1.9   A night shot of the Golden Gate International Exposition with the Tower of the Sun, 1939. The Bancroft Library, University of California, Berkeley.

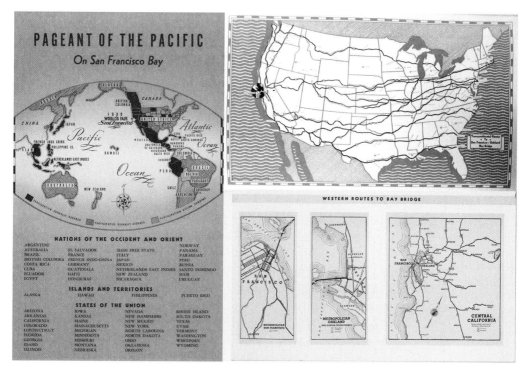

FIGURE 1.10   Maps illustrating the GGIE as part of the Pacific Rim and road networks linking the GGIE to the region and the continental United States, 1939. The Bancroft Library, University of California, Berkeley.

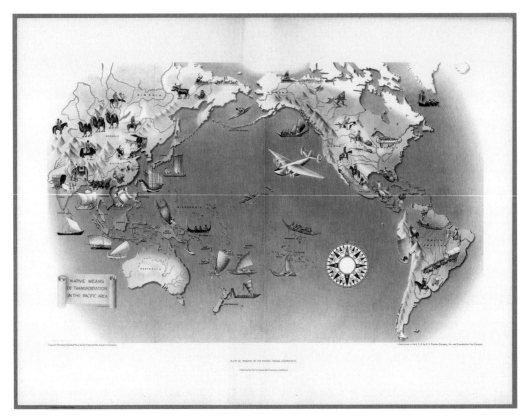

FIGURE 1.11   "Native Means of Transportation." One of six pictorial wall maps by Miguel Covarrubias installed in the
Pacific House at the Golden Gate International Exposition, 1939. David Rumsey Map Collection, http://www.davidrumsey.com.

(Shanken 2014, 10; Brechin 1999). Imaginatively extending the American frontier
ideologically and geographically, the GGIE contrasted with fairs of the 1930s that
projected visions of future worlds (see Schrenk, this volume). As may be seen in
Miguel Covarrubias' murals displayed in the Pacific House, official GGIE themes
mapped the diversity of modern and ancient cultures in the Pacific Rim drawing
from scientific ethnographic representations (Figure 1.11). In the Gayway, low cultural entertainment, such as Dancers of All Nations and the lascivious "bare facts"
of the Sally Rand Nude Ranch, combined with the GGIE's official images to enthrall
1.4 million visitors as World War II exploded in Europe and East Asia (Rydell, Findling, and Pelle 2000; James and Weller 1941).

   The initiation of a global and total war began to surface in the GGIE's utopian
visions as exhibits were closed or reorganized for the second opening of the fair
in March 1940. Japan had been engaged in a full-fledged war with China since
1937 and Germany had invaded Poland in 1939. Nearly all of Europe came under
German and Fascist control in 1940, transforming frontier boundaries and racialized national identities in both Europe and Asia. The impending conflict in the
Pacific could be seen at the GGIE in Japan's claim as the dominant foreign exhibit

and in their utopian narratives of colonization and imperialism promoting their Greater East Asian Co-Prosperity Sphere (see Horiuchi, this volume). Demonstrating San Francisco's reach from the local to the global, the Japan Pavilion's gendered orientalist visions included the all-female Japanese Takarazuka dance troupe in "The Grand Cherry" show, and its young female Japanese American staff in kimono spoke English and stood in for Japanese guides, metaphorically serving as bridges across the Pacific (see Horiuchi, this volume). By 1940, other harbingers of World War II were visible at the GGIE, such as the small replica of the cyclotron in the University of California's science exhibit, for which Ernest Livermore had received the 1939 Nobel Prize for Physics, and the closing of European exhibits whose nations had been invaded by Germany (Rubens 2004).

Naval Station Treasure Island and Military Occupation

In 1941, the Navy reinvented the Magic City into an intensive military space to serve the total war effort (Figure 1.12). A majority of the fair buildings, costing about $50 million, including *Pacifica*, which stood as a symbol of Pacific Rim unity, were dismantled. Even before the bombing of Pearl Harbor on December 7, 1941, and the US entry into World War II, the military's presence in the San Francisco Bay Area had surged with new bases planned and old ones expanded (United States and Sedway/Cooke 1985) (Figure 1.13). Naval Station Treasure Island, or NAVSTA, became a key component in the Bay Area arsenal of military bases, shipyards, repair docks, military personnel, and defense workers.

FIGURE 1.12   Aerial photograph of Naval Station Treasure Island in the 1940s. McDevitt 1946.

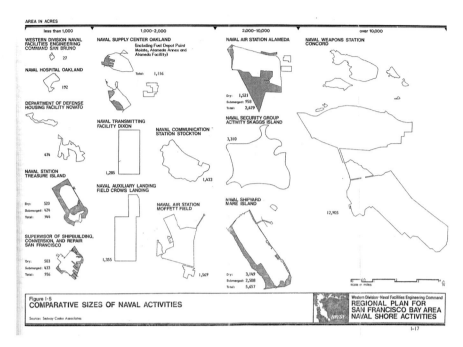

AREA IN ACRES

FIGURE 1.13 Comparative illustration of the sizes of naval bases in the San Francisco Bay Area in 1985. Naval Station Treasure Island in the lower left-hand corner. Draft Regional Plan, San Francisco Bay Area Naval Shore Activities, 1985.

Officially named the Naval Training and Distribution Center, Treasure Island, or TADCEN, TI, the base served as a distribution and training site. During World War II, 4.5 million US servicemen and servicewomen passed through Treasure Island on their way to and from the Pacific Theater, demonstrating the island's greatest global reach (McDevitt 1946) (Figure 1.14).

The transfer of land from the City of San Francisco to the US Navy was anything but smooth. The creation of a municipal airport, which had been the vision of the San Francisco Junior Chamber of Commerce a decade earlier, was to continue with the financial assistance of the Works Progress Administration during the Navy's temporary occupation of the island during 1941. However, on April 17, 1942, following Pearl Harbor, the Navy secured a federal court order to permanently acquire the island from the City of San Francisco (*San Francisco Examiner* 1962). In 1943, when plans for an airport had been permanently scrapped, the Navy transferred to the City of San Francisco, in exchange for Treasure Island, a large parcel of land near San Bruno that is now the site of San Francisco International Airport (MINS 1996).

By 1944, Treasure Island resembled a frontier town with land being cleared and new military facilities being built. Standard military buildings served as training schools, offices, embarkation barracks, galleys, dormitories, armories, theaters, sick bays, brigs, and recreational facilities for officers (Figure 1.15). Treasure Island even

hosted prisoner of war (POW) housing for 1,300 German POWs, mostly
members of General Rommel's Af-
rika Korps, between June 1945 and
March 1946 (MINS 1996).

Between 1941 and 1993—the
period during which Treasure Island
was an active naval base—the US
Navy, the Department of Defense,
and the City of San Francisco engaged in a struggle for control of the
island, proposing contrasting and often contradictory schemes. Considering its prime central location in the
bay, the contestation between gov-

FIGURE 1.14   Victory Day celebrations on Naval StationTreasure
Island, September 4, 1945. San Francisco History Center, San
Francisco Public Library.

ernment agencies over Treasure Island's jurisdiction and ownership became an important factor in claiming it for military use, public land, or real estate development.
The Navy saw the island as a central location where it could consolidate training
facilities and build a more permanent naval base for training. The Department of
Defense, at times, viewed the island as surplus to military operations and sought to

FIGURE 1.15   Construction of embarkation facilities on Naval Station Treasure Island, January 24, 1944.
Mare Island Naval Shipyard (MINS) 1996.

close the naval station. The City of San Francisco remained ambivalent about the island's role in its civilian economic geography. At once a source of jobs and construction contracts, San Francisco envisioned the island as a site for large transportation infrastructures or prime property for grand development schemes—a place on which to project the city's changing urban ambitions.

The powerful presence of the US Navy in the San Francisco Bay Area follows a long historical arc from the mid-nineteenth century of naval profiteering and land acquisition during the Gold Rush to the mid-twentieth century of the San Francisco Bay as a metaphorical "naval lake" with Treasure Island at its center. Within this spatial history is inscribed the US Navy's racist policies (see Arbona, this volume). These are most clearly defined in the historic mutiny trial, held in 1944 at Treasure Island, against fifty black sailors for their refusal to load arms in dangerous working conditions after an explosion at the Port Chicago Naval Magazine killed 320 sailors and coworkers. The traces of such an African American protest and racial injustice is an example of history that successive urban reinventions erase from places like Treasure Island (see Arbona, this volume).

The military's post–World War II planning for development in its naval lake was not entirely steady, but instead followed a boom and bust cycle spiking with the Korean War (1950–1953) and the Vietnam War (1966–1972) (United States and Sedway/Cooke 1985). Throughout the 1940s and 1950s, various technical training schools on bases around the Bay Area were consolidated into the Naval Schools Command at Naval Station Treasure Island (NSTI), providing the physical form for the Navy's Treasure Island university concept for its 1966 Master Development Plan (MINS 1996, 28; Armed Forces Directory Services 1966). An example of the unique training schools on NSTI, the Navy established the Damage Control Training School in 1947. Part of the military's Cold War nuclear warfare training, the school's mission was to instruct soldiers in atomic defense, particularly in decontamination procedures in the aftermath of a nuclear attack. For this training, the Navy built, from scrap material, a full-scale, above water, mock training warship called the USS *Pandemonium*. But this practice involved the actual contamination of places and people. This environmental dominance over the use of military property has resulted in a toxic past, which continues to plague current planning for the island (see Dillon, this volume).

By 1965, the US Navy wanted to solidify its presence on Treasure Island despite calls by a Navy survey board to declare the station surplus (*San Francisco Examiner* 1962). The Navy prepared a master development plan, published in 1966, that proposed replacing temporary barracks and structures with concrete buildings to create a permanent campus for the entire Fleet Training School in electronics for the Pacific (Ruth and Krushkov 1966; Armed Forces Directory Services 1966; Avery 1965), reflecting the military's participation in the development of the electronics industry in the Bay Area (Figures 1.16 and 1.17). Around the same time, the San Francisco Junior Chamber of Commerce proposed, yet again, an airport for small commercial planes, which resulted in another tussle over the future vision of the island (*San Francisco Chronicle* 1965) (Figure 1.18).

Although the Navy won out, new housing was constructed on sites laden with radioactive soils; many of these homes are now boarded and abandoned as soil remediation is under way.

Despite the master development plan of 1966, plans were afoot in the mid-1970s to eliminate the Twelfth Naval District at Treasure Island. The Department of Defense's plan was to streamline operations by creating four regional commands instead of twelve naval districts, which was to yield the federal government a savings of $3 million a year (*San Francisco Chronicle* 1973). During the 1970s other proposals were made to turn Treasure Island into a super port for giant tanker ships or into a fully operational solar station by the early 2000s that could power San Francisco's energy needs (Kusserow 1973; Irving 1979).

The contentious process of closing of military bases, which had begun with the Kennedy administration in the early 1960s, was somewhat resolved when Congress passed the Defense Authorization Amendments and Base Closure and Realignment Act in 1988 (P.L. 101-510) and Naval Station Treasure Island was marked for closure in 1993 (US Congress 1990). Yet the historical struggle between the various state actors for the control of Treasure Island meant that no clear plan for the future of the island existed (see Gillem, this volume). Procedural politics,

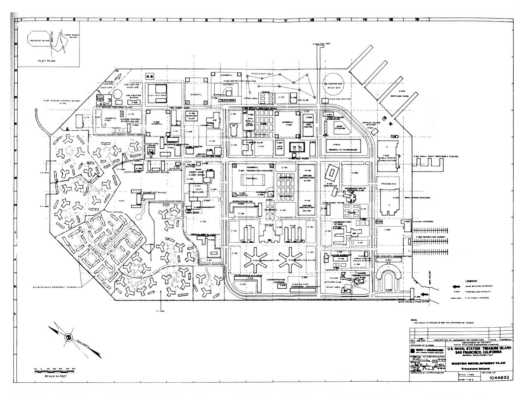

FIGURE 1.16   Master plan for Naval Station Treasure Island showing Treasure Island, 1966. Source: Ruth & Krushkov.

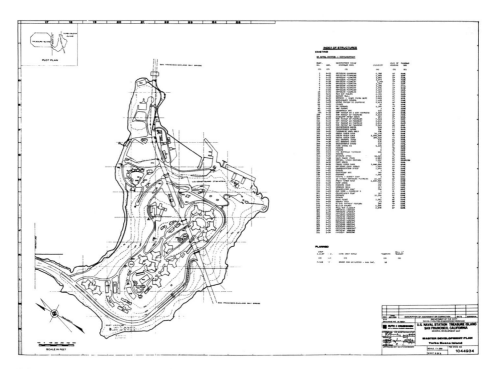

FIGURE 1.17 Master plan for Naval Station Treasure Island showing Yerba Buena Island, 1966. Source: Ruth & Krushkov.

FIGURE 1.18 Overlapping sites. The long rectangular site was marked as a runway for small planes proposed the by San Francisco Junior Chamber of Commerce, and the half octagonal site was delineated by the US Navy for permanent housing on Treasure Island. Aerial photo from the *San Francisco Chronicle*, February 16, 1965 Jaycee/ San Francisco Chronicle/Polaris.

lack of community participation, developmental economics, and conflicting visions have hampered the successful transition from a military base to new uses despite attempts on the part of city officials and developers to present Treasure Island's planned transformation as entirely seamless.

The Treasure Island–Yerba Buena Island Development Project

Treasure Island is poised for another radical reinvention with the planned Treasure Island–Yerba Buena Island Development Project (TIDP)—a spectacular green city envisioned in the middle of the San Francisco Bay (Figure 1.19). With its promise of a postcarbon ecotopia, the TIDP fulfills San Francisco's utopian ambitions to occupy the forefront of twenty-first century urbanism, one that is consistent with global trends toward large-scale, capital-intensive land developments marketed around ideas of sustainability.

In June 2011, the San Francisco City and County Board of Supervisors unanimously approved the TIDP, almost two decades after Treasure Island had been marked for closure in the third round of Base Realignment and Closure (BRAC) in 1993 (Figure 1.20). The road to the approval covered a long and convoluted planning process begun in 1995 (see Sankalia, this volume). Leading the effort has been a special planning and

FIGURE 1.19   Magic City 2.0. Photomontage of the Treasure Island Development Project with the San Francisco's Ferry Building and the Embarcadero in the foreground, 2005. Courtesy of Treasure Island Community Development.

FIGURE 1.20   Model of proposed development on Treasure Island and Yerba Buena Island. Treasure Island Community Development/Treasure Island Development Authority, 2005. Courtesy of Treasure Island Community Development.

implementation agency, the Treasure Island Development Authority (TIDA), controlled in large part by the San Francisco mayor's office. TIDA was charged with overseeing redevelopment of the island, managing interim uses, and negotiating the transfer of land from the Navy to the city. The authority was created by the San Francisco Board of Supervisors in 1997 and endorsed by the California State Legislature, underscoring powerful government agency control over the process.

Since the mid-1990s, Treasure Island has seen several visions for its reuse. Early proposals revolved around public uses, but the island's unique location, and the considerable cost of acquisition from the US Navy, swayed San Francisco city officials in considering the land for commercial property development (see Stehlin, this volume). However, Treasure Island is, arguably, not a suitable site for housing given its unstable landfill soil and its susceptibility to seismic liquefaction considering its proximity to some of Northern California's most dangerous earthquake faults. Moreover, the island's soils were contaminated by a host of pollutants, including radioactive waste, during the Navy's tenure. Data also suggests that, given predicted rising sea levels, a significant portion of the island will be submerged (SFBCDC 2011; Stark, Bird, and Stoll 2015). Despite warnings from some quarters of the Navy and even the Urban Land Institute that Treasure Island was not an ideal site for building, the prospect of easing San Francisco's incessant housing demand kept high-return residential property development on the table (Urban Land Institute 1996; Navy Department 2005).

In 2002, TIDA awarded the project to Treasure Island Community Development LLC (TICD) to serve as the master developer for both Yerba Buena Island and Treasure Island. TICD is a joint venture between Lennar Urban (a division of Lennar Corporation) and KSWM, which comprises Kenwood Investments LLC, Stockbridge Capital Group, and Wilson Meany LLC. Although TICD's early proposals for housing on the island were fairly modest—1,500 to 3,000 units—the 2011 plan calls for 8,000 units. In addition, retail spaces, offices, and hotel rooms are included, supported by large infrastructure improvements and several hundreds of acres of open space embellished by man-made wetlands (Figure 1.21). The increase in scope and building density has been necessary because of the enormous cost of overcoming

Treasure Island's physical constraints. In other words, the very problems associated with seismic instability, soil contamination, and sea level rise have taken the form of a series of "enabling constraints" that have driven a larger, high-risk project with potentially greater profits (see Stehlin, this volume).

Not only do physical constraints limit building on Treasure Island, but state law does as well. Treasure Island, which is entirely made of landfill, legally rests in the public trust under the California State Lands Commission (CSLC), which permits only certain maritime uses and prohibits residential use on fill lands (CSLC 2014). Nonetheless, substantial land for residential development on Treasure Island, one hundred acres in all, was carved out through a clever land swap by ostensibly forgoing housing development on the natural Yerba Buena Island, which is not subject to the CSLC public trust. Thus the problematic soils that make up the island and state law that governs building on it are intertwined with the larger structure of capital accumulation that grounds property development (see Stehlin, this volume).

Because a higher-risk, higher-density development was planned for Treasure Island, it had to be made palatable to lawmakers and the public at large. In 2005, TIDA and TICD turned to the idea of sustainability with a revamped development team and new leadership. But sustainability, which now drives the project, remains a largely contested concept. Its vague, unclarified significance is prone to be twisted by various groups—private corporations and the state—to serve their individual interests. At once a techno-scientific idea and a socioeconomic concept, sustainability forms a major theme of the TIDP, its advantages remaining unclear on Treasure Island but dominant in current discourses and practices of city planning and urban design (see Sankalia, this volume).

The use of a special planning agency (TIDA) controlled by the mayor's office and the absence of a well-entrenched local community has made Treasure Island's

FIGURE 1.21   Rendering from the Treasure Island–Yerba Buena Island Development Project showing the proposed transformation of Treasure Island, 2005. Courtesy of Treasure Island Community Development.

distinctive traits as a discontiguous, bounded island site even more clear. Seques-
tered under naval control, Treasure Island has never been subject to the City of San
Francisco's zoning laws or general plan requirements. It therefore remains outside
the normative planning practices of the City of San Francisco, giving it a special
status as an "other place," where formal experimentation that furthers the interests
of property capital becomes eminently possible (see Sankalia, this volume).

Between 2005 and 2011, the TIDP received a warm reception from urban design
critics, commentators, and segments of the local press. In 2008, it was awarded the
California Governor's Environmental and Economic Leadership Award as well as
local, regional, and state awards from the American Institute of Architects in 2006,
2008, and 2009. In part, the approbation for the project hinges on the manner in
which the project's developers have turned an underused, toxic-laden, derelict site
into a future vision, which is claimed in the imagination as a sustainable marketable
project even before it is realized in material form (see Crysler, this volume).

Herein lies the telos of modernist planning, which seems to ensure a flawless
transition from the past, to stable present, and ideal future. This process, the en-
visioning of a new city on Treasure Island, is steered by the idea of the blank slate
on which the past can be magically erased for a fresh future. In modernist planning
epistemologies, the conceit of abstraction flattens and empties out time and space—
man-made, planar, anachronistic, and physically disengaged—much like the place

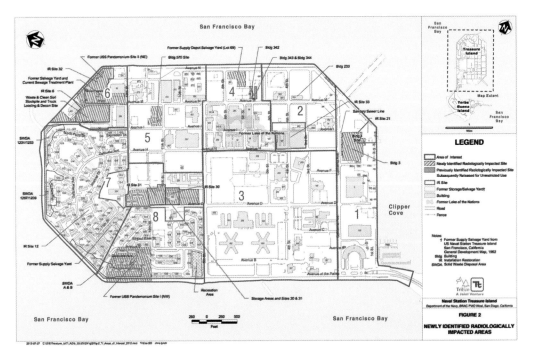

FIGURE 1.22   Map of Treasure Island with hatched portions showing "newly identified radiologically impacted areas."
2012. Source: US Navy image.

that is Treasure Island. Thus the notion of the tabula rasa realizes the site as an exploitable terrain: land that is created from fill, realized as property, built on, destroyed, redeveloped, and ultimately recovered as profit—a cycle of urban reinvention that ultimately produces an overabundance of waste (see Crysler, this volume).

Even if one concedes that the TIDP is a well-conceived, sustainable project, the question is still whether the project embodies the right ideas in the wrong place. The risk of seismic instability, toxic soils, and sea level rise places a cloud on whether the island should be a site of permanent habitation (Figure 1.22). The decision to pursue high-density residential development on the island has compelled the Treasure Island Development Authority, their planners, and developers to pursue a slew of contested ideas to justify building on Treasure Island.

Treasure Island—Past, Present, Future

As urban land, Treasure Island appears rife with the prospect of speculative development. One cannot escape the feeling when one visits Treasure Island that the site presents the possibility of being transformed into what planners call highest and best use of urban land. Even as early as 1992, when base closure was imminent, Treasure Island was seen as a "developer's dream," as a site for "something big." San Francisco's mayor at the time, Art Agnos, saw it as an "outstanding opportunity for new uses that would add to the city's tax roles [*sic*]" (Nolte 1991). Treasure Island's transitory status stretching back to the mid-1990s is already seen as the past, an empty container that is to be reinvented into Magic City 2.0.

As of 2016, Treasure Island remains a jarringly dissimilar landscape of dereliction and transitional use. Remnants of the GGIE's urban structure are still visible in the Avenue of Palms, which stretches north to south along the western side of the island; the iconic Art Deco air terminal building anchors the southwest corner and houses the Treasure Island Museum Association, among other nonprofit organizations. Boarded-up and derelict buildings from the Navy era dot the flat landscape; empty parking lots are interspersed among Little League fields, soccer pitches, and a quarter-acre urban agricultural patch. Wineries sit in converted military buildings, film production facilities and artists' workshops in former aircraft hangars. Some of the 2,500 people who occupied the low-density postwar Navy housing, allocated through the Base Closure Community Redevelopment and Homeless Assistance Act of 1994, have now moved out because environmental remediation activities are under way. The largest consolidated piece of land use on the island—about forty acres—is a youth job-training facility established in the 1980s and owned by the US Department of Labor, which will continue to function even as land around it is transformed with the new development. Water to the island is still brought in from pipes fastened to the underbelly of the San Francisco–Oakland Bay Bridge.

This brief overview of Treasure Island's successive historical periods demonstrates the linking of this small island's geopolitical and economic significance to the City of San Francisco's urban ambitions, the Bay Area region, the Pacific Rim, and US military power. The contributors to this collection probe this material history, in its planning processes and under the surface of the island, looking at waste products of its use and the exchange value of San Francisco Bay mud as property for ecological use and new housing. They also probe Treasure Island's political and utopian narratives of successive layers of urban reinventions that have generally remained unfiltered and underresearched. Many readers might have considered Treasure Island bounded by local or regional interests, but the essays stretch the geographical connections and their impacts outward from Treasure Island into the world—the inversion of the GGIE, which contained its fantasy world on the island within its ephemeral wind baffles. These periods of erasure and urban reinvention also serve as a backdrop against which the ecotopian plans for Treasure Island's future might be discussed and brought into public view. This focus on Treasure Island is particularly important given the paradoxes that it embodies: a peripheral and unassuming place abounding in geopolitical and economic significance and also a site projecting utopian visions with a dystopic material past. Our introduction of the concept of urban reinventions is meant as a skeletal framework, on which other studies may build to analyze similar projects globally, where state control and capital encourage the use of modernist tabula rasa planning.

References

Armed Forces Directory Services. 1966. "U.S. Naval Station Treasure Island San Francisco, California." Unofficial Directory and Guide. San Francisco History Center, San Francisco Public Library.

Associated Oil Company. 1936. *Tierra Nueva*. Pamphlet. Fang Family San Francisco Examiner Photograph Archive-Photographic Print Files, circa 1874–2000 (bulk 1911–2000), BANC PIC 2006.029—PIC, Box 080. The Bancroft Library, University of California, Berkeley.

Avery, Paul. 1965. "Navy Firm on T.I. Housing." *San Francisco Chronicle,* February 27, 1, 10.

Brechin, Gray A. 1999. *Imperial San Francisco: Urban Power, Earthly Ruin*. Berkeley: University of California Press.

California State Lands Commission (CSLC). 2014. "The Public Trust Doctrine." California State Lands Commission. http://www.slc.ca.gov/About/Public_Trust.html.

Irving, Carl. 1979. "A Treasure: Island Could Be a Solar Station." *San Francisco Examiner,* October 19.

James, Jack, and Earle Vonard Weller. 1941. *Treasure Island: "The Magic City," 1939–1940*. San Francisco: Pisani Printing and Publishing.

Kusserow, H. W. 1973. "Bay Superport on Treasure Island Urged." *San Francisco Examiner,* March 15.

Mare Island Naval Shipyard (MINS). 1996. *Historical Study of Yerba Buena Island, Treasure Island, and Their Buildings,* ed. Base Realignment and Closure Environmental Technical Division. Oakland, CA: Defense Printing Service.

McDevitt, E. A. 1946. *The Naval History of Treasure Island*. San Francisco: US Naval and Distribution Center.

Nolte, Carl. 1991. "Small Town in the Middle of the Bay." *San Francisco Chronicle,* June 4.

Progress. 1937. "Pacific Progress Inspires Fair: San Francisco Bay Area Represents the West and All of America in Creating a Pageant of the Pacific." Bulletin no. 1, 4.

Reinhardt, Richard. 1973. *Treasure Island: San Francisco's Exposition Years*. San Francisco: Scrimshaw Press.

Rubens, Lisa. 2004. "The 1939 San Francisco World's Fair: the New Deal, the New Frontier and the Pacific Basin." PhD thesis, University of California, Berkeley.

Ruth, H. D., and Abraam Krushkov. 1966. "Master Development Plan: U.S. Naval Station, Treasure Island, San Francisco, California." Berkeley, CA: Ruth & Krushkov.

San Francisco Bay Conservation Development Commission (SFBCDC). 2011. "Living with a Rising Bay: Vulnerability and Adaptation in San Francisco Bay and on its Shoreline." October 6. http://www.bcdc.ca.gov/BPA/LivingWithRisingBay.pdf.

San Francisco Chronicle. 1965. "Fight Opened for TI Airport." February 16, 6.

———. 1973. "12th Naval Districts to Vanish at T.I." October 19, microfilm.

San Francisco Examiner. 1962. "Treasure Island 'For Sale;' Surplus, Navy Board Rules." November 24, 1, 6.

Shanken, Andrew. 2014. *Into the Void Pacific: Building the 1939 World's San Francisco World's Fair.* Oakland: University of California Press.

Stark, Kevin, Winifred Bird, and Michael Stoll. 2015. "Major S.F. Bayfront Developments Advance Despite Sea Rise Warnings." *San Francisco Public Press*, July 29. http://sfpublicpress.org/searise.

United States and Sedway/Cooke. 1985. "Regional Plan for San Francisco Bay Area Naval Shore Activities." San Francisco: Sedway Cooke Associates.

Urban Land Institute. 1996. "Treasure Island Naval Station, San Francisco: An Evaluation of Reuse Opportunities and a Strategy for Development and Implementation." http://sf.uli.org/wp-content/uploads/sites/47/2011/06/San-Francisco-CA-1999.pdf.

US Congress. 1990. Defense Base Closure and Realignment Act of 1990 (P.L. 101-510). Washington, DC. http://www.brac.gov/docs/brac05legislation.pdf.

US Department of Navy (Navy Department). 2005. "Record of Decision for the Disposal and Reuse of Naval Station Treasure Island, California." Press Release. San Diego: US Department of Defense, Base Realignment and Closure West. http://www.sftreasureisland.org/Modules/ShowDocument.aspx?documentid = 74.

2. The Island at the Center of the Bay

RICHARD A. WALKER

In *The Island at the Center of the World,* Peter Shorto (2004) recovers the forgotten origins of New York, the Dutch colony of New Amsterdam that occupied Manhattan Island in the first half of the seventeenth century. His argument that the past still resonates today is music to the ears of any historian. More than that, it speaks to the geographer, for whom the distinctiveness of place is fundamental, as is the way every locale is connected to the wider world. How surprising what an unprepossessing little island can portend! As everyone knows, New York went on to become the center of the United States and, at times, the world (Burrows and Wallace 1998; Scobey 2002; Cassis 2006). But the elemental geographic truth of the power of place is all too often forgotten, along with the buried landscape of Manhattan and displaced Mannahatta Indians (Sanderson 2009).

In that spirit, I introduce Treasure Island as a foil for larger purposes. This odd little island at the center of San Francisco Bay has a surprisingly rich history, much in need of recovery at this moment when it is the target of fantastic plans for a gleaming urban hub. An otherwise modest mid-century artifact has a great deal to tell us about the past development and present state of the San Francisco Bay Area—the high-tech capital of the global economy. Moreover, this pancake of an island can be a launching pad for a wider inquiry into history and geography at scales far beyond the Golden Gate.

Treasure Island, like Manhattan, lies at the center of several worlds. One of these is San Francisco, once the queen city of the Pacific coast and full of global pretensions. Another is California, shining star of American capitalism and destined to become the biggest and most important state in the nation. A third world that once pivoted on San Francisco Bay is the American military projected across the Pacific Ocean. A fourth is the high-tech wonder world over which Silicon Valley and the Bay Area rule today. The fifth and final world is that of a globe beset by dramatic climate change, which may seal the fate of all low-lying islands.

Borrowing from Shorto's title is fruitful in another way. The Bay Area and New York have this in common: given their immense success as globalized cities, centers of capitalism, and cultural icons, they are both prone to building monuments to advertise their success. New York has the Brooklyn Bridge, Empire State Building, World Trade Center and memorial, Trump Tower, and much more. San Francisco has the Golden Gate Bridge, Transamerica pyramid, and Civic Center, among other things. Treasure Island and its world's fair fit into this cavalcade of monumental self-promotion.

At the same time, lurking behind the hubris is always a dark backstory of a blighted place. For Manhattan that backstory runs from slavery through Irish gangs and the wolves of Wall Street (Burrows and Wallace 1998). As for the City by the Golden Gate, we won't have to look far to see the buried skeletons popping up under our noses. In 2013, for example, as plans were being laid for the redevelopment of Treasure Island into a clone of the new San Francisco, radioactive contamination was discovered in the soil underneath playgrounds and parking lots of a residential area taken over from the US Navy (Lagos 2014). The dangerous particles embedded in the mud are a legacy that the San Francisco's elite, the island's developers, and the Navy would rather forget, but the past has a habit of coming back to haunt the present, "weighing like a nightmare on the brains of the living," as Karl Marx ([1852] 1963) so artfully put it.

The remembrance of things past triggered by these invisible messengers should alert us to the full array of problems plaguing this strange island at the center of the bay. Treasure Island may appear as beautiful, a tranquil scene illuminated by the bright California sunshine, touched by the magic of the Pacific fog sweeping in over the city, and offering splendid views of the urban and natural landscape on all sides—a place ripe with possibility for everyone. Nevertheless, as in the story penned by Robert Louis Stevenson from which it takes its name, Treasure Island is just as likely to be revealed as a cursed spot, doomed to disappoint our fantasies, reveal our follies, and ultimately fade beneath the waves.

Fantasy City

Treasure Island was born in fantasy as the site of the Golden Gate International Exposition (GGIE) of 1939, San Francisco's third entry in the lists of world's fairs.[1] Brash and beautiful, the exposition was a marvelous hodgepodge of buildings in Art Deco style and design bling borrowed from cultures around the Pacific Rim. At the center shone the spire of the Tower of the Sun, echoing the step-back skyscrapers of the 1920s. Within the great halls of Industry, Science, and Homes and Gardens were showcased exhibits from some forty nations and as many US states. Ironically, the most popular part of the fair was the Gayway amusement area, especially Sally Rand's naked girls in cowboy hats, bringing back memories of San Francisco's Old Barbary Coast (James and Weller 1941; Rydell 1993; Pipes 2007).

The GGIE fit the model of world's fairs in proclaiming a kind of utopia of modern living and global fraternity. Over the previous century, world's fairs had been the principal showplaces of industrial accomplishment and unrelenting modernity in the advanced capitalist countries, yielding such wonders as London's Crystal Palace, Paris' Eiffel Tower, and Chicago's White City. San Francisco got in on the act with the Midwinter Fair of 1894, which left the Japanese Tea Garden in Golden

Gate Park, and the Panama Pacific International Exhibition of 1915, of which the Palace of Fine Arts remains in the Marina District on the city's northern waterfront (Ackley 2015). World's fairs were meant to be ephemeral, throwing up wonderful meringues of faux palaces, exhibit halls, and amusements that melted away after the fair's close (Rydell 1984). The GGIE opened in 1939 and lasted just two seasons. Treasure Island remained.

The original excuse for the GGIE was the opening in the mid-thirties of the Golden Gate Bridge and the San Francisco–Oakland Bay Bridge. The site chosen at the midpoint of the Bay Bridge—by far the more important of the two bridges—was certainly appropriate. One can well understand the local pride in the world-class accomplishments of the Bay Area engineers who had designed and built the two massive bridges in record time and under budget. The twin bridges were, furthermore, a powerful statement of the region's expanding network of highways and connections to the rest of the country in the automobile age.

In the course of planning the exposition, its purposes were expanded to take in the entire Pacific basin, making it an international fair. It was therefore festooned with imagery from Asia and the South Pacific, all presented in the spirit of unity and cooperation. Not coincidentally, the proposal for an artificial island in the middle of the bay was born as a plan for an airport to serve the international ambitions of San Francisco—fully a decade before the fair of 1939. The idea was that seaplanes plying the Pacific mail routes could take off and land in the bay and that regular planes would use the flatscape of Treasure Island. In keeping with this joint project, some of the fair's buildings were designed to serve as terminal and hangars for the future airport.

The GGIE was a cheerful veneer over the serious intentions of San Francisco capitalists to promote American domination of the Far East (Brechin 1999). Those ambitions ran into a brick wall with the rise of the Japanese empire, and the Treasure Island fair closed hastily under the cloud of approaching war in 1941. The Japanese attack on Pearl Harbor snuffed out happy notions of a harmonious Pacific basin. Fittingly, the Navy took over the island to serve the war effort, and the civilian airport project for Treasure Island was shelved. Instead, the airport moved to its present location on the Peninsula.

Just as galling to San Francisco's bloated self-regard was that New York mounted a parallel world's fair in 1939–1940 that put the Golden Gate International Exposition in the shade. New York's fair grabbed the headlines and the credit for imagineering the American Century (Gelernter 1995). The General Motors Pavilion, in particular, won all the plaudits for its gigantic Futurama model of an "autotopic" city, designed by Norman Bel Geddes, which presaged the glory days of American suburbanization of the postwar era.

The kicker is that New York had much less to do with the invention of postwar suburbia than California. It was here that television was invented and sitcoms mass produced, catalytic cracking for cheap gas was introduced and the car culture farthest advanced, and single-story bungalows and mass-produced tract housing were perfected (Walker 1995, 1996). Los Angeles took the prize as the postwar suburban paradise, but the Bay Area was exploding outward just as rapidly (Walker and Schafran 2015).

In the end, the Bay Area has grabbed bragging rights from both Los Angeles and New York over the last generation (Storper et al. 2015). Silicon Valley is the acknowledged world center for the fantasies of electronic modernity today, from personal devices to internet portals to social media. Today's equivalents of the world's fairs of the past are the great electronics extravaganzas, such as Oracle OpenExpo and Apple's showcases (formerly MacWorld) held annually in San Francisco. Indeed, the whole city has become a kind of fantasyland of new companies and young techies and the landscape of trendy cafes and restaurants.

Today, Treasure Island is being extolled as the latest and largest bauble in the diadem of San Francisco's new fantasy world. The city has been booming ever since the crash of 2008–2009 and has added new companies, jobs, and workers at a dizzying pace since 2010. Now promoters are targeting the island for a vast new urban development scheme, complete with offices, hotels, and high-rise condos, as well as low-rise housing, commercial space, and a bit of environmentally friendly wetlands. Given that Treasure Island is more central to the whole Bay Area than downtown San Francisco, the new plan appears to be nothing less than a play to make it the new downtown of the metropolis—the island at the center of the center of the high-tech world.

Treasure Islands

When the promoters of the GGIE named the reclaimed land Treasure Island, they were echoing the legacy of the California Gold Rush, the event that put San Francisco on the map. The Gold Rush has remained the founding myth of the city and Northern

California, endlessly revisited and celebrated (see, for example, Caughey 1948; Rohrbaugh 1997). The California Gold Rush was a global event that the imagination of people around the world with the promise of easy fortunes for hardy adventurers (Chinese Argonauts called it Gold Mountain). More than that, California gold and silver infused a rapidly industrializing country and Atlantic economy with much-needed money to grease the wheels of commerce.

Treasure Island is, of course, the title of a children's adventure book by Robert Louis Stevenson published in 1883, but the connections are closer than it might seem. Stevenson was drawn to California from his native Scotland after falling in love with a miner's wife. They married in San Francisco in 1880 and took up residence for a summer in the Napa Valley, where Stevenson wrote *The Silverado Squatters*. A decade later, they returned to sail from San Francisco to the South Pacific in Stevenson's continuing search for fantasy. Meanwhile, San Francisco capitalists were gaining control over much of Hawaii and the Philippines. Another parallel is the mythology of the pirates of the Caribbean on which Stevenson drew in *Treasure Island*, the British equivalent of the glorified tales of the Old West that were at the time common currency of San Francisco literature and, later, Hollywood films and TV.

California went on to be much more than a gold mine, growing into a prosperous region on the strength of its trading networks and manufacturing, centered on the Bay Area. As the mining era wound down, a new source of wealth was revealed in the immense productivity and diversity of the state's agriculture and food processing. It went on to be the greatest agricultural state in the nation in the twentieth century and the leading force in modern agribusiness based on advanced organization, aggressive marketing, massive irrigation, hybridization, and petro-farming (Walker 2004; Romero 2015).

San Francisco ruled over all it surveyed in the nineteenth century as the commercial and banking hub of the state and of the Pacific slope. The city was a virtual Treasure Island of finance that lent and invested its accumulated capital to build up enterprise throughout the American West and across the Pacific basin. As the twentieth century dawned, a new innovation, branch banking, was taken up by San Francisco's A. P. Giannini, and it propelled him to the apex of US finance. By the time of the Golden Gate International Exposition, Bank of America had become the largest in the world (Nash 1992).

Meanwhile, Los Angeles grew rich on citrus farming and oil in the early twentieth century, exploding across the Southern California landscape and doubling the Bay Area in size. The City of Angels industrialized by canning foods, making equipment for the oil industry and refining petroleum, building aircraft and vehicles, and mass-producing films in the studios of Hollywood (Hise 2004). Los Angeles' rapid growth demonstrated another force in the prosperity of the Golden State: immigration. Workers of every stripe have poured into the state since the Gold Rush, lending their skills and initiative to the booming enterprise that is the California economy. By the end of World War II, Los Angeles was poised to overtake Chicago as the number one industrial city in the country.

Much less well known than mining, agriculture, or movies in the history of California is the role of the construction industry, both residential and commercial. At the time of the building of Treasure Island, the state was the construction capital of the country and probably of the world. In the middle of the twentieth century, Californians invented or perfected most of the technologies used to build modern highways, tunnels, dams, aqueducts, airstrips, and refineries. Leading engineering companies of the era included Kaiser, Bechtel, Utah Construction, and Morrison-Knudsen (Walker 1996). For example, Oakland-based Henry Kaiser built highways in the 1920s, dams in the 1930s, ships during the war, and housing tracts and cars afterward; in the process, by 1950, he assembled one of the greatest industrial empires in the world (Foster 1989).

The New Deal era under President Franklin Roosevelt in the 1930s greatly augmented the federal government's willingness to fund infrastructure and regional development projects. The construction of an airport for the Pan American fleet provided a perfect justification for federal support. The US Post Office was already subsidizing the Pacific mail service, the first regularly scheduled air routes in history, and the New Deal was investing in airports around the country (Leighninger 2007). Not only did this signal the rising star of air travel in general, it also spoke to the pivotal place of California in the age of aeronautics and the growing heft of California in national politics. Exemplifying the latter, Henry Kaiser was one of the few big capitalists to support Roosevelt and was amply rewarded with federal contracts for everything from the Grand Coulee Dam to the Bay Bridge. So, not

FIGURE 2.2. Berkeley landfill, June 1987. Photo: Bob Walker. Courtesy of Bob Walker Collection, Oakland Museum of California.

surprisingly, the New Deal paid the tab and the Army Corps of Engineers undertook the reclamation work for what was to become Treasure Island.

After World War II, California surged to head of pack to become the leading state in the nation in terms of economic output and population. The triumph of the Golden State was driven by a fruitful combination of Los Angeles manufacturing, aerospace, and entertainment industries; Bay Area finance, food, and early electronics; and Central Valley agribusiness. To add to the propulsive mix, California hitched its wagon to resurgent Japan and other rising industrial powers of East Asia.

This tight intersection with the booming trans-Pacific economy continues today with the state's links to China, from handling containers passing through the largest ports on the West Coast to cutting deals for local architects, engineers, and financiers to help build the booming cities of the east. No other part of the United States has deeper connections across the Pacific in trade, technology, finance, business services, and corporate linkages (Walker and Lodha 2013). This is not such a far cry from Stevenson's fascination with the South Pacific first gestated in nineteenth-century San Francisco and the dreams of far-off adventures that filled the imaginations of the reading public in an age of imperialism, which he captured so brilliantly in *Treasure Island.*

The Arsenal of Democracy

For half a century, Treasure Island was part of a different imagination—that of the United States military—as the Navy took over and refused to budge. The naval installation is an apt metonym for the military occupation of the entire San Francisco Bay since the dawn of the American conquest of California and for the country's repeated confrontations across the not-so-Pacific Ocean in the twentieth century.

One of main reasons for the forcible seizure of the northern half of Mexico between 1846 and 1848 was that the United States coveted San Francisco Bay, the best natural port on the Pacific coast of the Americas. California bookended the US continental empire-state and gave Washington an open door to Asia. With the annexation of California in 1846, the US Army immediately took over the Spanish-cum-Mexican garrison at the Presidio and built Fort Point to guard the newly christened Golden Gate. Soon, a military archipelago developed on the islands and promontories around San Francisco Bay, which served as the US military launching point for a century of warfare around the Pacific.

From early on, the Army ran logistics from Black Point (Fort Mason) between North Beach and Cow Hollow and grabbed Alcatraz for a prison. Later, it used Angel Island for mustering troops, along with a string of bases around central California. The Marin headlands bristled with artillery batteries at Forts Cronkite and Baker, as did the Presidio and Fort Funston on the San Francisco side. From the Presidio, the Army could oversee an empire, whether commanding Indian wars around the

West or the conquest of the Philippines after the Spanish-American War of 1898 (Walker 2001).

In 1850, the Navy moved upriver to Vallejo, a better landing site than San Francisco itself, and established its first base at Mare Island. There was some naval posturing during the Civil War, but the real naval buildup came around 1900 with the projection of American power in the Pacific under Teddy Roosevelt. The showpiece of this effort was, of course, parading the Great White Fleet around the world, with a notable passage through San Francisco Bay before crossing the ocean. After World War I, the Navy chose San Diego as its West Coast headquarters, much to the disappointment of the Bay Area, but despite this setback naval operations expanded around San Francisco Bay, particularly during World War II (Lotchin 1992). During the war, the bay became the Navy's biggest operations center, a kind of naval lake (see Arbona, this volume). Logistics were run out of the base at the Port of Oakland, submarine operations and repair from Mare Island, ship outfitting and repair at Hunters Point, and ammunition storage and loading at Port Chicago. The rapid growth of naval air power created a need for new Navy airfields at Treasure Island, Alameda Point, and Mountain View. The latter, Moffett Field, was named for the admiral who guided the interwar development of Navy aircraft and served chiefly for antisubmarine operations.[2] The Navy also took charge of Oakland airport during the war. The Bay Area continued to serve the military's purposes right through the Korean, Vietnam, and Gulf Wars, and Treasure Island served as a Navy training and education center.

FIGURE 2.3   San Francisco–Oakland Bay Bridge under construction, 1933–1936. The Bancroft Library, University of California, Berkeley.

The link of Treasure Island to US military aviation was more than a tactical matter. The Bay Area had been an early site of experimentation in aviation, starting from the Army's airfield at Crissy Field in the Presidio. Some of the first stunt flyers entertained at the 1915 fair, but more serious were such avionics pioneers as the Loughhead brothers, who founded Lockheed Aircraft in 1912 before moving it to Southern California during the war. Oakland put in one of the first modern civic airfields in the mid-1920s, with the longest runway in the world, from which Amelia Earhart and other air pioneers launched their transpacific flights. The Boeing Aeronautics School there trained hundreds of the first generation of commercial airline pilots. During World War II, Hewlett-Packard and Litton Industries made the tubes that powered radar and sonar systems for the Allies (Leslie 2000).

In the Bay Area, technology is destiny. But the technology of greatest import to the creation of Treasure Island and the geography of the bay shoreline has not been aviation or bridge building but the humble practice of earth moving. Treasure Island lay at the center of a new post–World War capacity for reworking landscapes, which has had catastrophic effects on the bay environment.

The Broken Shore

A clear link between the building of Treasure Island and the Gold Rush is the way the landscape around the edge of the bay has been reengineered to make way for the civilization that California's mineral treasure unleashed. At the time Treasure Island emerged from the shoals, no one thought twice about filling San Francisco Bay. Bay fill had been a way of life for a century, driven by the lure of making new land from mudflats (Booker 2013). San Francisco's waterfront, filled for docks, warehouses, factories, and houses, bears no resemblance to the craggy outline on early maps. Yerba Buena Cove, Mission Bay, and Islais Creek were all filled in, and the waterfront smoothed out, with most of the material coming from chopping down massive sand dunes and taking huge bites out of Telegraph Hill, Rincon Hill, and Potrero Point (Dreyfus 2008).

The technology of bay fill is simple: construct a dike, dump or pump fill behind the barrier, then compact the material. Builders love bay fill because it is cheap and flat. San Francisco is less Baghdad by the Bay than Kansas on the Mudflats. Other cities around the bay are similarly altered. Along the agricultural frontiers of the bay, the method was even simpler: build a levee around a marsh and pump out the water. The entire Sacramento–San Joaquin River Delta—itself as big as the bay—was reclaimed for farming by this method (Thompson 1959). Thousands of acres of marshes around the bay became cow pastures, and, in the far South Bay, where freshwater inflow is minimal, salt drying beds (Booker 2013).[3]

Most of the islands within San Francisco Bay have been dramatically reshaped by quarrying and filling. To shippers, islands were simply impediments to commerce; to quarrymen, they were sources of stone; and to the government, they were isolated sites for prisons and quarantine. Blossom Rock was blown up entirely. Alcatraz was diced and sliced into a rocky nub. Plans were afoot after World War II to tear down Angel Island and dump it into Richardson Bay to build a New Town. Yerba Buena Island was, at least, useful for holding up the Bay Bridge, so it survived. Hills around the bay fared even worse. Telegraph Hill was mercilessly quarried, mostly to build the seawall; Rincon Hill, cut down over the years, is barely visible under the Bay Bridge landfall; half of Candlestick Hill disappeared into the city's garbage dump; and Mount San Bruno, now revered for its unique ecology, was destined to be deposited into the South Bay as Redwood Shores New Community.

In short, the Bay Area provides a perfect example of how capitalist expansion has always brought a dramatic reworking the face of the earth at its spatial frontiers (Walker and Moore 2015). The result was that the bay ended up the most altered major estuary in North America, its size reduced by almost half through filling and diking. Bay fill looks innocent enough after the fact, but the process of filling has wrecked havoc on the bay's ecology, smothering oysters and other benthos and choking the waters with sediments.

Furthermore, it means reduced areas of mudflats and wetlands where shellfish and plankton are most prolific, shorebirds feed and nest, and fish breed and grow. Add unchecked urban pollution and overfishing, and you have a recipe for a catastrophic decline in the bay's once-abundant fish and wildlife, which have been replaced over the years by a myriad of exotics (Dow 1973; Cohen and Carlton 1995).

A tangible link between California gold and Treasure Island is humble mud and gravel. After the easy pickings of the Gold Rush were exhausted, companies with deep pockets turned to hydraulic mining in the Sierra foothills, washing billions of tons of soil and gravel off the mountains and into valleys and streams. Riverbeds in the Central Valley were raised by several feet of new gravels, and the lighter materials were carried farther downstream to deposit a thick layer of mud on the floor of San Pablo Bay and beyond (Brechin 1999; Beasley 2004). It is possible, therefore, that some of the goop that created Treasure Island came from the goldfields.

Turning goop into gold at Treasure Island required another technology of the mining era: dredging. After hydraulic mining was terminated by court order in the 1880s, miners looked downstream to the gold-laden river gravels of the Sierra rivers, from the Feather to the Tuolumne. River dredging took off around 1900 and, in the process of yielding millions of dollars of gold, destroyed hundreds of miles of riverbed and left thousands of acres of denuded gravel piles, still visible along the riverbanks of Northern California. Dredging was an environmental disaster every bit as great as hydraulicking, but much less well known (Hayes, n.d.; Beasley 2004).

Treasure Island kicked off a new and more devastating era of bay fill in the middle of the twentieth century. The Army Corps of Engineers did a bang-up job, building a three-mile-long rock wall enclosure and filling it with twenty-five million cubic yards of muck dredged from sediment accumulated on the bottom of the bay. It was not the biggest man-made island in the world, as boosters claimed, but it was big and bad enough. The Flat Earth Age of Bay Area expansion was launched.

The war brought huge new military landfills all around the bay, including the Oakland Army and Navy logistics centers at the port of Oakland and the naval air stations at Alameda and Moffett Field. These were followed in the postwar era by massive expansions of the San Francisco and Oakland airports far out into the bay. Alongside these came gargantuan New Town developments on former marshlands and mudflats of the South Bay: Foster City on the Peninsula and Harbor Bay Isle at the south end of Alameda, next to the Oakland airport. These were suburbs destined for tens of thousands of new commuters.

The worst postwar assaults on the bay came in the form of so-called sanitary landfills. The old-fashioned garbage dump was refashioned as way for every city around the bay to buy a free ticket to new beach frontage. The sanitary landfill was developed in Fresno by an Army engineer during World War II, and it was a fitting technology for the Cold War era: "dump and cover." The new dumps were gigantic. San Francisco consumed the whole of Candlestick Cove with its refuse; San Jose smothered hundreds of acres of South Bay sloughs; and East Bay cities like Emeryville, Berkeley, and Albany nearly doubled in size as their dumpsites spread out into the bay. Worse, the sanitary landfills were anything but, and over time they have allowed a vile stew of toxic chemicals to leach out into the bay through their porous barriers.

The airports, New Towns, and sanitary landfills were all made possible by the invention of a new machine, the bulldozer, in the 1930s. Bulldozers replaced dynamite, steam shovels, and Fresno scrapers in the arsenal of earthmoving equipment, and nicely complemented the waterborne dredges as weapons of mass destruction of San Francisco Bay and its surrounding hills. Where else would the bulldozer have been invented but here in the Bay Area, construction capital of mid-century America? Indeed, bulldozers were just a Fresno scraper, invented for leveling fields in the nineteenth century, attached to a caterpillar tractor, invented in Stockton in 1901 for working on marshy Delta islands. Henry Kaiser, the great Oakland builder, bought out the first bulldozer company and made it his talisman (Foster 1989).

The logical endpoint of a century of bay fill was the Reber Plan, the boldest of many proposals to dam and fill the bay until it would have been no more than a fabric of rivers and ponds (Wollenberg 2015). But before Reber could realize his dream, times changed again, and a rebellion broke out against untrammeled bay fill. What had once been seen as potential dry land, a handy dumpsite, and an industrial highway began to be appreciated as a scenic delight and public treasure.

A massive popular backlash, led by the Save the Bay Association, brought a halt to the madness in the 1960s and put the Bay Conservation and Development Commission (BCDC) in charge of the bay and its shoreline (Walker 2007). In the eyes of today's environmentalists, Treasure Island is less of a centerpiece of San Francisco's global ambition than an ineffable eyesore and reminder of the blunders of the past. Yet the island has escaped the curfew on bay development and the progress of returning bay flats to marshland. It now awaits a new urban makeover, if the developers have their way.

They are again looking to its homely flatness to yield a wealth of treasure just like the gold diggings and New Towns of yesteryear, but aiming to do so by selling their plans as the Brave New World of Smart Urbanism and sensitivity to climate change.

FIGURE 2.4   Douglas Skyhawk at the former Alameda Naval Air Station, 2015. Photo: Lynne Horiuchi.

The Ultimate High-Rise

What are we to make of the fantasy of developing Treasure Island as a high-rise mini-city in the twenty-first century? In one sense, it is the predictable outcome of an abandoned world's fair site, as has happened time and again in cities around the world—most recently in Beijing. San Francisco's Marina District was built on the site of the 1915 Panama Pacific International Exposition, a nice moneymaker for the family of one of the city's former Silver Kings, James Fair. If only the Navy had not gotten in the way, Treasure Island might have been developed as another Foster City of tract homes in the postwar wave of suburbanization. But times have changed, and Treasure Island is coveted for a different kind of development today, one suitable to a very different San Francisco and Bay Area.

The Bay Area is the electronics and information technology capital of the world, a place without peer in the global economy (Storper 2013; Storper et al. 2015). The business of high tech has been so good that Silicon Valley is now the economic core of the bay region, not San Francisco (Walker and Schafran 2015). But the old city has made a comeback and has become the start-up center of the electronic metropolis in the 2000s. With changing tastes in urbanity, the young and the restless who populate the offices of firms like Reddit and Twitter prefer to live in a dense, lively city rather than a flat, boring Valley of the Engineering Nerds. San Francisco is bristling with vibrant, fast-growing firms that are changing the way people live, from LinkedIn and Instagram to Airbnb and Uber. Plus, Silicon Valley giants like

Google and Facebook have opened branch plants in San Francisco and even run private bus services for workers commuting from the city to their main offices thirty miles to the south.

Three high-tech booms have hit the Bay Area since 1995, and, despite spectacular crashes in 2000 and 2008, each new upswing has boosted the San Francisco tech economy to new heights. Tech offices have been crowding into the city's central business district, driving up commercial real estate prices. Because office building was blocked from expanding to the west and north of downtown by the anti-high-rise movement of the 1970s and 1980s, San Francisco's downtown has had to push southward. New offices first leapt across Market Street in the 1980s, then on to Mission Bay (a former rail yard) and the Inner Mission in the late 1990s and early 2000s (Walker 2006). More recently, the whole downtown has been recentered in a cluster of skyscrapers along Mission Street, including a Salesforce headquarters that is the first San Francisco building to exceed one thousand feet. Along with this expansion has come new housing for the tech workforce in repurposed warehouses and condominium clusters and high-rises in the South of Market, Mission District, Mission Bay, and the whole eastern belt down to Bayview-Hunters Point.

Along with this growth has come an immense surge in land values in San Francisco and all around the Bay Area. Not only has demand for office and residential space gone up, it has been multiplied exponentially by the immense enrichment of the tech sector and everyone around it. The Bay Area has the highest average wages in the country, but that barely begins to tell the story. With every new tech bubble has come a flood of venture capital and investment capital into local companies, driving up their stock values, making their owners and executives wealthy, and fueling six-figure salaries for twenty-something tech workers (Walker 2006, 2010). The result is that San Francisco—indeed, the whole Bay Area—is the hottest real estate market in the country and among the top five in the world. Average rents and house prices run neck and neck with those in Manhattan.

Meanwhile, people with modest salaries and families with kids have been moving out of the city in droves, landing in Oakland, Daly City, the outer suburbs like Brentwood, and even as far out as the Central Valley (Schafran 2012).[4] Given the price of land in the city, far-sighted developers naturally asked, "Why not make the leap to Treasure Island?" The idea first surfaced in the 1990s at the height of the dot-com boom, as promoters realized that the surplus Navy base could add a nice new slice of territory adjacent to San Francisco's high-priced downtown. Over time, the plan has become more ambitious and elaborate. The current developer, Treasure Island Community Development LLC (TICD), a consortium of Lennar Corporation, Wilson Meany LLC, and Kenwood Investments LLC, proposes to build a virtual new city on the island, including the whole package of residential, office, and retail space for tens of thousands of future San Franciscans.

The idea of a boomtown in the bay was, of course, too much for the politicians of San Francisco to resist. A supremely crafty political operator, Willie Brown, had been elected mayor in 1992 and was presiding over the dot-com bubble of the 1990s. Brown, who ran the state legislature for years as speaker of the assembly,

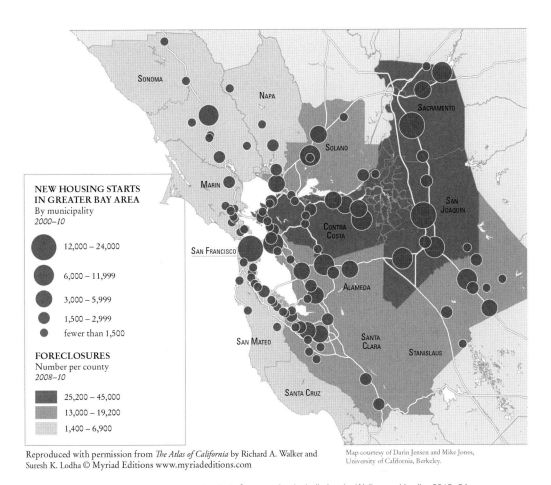

NEW HOUSING STARTS
IN GREATER BAY AREA
By municipality
2000–10

- 12,000 – 24,000
- 6,000 – 11,999
- 3,000 – 5,999
- 1,500 – 2,999
- fewer than 1,500

FORECLOSURES
Number per county
2008–10

- 25,200 – 45,000
- 13,000 – 19,200
- 1,400 – 6,900

Reproduced with permission from *The Atlas of California* by Richard A. Walker and
Suresh K. Lodha © Myriad Editions www.myriadeditions.com

Map courtesy of Darin Jensen and Mike Jones,
University of California, Berkeley.

FIGURE 2.5   Bay Area housing starts, 2000–2010. Cartography: Isabelle Lewis. Walker and Lodha 2013, 64.

was nothing if not a friend to developers. He quickly turned back the tide of the
anti-high-rise forces of the previous decade by booting out the planning commission, ending all regulation of loft developments, and winning approval of the Mission
Bay redevelopment plan on the city's old rail yards after years of controversy. The
chance to grab Treasure Island brought a gleam to Willie's eye. By a happy chance
of history, the boundaries of the city and county extend halfway across the bay to
include Yerba Buena and Treasure Island (much to the chagrin of Oakland).

Then the dot-com bubble burst, putting all development plans on hold. A revolt
against Willie's Way peaked along with the dot-com bubble in 1999 and led to a
near sweep of the board of supervisors election in 2000 by candidates from the
Left (Carlsson 2004). Brown's chosen successor as mayor, Gavin Newsom, barely
squeaked into office. Nevertheless, the tech economy recovered after a few years,
along with commercial development and business-friendly government under
Mayor Ed Lee, after Newsom went on to higher office. Unsurprisingly, the Treasure
Island–Yerba Buena Island Development Project was finally approved in 2011.

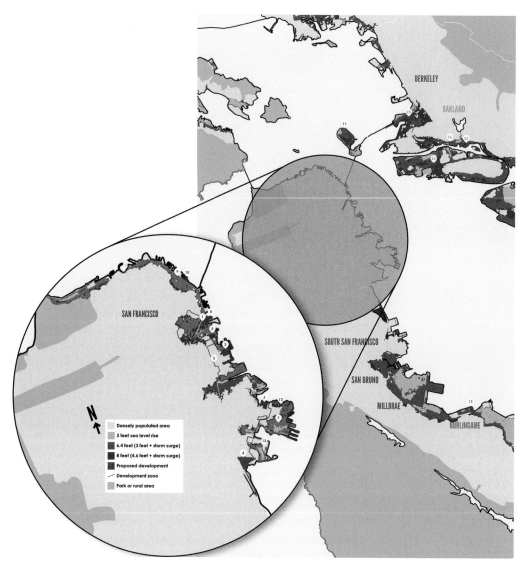

FIGURE 2.6   Sea-level rise around San Francisco Bay. Cartography: Maia Wachtel, Marcea Ennamorato, and Brittany Burson. Courtesy of *San Francisco Public Press*, special issue, summer 2015, B4.

Once upon a time, in the 1970s, many of San Francisco's elite were shocked by high-rises and fought to limit the "Manhattanization" of the city's downtown (Brugman and Sletteland 1971). A lot of folks, high and low, loved the views of the cool grey city draped over its many hills and did not share the corporate enthusiasm for skyscrapers (Walker 1998). By the 1990s, however, a new rallying cry of gentrification arose against unrestrained development, with most of the opposition coming from the city's artists, bohemians, and working people of color (Solnit 2001). That rebellion was quelled after a few years, but the problem of mass displacement by high rents and unscrupulous landlords is back with a vengeance, along with serious unrest from below. The most notable sign of discontent has been the attacks on unmarked Google buses making their stealth runs through the city (Solnit 2013; Fimrite 2014).

Willie Brown's popularity has never waned among the city's elite. In 2014, his many friends in high places pulled off the remarkable coup of having the western half of the Bay Bridge named after him, just as the new eastern half of the bridge connecting Oakland and Yerba Buena Island was completed (and remained nameless). This came as a nasty shock to many people around the Bay Area less enamored of Willie. The city's swells turned out in force for the naming ceremony to bask in Willie's reflected glory, and, naturally, the festivities took place on Treasure Island.

Although San Francisco remains captive to the purveyors of development, the new Treasure Island plan will have to reckon with larger forces than Willie Brown. One of those is the powerful Bay Area environmental movement and particularly its keystone organization, Save the Bay, which will undoubtedly have trouble swallowing the idea of a high-rise heaven in the center of the bay. Save the Bay will be able to mobilize the powerful Bay Conservation and Development Commission, which has oversight of all development around the shores of the bay, to cast its flinty eye on the whole notion. The other major difficulty facing the developers is the unstoppable force of rising sea levels, a matter to which we now turn.

Down by the Bay

The ambitious mega-development plan on Treasure Island is supposed to be a model for twenty-first-century sustainable urbanism. This echoes the Bay Area's wider claim to be the green capital of the world, marrying its reputation for environmental activism to its electronic competence to give birth to a new era of Smart Buildings and Smart Cities (Knuth 2014). But the hard reality of global climate change is likely to trump the optimistic plans of the island's promoters. Sustainable urbanism may or may not sink for economic and political reasons, but natural forces are very likely to have the last word.

Adding Kansas to the United States made sense, but making it oceanfront property was not such a great idea. The north end of Treasure Island was never terribly stable to begin with, because solid rock slips away the farther one gets from Yerba Buena Island; that part of the artificial island began to sink as soon as it was finished. The rest of Treasure Island may not be sinking absolutely, but it certainly is with respect to the water in the bay as the world's glaciers, the Greenland icecap, and the northern tundras gradually melt. The question is not if but when it will be below sea level.

The grim reality of global warming is signaled by the rising seas, which pose a number of dangers around the fringes of San Francisco Bay (BCDC 2009). Conservative estimates are in the range of seven to twenty inches by the end of the century, which doesn't sound like much until you factor in wind and waves when the Pacific blows up the kinds of storms that drive the fifty-foot mountains of water beloved of surfers at Mavericks on the San Mateo coast. The bay is more protected, of course, but ten-foot waves might well occur in extreme circumstances. More telling will be the effects of winter high tides, which are never factored into popular estimates of sea-level rise, and which add two feet to the normal five- to six-foot high tides at the Golden Gate. Levees can be raised, of course, but when they sit on a mud base, their resiliency is always compromised, as witness the Sacramento Delta and New Orleans (Booker 2013).

One would think that this might be an obvious concern for government planners and regulators in a state like California. After all, the Golden State has long been a national leader in environmental protection and energy conservation. Energy consumption per capita is among the lowest in the United States and even measures up to European countries. A bellwether law to reduce carbon emissions, the California Global Climate Solutions Act, was passed in 2006, followed by various energy conservation measures. The Bay Area is well ahead of other parts of the nation in cultivating so-called Green Tech companies, from solar power to instrumentation, construction to electric cars (Walker and Lodha 2013; Knuth 2014).

But not so fast. It seems that climate change denial is prevalent even in California. A good example is the recent drought, a clear marker of natural variability in a Mediterranean climate zone, where long droughts are normal in the record laid down by tree rings. The problem of drought (and flood) will only get worse in a warmer world. The response of agribusiness in the Central Valley and developers in Southern California has been to insist on more of the same water-fed wonderland they have always feasted on. They think the failure of the state to deliver water in 2013 through 2015 is due to environmental protections rather than lack of rain and snow. The liberal governor, Jerry Brown, is determined to build two giant tunnels under the Delta to deliver the entire flow of the Sacramento River to them (Palomino 2013). This is both a recognition that the Delta farmlands are doomed by sea-level rise (which would put salt water into the pumps) and a catastrophe for the bay-delta estuary, which lives on the mixing of fresh and saltwater across the seasons and years. Treasure Island, if it survives sea-level rise, will sit astride an ecologically dying bay.

Even the Treasure Island plan approved by San Francisco designated one-quarter of the island as wetlands—a clear admission of the futility of guarding the whole terrain against the rising waters. Perhaps a perfect system of enclosure can be engineered, but will it be worth the cost? And, given the long list of engineering cock-ups on the new eastern span of the Bay Bridge, who would be willing to bet on those odds (Van Derbecken 2015)? These may be the glory days of Silicon Valley, but the glory days of California construction appear to be dead and gone if the new Bay Bridge is any indication. Treasure Island may attach itself to the core of global high-tech, but IT cannot do much to levitate mud.

What does the future hold for Treasure Island as cipher for San Francisco, California, and the larger world? The forces that created Treasure Island and much of the Bay Area appear to have left it behind. The Golden Gate International

Exposition is long gone. The Navy and the rest of the military fled the Bay Area during the 1990s as the Cold War wound down, the American empire shifted its military bases toward Africa and the Indian Ocean, and the Pentagon got tired of protests against its battleships and bases by Bay Area leftists (the only remaining outpost is up the river at Port Chicago). Kaiser Industries fell apart in the 1960s and the vanguard of urban construction has moved on to Japan, China, and Dubai.

Treasure Island is left as a sinking symbol of past glories, from the Gold Rush to the postwar Golden Age. Environmentalists, still a potent force in bay affairs, would certainly prefer to see it meet the same fate as the South Bay salt flats or the Army's former Crissy Field: a return to marshlands and meandering sloughs. If you want a truly vanguard project in terms of adaptation to global climate change, then do nothing and let Treasure Island melt away. Dust to dust, mud to mud.

Notes

1   I borrow my section headings, with thanks, from the titles of admirable urban books: Hannigen (1998), Shaxon (2011), Baime (2014), Quinn (1981), Brugmann and Sletteland (1971), and Booker (2013).

2   Merchant ships were also constructed and repaired all around the bay during the war, by Kaiser, Bechtel, Bethelem and Moore, making the Bay Area briefly the largest shipbuilding center in the world (Wollenberg 1990).

3   Robin Grossinger and his team at the San Francisco Estuary Institute are engaged in a long term effort to reimagine the bay's coastline as it was circa 1850 (see http://www.sfei.org/cb). See also the bay atlases by Prelinger and colleagues (2013–2014).

4   The San Francisco and San Jose metropolitan areas came in as the third and fourth most unaffordable major housing markets of eighty-five rated in the tenth Annual Demographia.com International Housing Affordability Survey, trailing only Hong Kong and Vancouver. This is due not just to income and wealth, but also to hyperactive lending in booms (Walker 2006; Bardhan and Walker 2011).

References

Ackley, Laura. 2015. *San Francisco's Jewel City: The Panama Pacific International Exposition of 1915.* Berkeley and San Francisco: Heyday Press and California Historical Society.

Baime, Albert. 2014. *The Arsenal of Democracy: FDR, Detroit, and Their Epic Quest to Arm an America at War.* Boston: Houghton Mifflin Harcourt.

Bardhan, Ashok, and Richard Walker. 2011. "California Shrugged: The Fountainhead of the Great Recession." *Cambridge Journal of Regions, Economy and Society* 4, no. 3:303–322.

BCDC. 2009. "San Francisco Bay: Preparing for the Next Level." Technical Report No. C03021/CE9/0E0/000009. Oakland, CA: Bay Conservation and Development Commission.

Beesley, David. 2004. *Crow's Range: An Environmental History of the Sierra Nevada.* Reno: University of Nevada Press.

Booker, Matthew. 2013. *Down by the Bay: San Francisco's History between the Tides.* Berkeley: University of California Press.

Borchert, John. 1978. "Major Control Points in American Economic Geography." *Annals of the Association of American Geographers* 68, no. 2 (June): 214–232.

Brechin, Gray. 1999. *Imperial San Francisco: Urban Power, Earthly Ruin.* Berkeley: University of California Press.

Brugmann, Bruce, and Greggar Sletteland, eds. 1971. *The Ultimate Highrise: San Francisco's Mad Rush toward the Sky.* San Francisco: Bay Guardian Books.

Burrows, Edwin, and Mike Wallace. 1998. *Gotham: A History of New York City to 1898.* New York: Oxford University Press.

Carlsson, Chris. ed. 2004. *San Francisco: The Political Edge.* San Francisco: City Lights.

Cassis, Youssef. 2006. *Capitals of Capital: A History of International Financial Centres, 1780–2005.* New York: Cambridge University Press.

Caughey, John. 1948. *Gold Is the Cornerstone.* Berkeley: University of California Press.

Cohen, Andrew, and James Carlton. 1995. *A Case Study of the Biological Invasions of the San Francisco Bay and Delta.* Washington, DC: US Fish and Wildlife Service. https://nas.er.usgs .gov/Publications/SFBay/sfinvade.html.

Dow, Gerald Robert. 1973. *Bay Fill in San Francisco: A History of Change.* Master's thesis, California State University, San Francisco.

Dreyfus, Philip. 2008. *Our Better Nature: Environment and the Making of San Francisco.* Norman: University of Oklahoma Press.

Fimrite, Peter. 2014. "Google Barge Must Be Moved, State Says." *San Francisco Chronicle*, February 3.

Foster, Mark. 1989. *Henry J. Kaiser: Builder in the Modern American West.* Austin: University of Texas Press.

Gelernter, David. 1995. *1939: The Lost World of the Fair.* New York: The Free Press.

Hannigan, John. 1998. *Fantasy City: Pleasure and Profit in the Postmodern Metropolis.* New York: Routledge.

Hayes, Gary. n.d. "Mining History and Geology of the California Gold Rush." Modesto Junior College. http://hayesg.faculty.mjc.edu/Gold_Rush.html.

Hise, Greg. 2004. "'Nature's Workshop': Industry and Urban Expansion in Southern California, 1900–1950." In *Manufacturing Suburbs*, ed. Robert D. Lewis, 178–199. Philadelphia: Temple University Press.

James, Jack, and Earle Weller. 1941. *Treasure Island: "The Magic City," 1939–1940.* San Francisco: Pisani Printing and Publishing.

Knuth, Sarah, 2014. *Speculating on the Green City: Property and Finance in the Clean Energy Economy.* PhD diss., Department of Geography, University of California, Berkeley.

Lagos, Marissa. 2014. "Is Treasure Island Toxic? Residents Worries Grow." *San Francisco Chronicle*, February 16.

Leighninger, Robert, Jr. 2007. *Long-Range Public Investment: The Forgotten Legacy of the New Deal.* Columbia: University of South Carolina Press.

Leslie, Stuart. 2000. "The Biggest 'Angel' of Them All: The Military and the Making of Silicon Valley." In *Understanding Silicon Valley*, ed. Martin Kenney, 48–70. Stanford, CA: Stanford University Press.

Lotchin, Roger. 1992. *Fortress California, 1910–1961: From Warfare to Welfare.* New York: Oxford University Press.

Marx, Karl. (1862) 1963. *The Eighteenth Brumaire of Louise Bonaparte.* New York: International Publishers.

Nash, Gerald. 1992. *A. P. Giannini and the Bank of America.* Norman: University of Oklahoma Press.

Palomino, Joaquin. 2013. "Tunnel Vision Part One: Delta in Peril." *East Bay Express*, June 12. http://www.eastbayexpress.com/oakland/tunnel-vision-part-one-delta-in-peril/ Content?oid = 3577110.

Pipes, Jason. 2007. *San Francisco's Treasure Island.* Charleston, SC: Arcadia Publishing.

Prelinger, Megan, Rick Prelinger, and Stacy Kozakavich. 2013–2014. *Watersheds, Islands, Shorelines, San Francisco, and East Bay.* Folio atlas series on permanent exhibit at the Bay Observatory Gallery. San Francisco: Prelinger Library and Archives Working Group for the Exploratorium Museum.

Quinn, Arthur. 1981. *Broken Shore: The Marin Peninsula, a Perspective on History.* Layton, UT: Peregrine Smith.

Rohrbaugh, Malcolm. 1997. *Days of Gold: The California Gold Rush and the American Nation.* Berkeley: University of California Press.

Rydell, Robert. 1984. *All the World's a Fair: Visions of Empire at American International Expositions,* 1876–1916. Chicago: University of Chicago Press.

———. 1993. *World of Fairs: The Century of Progress Expositions.* Chicago: University of Chicago Press.

Sanderson, Eric. 2009. *Mannahatta: A Natural History of New York City.* New York: Abrams.

Schafran, Alex. 2012. "Origins of an Urban Crisis: The Restructuring of the San Francisco Bay Area and the Geography of Foreclosure." *International Journal of Urban and Regional Research* 37, no. 2 (March): 663–688.

Scobey, David. 2002. *Empire City: The Making and Meaning of the New York City Landscape.* Philadelphia: Temple University Press.

Shaxson, Nicholas. 2011. *Treasure Islands: Tax Havens and the Men Who Stole the World.* New York: Palgrave Macmillan.

Shorto, Russell. 2004. *The Island at the Center of the World: The Epic Story of Dutch Manhattan and the Forgotten Colony that Shaped America.* New York: Vintage.

Solnit, Rebecca. 2001. *Hollow City: Gentrification and the Eviction of Urban Culture.* Photos by Susan Schwartzenberg. London: Verso Press.

———. 2013. "Diary." *London Review of Books* 35, no. 3 (February): 34–35.

Storper, Michael. 2013. *The Keys to the City: How Economics, Institutions, Social Interaction, and Politics Shape Development.* Princeton, NJ: Princeton University Press.

Storper, Michael, Thomas Kemeny, Naji Makarem, and Taner Osman. 2015. *The Rise and Decline of Great Urban Economies: Los Angeles and San Francisco since 1970.* Stanford, CA: Stanford University Press.

Thompson, John. 1959. "How the Sacramento–San Joaquin Delta Was Settled." *Pacific Historian* 3, no. 3 (August): 49–58.

Van Derbecken, Jaxon. 2015. "Plague of Problems Puts Bay Bridge Seismic Safety in Question." *SFGate,* May 11. http://www.sfgate.com/bayarea/article/Plague-of-problems-puts-Bay-Bridge-seismic-safety-6253577.php.

Walker, Richard. 1995. "Landscape and City Life: Four Ecologies of Residence in the San Francisco Bay Area." *Ecumene (now Cultural Geographies)* 2, no. 1: 33–64.

———. 1996. "Another Round of Globalization in San Francisco." *Urban Geography* 17, no. 1 (May): 60–94.

———. 1998. "An Appetite for the City." In *Reclaiming San Francisco: History, Politics and Culture,* ed. James Brook, Chris Carlsson and Nancy Peters, 1–20. San Francisco: City Lights Books.

———. 2001. "A Hidden Geography." In *The Golden Gate,* ed. Richard Misrach, 145–158. Santa Fe, NM: Arena Editions.

———. 2006. "The Boom and the Bombshell: The New Economy Bubble and the San Francisco Bay Area." In *The Changing Economic Geography of Globalization,* ed. Giovanna Vertova, 121–147. London: Routledge.

———. 2007. *The Country in the City: The Greening of the San Francisco Bay Area.* Seattle: University of Washington Press.

———. 2010. "The Golden State Adrift." *New Left Review* 66 (November–December): 5–30.

Walker, Richard, and Suresh Lodha. 2013. *The Atlas of California: Mapping the Challenge of a New Era.* Berkeley and London: University of California Press and Myriad Editions.

Walker, Richard, and Jason Moore. 2015. "Capital in Nature: The Unending Vortex of Exploitation." Paper for the conference Anthro-Obscene. Stockholm (September 17).

Walker, Richard, and Alex Schafran. 2015. "The Strange Case of the Bay Area." *Environment and Planning A* 47, no. 1 (January): 10–29.

Wollenberg, Charles. 1990. *Marinship at War.* Berkeley, CA: Western Heritage Press.

———. 2015. "The Man Who Saved the Bay by Trying to Destroy It." *BOOM: A Journal of California.* http://www.boomcalifornia.com/2015/04/the-man-who-helped-save-san-francisco-bay-by-trying-to-destroy-it/.

Part I

TREASURE ISLAND, AN AIRPORT, AND THE GOLDEN GATE INTERNATIONAL EXPOSITION

3. How to Celebrate a Bridge

ANDREW M. SHANKEN

Treasure Island, that artificial island built on the shoals of Yerba Buena Island, is now a minor curiosity of windswept fields, aging housing, and an odd hodge-podge of postmilitary institutions. But in its day it ranked among the visionary projects that aimed to transform San Francisco into a metropolitan area that could compete with Los Angeles. The largest human-made island in the world when it was completed, it took its place among the most ambitious public works projects in the nation. In the mid-1930s, the San Francisco–Oakland Bay Bridge (1933–1936), or SFOBB, and the Golden Gate Bridge (1933–1937) tied Marin and the East Bay to San Francisco by car. These spans created a coherent re-gion out of a disjointed geography just as regionalism became a cause célèbre among planners and New Deal writers and artists. The Golden Gate Bridge was the longest suspension bridge of its time, the SFOBB the longest span of any kind. They joined the San Francisco Bay Toll Bridge (now the San Mateo Bridge), which had been the world's longest span when it was completed in 1929. The tens of thousands of boats that crossed the bay each day were gradually re-placed by hundreds of thousands of cars, and trains that ran on the lower deck of the SFOBB. The Caldecott Tunnel (1937) extended the reach of commerce and commuters, allowing traffic to bypass the inner East Bay for the towns and more spacious suburbs east of the hills.

Treasure Island was of a piece with these extraordinary Depression-era public works projects—and part of what Roger Lotchin has called the "Tournament of Cities," an intermetropolitan competition for control of resources and trade on the West Coast (1997, 365). Such visionary projects were often born of in-security in an era when cities proposed momentous, sometimes radical, and even economically destabilizing interventions as a way of spurring growth and upstaging rival cities. San Francisco overcompensated for its waning economic status with outsized visionary projects. In other words, the city's attitudes about the nature of urban land and its transformation were part of a larger regional dynamic of business, governance, and infrastructure that varied throughout the West. In this context, an island exposition-cum-airport was both extraordinary and normative. San Francisco repeatedly "doubled down" on grand infrastruc-tural projects. It is a legacy still visible today, both in the built environment and in the city's willingness to stake its future on large gambits.

A Golden Gate Air Terminal

The origins of the island reach back to 1929, when the idea of filling in the shoals for an airport first took hold. Even then it had become obvious that San Francisco lacked the sort of airport that would help the city realize its ambition to be the center of trade on the West Coast. Although blessed with a large deepwater port and soon to be laced with bridges and tunnels that would give it room to grow, the city had few suitable sites for airports. Mills Field, on the site of the present airport south of the city, had opened in 1927 as a temporary site until a permanent one was located. Relatively far from downtown by the standards of the day, it had little room for growth without encroaching on privately held land or expensive reclamation projects.

The quandary over the airport was especially poignant in San Francisco, whose business community was obsessed with aeronautics as a way of extending its far-flung economic ties. Convinced that air traffic would supplant shipping, business leaders angled for a state-of-the-art airport in order to control Pacific trade. Beginning in 1927, articles and images of airplanes filled the pages of *Pacific Commerce* and *San Francisco Business,* the magazine of the Chamber of Commerce (Figure 3.1). Images like this were overtly anticipatory: the two great bridge projects, still years from completion, are both drawn in. Yet where would the planes land in this future metropolis? Oakland, Alameda, or the Army's Crissy Field? Tellingly, the plane's right wing blocks out the site of Mills Field.

The image was a forecast and an indictment. From the outset, Mills Field was beset with troubles. The Airport Committee of the San Francisco Board of Supervisors, who supported the site, admitted that it was "held up to ridicule and contempt" (Airport Committee 1931, 25). In 1928 it lost Western Air Express and Maddux Air Lines to Oakland, two of the major regional carriers, a significant blow in an era of intra-bay competition. The same year a $1 million bond issue failed in a public referendum, leaving the city short of the funding it needed to bring the field up to date. (Voters rejected the airport even as they supported the bridges and tunnels.) Making matters worse, in 1929 Charles Lindbergh crashed on take-off because his plane, the largest one in the world, sank into a soft spot on the runway (Airport Committee 1931, 25). The newspapers pilloried the city (*San Francisco Chronicle* 1929b, 22). When Lindbergh's wheels got stuck, the *San Francisco Chronicle* editorialized: "What did he do? He sent his passengers over to Oakland in a smaller plane." A tractor pulled his plane out of the mud, then he flew to Oakland, picked up his passengers, and flew from there (1929a).

In a moment of explosive growth in air travel, while dozens of airports were being built across California, San Francisco muddled about. Oakland had just finished a modern airport, located just minutes from its downtown, with speedboat service to San Francisco. In March 1929, nearby Alameda inaugurated a small municipal airport and in August of the same year the San Francisco Bay Airdrome, a privately

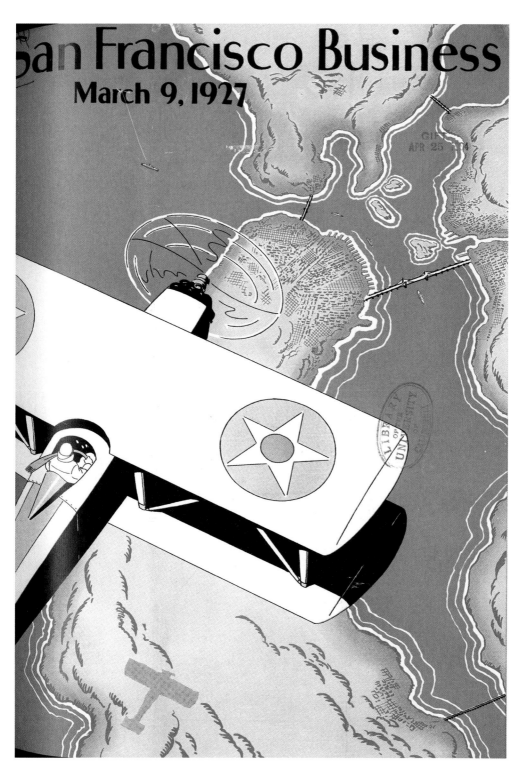

FIGURE 3.1 Cover of *San Francisco Business* 14 (March 9, 1927), 9.

run company that competed with Oakland's municipal airport, also opened in Alameda—it cleverly appropriated the name San Francisco even though it was on the
other side of the bay. These three airports had absorbed "practically all of the air
traffic that [was] aiming for San Francisco" (Baldwin 1932, 20). By 1932, all commercial carriers in the Bay Area used East Bay airports. The *Chronicle* tried to em-
barrass the city into action: "The Boeing airmail transport tried to use Mills Field in
the beginning. So did other big air companies. One by one they have given up and
moved on. . . . . Traffic is forced away . . . because the field is well, ask Lindbergh.
He knows" (1929b).

The Lindbergh debacle reinforced what was long in coming. In 1925, the
US government had begun contracting with private carriers to deliver airmail,
greatly expanding the demand for landing fields. The Air Commerce Act of 1926
led to a flurry of reports, scholarly and architectural studies, and municipal
attempts to figure out exactly where airport planning fit amid park systems, infrastructure and transportation, and city planning (Goodrich 1928; Nolan 1928;
Bednarek 2005). Lindbergh's flight across the Atlantic in 1927 awakened interest in aviation and inspired "cities across the country to plunge into the business
of building airports" (Bednarek 2005, 351). Many of the most successful commercial airlines were founded in the wake of his flight, including Pan-Am and
TWA in 1928, Delta in 1929, and American Airlines in 1930, as well as scores
of now obscure regional carriers.

By the end of the decade, airports were far more than business propo-
sitions or technical achievements. They had become a cultural phenomenon
and a symbol of the age. Architects, planners, landscape architects, and engineers took up airport design. The Beaux-Arts Institute's annual competition
in 1927 for the design of "an Air Transport Terminal" was part of an attempt
to advance the cause of the Beaux-Arts into modern life. In 1929, both *Architectural Forum* (December) and the California-based *Architect and Engineer*
(November) devoted entire issues to airport design, and in 1930 the Lehigh
Portland Cement Company sponsored a national competition for the design
of airports (*Bulletin of the Beaux-Arts Institute* 1928, 5–13). The plane held out
hope for an economic recovery and thus became a symbol of relief from the
Depression.

In San Francisco, the Junior Chamber of Commerce took up the issue.
Formed only in 1927, by late 1931 its Aeronautics Committee began to press
the idea for an airport on the "wastelands" north of Yerba Buena Island. They
invited military, civic, state, and bridge officials, aeronautics experts, Mayor
Angelo Rossi, congressional representatives, and more than fifty city, state, and
commercial leaders to discuss the idea with a formidable group of experts who
they had assembled (*San Francisco Chronicle* 1931, 16). Architect Mario F. Cor-
bett, who would later become well known for his modernist houses, prepared
maps; engineer Lochiel M. King provided estimates on filling the shoals; and engineer B. G. Hindes proposed a layout for the airport that roughly corresponded
to the shape the island would eventually take. By May 1932, they had settled

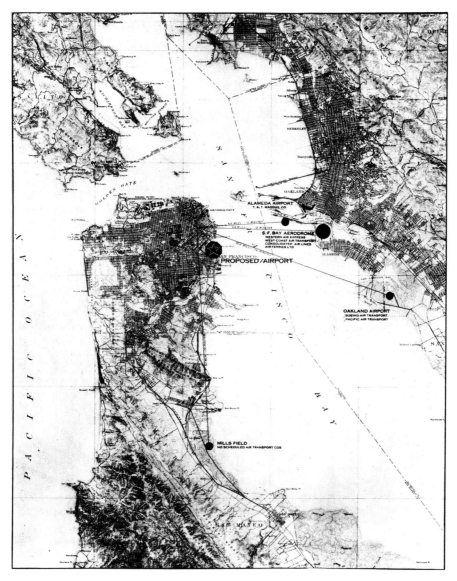

FIGURE 3.2   Map of proposed airport near China Basin. Charles Hobart Baldwin, "Proposed Airport of San Francisco," *Architect and Engineer* 103, no. 2 (November 1930): 52.

on the site and strategically lined up the most important local authorities to appeal to Mayor Rossi, including B. M. Doolin, the superintendent of Mills Field, and E .G. Cahill, the manager of San Francisco Public Utilities Commission (*San Francisco Chronicle* 1932, 17). The Junior Chamber of Commerce endorsed the project as a way of "solidifying San Francisco's paramount position as the focal point for every air line operating in the Pacific Empire" (San Francisco Airport Museum 1932).

Charles Hobart Baldwin, a member of the Junior Chamber of Commerce, laid out the stakes. San Francisco's "mercantile preeminence," he wrote, "is in danger of being transferred to rival cities across the Bay" (1932, 4). Baldwin, who was both an aviator and had architectural training, reviewed the exhaustive search for suitable sites, including McLaren Park, Marina Park, Twin Peaks Mesa, the Marina, China Basin, State Islais, Bernal Heights, Hunters Point, the shoals of Goat Island (later renamed Yerba Buena Island), as well as sites in San Mateo, Millbrae, and Bay Farm Island. These competed with proposals to build great platforms over piers and train sheds (Dohrmann 1927, 22–23). Most of these sites were dismissed because they lacked sufficient land, were too crowded, or presented insurmountable technical challenges. Baldwin urged the abandonment of Mills Field, which by 1932 hosted no commercial flights.

Baldwin had been agitating about the airport for several years. Two years before, in an article for the *Architect and Engineer,* he presented a map that made clear just how remote the South San Francisco site was to the city (1930, 52–60) (Figure 3.2). At the time, he favored a site near China Basin, but by 1932 his vision had evolved. In place of Mills Field, he proposed a "system of airports" unlike existed anywhere in the country, which would turn San Francisco into "the aviation center of the entire Pacific Coast" (1932, 19). The various airports would serve different functions and parts of the city and region. To the north, a small airport on the Marina would cater to private flyers, and the top of Hunters Point would be leveled to serve the south parts of San Francisco. It was a solution born of the logic of zoning.

Meanwhile, Baldwin and the Junior Chamber of Commerce took up Major Harvey S. Burwell's idea to fill in the Yerba Buena shoals for "a unified terminal for commercial air lines serving the Bay district" (Baldwin 1930, 59). In fact, Burwell's idea was simultaneously narrower and more ambitious. He called for a naval air base on the shoals site as part of a regional approach to air transit that would cut through competition between Bay Area cities. He imagined a "central base terminal" within minutes of the "center of business," with "suburban ports" arrayed throughout the bay (*San Francisco Chronicle* 1929c, 11). Burwell, an aviator who served as the commanding officer of the air corps unit of the ROTC of the University of California, Berkeley, was among the earliest proponents of a system of airports. Henry V. Hubbard, a national figure in city planning based at Harvard University, argued for a "regional system of airports" in 1930 (Hubbard, McClintock, and Williams 1930, 20–36). The same year, the US Department of Commerce came out in support of the same idea, categorizing airports into three distinct types: smaller airports for private aviators; service airports for shipping, mail, and similar business activities; and terminal airports that took most of the commercial air traffic of a city (1930, 2). The Commerce report matches Baldwin's vision: he was applying national ideas to the local situation in San Francisco.

An airport on the shoals could only work, of course, after the city had chosen the Bay Bridge route over Goat Island (now Yerba Buena Island). Congress approved the bridge site in February 1931, and within a year the San Francisco Board of

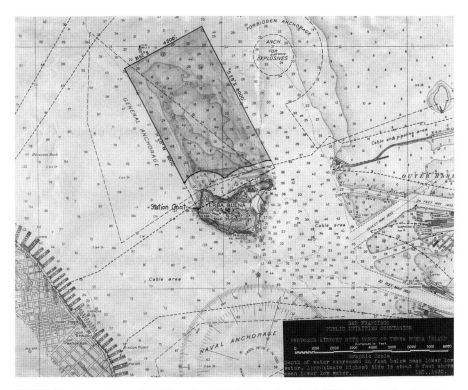

FIGURE 3.3   Proposed airport site, December 1932. San Francisco Public Utilities Commission. Donald D. Larson Collection on International Expositions, Special Collections, Fresno State University.

Supervisors voted unanimously to support the proposal for a mid-bay "Golden Gate Air Terminal." City officials hoped that the future airport could be incorporated into the construction of the bridge. By May 1932, officials had begun to sketch out a vision for the island. That December, the San Francisco Public Utilities Commission roughed out its plan for a rectangular shaped island, which shows that the key municipal players were committed to the site long before it had been officially sanctioned (Figure 3.3). Separated from Yerba Buena Island by a channel, and lacking the causeway and bridge that would connect it to both sides of the bay, the new island was little more than a sounding, as the depth marks suggest, yet in outline it anticipated the basic shape and dimensions. As the bridge moved forward, the supervisors commissioned engineering studies from Charles H. Purcell, chief engineer for the SFOBB, for traffic connections to the proposed airport (Board of Supervisors, 1933, 215). A host of civic groups threw their weight behind the idea, and Rossi soon appealed to the state to cede the land to the city and county of San Francisco. The most important were the Columbus Civic Club, Haight-Ashbury Improvement Association, Property Owners' Association of North Beach, Eureka Valley Promotion Association, and the California Court (*San Francisco Chronicle* 1932c, 17). The support compelled Governor James Rolph, San Francisco's previous mayor, to grant 720 acres of submerged land to the city in June 1933.

From Airport to Fair

Within a month, the idea for hosting an exposition as a bridge celebration on the shoals site had been proposed and published in the newspapers (*San Francisco Chronicle* 1933, 5). The airport and fair converged. Local interests battled for two years before the site was officially chosen, but the airport and exposition had been linked in the popular imagination in a way that made it seem like a foregone conclusion. Yet the San Francisco Board of Supervisors was divided (*San Francisco News* 1934). The Advisory Planning Committee for the Bridge Celebration, as the exposition was first known, was formed at the beginning of 1934. In February, the committee came out in favor of the shoals, in part because it minimized the "risk of sectional antagonism . . . [and] community jealousies" in the Bay Area (Advisory Planning Committee 1934, 4). The site, moreover, had the advantage of being directly connected with the bridges—the object of the celebration and the means by which many people would get to the fair (4).

One month later, Mayor Rossi authorized architects W. P. Day and George Kelham to study potential sites for the fair. Day was an experienced establishment architect and engineer. As superintendent of building permits in San Francisco, he had designed several landmark buildings, including the Mark Hopkins and Sir Francis Drake Hotels, the Chronicle Building, and the cathedral, and in Sacramento the state library and courts building. Day had the technical skill to test the site himself and the design background to project how the fair might look. Kelham was a versatile traditionalist who could move freely between the Beaux-Arts classicism of his training and Art Deco. He had been supervising architect for the 1915 exposition, as well as for the UC Berkeley campus, and designed the San Francisco Public Library and the Federal Reserve Bank. They were among the elite and enterprising architects who had rebuilt San Francisco after the earthquake and fire of 1906. Day would go on to be the director of the Department of Works for the Golden Gate International Exposition (GGIE), and its vice president. Kelham would head the Architectural Commission until his death in 1936. Along with their colleague Arthur Brown Jr., most of the architectural cadre that would design the fair was in place from its inception.

Time was short and events moved quickly in 1934 and 1935. In May 1934, Day and Kelham published a proposal for the fair in the *San Francisco Chronicle*. It showed the characteristic rectangular island with its corners chamfered off and filled with a thick poché of Beaux-Arts palaces and courts sheltering the fair against westerly winds—the fair in embryo (*San Francisco Chronicle* 1934, 11). In July, they released their official report, which argued compellingly for the artificial island and dismissed all other sites (Day and Kelham 1934). Urban infrastructure was of paramount importance: the island's eventual use as an airport made it especially desirable. The rest of the report set down in detail a surprisingly complete description of the plan of the fair, including plans for dredging and filling, fog calculations, how to bring water to the artificial island, and other technical details. Empirical data and expert opinion were thus added to the emerging preference for the shoals site (Day and Kelham 1934, 2–3). Day had the gravitas as an architect and administrator, and the technical chops as an engineer, to have his findings taken seriously (*Architect and Engineer* 1938, 38). The also-rans had little chance.

Day and Kelham quickly worked out the main aspects of what would become the Key Plan: "The palaces are grouped around a central tower . . . with intervening courts of great width." The tower would be "of commanding height," with the buildings to the southwest built "high enough to act as barriers to the wind, enabling the entire area, with the exception of the auto parking space, to be in the lee" (*Architect and Engineer* 1938, 15–16). Modifications would be made, but here was the kernel of the plan before the exposition had been approved, the site chosen, or an official administrative body sanctioned by the city to create the fair (Bottorff, n.d., 31). Arthur Brown Jr., acting in his double role as a city supervisor in San Francisco and an architect of international repute, exerted his influence. He helped orchestrate a set of studies that made the alternative sites seem expensive or impractical (Board of Supervisors 1935, 399, 1099–1100). Although many details remained, the project had the feeling of a fait accompli.

In April 1935, city leaders delivered an ultimatum: "If use of the shoals is refused it is safe to say there will be no exposition—unless the Board of Supervisors themselves promote and finance one" (Board of Supervisors 1935, 399, 437). The matter was put to a public referendum in May 1935—the same public that had rejected the expansion of Mills Field. San Franciscans came to the polls in a "record-breaking turnout" and the shoals site passed with a resounding majority (*San Francisco News* 1935).

Brown, in his role as supervisor, quickly motioned to appoint the Exposition Company, which already employed him as architect, to plan and conduct the fair on the shoals (Board of Supervisors 1935, 475, 1513). Day was immediately appointed director of the works; soon after Kelham became chief of architecture. The first dated sketch of the fair was made on July 8, 1935, days before the Exposition Company was made official. It was by Arthur Brown Jr., who was already tinkering extensively with the plan.

Artificial Islands

How did a group of conventional architects and civic leaders come to support and even obsess over a visionary plan to build an island in the bay for an airport and exposition? What appears at first blush to be an outlandish scheme was in fact a common way of thinking about land, airports, and municipal infrastructure. Much of the coastline of the San Francisco Bay had been reclaimed using the same methods needed to create Treasure Island. The marina was built on the tidal flats, marshes, and dunes that were "improved" for the 1915 exposition. With a number of holdovers from the earlier fair in charge of the GGIE, it is not surprising that they would again link civic improvement and reclamation to the exposition. The great bridge projects made dredging and filling a part of everyday life in the Bay Area.

Cities, moreover, had used fairs as pretexts to improve infrastructure and as a form of civic improvement. Most recently, the 1933–1934 Century of Progress Fair in Chicago—one of San Francisco's models—took place on Northerly Island, an artificial island built in the early 1920s that realized part of Daniel Burnham's Chicago Plan of 1909. Even before the island was finished, a plan to locate Chicago's airport there was widely approved by the business community, Mayor William Hale, and the Chicago South Park Commission.

Throughout the period, airports were proposed on reclaimed shoreline, including San Francisco's airport, which was extended into the bay from the original site of Mills Field. In fact, the shallows there were being dredged and filled using Works Progress Administration (WPA) funding at the same time that Treasure Island was being built. Experts favored shoreline sites because they were free of obstructions and open to easy expansion (Hubbard, McClintock, and Williams 1930, 22). In the late 1920s, San Diego and Portland both built airports on sites reclaimed from water, the latter by tripling the size of tiny Swan Island, which sat in the Willamette River, and connecting it to the mainland via a causeway, as would happen later at Treasure Island. The Chamber of Commerce knew this project well. In 1927, D. R. Lane, one of its members, flew the western airmail route and wrote a series of articles about the airports he saw for *San Francisco Business*. He found Portland's airport "most striking," in part because its financial situation resembled that of San Francisco, but Lane was especially enamored of the creative and spectacular reclamation of land so near the downtown (Lane 1927).

Other cities had used similar strategies. In Los Angeles, San Francisco's main competition for control of air-based commerce, Allen Field began operating as a civilian airport in 1927 on Terminal Island, an artificially enlarged island that had originally hosted the Los Angeles Terminal Railway. Day and Kelham later looked to New Orleans, where the newly finished Shushan Airport was built on land reclaimed from Lake Pontchartrain (1934). Creating land was one of the few ways that cities could find sites near commercial centers without resorting to eminent domain.

Simultaneously, an interest in floating airports or seadromes and island airports arose in the 1920s and gained momentum in the early 1930s, just as the Yerba Buena shoals were being proposed as a site for the airport. Engineer Edward Robert Armstrong widely published his ideas for a floating platform or seadrome akin to an oil platform that could be placed in deep water, allowing aircraft to island hop their way across the oceans (*Architectural Record* 1934, 344). The idea of island airports was widely disseminated in magazines like *Popular Mechanics*, architecture journals, and news magazines (see, for example, *Architecture* 1928; White 1929; Salamanca 1930). In 1933, the German airline Lufthansa retrofitted the *Westfalen* as an aerodrome and floated it to the mid-south Atlantic so that Germany's planes could jump between West Africa and South America. The next year, Norman Bel Geddes, the audacious industrial designer, proposed a floating airport for New York City (*Literary Digest* 1933, 14).

In these early years of aviation and city planning, the real and the visionary often blended. Treasure Island was part of this moment of overheated speculation, putting it in dialogue with national issues of aviation and land use, as well as international issues of commerce and culture. In an age when smaller airplanes could travel only hundreds of miles without refueling, a trail of small floating airports spanning the Pacific would have been a powerful vision, especially to the San Francisco business elite wishing to tap into the commercial potential of Pacific markets. They imagined their artificial island as the West Coast terminus of a great system spanning the Pacific. In other words, Baldwin's idea for a regional system of airports grew quickly into a vision for a network that would span the globe.

With the concept of island hopping coming into vogue, the idea of holding the exposition on the island also would have resonated on other levels. San Francisco, isolated on its peninsula, often thought of itself as an island. Competition between the cities of the Bay Area, moreover, made a mid-bay island all the more appealing as a way to calm interurban rivalries. A less obvious frame of reference is Pacific Island culture. Although the fair was not given its thematic name, Pageant of the Pacific, until 1936, from the beginning it aimed itself at cultures that ringed the Pacific Ocean—in part to distinguish itself from the New York fair of the same year. Treasure Island would thus join Angel Island and Alcatraz Island in recalling the archipelagos of Asia and the South Pacific. Interest in Pacific Island culture had grown in the late 1920s and early 1930s. San Francisco's business community sought a stable, peaceful Pacific theater. As Chamber of Commerce member Robert Newton Lynch wrote at the time,

> When two intrepid flyers crashed into Molokai, having made the trip from San Francisco to the Hawaiian Islands in a single day . . . [they] annihilated the element of time in transportation across the Pacific. Heretofore the element of time has been the determining factor in solving and adjusting the relationship of nations . . . We have now come into an age when there will not be time to get ready for the inevitable. (1927, 6)

The ominous last sentence, written fourteen years before the attack on Pearl Harbor, shows the extent to which the San Francisco business community had anticipated the new dynamics of air travel. Preoccupied with the intertwined prospects of aviation and the Pacific, its members were willing to go to great lengths to defend their economic interests from competition and war. This dynamic between flight, Pacific commerce, the community of nations, culture, and the specter of war built Treasure Island. Its name famously invoked the gold dust that floated down the Sacramento River into the Bay in the nineteenth century. But it just as easily could have referred to the untapped commercial riches that lay west of the Golden Gate—a modern Gold Rush waiting to be mined by intrepid aviators.

Building the Island

Bids went out for the dredging in August 1935. The work proceeded at a blistering pace. The WPA provided funding, but it hinged on making land available for the first buildings no later than July 1936 (Corps of Engineers 1937; James and Weller 1941). Contracts were only advertised in February of that year, the same month that the overmatched WPA handed the work over to the Army Corps of Engineers. Dry land had to rise in mere months. The plan involved building a seawall to provide still water for the fill and shelter for the dredges. The perimeter acted like an enclosure dike and resisted the lateral movement of the fill (Corps of Engineers 1937, 11) (Figure 3.4). The workers then filled in the area from south to north. Land for the three permanent buildings—the Administration Building, Hall of Transportation, and Palace of Fine and Decorative Arts—emerged on the south edge of the island, where the shoals were shallowest. An aerial photograph from August 1936 reveals the first building foundations. These were to become the terminal and hangars for the airport.

By April 1936, the first bump of land appeared amid dredges as slotted pipes discharged sand. The *Sacramento* dredge made its first fill on the southwest corner of the shallows, and the *San Joaquin* dredge built the causeway, discharging sand

FIGURE 3.4 Construction of perimeter wall and first building foundation, August 27, 1936. Yerba Buena Shoals Project, National Archives and Records Administration, San Bruno.

through slotted pipe laid out along its length (Figure 3.5). The *Monarch*, a clamshell dredge, placed foundation for the upper section of rock wall and *Culebra*, a hopper dredge, collected material from a borrow area near Alcatraz Island and discharged it on the shoals. The *Multnomah* rehandled this material on the eastern side, extending it north, and pipeline dredges pumped it over the seawall. Meanwhile, derrick barges helped build the seawall, their cranes swinging cyclopean rocks from boat to shoal.

FIGURE 3.5   Boy on pipe discharging sand, July 28, 1936. Charles H. Lee Papers, Special Collections and University Archives, University of California, Riverside.

As the island slowly emerged, workers suspended a pipeline for water across the unfinished bridge. The two projects had been linked in the imagination; now they were to be connected as infrastructure. In August, piles had been driven into the new soil and foundations for the hangars rose improbably above the waterlogged fill. By September, the causeway had been filled, partially banked for its roadway, and a strip of land continued northward, forming a spit where the roadway would eventually continue. By the end of 1936, the perimeter was fixed everywhere but on the northern edge, where the shoals were deepest and the sand most liquid (Figure 3.6). About one-quarter of the island had emerged above the water.

The entire perimeter was firm by the first of June 1937 and buildings began to emerge. The land was mostly level, the terminal and hangars largely

FIGURE 3.6   Laying pipes on the emerging island, 1936–1937. Photo: Don K. Oliver. Donald D. Larson Collection on International Expositions, Special Collections, Fresno State University.

finished, and the outlines of the main buildings visible on the ground. But the northern part of the island was still waterlogged and unready to receive the thousands of cars that would park there. Then technical issues threatened to halt the project. The northern edge lay on the most plastic mud. A stretch of some five hundred feet began to heave and settle as much as fifteen feet in elevation (Corps of Engineers 1937, 19). Engineers trenched a four-hundred-foot cut to a depth of twenty to thirty feet, undercut the muddy bottom, and backfilled it with heavy hopper sand. The interior was compromised as well. There "the mud stiffened and would neither move ahead through the spillway" as they tried to push it out with sand from the borrow areas. Nor would it sink under the weight of the new fill (19). Instead, the concentrated mud simply rose above the sand, as high as eighteen feet, five feet above the planned height of the island. A dredge called the *Pronto*, then at work in the Sierra Nevadas, had to be dismantled, shipped to the site, "raised unit by unit over the rock wall," and reassembled over the mud (20). For days, as the *Pronto* dredged out the mud, the *Sacramento* filled the hole with heavy hopper sand and the island rapidly grew firm.

Other more delicate operations then stole the attention of the engineers and workers. Because they dredged soil from the bay and delivered it by saltwater suspension, it had to be leached and treated before it would be fertile. Time again became taskmaster. The soil had to be ready for planting by May 15, 1938. Treatment began in August 1937. Under the direction of Charles H. Lee, a leading hydraulic engineer in California and the chief of the Division of Water Supply and Sanitation for the GGIE, they lowered the water table by pumping, and then leached out salt, but they also had to replace soil that was resistant to leaching. The water table was highest in the center of the island, creating a dome of salt water in the fill. With few precedents for how to go about this work, after several false starts, they began drilling wells (see Lee 1938a, 13; 1940). Volume pumping began on January 11, 1938, and ended four months later. They drilled more than two hundred wells to a depth of twenty-five feet, spaced about sixty feet apart, and grouped around pumps, which drained millions of gallons of briny water from the sand (Figure 3.7). Simultaneously, they "backfilled with coarse sand to form a collecting envelope" (Lee 1938b, 4). This allowed them to pump water out of the ground and lower the water table. They then set up sprinklers to dissipate the clay, replaced areas of clay with soil when necessary, and amended it with gypsum.

Even as the water retreated, workers had to insert infrastructure. They laid forty miles of steel pipe in seven systems for the water supply (Lee 1940). On July 22, 1938, a few months before the fair opened, Lee found that the pipes had begun to corrode and leak. The same held for the gas lines. By September 1938, the fair due to open in February, the rate of leakage had increased to fifteen new leaks per week, a veritable crisis for an island exposition with one source of water. Lee found the cause of the pitting was soil corrosion: "pipes acted as conductors between sand and clay, which had different charges, picking up electric

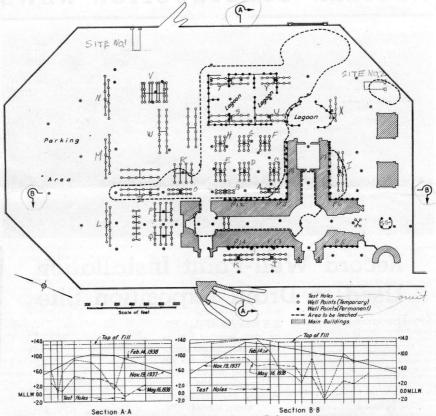

FEATURES of well-point drainage system indicated on map of Exposition site. Each of the groups of points was connected to a pump discharging into the storm drain system on the island. Only the main building units are shown and these are provided with permanent installation of well-points. Other buildings will occupy the remainder of the island, except for the parking area at the north. The test holes were used to determine water level.

RESULTS of the well-point drainage are shown on the two typical profiles. Measured by means of the test holes the progressive lowering of the saltwater table is shown approaching or below the required El. 6.

plished and the other elements of the construction program which had to be carried forward simultaneously.

The absolute necessity for the installation of an elaborate drainage system was apparent from the studies showing the relatively small amount of natural drainage which had taken place following the completion of the fill. Observations confirmed the fact that the central section of the island would not lose its salt water content for many years, and that ground water would not be low enough to permit necessary work during 1938.

Sinking the points

Points were installed in sand-filled holes which were jetted down to a depth of about 23 ft. below the surface of the fill. The installing of these points was a relatively simple and rapid operation, the crew of four completing from 10 to 20 installations in an 8-hr. shift.

An A-frame of timber was used to support the jet pipe. This pipe was 22 ft. long, of 1¼-in. diameter, and connected by rubber hose to the fire hydrants available on the island. These hydrants, with 125-lb. static head, develop a jetting pressure of between 90 to 100 lb.

The end of the jet pipe (see illustration) was provided with an 8-in. diameter piece of pipe, open at both ends, which extended back from the discharge end for a distance of 2 ft. This outer shell was held in position by welded

current from sandy areas and discharging it locally into clay balls . . . with resultant pitting at the points of discharge." It essentially acted like a wet cell battery, eating away the metal as it conducted between these two soil environments (Lee 1940, 316, 318).

The pressure on the engineers was immense. With only months to finish dozens of buildings and plant a million plants, leaks were springing up throughout the system. Lee convinced W. F. Day to use a process called cathodic protection, which involved changing the electrical charge of the soil, thus rendering the pipe negative to the soil. They introduced direct current into the surrounding soil by sinking used heavy pipe at some distance from the pipeline itself. These acted as anodes, which were quickly corroded, after which the charge flowed through the soil and back into the pipe, converting anodic areas to cathodic ones, and balancing out the charge (Lee 1940, 319).

FIGURE 3.8   Mature trees barged in to Treasure Island, 1938. Harry W. Shepherd Collection, Environmental Design Archives, University of California, Berkeley.

After the soil was treated, 2,115 trees were barged in, the most abundant of which were acacia (630), eucalyptus (360), olive (271), palms (186), and pittosporum (157) (Figure 3.8). Most were full-grown specimens, dug up from their locations and transported with their roots in attached soil encased in wooden boxes, in which they would be planted. This presented problems because many of the roots extended as far as five feet but had to remain above the water table, where they might come into contact with saline water (Lee 1938b, 4). Every hole had to be prepared with gypsum-enriched backfill surrounding each box to serve as a buffer against the migration of salinity. They drilled casing wells with gravel envelopes. If water were to seep into the well, the gravel was there to prevent briny sand from being carried with the water (Lee 1938b, 27). The island—now artificial in several ways—was ready.

A Pacific Island

As is well known, after the fair the Navy took over Treasure Island, which was almost immediately rendered unusable as an airport by the larger and faster planes developed to fight the war. There would be no Golden Gate Air Terminal. This apparent failure, however, is almost entirely overlooked, partly because the city put almost no money into it in the first place. Financially it was as dispensable as the fair. As infrastructure it became redundant, as well. Mills Field, now expanded with WPA funding, became viable and has served as San Francisco's airport since the war.

In the moment of its creation, however, Treasure Island provoked other issues. San Franciscans had been sold on the shoals site for the exposition based on a vision of a mid-bay airport, one that would unite the cities of the bay as it helped the region compete with other cities on the West Coast for dominance in the Pacific. Some of this vision played off of larger urban and regional concerns involving labor, economic growth, and interurban competition. In the mid-1930s, the stakes were high. As the fair was being proposed, the Waterfront Strike of 1934 paralyzed San Francisco. The fear of violence and communist agitation, let alone a work stoppage, would have ruined the fair. The city reached an agreement with the unions to guarantee that exposition workers would not strike so long as union labor was used and 60 percent of the workforce was drawn from public relief rolls (Rubens 2004, 20–23).

Treasure Island is the swan song of these political and economic processes. As bold as the bridges, exposition, and airport appear, they were born of anxiety. Before World War II, the intense competition between western cities for resources created a system of metropolitanism, by which cities essentially operated as city-states waging commercial wars for regional dominance. Growth became the central mechanism through which a city could make vast claims (Lotchin 1979, 360–362). This was not just a matter of elites and boosters having their way. Ordinary citizens elected booster mayors and ratified public works projects. This is particularly important for understanding the morass surrounding the San Francisco airport, which, as infrastructure, was as essential as the bridges to the growth of the city. The same citizens that supported two of the most dramatic bridge projects in the world balked at turning Mills Field into a major airport. Simultaneously, they backed building an artificial island for the fair and airport. In other words, San Franciscans sometimes rejected pragmatic local projects in favor of risky, visionary, and symbolic projects.

San Francisco's waning influence prompted this state of affairs. The grand projects reflect the last gasp of early twentieth-century urban competition—something San Francisco appeared destined to lose in the 1930s. The city no longer had the raw population necessary to compete with Los Angeles. The ebb of San Francisco's power spurred a self-sustaining dynamic in the city (Lotchin 1979, 364).

> As the size of government grew in response to San Francisco's relative economic decline, more power over the creation and implementation of policy fell into bureaucratic and supposedly expert hands, like those of the chief engineer, the airport manager, and the head of the Public Utilities Commission. This windfall gave

the bureaucrats an incentive to favor still more urban competition, thereby placing further power within their spheres. (369)

Arthur Brown Jr. demonstrates this crossover from professional expertise to bureaucratic power, as does W. P. Day with his wealth of managerial expertise. Brown and Day were servants of the larger phenomenon of urban competition. Roger Lotchin aptly calls this a "defense mechanism" in a moment of "urban status anxiety." One of the outcomes of these urban battles in the early twentieth century was a remarkable string of public works, much of which brought employment to the Bay Area during the Depression (369) (Figure 3.9).

Interurban competition manifested itself most often in San Francisco's attempts to overcome its geographical limitations with bridges, highways, and tunnels (Lotchin 1979, 375). Air travel, of course, became an indispensable element of transcending the city's physical boundaries. A great airport linked to the bay's advantages would draw commerce regardless of the size of the city. This explains why the tone of the Chamber of Commerce was so urgent in the early 1930s, and why otherwise prudent city supervisors, businessmen, and architects put an airport in the middle of the bay. Finally, it also explains the compelling necessity of an exposition to celebrate the bridges and the coming of age of San Francisco as an international metropolis.

Might we see similar gambles, in spite of vast cultural, economic, and political differences between then and now, in how the city currently treats its infrastructure

FIGURE 3.9   Major public works in the Bay Area in the early twentieth century. *The Argonaut*, May 28, 1937, 18.

and resources? Conscience now disallows scraping the bottom of the bay to create new islands or filling it for an airport. Radical political antagonism to federal government makes the possibility of finding public funds for new bridges and tunnels remote. With regional thinking withered on the vine, the sort of infrastructure that could redefine a metropolitan area is also moribund—replaced, perhaps, by the California high-speed rail project, a vision that speaks to the end of the tournament of cities. Yet, Treasure Island still embodies the earlier impulses. How deeply impractical to house thousands of people on unstable landfill in the middle of the bay, linked only by a single causeway and ferries. Looking beyond the island to how the city goes about its business, what a thin economic premise it is to base a city's fortunes on the vicissitudes of silicon. Instead of great bridges, open to the multitudes, Google and Apple buses transform neighborhoods. The difference is dramatic, but the scale of the gamble is similar. Will the promise, hatched in the 1930s, of creating a global city through aviation be fulfilled through information technology? The early indications are bleak. Private projects backed by global resources have indeed replaced civic projects launched with federal funds. It is a global wager anted up with local assets. Time will tell whether these silicon bridges and tunnels will leave a legacy as enduring as the physical infrastructure of the 1930s.

References

Advisory Planning Committee for the Bridge Celebration Founding Committee (Advisory Planning Committee). 1934. "Report to J. W. Mailliard, Jr." William G. Merchant Collection, Environmental Design Archives. University of California, Berkeley.

Airport Committee of the Board of Supervisors. 1931. "San Francisco Airport: A Report." San Francisco: Airport Committee, Board of Supervisors.

Architect and Engineer. "World's Fair Builders: William P. Day." March 1938, 38.

Architectural Record. 1934. "Transatlantic Seadrome Design by E. R. Armstrong." Vol. 76 (November): 244.

Architecture. 1928. "Plan for a Floating Airport by Henri Defrasse." Vol. 41 (June 15): 185–186.

Baldwin, Charles Hobart. 1930. "Proposed Airport of San Francisco." *Architect and Engineer* 103, no. 2 (November): 52–60.

———. 1932. *The Urgent Importance of Taking Immediate Steps to Provide Airports for San Francisco*. San Francisco: C. H. Baldwin.

Bednarek, Janet R. Daley. 2005. "The Flying Machine in the Garden: Parks and Airports, 1918–1938." *Technology and Culture* 46, no. 2 (April): 350–373.

Bottorff, H. C. n.d. "Closing Report, San Francisco Bay Exposition, Sponsor for the Golden Gate International Exposition." The Bancroft Library. University of California, Berkeley.

Bulletin of the Beaux-Arts Institute of Design 4, no. 9 (1928): 5–13.

Day, W. P., and George Kelham. 1934. "Report on Investigation of Sites for a Proposed Exposition to Commemorate the Completion of the Golden Gate Bridge and the San Francisco-Oakland Bridge." Manuscript. William G. Merchant Collection. Environmental Design Archives. University of California, Berkeley.

Dohrmann, Fred. 1927. "The Future of the Waterfront—Aviation Landing and Elevated Highway." *Pacific Commerce,* January 5, 22–23.

Goodrich, E. P. 1928. "Airports as a Factor in City Planning." Supplement to *National Municipal Review* 17:181.

Hubbard, Henry V., Miller McClintock, and Frank B. Williams. 1930. *Airports: Their Location, Administration and Legal Basis.* Cambridge, MA: Harvard University Press.

James, Jack, and Earle Weller. 1941. *Treasure Island: "The Magic City," 1939–1940.* San Francisco: Pisani Printing and Publishing.

Lane, D. R. 1927. "The Airport Problems of Other Cities." *San Francisco Business,* February 9.

Lee, Charles H. 1938a. "Draining and Leaching Treasure Island." *Engineering News-Record,* October 13, unpaginated reprint. Charles H. Lee Papers. Water Resources Center Archives. University of California Riverside.

———. 1938b. "Report on Soil Drainage and Leaching at Treasure Island." January 12, 4. Charles H. Lee Papers. Water Resources Center Archives. University of California, Riverside.

———. 1940. "Cathodic Protection on Domestic Distribution System at Treasure Island." *Journal of the American Water Works Association* 32, no. 2 (February): 305–338.

Literary Digest. 1933. "A Mid-Ocean Port for Airplanes." June 3, 14.

Lotchin, Roger W. 1979. "The Darwinian City: The Politics of Urbanization in San Francisco between the World Wars." *Pacific Historical Review* 48, no. 3 (August): 357–381.

Lynch, Robert Newton. 1927. "Working for Peaceful Commerce in the Pacific." *San Francisco Business,* September 14.

Nolan, John. 1928. "City Planning for Airports and Airways." *SAE Journal* 22:411–413.

Rubens, Lisa. 2004. "The 1939 San Francisco World's Fair: The New Deal, the New Frontier and the Pacific Basin." PhD diss., University of California, Berkeley.

Salamanca, L. 1930. "Way Stations on the Ocean." *National Republic* 18 (November): 16–17.

San Francisco Airport Museum. 1932. "1932 Concept of Golden Gate Air Terminal on Shoals." San Francisco: SFO Museum.

San Francisco Board of Supervisors (Board of Supervisors). 1933. *Proceedings.* San Francisco Public Library.

———. 1935. *Proceedings.* San Francisco Public Library.

San Francisco Chronicle. 1929a. "Truth to Rouse City to Provide for Genuine Airport." March 27.

———. 1929b. "San Francisco Gets Elegant Black Eye upon the Air Map." April 6.

———. 1929c. "Air Base Not Ladies' Aid Job Club Told." November 1.

———. 1931. "Yerba Buena Airport Plan to Be Pressed." October 12.

———. 1932a. "Yerba Buena Selected for Air Terminal." May 17.

———. 1932b. "Yerba Buena Airport Site Urged on Rossi." August 20.

———. 1932c. "Civic Groups Boost Yerba Buena Air Site." December 28.

———. 1933. "Fair to Mark Completion of Spans Planned." July 13.

———. 1934. "Site Proposed for 1937 Bridge Fair." May 27.

San Francisco News. 1934. "Groups Make Island Fair Site Protest." August 31. Oakland, CA: Vertical Files, History Room, Oakland Public Library.

———. 1935. "24,747 Majority at Polls Spurs Start of Exposition." May 3. Oakland, CA: Vertical Files, Oakland Public Library.

US Army Corps of Engineers (Corps of Engineers). 1937. "Yerba Buena Shoal Reclamation Project." Manuscript. The Bancroft Library, University of California, Berkeley.

US Department of Commerce, Aeronautics Branch. 1930. *Report of Committee on Airport Zoning and Eminent Domain.* Washington, DC: Government Printing Office.

White, P. W. 1929. "Bridging the Ocean with Man-Made Islands." *American Magazine* 208 (November): 46–49.

4. Visions of *Progress* and *Peace*

Foreign Architectural Representations at the Century of Progress and Golden Gate International Expositions

LISA D. SCHRENK

> *. . . the warp and the woof of the foreign participation in the Pageant of the Pacific has been woven into a broad tapestry steeped in the chrome of nearly two score nations, with the pulse of each sounding a call to millions of people in America to "see the whole world" on Treasure Island at the Golden Gate International Exposition in 1939.*
>
> JOHN RICHARD FITCH

The 1930s was the most active era of American world expositions.[1] Within a span of only five years, six major fairs, including the Golden Gate International Exposition (GGIE) on Treasure Island, were held in the United States.[2] All were attempting to emulate the economic success of the 1933–1934 World's Fair in Chicago. Held at the nadir of the Great Depression, A Century of Progress looked to American corporations to fill a gap left by foreign countries, which, facing economic difficulties of their own, had in many cases declined to sponsor individual buildings. As at Chicago, large, modern corporate pavilions housed dramatic displays of new commercial products on the fairgrounds in Dallas, Cleveland, San Diego, and New York. Full-scale production lines and interactive exhibits were favorite methods to entertain and educate the public about recent advances in scientific technology and to the benefits of modern commercial goods, including their role in stimulating a still sluggish economy.

American corporations were less prominently featured at the sixth exposition held during the decade. In contrast to focusing on scientific developments and manufactured products, organizers of San Francisco's 1939–1940 Golden Gate International Exposition were more interested in boosting the status and economy of the West Coast by promoting peaceful relationships and trade between countries around the Pacific Ocean at a time of growing tensions. This objective, along with a strong paternalistic view toward the various peoples of the Pacific Basin among US

politicians, produced an event that was more in keeping with recent European expositions held to increase foreign trade and generate support for imperial policies.
The GGIE organizers themselves claimed that "the World's Fair at San Francisco
was to be a cultural rather than a commercial Exposition."[3] Domestic business
interests dominated the other fairs, but in San Francisco foreign pavilions far out-
numbered those constructed by US companies.

This essay presents a comparison between the foreign architectural presentations at the Century of Progress and the Golden Gate International expositions. It
explores, in the context of economic and political conditions, how and why Treasure Island played host to an event that was so different in character than the other
US expositions of the era.

Foreign Presentation at International Expositions

The introduction of international expositions in the mid-nineteenth century coin-
cided with the rise of industrialization and with a growing desire of major national
governments to project unique identities as they competed for economic power in
a rapidly changing world. In attempting to bring their citizens together peacefully
and to formulate strong identities, countries rely upon elements of the humanities,
including the arts, music, and literature, even sports. By serving as gathering places
for the world, international expositions, similar to the modern Olympic Games,
provide ideal settings for participating governments to present political messages
designed to stimulate the morale of their citizens and to elevate the country's pres-
tige in the eyes of other nations.

As places to house exhibits of indigenous arts, commercial products, and scientific advances, foreign pavilions are one of the most visible representations of
nations at world's fairs. In the past, exposition organizers advertised that visitors could *tour du monde en un jour*. For example, the fairgrounds of the 1931
Exposition coloniale internationale, located in the Bois de Vincennes on the out-
skirts of Paris, prominently featured traditional building forms and recreations of
historic landmarks representing different nations of the world, such as the Pavillon
de l'Indochine, an imposing replica of the central core of Angkor Wat. Through
this type of architectural appropriation participating nations reinterpreted distant lands to fit various political and commercial agendas. Along the Avenue des
Colonies, for example, smaller buildings of historical pastiches held exhibits that
encouraged support for trade and colonialism by romanticizing the exotic qualities
of the individual dependencies and highlighting the potential benefits of exploiting
their resources.

In addition to individual foreign pavilions, entire historic villages celebrating
different cultures became popular venues. Poble Espanyol at the 1929 Exposició
internacional held in Barcelona included more than one hundred buildings that
featured design elements characteristic of different regions in Spain (Figure 4.1).
Within the buildings were cafés and shops that celebrated the epicurean

specialties and handicrafts of the
area. An open square in the center
of the village served as a focal point
for the attraction and provided a setting for ethnic dance and ceremonial
performances.

The United States sponsored
similar exhibits to help promote its
own imperial policies. Most prominent was the Philippine display at
the 1904 Louisiana Purchase Exposition in St. Louis. One of the greatest spectacles of the fair, the living
panorama consisted of more than
one thousand Filipinos in their "native habitat." These scantily clothed
members of the territory's rural tribes
came to represent the whole of the
Philippine population in the minds
of many Americans. In keeping with
views expressed by future US president Woodrow Wilson and others
in Washington, the fair presented
the Filipinos as childlike primitives
not capable of self-governance, but
in great need of assistance from the
United States to tutor and guide them

FIGURE 4.1   Poble Espanyol at the 1929 Exposició internacional
held in Barcelona. Photo: Lisa Schrenk.

down the proper path toward civilization (Rydell and Kroes 2005). Political agendas might not have been so unabashedly displayed at American expositions of the
1930s, but the underlying messages presented were often just as strongly shaped
by a need to justify and promote various existing or desired power structures by fair
organizers, host governments, and pavilion sponsors.

A Century of Progress

The Century of Progress Exposition was largely a corporate fair held on the western
edge of the industrial heartland of the United States. Much of the original financial
backing for the event did not come from government sources, as it had for earlier
expositions, but from Chicago's elite business leaders, including Julius Rosenwald,
Robert McCormick, and Philip K. Wrigley, hoping to stimulate the dismal local
and national economies, encourage greater consumption of their products, and
strengthen bonds between government, educational institutions, and industry. The
planners offered a positive environment for businesses to exhibit by eliminating

direct competition between companies for major awards—a common practice at earlier expositions. They also encouraged corporations to construct their own pavilions by providing building sites free of charge (Lohr 1952, 34–35). Prominent edifices by Sears and Roebuck, General Motors, and other companies filled the fairgrounds.

From the start organizers stated that they had "high hopes" for a large foreign presence at the Chicago fair, but by this they meant primarily a European one. In the fall of 1930, a group of exposition officials toured Europe to study current and recent expositions and make potential contacts among government officials. At the same time, a London office was established from where a campaign was launched to encourage foreign participation (Lohr 1952, 153–155).

During their travels, fair officials were captivated by Poble Espanyol and the other historic venues they witnessed at European expositions. They believed that this type of presentation would be an ideal way for "old world" countries to represent themselves in Chicago. Architect Daniel Burnham Jr., a member of the fair's board of directors, oversaw the creation of a pamphlet titled *Old Europe* designed to encourage European nations to sponsor historic villages. Intended as one of the most important features of the fair, planners envisioned Old Europe as a series of small national villages consisting of "mediaeval buildings of outstanding character and interest" grouped together on Northerly Island, a section of the fairgrounds that projected into Lake Michigan. The design called for the individual villages, situated along picturesque streets and waterways, to surround a central "Grand Place" where fêtes, dances, and other traditional forms of entertainment could be held. As with exposition attractions like Fort Dearborn that tied directly to Chicago's early history and foreign historic recreations, such as the Mayan Nunnery at Uxmal, organizers believed that the Old Europe area would allow visitors to make chronological and developmental comparisons in the context of ethnic and cultural heritage (Schrenk 1999).

The promotional material revealed a rather myopic viewpoint that gave preference to the American gaze. The writer of the *Old Europe* brochure proclaimed that such presentations would "enable American citizens of European descent to see for themselves how their European ancestors lived" in contrast to "the modern [American] cities in which they now live," thereby giving them "a good idea of the changes that have occurred during the last hundred years" (*Old Europe* 1932).

Although historic villages provided some of the most popular and financially successful attractions at earlier European expositions, the official invitation to build such exhibits in Chicago fell largely on deaf ears in Europe. Having no desire to distinguish themselves as "quaint custodians of a picturesque past" and presented in a way similar to how they had often represented their colonies, European governments declined the offer (Doordan 1993, 222). They wanted the world to recognize their recent achievements in the sciences and industry and not be viewed as stagnant societies against which Americans could measure their own development (Lohr 1952, 155).

After it became clear that the Old Europe concept was not going to be accepted by European governments, Chicago fair organizers suggested creating a Hall of

Nations to house foreign participants. Some nations, however, had already committed to building their own pavilions. Other governments feared that the Hall might not "constitute [a] sufficiently dignified form of participation," so, like the Old Europe scheme, the plan was dropped.[4] Those countries interested in exhibiting, but not in constructing their own pavilions, were accommodated with display space in one of the fair's large thematic pavilions. Several nations sponsored other forms of exhibits. The Dominican Republic built a 250-foot-long model of the proposed Columbus Memorial Lighthouse; Norway exhibited the *Sorandet,* a three-masted training vessel in the fair's lagoon.

The few national pavilions that were built in Chicago, such as those of Sweden and Czechoslovakia, received significant support from local immigrant communities. Far from the historic representations envisioned by fair organizers, the countries built austere, box-shaped buildings, labeled ultra-modern in fair publicity. Members of Benito Mussolini's government in Italy vehemently opposed the idea of an Italian village. They informed exposition officials that Italy's representation at A Century of Progress would be "entirely modern in character and that it was no use thinking that they would go in for reproductions of old buildings which would give a false impression of the high degree of modern efficiency which has been reached by the Italian state."[5] In place of visions of Venice or ancient Rome, Mussolini personally approved funds to construct a dynamic Italian Pavilion (Mario de Renzi, Antonio Valent, and Adalberto Libera) consisting of easily recognizable symbols of Italy's recent transportation achievements and its political ideology (Figure 4.2).[6] The building's prominent eighty-foot-high steel-and-prismatic-glass tower in the shape of a *fascio littorio* (the ancient Roman symbol of power and authority adopted by Italian fascists) reflected the major political goal of the displays inside: to increase support for fascism among Americans (Schrenk 2007, 93).

One European country to be represented at the fair in 1933 by a historic village was Belgium. La Belgique Pittoresque, however, was not sanctioned by the Belgian government, which had officially declined to participate in the event. Flemish and Chicago businessmen, who witnessed the financial benefit of similar ethnic venues at recent expositions in Belgium, erected a "medieval" town, designed by Belgian Alfons de Rydt (Alphonse De Rijdt) and the local Burnham Brothers. It consisted of an artificial assemblage of major architectural landmarks from different historic eras and divergent sites to create a romantic, picturesque vision of the nation's past. As at earlier venues, the authenticity of the attraction was reduced further through the elimination of unpleasant or troublesome elements, such as dirt, crime, and, in this case, even the use of foreign language.

The Belgian Village earned significant profits during the 1933 fair season, leading to what one contemporary writer in *Architectural Forum* called a "village epidemic" (1934, 376). When the exposition reopened in 1934 for a second season, a whole series of new historic towns appeared (Figure 4.3). These attractions, like Picturesque Belgium, were not sponsored by national governments, but instead were largely constructed by Daniel Burnham Jr. and other underemployed

FIGURE 4.2   Italian Pavilion at A Century of Progress Fair, Chicago, 1933. Photo: Kaufmann and Fabry, photographers.

local architects hoping to supplement their diminished incomes during the Great Depression (Schrenk 2007, 9). Although the villages were often built with financial help from local expatriates, the vision of these historic towns was largely American in origin. The Chicago fair organizers' great desire to see such attractions realized lay not in the underlying political messages the villages could express, but in their potential ability to attract crowds and thus bring financial return to investors. Unfortunately, most of the new village attractions ended the fair season deep in the red. There were just too many similar venues competing for a limited amount of visitor resources.

Although European participation was central in their minds, organizers did eventually encourage other nations of the world to exhibit at the fair. Emissaries of A Century of Progress made visits to Turkey, Persia, Siam, China, Japan, Mexico, and a number of South American countries.[7] Despite these efforts, most countries declined official representation, many citing dismal economic conditions at home. The only Asian nations to have a significant architectural presence in Chicago were China and Japan. Their main official venues were centrally located just south of Soldier Field next to another attraction from the Far East that saw far more publicity than the government-sponsored venues: the Chinese Bendix Lama Temple, a fully furnished reproduction of the ornate eighteenth-century gold-roofed Wanfaguiyi Hall at Jehol, the summer palace of the Manchu emperors (Figure 4.4).[8] The building was carefully reproduced, disassembled, and then brought from Inner Mongolia to Chicago by the Swedish explorer Sven Hedin for Chicago businessman Victor Bendix, a Swedish American and the funder of the enterprise. The presence of the Lama Temple must have been bittersweet for the Chinese because in addition to celebrating the elegance of Manchu court temple architecture, it served as a physical reminder of the recent seizure of Jehol by Imperial Japanese Army troops attempting to create a buffer zone between the Japanese-controlled area of Manchukuo and the rest of China.

In April 1931 the Chinese government accepted an official invitation to exhibit at A Century of Progress and the following year sent a diagrammatic plan for a compound consisting of narrow streets "in the nature of a Chinese village" designed by the American expatriate Henry K. Murphy (Findling 1994, 53). In early 1933, however, Exposition president Rufus C. Dawes received a cable announcing that the funds appropriated for the fair had been "absorbed by the military situation" with Japan after continued Nippon offensives into China (Duffy 1933). According to a news report, three hundred bales of exhibits weighing seventy-five tons, including works of jade, ivory, lacquer, and brass, were already on their way to Chicago (Duffy 1933). Organizers initially planned to make room for the items in the Travel and Transport Building, where displays from several other countries were located, but last-minute support from the Chamber of Commerce and several provincial governments in China allowed for the construction of a Chinese attraction to take place (Duffy 1933; Lohr 1952, 156–157). An elaborately carved *pailou* gateway from Shanghai that had previously appeared at the 1915 Panama-Pacific Exposition fronted the one-acre complex, which contained shops, an open-air theater, a restaurant, and a tea garden. Exhibits featured a fifty-inch-tall, intricately carved jade temple (Findling 1994, 53; Ho and Moy 2005, 123).

When the exposition reopened for a second season in 1934, fairgoers were also able to visit a competing Chinese attraction. The local Chinese American community had financed an entertainment venue located next door to a new Dutch Village on the site initially designated for Old Europe. The Streets of Shanghai concession, "where West meets East," was designed as a walled Chinese city by the local Burnham Brothers and C. Herrick Hammond, assisted by

FIGURE 4.3   Poster of the 1934 Century of Progress Fair. Photo: Weimer Pursel.

FIGURE 4.4   Chinese Bendix Lama Temple at A Century of Progress, Chicago, 1933. Photo: Kaufmann and Fabry, photographers.

Chinese architect See Wing Louie. Two brightly painted pagodas eight stories high marked the entrance. Inside visitors could experience the Buddhist Lo Han Temple, watch the operations of a noodle factory, and be entertained by Chinese American blues singer and actress Olive Young Lum. Like most of the village venues, Streets of Shanghai faced major financial difficulties and entered bankruptcy in late July, though it continued to remain open for the duration of the exposition (*Chicago Tribune* 1934, 6).

Japanese culture was also represented at the fair by iconic historic forms. In September 1932 the Japanese Diet authorized official participation at A Century of Progress (Findling 1994, 53). The following spring "an army of Japanese workmen and engineers" constructed a three-hundred-foot long building in the twelfth-century Kamakura-era style, designed by Iwakichi Miyamoto, right next door to the official Chinese concession. Exhibits included handicrafts and industrial and agricultural products. "Dainty Geisha Girls" held tea ceremonies in a Japanese garden (*Official Guide Book of the Fair* 1933, 93). A small adjacent pavilion with a traditional Japanese roof and a large, modern plate-glass window held displays, including a large three-dimensional topographical map and dioramas, that featured the agricultural and industrial resources of Manchuria and the building of the South Manchurian Railway in an attempt to gain legitimacy for the recent creation of Manchukuo (Lohr 1952, 157–158).

A variety of other foreign attractions at A Century of Progress helped present an international vision to fairgoers. Most were independent venues, such as the Chinese Bendix Lama Temple, with no official foreign sanction. Egypt, however, built a small pavilion with four large lotus columns recalling the Temple of Philae to promote tourism. Poland had initially planned to host a modern pavilion but withdrew, and the building opened as the German-American Restaurant. The large, long Ukrainian Pavilion, sponsored by immigrant societies in America and Europe, included exhibits presenting folk and high art, most notably a group of modern figurative sculptures by Aleksandr Archipenko. One of the most visible foreign attractions was the Mayan Nunnery of Uxmal. Under the direction of Danish explorer and archaeologist Frans Blom, the prominent wood and plaster reconstruction, consisting of just one wing of the nunnery, was built as accurately as possible to the original stone building using measured drawings and casts created during a Tulane University expedition to the Yucatan in 1930.

Fairgoers could find other, less academic foreign presentations in the midway area among Ripley's Believe-It-or-Not Odditorium, an exhibit of incubator babies, and a midget village. These commercial attractions were designed to titillate and transport people's imagination to foreign locals. One of the most popular was the Streets of Paris, where visitors could sit outdoors at Parisian cafés and watch Sally Rand strut her stuff, often wearing little more than large ostrich feather fans. At the Moroccan Village, visitors sipping mint tea or thick black coffee could watch the intricate gyrations of exotic dancers while listening to "weird desert strains from queer Moorish instruments" in the shadow of a muezzin's tower (Lohr 1952, 176; Duffy 1933). The strange and mysterious Oriental Village, operated by International Bazaars, was designed from photographs of sites as diverse as Cairo, Jerusalem, and Constantinople, and featured Egyptian dancers and Moorish jugglers (McDowell 1933). Nearby was Darkest Africa, a sideshow-esque concession à la the Philippines display at the 1904 St. Louis fair in the guise of an anthropological exhibit, owned and operated by showman Louis Dufour. Labeled on the map in the 1933 official guidebook as "Dufour's Freak Show," the venue featured huts inhabited by people representing different areas of Africa, including royalty from Nigeria and a pygmy tribe from the Belgian Congo (*Official World's Fair Weekly* 1933, 10; Ganz 2008, 112). These venues featured caricatures of faraway places, populated by natives who were usually presented as exotic and uncivilized, as a way to both entertain fairgoers and help justify colonialism and Western domination of those cultures.

Although A Century of Progress was grounded in industrial modernity, organizers largely favored these forms of historic or exotic foreign representation due to their perceived ability to attract fairgoers and for their role as contrasting backdrops to the celebrated advancements in science, technology, and consumer goods showcased in the large, modern thematic and corporate pavilions. Along with local conditions of the host city, the changing economic and political situations at the end of the decade, as the world moved out of the Depression and into a state of conflict, contributed to the central underlying emphasis on industrial progress in Chicago being replaced by a focus on international trade and peace in San Francisco. A major outcome of this shift was a greater acceptance among organizers to a wide range of foreign architectural voices contributing to the GGIE.

Golden Gate International Exposition

Initially organized to celebrate the completion of the Golden Gate and the San Francisco–Oakland Bay bridges, the GGIE quickly projected a broader theme to the world: Pageant of the Pacific. While A Century of Progress and the other American expositions of the 1930s focused largely on the promotion of scientific advances and manufactured goods, local organizers of the San Francisco fair were more interested in marketing the West and increasing foreign trade in the Pacific at a time of growing competition for resources, especially from Japan.

East Asia had become the fastest growing market for US investment since the arrival of the Depression, and a major goal of the exposition was to encourage additional investment and construction of infrastructure to support America's expanding presence in the region (Rubens 1991). In part to sustain this growing market, the exposition helped to promote the United States government's policy of peace and neutrality despite rapidly escalating political tensions around the world. From President Franklin Roosevelt's 1936 invitation to the countries of the world to come to the fair, which talked about the exposition contributing "to cordial relations among the nations of the world"—echoing his Good Neighbor policy in the Americas—to the text of the souvenir pamphlets passed out in foreign pavilions at the event that highlighted the peaceful and romantic qualities of the locale as well as its major resources, fair organizers reinforced the economic importance of a peaceful Pacific region.[9]

With construction of a competing exposition under way in New York City, many people felt that the San Francisco exposition should not be held. Organizers feared it would draw exhibitors and visitors away from the East Coast event. An adamant supporter for holding the GGIE was President Roosevelt, who authorized significant New Deal funds for both fairs. At a luncheon attended by a thousand California civic and business leaders on Treasure Island the summer before the expositions opened, Roosevelt predicted that "1939 would go down in history not only as the year of the two greatest American fairs, but would be a year of world wide rejoicing if it could also mark definite steps toward permanent world peace" (James and Weller 1941, 55). One of the steps he envisioned was the realization of the GGIE.

To help differentiate their event from the coinciding world's fair in New York, San Franciscans focused the exposition on increasing trade and tourism in the western states and throughout the Pacific region. Local organizers, who viewed their city as the maritime capital and gateway to the Pacific, wrote "the course of empire moves West, and the future greatness of San Francisco and her neighboring communities in the bay area is bound up in a great measure with growth and development of our trade and commerce with the nations of the Pacific."[10] Business leaders wanting to attract as much publicity as possible realized that also highlighting foreign travel and tourist sites would help draw the greatest number of people to the fair. The rewards of foreign participation, fair planners claimed, would be mutually beneficial due to increased trade and industrial production (San Francisco Bay Exposition 1939). The message was convincing, as more Pacific Rim nations sponsored pavilions and exhibits at the GGIE than at any previous world's fair.

In his influential paper "The Significance of the Frontier in American History," presented at the American Historical Association meeting held in Chicago in 1893 during the first Chicago World's Fair, Frederick Jackson Turner promoted the view that America's identity and success were defined by what occurred in the juncture between the civilization of settlement and the savagery of wilderness during the nation's expansion westward (1920, 3). Achieving the ability to continually tame a wild, uncivilized land as the frontier moved farther and farther away from the established social structure and authority of Europe, he argued, led Americans to build a unique national character marked by strength and the resourcefulness of the individual. This speech, along with a belief that frontier expansion was coming to a close, prompted those in power at the end of the nineteenth century to search for a new frontier that would allow the United States to sustain its energy and unique character into the twentieth century.

An obvious solution was to continue westward momentum beyond the California coast into the Pacific. This notion built upon ideas promoted by other contemporary strategists, such as Alfred T. Mahan, who believed that the establishment of a major military presence in the Pacific was crucial to the nation's ascension into a position as a world power. Major political leaders, including President Theodore Roosevelt, concurred, and by the start of the twentieth century the United States' growing presence in the Pacific included acquiring the Philippines, Guam, Samoa, and the Hawaiian Islands. By the 1930s, however, US policy had shifted away from practicing expansionism to increasing influence and power through economic gains resulting from the "mutual beneficial" actions of trade. According to a publicity brochure, the GGIE would "lay the cornerstone of a new Pacific Empire, united in a common bond of social and commercial well being."[11]

The utopian environment of a world's fair offered an ideal backdrop for the celebration of America's expanding political and economic roles in the Pacific. Realizing this fact, George Creel, US commissioner to the GGIE, exclaimed that the fair would prominently showcase America's growing "Western Empire in every sense of the term."[12] For the local businessmen organizing the exposition, this meant promoting a peaceful, resource-rich, Pacific realm where trade could take place without the distraction or inconvenience of war. The vision of peace in the Pacific was presented through the guise of a happy family of trade partners. The US government viewed itself as that family's patriarch.

In reaction to the progressive pavilion designs of Chicago's Century of Progress Exposition, a major aim of the architecture of the San Francisco fair, according to event organizers, was "not to resort to shock or strange idiom," but instead to develop a more conservative architectural language that would reflect the diversity of the Pacific Rim nations (Jones 1939, 18). Members of the exposition's architectural commission, led by Arthur Brown Jr., who had served on similar commissions for the 1915 and 1933–1934 expositions, stated that they derived the basic style of the fair's main architecture from Mayan precedents.[13] Underneath the major pavilions' ornamental elements, however, were solid, classical forms that were then decorated with a "mingling" of modern interpretations of both Asian and pre-Columbian details to create a new, exotic style christened *Pacifica*.

In contrast to the modern, asymmetrical layout of the Chicago fair, which allowed for each building to be its own architectural entity, the aesthetics of the GGIE were much more highly controlled by its organizers (Figure 4.5). The fair's so-called Key Plan for Treasure Island incorporated a strong formal Beaux-Arts composition that took climatic conditions of the site (particularly the prevailing trade winds) into consideration and reflected the formal educational backgrounds of the fair's architectural commissioners.[14] According to the designers, the plan, however, was "sufficiently elastic enough to permit many modifications to meet changing conditions, at the same time losing none of its essential characteristics" (Brown 1939, 19).

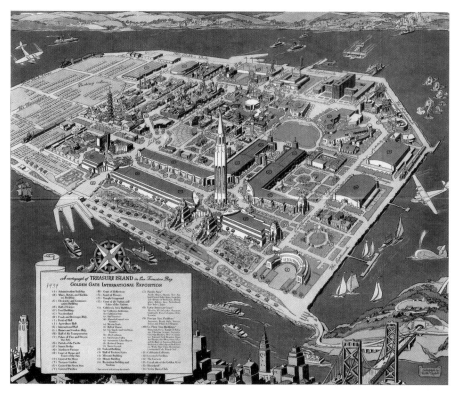

FIGURE 4.5   Aerial view of the Golden Gate International Exposition, 1933. *Official Guide Book of the Fair.*

In the realized scheme, major thematic buildings were laid out along two major axes in a cruciform plan located toward the western front of the island. The exterior façades of the pavilions served as a backdrop for elaborate promenades of formal gardens and fountains. At the crossing the four-hundred-foot-tall Tower of the Sun (Arthur Brown Jr.) marked the central Court of Honor and functioned as a vertical focal point for the exposition. The fairgrounds included three permanent concrete and steel buildings at the south end of the island, part of the plans for a future airport: a semicircular terminal and two large barrel-vaulted airplane hangers. Beyond the central core area of buildings was the "arterial girdle," a roadway that joined a series of secondary zones that incorporated informally composed elements within themselves.

A second major vertical feature in the central court area was the eighty-foot-high figure *Pacifica* (Ralph Stackpole), the focal point of a grouping of sculpture at the north end of a long promenade (Figure 4.6). *The Peacemakers,* a massive bas-relief mural 144 feet long (Margaret, Helen, and Esther Bruton) served as a companion piece for *Pacifica.* The mural consisted of registers of figures representing eastern and western races marching from each side toward two larger central figures symbolizing peaceful ideals: Buddha representing peace in the eastern realm and a toga-clad female signifying peace in the western world. Although the basic subject of *The Peacemakers* emphasized the fair's utopian goal of unity in the Pacific, below the mural was the *Fountain of the Western Waters,* decorated with small sculptures representing South America, North America, Oceania, and Asia. Except for one figure symbolizing the modern American woman, the sculptures presented idealized figures from Pacific nations engaged in rudimentary human activities such as hunting, cooking, and music making. Towering over the fountain, *Pacifica* represented the Pacific region, but could just as easily be read as a personification of the US government carefully watching over and protecting the peoples of the Pacific characterized below.[15]

To control the overall aesthetic quality of the fairgrounds, organizers instituted a policy that required most exhibitors to use space provided by the exposition. This resulted in few businesses constructing their own pavilions. In contrast, countries were strongly encouraged to sponsor freestanding buildings. Unlike the Century of Progress Exposition, where foreign pavilions and other exhibits were scattered throughout the fairgrounds, more than twenty nations were clearly organized into three zones within the arterial girdle. Most prominent were the Asian countries arranged around a picturesque basin of water in the Pacific Area. Adjacent was a significantly smaller site reserved for Central and South American nations that bordered the Pacific Ocean. To the west, a strip of land housed European countries, along with the Atlantic-bordering American nations of Brazil and Argentina. The massive US Federal Pavilion was located on its own on a prominent seven-acre site at the culmination of a major east-west axis.

Early on fair organizers envisioned the inclusion of an International Palace for countries not interested or able to construct their own pavilions. Similar in concept to the Hall of Nations in Chicago, the palace was initially to be housed in one of the permanent future airplane hangers. Rejecting the term "palace," which seemed a bit extravagant for a concrete and steel hanger, the idea eventually evolved into the creation of an International Hall located in one wing of a central thematic building.[16]

Both Sweden and Czechoslovakia, who had built modern pavilions in Chicago, presented simple, clean-lined displays in the hall. The Czech exhibit included large photomurals illustrating historic images of the country, a presentation technique that was introduced at the Chicago exposition by Henry Ford. Perforated sheets of metal used for tabletops and dividers gave the exhibit a progressive feel. Tragically, Germany invaded Czechoslovakia the day after it opened and

FIGURE 4.6   Statue *Pacifica*. The Bancroft Library, University of California, Berkeley.

the display was turned over to the local Czech community to operate (*Architectural Forum* 1939, 498–499).

A series of preliminary plans of the fairgrounds, many signed by Arthur Brown Jr., provide clues to the development of other foreign exhibits.[17] A plan dated January 4, 1937, suggests that the exposition's architects originally envisioned a foreign presentation similar in composition to that found at A Century of Progress: a few large national pavilions, a series of ethnic villages, and available exhibit space elsewhere for those countries not hosting their own buildings. The layout identifies the eastern airplane hanger as the location of the International Palace. To the east of the hanger, an area labeled Foreign Governments includes the outline of three large buildings (Figure 4.7). North of this section, at the eastern edge of the island, the plan identifies three large groups of small buildings as Foreign Villages. The area that eventually housed foreign pavilions located near the center of the fairgrounds was covered with a series of large buildings identified as Industrial Exhibit Sites, recalling the prominent corporate presence in Chicago.

By February 15, designers had reserved a second area north of the airplane hangers for additional foreign pavilions. The ethnic villages were relocated inland near the final location of the Gayway, the amusement zone for the exposition, recalling the novelty role of such venues at earlier fairs. The Industrial Exhibit Sites area was further developed following an underlying grid consisting of a three by four matrix of blocks, with the four northeastern squares unified into a large superblock.

A number of drawings produced from the summer of 1937 through 1938 reveal that Brown and his colleagues paid significant attention to the development of the

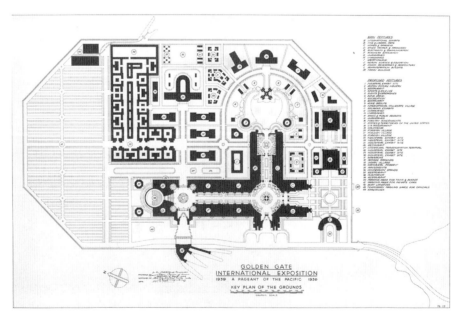

FIGURE 4.7   GGIE plan, January 1937. The Bancroft Library, University of California, Berkeley.

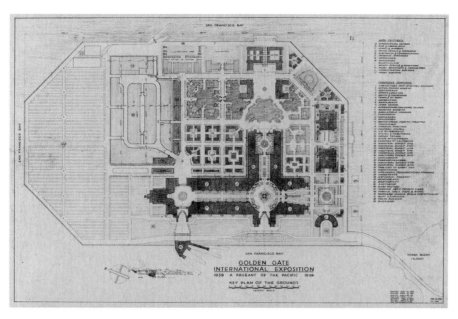

FIGURE 4.8   GGIE plan, May 1937. The Bancroft Library, University of California, Berkeley.

Pacific Area located at the site of the earlier super block and parts of the neighboring blocks to the south. An early revision dated May 5, 1937, shows the pavilions lining the periphery, allowing space in the center for a basin of water that was divided by a major east-west path. The drawing noted that other foreign pavilions would still be located at the south end of the fairgrounds near the east hanger, a remnant of the International Palace concept (Figure 4.8).

Brown explored various solutions for the central focal point of the zone that were documented in a series of drawings. Concepts included creating an archway or other landmark at the central point of the intersecting road on a bridge over the waterway, projecting sections of land from the north and south sides opposite the bridge for gazebos and other structures, and creating one central island connected from the east and west by the central pathway.[18] The final design developed out of the last two concepts. It included a central landmass that projected from the bridge into the larger northern basin for Pacific House (a hospitality center for foreign visitors), smaller projections for the Johor Pavilion, and structures linked to the Japanese and Philippines buildings. Large undated drawings, most likely from the second half of 1938, illustrating rows of different foreign pavilion elevations, suggest that the architects were especially interested in the overall composition, particularly in balancing the building massings and creating attractive views from different vantage points. By June 1938, the architects had begun to develop the zone designated for the Latin American pavilions at the far northwest quadrant of the Pacific Area. It was not until later in the year, however, that they finally turned their attention to the strip of land west of the Pacific Area for European nations and the Atlantic-facing South American countries and began to finalize exhibit designs for the US Pavilion.

FIGURE 4.9   United States Pavilion building showing mural and parade, 1939–1940. Library of Congress.

In his opening day radio address, President Roosevelt proclaimed, "Unity of the Pacific nations is America's concern and responsibility" (James and Weller 1941, 89). The formal qualities of the US Federal Building, and selection of exhibits held within, reinforced this belief while projecting an imposing message of power and awe to both citizens and foreign visitors alike. According to an exposition press release, the theme Pageant of the Pacific was "presented to architects as an example of natural selection."[19] The colorful, massive US Pavilion reflected the country's prominent place in that evolutionary selection process and contrasted sharply with the iconic designs of pavilions representing Pacific nations (Figure 4.9). Exhibiting the United States architecturally with a modern design while encouraging other countries to build historically based structures was not a new concept, as witnessed in the Old Europe scheme for A Century of Progress almost a decade earlier.

The 265-foot-long Federal Building (Timothy Pflueger), like most of the other fair pavilions, was constructed of Douglas fir. It consisted of a central outdoor Colonnade of the States comprised of forty-eight 104-foot-high columns representing the individual states. The columns were arranged in three aisles symbolizing the three branches of the federal government (San Francisco Bay Exposition 1940, 76). Flanking the colonnade were two large projecting porticos with delicate, triangular columns recalling the more traditional classical vocabulary found on most permanent federal buildings in Washington, DC. Two 190-foot-long, intensely colored murals covered the façades of the wings. Their subject matter—"Conquering the West by Land" and "Conquering the West by Water"—celebrated past efforts of expansionism and reinforced Washington's desire to continue frontier development, at least economically, into the Pacific.

Exhibits relating to the theme of the pavilion, such as the popular multivisual extravaganza Cavalcade of the West, graphically intertwined the stories of the nation's march westward and its progress forward as a major modern world power (James and Weller 1941, 89). A deliberate attempt was made to unite the individual displays through the development of a series of general exhibits into which was "woven the story of the essential services of the government" (Gutheim 1939, 615). The displays were clearly laid out within the pavilion to impress upon fairgoers the importance of the country's role in the Pacific. The main exhibits of the Pageant of America focused on national defense and the march of science; other exhibits addressed social and economic affairs, conservation, housing, recreation, the Works Progress Administration, and the Coast Guard.

A large exhibit presented six different civilizations of the American Indian. Although the fair did not have an American Indian village concession, Native American artisans in tribal dress presented demonstrations of weaving blankets and baskets, making pottery, and engaging in other traditional pursuits. According to a Northern Pacific Railway brochure on the exposition, the exhibit illustrated that American Indians were not "a vanishing race" but "a vital, worthwhile force in modern America" despite the fact they continued to be exhibited in ways that reinforced the prevailing belief among many in the United States that Native Americans existed outside the realm of modern American society (Northern Pacific Railway 1940).

Rallies and exhibits surrounding the US Pavilion reflected fair exhibitors' desire for a peaceful Pacific. The Temple of Religion included a massive Tower of Peace that served as a monument to worldwide humanitarianism, and in the Hall of Western States, among displays featuring the natural resources and tourist destinations of New Mexico and Oregon, the organization Peace Projects presented a plea for international peace. The human cost of war was dramatically illustrated in their exhibit through the display of the large mural *Peace or War* by Ray Strong, which graphically presented the negative consequences of military conflict. Reproductions of the mural were widely distributed in pamphlets given out to fairgoers at both the GGIE and the New York world's fairs.

A 1939 guidebook to the exposition pointed out that Americans were both uninformed and misinformed about the "home lands of our international friends." To help remedy this situation, it went on to state that fairgoers could find on Treasure Island "significant and worthwhile contributions each country has to offer in resources, industry, the arts, recreation and attractions to travelers" (San Francisco Bay Exposition 1939, 10). Organizers wanted the foreign pavilions to "reflect the traditional architecture of various Pacific nations, yet also to lend themselves to a harmonious whole."[20]

In contrast to the Chicago fair, where planners first focused their efforts on attracting foreign exhibitors from Europe, the organizers for the GGIE looked primarily south and west for countries to partake in their event. In an attempt to meet a goal of 100 percent participation from Asia and South and Central Americas, the exposition president, Leland Cutler, along with five commissioners, including the noted English exposition organizer O. J. Keatings, traveled extensively throughout these regions, encouraging countries to sponsor exhibits in San Francisco. During their travels, they met with government officials and business leaders. In addition to the construction of foreign pavilions, the commissioners also explored the possibility of including original or recreations of exotic historic buildings from the Pacific region similar to the nunnery from Uxmal at the Chicago fair. Looking for an alternative to the Chinese Bendix Lama Temple, which was headed eastward to be exhibited at the New York World's Fair, organizers of the San Francisco exposition considered shipping over an actual "Llama [sic] temple from China." They envisioned the temple being used by Tibetan monks during the fair to "conduct the regular rituals and services of the Mysterious Asian sect."[21] A plan to exhibit a Buddhist temple from Siam to show "the ordinary Siamese life in all strata," including through Technicolor movies, was also explored.[22] Neither plan, however, was realized.

In addition to personal visits to countries by the commissioners, in late 1936 the exposition's "Department of Exploitation" decided to produce a deluxe brochure to help sell foreign government officials and other potential international exhibitors on the benefit of participating in the exposition. Although emphasis was placed on encouraging Pacific nations to exhibit, plans were to publish the brochure in four European languages: English, Spanish, French, and Italian. Organizers did propose to include personalized translations for "single-language nations" such as Japan, and conclude the brochure with a personalized message for the intended recipient about the benefits of exhibiting. As planned, the printed brochure contained pages that addressed reasons for holding the fair. It explained the economic significance of the event, provided details on exposition organizers, and described main features of the fairgrounds.[23]

Echoing Chicago, the exact list of foreign participators was constantly changing almost up until opening day. By January 1, 1939, just seven weeks before the exposition officially commenced, the count included thirty-five foreign lands exhibiting, twenty-two nations represented by individual pavilions.[24] The Pacific Area formed the centerpiece of the foreign exhibits with the buildings of Eastern nations arranged around the small, picturesque Medial Lake. Each pavilion was identifiable through the use of traditional architectural elements and forms. The independent Malay state of Johor, for example, built an overscaled, modernized version of a traditional Menangkabau-style Malay council house, complete with a dramatically swooping roof. Financed by the "enlightened and democratic" Sultan Ibrahim II of Johor, one of the wealthiest men in the world at the time, the pavilion housed the ruler's impressive jewel collection and hunting trophies, as well as displays of native species and local crafts. It also offered exhibits on the country's rubber and tin mining industry to show the "effect on its people of the progressive and enlightened policies of the government," and the state's contribution to the world economy (San Francisco Bay Exposition 1939, 85).

Despite recent horrific military actions in China, including the Rape of Nanking, Japan presented a benevolent, yet commanding, face at the exposition. Its venue (George Gentoku Shimamoto) was one of the largest foreign exhibits at the fair, with buildings designed to recall a fourteenth-century feudal castle, a traditional Samurai house, and a Buddhist temple (also see Horiuchi, this volume). A pagoda, which provided the most identifiable element of the Japanese ensemble, balanced the taller multilevel *shikhara* of the Dutch East Indies venue next door as the main vertical landmark of the zone. The architect of the latter, Robert Deppe, modeled the pavilion after a mid-fourteenth-century Hindu-Javanese building in the Penataran Temple complex near Blitar in East Java. The life of the designer, born and educated in Amsterdam, but living at the time in Batavia (Jakarta), Java, reflects the often complicated intermingling of eastern and western worlds and cultures in the modern era that was typically lost in foreign presentations at expositions. Within the pavilion, recorded sounds of exotic gamelan and *kroncong* music filled the air as visitors watched performances of traditional *wayang* shadow puppets or viewed an illuminated mural of the longest air route in the world (San Francisco Bay Exposition 1939, 86).

Echoes of colonialism and Western conquest filled a number of the Asian buildings in the Pacific Area. For example, fairgoers could taste the Dutch colonial dish *rijsttafel* in the Javanese restaurant next door to the Dutch East Indies pavilion. The Australian and New Zealand buildings, designed by Edward L. Frick, an American and head of the Division of Architecture for the exposition, featured exhibits of dioramas, photographs, and handicrafts highlighting native tribal groups. The New Zealand Pavilion was based on the design of a Maori meetinghouse; Australia was represented by a simple, neoclassical design. Georges Besse and Claude Meyer-Levy designed both the French and the French Indo-China buildings at the fair. The latter, closely modeled on the Indo-China Pavilion at the 1931 Exposition coloniale internationale in Paris, was labeled as being designed in "true Annamese style." In reality, it consisted of a modern French Beaux-Arts design decorated with traditional motifs, including what was identified in the guidebook as an "authentic bas-relief inspired by the famous ruins of Angkor."[25] Exhibits inside featured decorative works of silk, silver, and lacquer, and displays of hand-carved objects, including a thirty-foot-long dragon produced by "wards of the French Colonial Government" (Pavilion of French Indo-China 1939) (Figure 4.10).

Both the Dutch and the French promoted their beneficial roles in Southeast Asia at the exposition, in part to counteract growing Japanese interests in the

FIGURE 4.10   Pacific Area rendering by Arthur Brown Jr., 1937. The Bancroft Library, University of California, Berkeley.

region. A related brochure on the French Indo-China Pavilion stressed the work the French government had done in modernizing the colony, including building airports, highways, and railroads, and establishing schools and medical facilities throughout the colony.[26] Responding both to the underlying emphasis of the exposition on Pacific harmony and the growing threat of Japanese aggression at home, the brochure went on to exclaim that "French Indo-China is a quiet country, whose friendly population has for its motto: 'Peace and Work'" (Pavilion of French Indo-China 1939).

The Philippines Pavilion, by Filipino architect Gregorio P. Guttierrez, contrasted sharply with the territory's presentation at the 1904 St. Louis exposition. This reflected changes in Western perceptions of the country as it moved toward independence and the shift away from placing groups of native people "going about their daily lives" on exhibit at world's fairs. In place of the earlier tribal display, the simple L-shaped pavilion featured modern furniture of bamboo, rattan, and hardwood, and highlighted natural resources and recreation activities in one wing and manufactured products in the other (James and Weller 1941, 108). An exhibit telling the story of gold production in the central rotunda emphasized that the territory had developed into the second largest source of gold production under the US flag (San Francisco Bay Exposition 1939, 82). Instead of traditional music, fairgoers were entertained with symphonic concerts given by the 110-piece Philippine Constabulary Band from a bandstand in the north lagoon.

In the center of the Asian pavilions situated on an island in the middle of Medial Lake was Pacific House (William G. Merchant), headquarters for the Pageant of the Pacific. Described as an "extremely modern construction," the building stood out from the historically derived Asian pavilions nearby (Figure 4.11). With its progressive design and impressive scale, the Pacific House, like the statue *Pacifica,* could be read as a visual symbol of the host's desire for a dominant role in the Pacific region. The building housed exhibits that stressed "the common interests of [the] peoples of the Pacific hemisphere and demonstrates their contributions to contemporary civilization" (San Francisco Bay Exposition 1939, 79). Six pictorial wall maps by muralist Miguel Covarrubias highlighted the various arts, native plants, peoples, animals, and architecture of the region. The classification of subject matter by type, in this case via location on maps, evoked the popular practice of categorizing objects (Covarrubias 1940). This organizational methodology, which developed along side the rise of scientific inquiry in the modern era, was clearly reflected in the

FIGURE 4.11   Pacific House and Asian pavilions, 1939. Northern Pacific Railway brochure.

arrangement of exhibits at earlier international expositions. Covarrubias' mural *Peoples of the Pacific,* which identifies different groups by representational figures, recalls Malvina Hoffman's *Races of Man,* approximately one hundred busts and statues of people from around the world, commissioned by the Field Museum in 1930 and first exhibited at A Century of Progress. In creating their works, both artists responded to the growing realization among anthropologists at the time of the difficulties in categorizing people by race and ethnicity, especially by skin color (Covarrubias 1940; Kinkel 2011). The large windows on Pacific House that project outward from each of the four façades of the building helped visually link the interior displays with the architectural exhibits outside (James and Weller 1941, 102). However, unlike the orderly classifications based on the geographical structure in Covarrubias' murals, the pavilions formed a picturesque assemblage of architectural forms that only minimally reflected the real geographical relationships of those nations.

One country missing from the Pacific Area was China. In 1915, the new Republic of China had prominently participated at the Panama-Pacific Exposition, using the earlier San Francisco fair to promote an image of a modern nation through the presentation of approximately two thousand tons of displays (Wang and Song 2008, 136). In contrast, two decades later, the beleaguered country sponsored no official representation. Instead their presence at the exposition consisted most visibly of the Chinese Village, a three-and-a-half acre commercial attraction located in the Gayway similar to Chicago's Streets of Shanghai. The walled compound, sponsored by Chinese Factors, Inc. and merchants from the local ethnic community, contained a large pagoda, a version of the Temple of Heaven, and shops, a restaurant, a tea pavilion, and a cocktail lounge. Exhibits ranged from the jade pagoda previously exhibited at A Century of Progress to the personal effects of the late empress dowager. Fairgoers were entertained by performances of Chinese actors, dancers, acrobats, and puppets (San Francisco Bay Exposition 1939, 102). Nearby, in the midst of attractions similar in scope to those of Chicago's midway, including incubator babies and an updated version of Ripley's Odditorium, were commercial venues based on Old World visions, including an Estonian Village, a Scottish Village, and the Holy Land Building.

The East Pacific pavilions were scattered in a pleasing informal arrangement around Medial Lake, but the buildings in the smaller Latin American Court to the northwest presented a more compact and controlled, inward-looking composition. The unity between the individual pavilions was largely due to the fact that all but one of the buildings (Columbia by Pablo de la Cruz and Rafael Ruiz) were designed not by different architects native to those countries, but by Edward L. Frick and his Division of Architecture staff (Figure 4.12). The court consisted of eight buildings representing Central and South American countries arranged around an open courtyard that held cultural performances and displays of traditional handicrafts. Inside each pavilion was the usual collection of exhibits highlighting the country's natural resources, artistic and cultural heritage, and tourist destinations.

Exposition scholar Robert Rydell observes that the inward design of the Latin American Court with its "exhibits of natural resources and aboriginal artifacts" helped reinforce "American images of Latin American nations as culturally

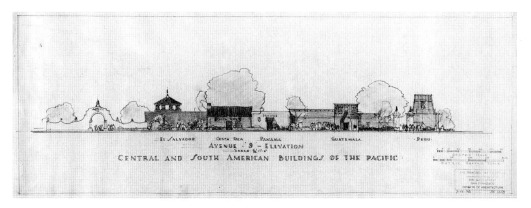

FIGURE 4.12 Central and South American Buildings by Arthur Brown Jr., 1938. The Bancroft Library, University of California, Berkeley.

backward and economically valuable producers of raw materials and potential con-
sumers of industrial surplus." The displays, though, were not so different from how
many of the other countries in the rest of the Pacific Area presented themselves to
fairgoers (Rydell 1989, 349). Frick's designs for the Latin American Court, however,
did exhibit less sophisticated exterior forms than many of the other foreign buildings. The pavilions typically consisted of basic geometric massing with façades of
large, flat, unadorned spans highlighted by areas of traditional decorative details,
such as the corbel vault and heavy Mayan-style frieze on the Guatemalan Pavilion.
The decorative elements served as shorthand identification markers for the buildings, giving the Latin American Court the ambience of a Midway venue similar to
the ethnic villages at A Century of Progress or Poble Espanyol in Barcelona.

In contrast to the Pacific-facing South American countries, Brazil and Argentina
were not relegated to representing themselves with traditional building forms in
the Latin American Court. Fair organizers instead located the countries' strikingly
modern pavilions alongside the few European participants in the Foreign Area.
Although the Brazilian Pavilion, designed by American architect Gardner A. Dailey,
might have not been as dramatic as its companion at the New York World's Fair
(Oscar Niemeyer and Lúcio Costa), which featured pilotis and a curving ramp, the
San Francisco building did adopt its modern vocabulary. Two forty-foot-high murals
(Robert B. Howard) on the exterior celebrated coffee production and the scenic and
recreational resources of the country. The Argentine Pavilion also had visual ties to
its sister pavilion in New York, given that both buildings were designed by Armando
d'Ans and featured huge maps of the nation on their façades. Exhibits within the
South American buildings in San Francisco, as with their European neighbors, highlighted modern commercial products and manufacturing industries, as well as natural resources like coffee and rubber. Instead of live performances of traditional
music as was popular in the Latin American Court, a sound system in the Brazilian
Pavilion broadcasted the latest popular and classical music by national composers
as tangos sounded from the Argentine Pavilion (Figure 4.13).

Both France and Italy built austere modern buildings, as was in vogue at the time among progressive architects in Europe. The French Pavilion housed displays of high fashion and fine art, including sculptures by Rodin and Bourdelle. Italy exhibited information on Italian tourist destinations. Architect Alfio Susini, assisted by Peter Canali, exchanged the Fascist axe and transportation motifs of the Italian Pavilion in Chicago with a more neutral design consisting of an oval building fronted by a sleek, marble portico and topped by a 115-foot tower decorated with the lists of names of major Italian tourist destinations (James and Weller 1941, 113). The tower held its own in the sky above the foreign venues as it competed for fairgoers' attention with the multilevel towers of the Japanese, Dutch East Indies, and Chinese venues. Next door, the Norwegian Pavilion stood in sharp contrast to the modern buildings lining the Atlantic area. Built by the Norwegian Ship Owner's Association, the pavilion represented a traditional log ski and sports lodge complete with a sod roof (San Francisco Bay Exposition 1939, 91).

Although the modern pavilions built by Italy, Brazil, and Argentina sharply contrasted with the historic pastiches of the Pacific Area, an even greater divergence arose between how the United States and Pacific nations were exhibited after the fair reopened for a second season in 1940. Growing concern regarding world events led to changes in displays that reflected a move further away from the exposition's utopian vision of a peaceful Pacific. Exhibits such as Peace Projects disappeared. In their place were greatly enlarged national defense displays that reflected an increased desire among organizers to use the exposition as a deterrent against the growing threat of war through the exhibition of the United States' military might. Prominent exhibits included demonstrations of "the newest weapons used by Uncle Sam for preparedness in the air and on land and sea," including a "Flying Fortress" bombing plane, a submarine, and numerous displays of other fighting machines (Northern Pacific Railway 1940). Pageants and military maneuvers were held along the road in front of the Federal Building. Even changes to the Native American exhibit that expanded to include displays of Inca, Maya, and Aztecs handicrafts, cultures that had no direct tie to the United States, seemed to subliminally reflect the government's agenda of presenting itself more as a political force in the Pacific and less as a promoter of peace (San Francisco Bay Exposition 1940, 77).

Evolving political and economic conditions across the world also led to significant changes for the foreign exhibits between fair seasons. Because

FIGURE 4.13   Brazil Pavilion at the GGIE. 1939. The Bancroft Library, University of California, Berkeley.

of growing tensions in both Europe and Asia, a number of nations were not in the position to return to San Francisco when the exposition reopened; others continued to be represented, but, like the Czech exhibit the year before, switched from official presentations to ones sponsored by local ethnic communities (James and Weller 1941, 100). France, which had with Britain declared war on Germany almost two months before the fair closed in 1939, had more on its mind than reopening an exhibit in San Francisco. Norway ended its official representation after Germany invaded the country in April 1940, and its log pavilion was disassembled. Norwegian Americans, who still wanted their homeland to have a presence at the fair, took over the New Zealand Pavilion and altered it from a Maori meetinghouse into "a typical Scandinavian structure" (San Francisco Bay Exposition 1940, 71). Dedicated to the ideals of peace and progress, the building served as the center of Norwegian war relief efforts while the exposition was in operation (James and Weller 1941, 115–116).

Several Pacific Area buildings were also repurposed for the 1940 fair season. The Philippine Pavilion was transformed into the new International Market, a *caravanserai* of wares from more than two dozen countries exhibited to "tempt and exhilarate" (San Francisco Bay Exposition 1940, 70). In a similar fashion, the Dutch East Indies building was reincarnated as the Treasure House, hosting craft demonstrations and displays of art objects from all over the world. The Johor Pavilion, meanwhile, broadened its scope to represent all of the Malay states.

The Latin American area, rechristened the International Court, also underwent a major transformation and became more geographically diverse by welcoming several European countries. Switzerland took over the Chilean Pavilion, the Netherlands moved into Panama's former home, and Portugal adopted the Guatemalan Pavilion. Uruguay, meanwhile, replaced El Salvador. Unlike the dramatic alterations that the Norwegian Americans made to the New Zealand Pavilion, the exteriors of the Latin American buildings remain largely unchanged.

With the closing of the San Francisco exposition in the fall of 1940, the utopian vision of a peaceful, international marketplace in the Pacific evaporated as expanding political tensions reached the shores of the United States. Although the Roosevelt administration largely failed in its mission to use the GGIE as a venue in which to project a peaceful Pacific, the event did help publicize America's growing role in the region. It also introduced the character, products, peoples, and sites of the countries of the Pacific to millions of fairgoers and many more through secondary sources, such as newsreels and souvenirs.

A major goal of the Century of Progress International Exposition's modern vision for corporate America was to bring the United States out of the Great Depression. The event's financial and commercial triumph led a series of other American cities to attempt to emulate its success in hopes of improving their own local economies. The character and aims of the GGIE, however, were quite different. With world tensions sharply rising at the end of the 1930s and the US government desiring to increase its role in the Pacific region, the fair on Treasure Island was less about promoting an American consumer culture and more about establishing a dominant role in the Eastern Hemisphere as a way to secure accessibility to resources and promote international trade. The rise of political confrontations outside the fairgrounds directly impacted the exposition, particularly in how countries were presented, if they were represented at all.

The failure to achieve the Roosevelt administration's utopian vision of Pacific unity as the world's nations were being drawn into war was made abundantly clear when, after the close of the exposition, Treasure Island was not turned into a regional airport as planned, but instead was appropriated by the Navy and transformed into a military base. The island served as a major headquarters for the United States' involvement in the Pacific Theater during World War II. The Tower of the Sun and the fantastic foreign pavilions vanished. Soon, up to twelve thousand men a day were processed on the island as they made their way to fight the Land of the Rising Sun (Miller 2010). The utopian vision of a Pacific of Peace had turned into the horrific reality of a Pacific of War.

Notes

Epigraph. John Richard Finch, "Summary of Foreign Participation: Corrected to January 1, 1939," press release, Golden Gate International Exposition, Publicity Files, San Francisco Public Library.

1 The author is grateful to Lynne Horiuchi, Melissa Jensen, Lorenz Schrenk, and Steven Weis for their assistance with this essay.

2 The other expositions include the California-Pacific International Exposition in San Diego (1935–1936), the Texas Centennial Exposition in Dallas (1936), the Great Lakes Exposition in Cleveland (1936–1937), and the New York World's Fair in New York City (1939–1940).

3 John Richard Finch, "Summary of Foreign Participation: Corrected to January 1, 1939," press release, Golden Gate International Exposition, Publicity Files, San Francisco Public Library.

4 "Foreign Participation," Folder 15–121, Century of Progress Records (CoPR), University of Illinois at Chicago (UIC).

5 O. J. Keatings, letter to Henry Cole, March 10, 1932, Folder 2-1106, CoPR, UIC.

6 "Italy," memo chronicling contact with the Italian government regarding its participation in the exposition, CoPR, UIC.

7 "Foreign Participation," Folder 15-121, CoPR, UIC.

8 For more information on the Chinese Bendix Lama Temple, see Roskam 2014.

9 Press release, June 17, 1936, Publicity Files, Golden Gate International Exposition (GGIE), San Francisco Public Library (SFPL).

10 Ibid.

11 *Golden Gate International Exposition, 1939 on San Francisco Bay,* brochure, circa 1937, 10, 4. Arthur Brown Jr. Papers, Folder 240, MSS 81/142, The Bancroft Library, University of California, Berkeley.

12 "Talk by George Creel before Commonwealth Club," August 26, 1938, Box 5, Speeches 1938–40, George Creel Papers, Library of Congress.

13 The architectural commission included George W. Kelham, Arthur Brown Jr., Lewis P. Hobart, William G. Merchant, Timothy L. Pflueger, and Ernest E. Weihe. Kelham chaired the committee until his untimely death in 1936. Brown then took over the leadership position. W. P. Day served as director of works.

14 All of the members of the architectural commission except Timothy L. Pflueger had either attended the École des Beaux-Arts in Paris as part of their architectural education or had worked for someone who had been educated at the institution.

15 The artist Robert Stackpole envisioned *Pacifica* to suggest the Pacific as a whole, as an embodiment of Pacific Basin cultures, but recognized that the viewer "reads his own symbolism and it is not likely to coincide with that of the artist" (1939).

16 The exhibition space could have been more correctly labeled the European Hall because all the nations hailed from Europe.

17 These drawings are located in the Arthur Brown Jr. Archive at the Bancroft Library.

18 Different preliminary variations of the Pacific Basin Area appear in drawings Brown worked on dated October 26, October 27, November 17, November 26, and December 17 of 1937, and January 19, March 24, June 22 of 1938 (Arthur Brown Jr. Papers, Folder 251, MSS 81/142, the Bancroft Library).

19 "Pageant of the Pacific," press release circa 1938, Publicity Files, GGIE, SFPL.

20 Ibid.

21 "Ancient Temple May Be Brought to S. F. Exposition," circa 1939, Golden Gate International Exposition newspaper clip sheet no. 3, Publicity Files, GGIE, SFPL.

22 "Native Temple for 1939 Fair," newspaper clip sheet no. 4, Publicity Files, GGIE, SFPL.

23 *Foreign—Exhibitors De Luxe Booklet*, October 21, 1936, Publicity Files, GGIE, SFPL.

24 Finch, "Summary of Foreign Participation."

25 "A Handy Key to 12 Enchanting Days at the Golden Gate Exposition," San Francisco: Recorder Printing and Publishing, 1939, Publicity Files, GGIE, SFPL.

26 Finch, "Summary of Foreign Participation."

References

Architect and Engineer. 1936. "World's Fair Buildings." Vol. 125 (May): 63–64.

Architectural Forum 1934. "A Century of Progress Paradox." Vol. 61 (November): 376.

———. 1939. "San Francisco Golden Gate Exposition." Vol. 70 (June): 498–499.

Brown, Arthur, Jr. 1939. "The Architectural Planning of the Exposition." *Architecture and Engineer* 136 (February): 18–20.

Brown, Arthur, Jr. Papers. BANC MSS 18/142c. The Bancroft Library, University of California, Berkeley.

Century of Progress. Records, 1927–1952. Special Collections and University Archives, University of Illinois at Chicago.

Chicago Tribune. 1934. "Ask Bankruptcy for Streets of Shanghai." July 20.

Covarrubias, Miguel. 1940. *Pageant of the Pacific*. San Francisco: Pacific House.

Creel, George. Papers. Library of Congress. Washington, DC.

Doordan, Dennis P. 1993. "Exhibiting Progress: Italy's Contribution to the Century of Progress Exposition." In *Chicago Architecture and Design, 1923–1993: Reconfiguration of an American Metropolis,* ed. John Zukowsky, 219–231. Munich: Pretel-Verlag for the Art Institute of Chicago.

Duffy, Sherman R. 1933. "France Out as World Fair Exhibitor." *Chicago American,* March 3.

Findling, John E. 1994. *Chicago's Great World's Fairs*. New York: Manchester University Press.

Ganz, Cheryl R. 2008. *The 1933 Chicago World's Fair: A Century of Progress*. Champaign: University of Illinois Press.

Golden Gate International Exposition. Publicity Files. San Francisco Public Library.

Gutheim, Frederick A. 1939. "Federal Participation in Two World's Fairs." *Public Opinion Quarterly* 3, no. 4:608–622. doi:10.1086/265343.

Ho, Chuimei, and Soo Lon Moy, eds. 2005. *Chinese in Chicago, 1870–1945*. Mount Pleasant, SC: Arcadia Publishing.

James, Jack, and Earle Vonard Weller. 1941. *Treasure Island, "The Magic City." 1939–1940: The Story of the Golden Gate International Exposition*. San Francisco: Pisani Printing and Publishing.

Jones, Fred W. 1939. "The Exposition." *Architect and Engineer* 136 (February): 18.

Kinkel, Marianne. 2011. *Races of Mankind: The Sculptures of Malvina Hoffman*. Champaign: University of Illinois Press.

Living New Deal Project. n.d. "Treasure Island—Golden Gate International Exposition—San Francisco CA." Berkeley: Institute for Research on Labor and Employment, University of California. http://www.irle.berkeley.edu/livingnewdeal/.

Lohr, Lenox R. 1952. *Fair Management: The Story of A Century of Progress.* Chicago: Cuneo Press.

McDowell, Malcolm, 1933. "Oriental Village to Show Life of East at Fair." *Chicago Daily News,* February 6.

Miller, Richard. 2010. "Treasure Island Music Festival." .

Northern Pacific Railway. c. 1940. *San Francisco World's Fair 1940.* Brochure. Collection of Lorenz P. Schrenk.

Official Guide Book of the Fair. 1933. Chicago: A Century of Progress.

Official World's Fair Weekly. 1933. "Anthropology in Africa." October 14.

Old Europe. 1932. "London: A Century of Progress." Chicago: Burnham Library, Art Institute of Chicago.

Pavilion of French Indo-China. 1939. *1939 Golden Gate Exposition, Treasure Island.* Brochure. Arlington, VA: Society of Indo-China Philatelists Archive. http://www.sicp-online.org.

Roskam, Cole. 2014. "Situating Chinese Architecture within 'A Century of Progress': The Chinese Pavilion, the Bendix Golden Temple, and the 1933 Chicago World's Fair," *Journal of the Society of Architectural Historians* 73, no. 3 (September): 347–371.

Rubens, Lisa. 1991. "The 1939 San Francisco World's Fair: The New Deal, the New Frontier, and the Pacific Basin." PhD diss., University of California, Berkeley.

———. 1994. "Re-presenting the Nation: The Golden Gate International Exposition." In *Fair Representations: World's Fairs and the Modern World,* ed. Robert W. Rydell and Nancy Gwinn, 121–139. Amsterdam: VU University Press.

Rydell, Robert W. 1989. "The 1939 San Francisco Golden Gate International Exposition and the Empire of the West." In *The American West, as Seen by Europeans and Americans,* ed. Rob Kroes, 342–359. Amsterdam: Free University Press.

Rydell, Robert W., and Rob Kroes. 2005. *Buffalo Bill in Bologna: The Americanization of the World, 1869-1922.* Chicago: University of Chicago Press.

San Francisco Bay Exposition. 1939. *Official Guide Book: 1939 Golden Gate International Exposition on San Francisco Bay.* Rev. ed. San Francisco: The Crocker Company.

———. 1940. *Official Guide Book: 1940 Golden Gate International Exposition on San Francisco Bay.* San Francisco: The Crocker Company.

Schrenk, Lisa D. 1999. "From Historic Village to Modern Pavilion: The Evolution of Foreign Architectural Representation at International Expositions in the 1930s." *National Identity* 1, no. 3: 287–311.

———. 2007. *Building a Century of Progress: The Architecture of Chicago's 1933–34 World's Fair.* Minneapolis: University of Minnesota Press.

Shanken, Andrew. 2015. *Into the Void Pacific: Building the 1939 San Francisco World's Fair.* Berkeley: University of California Press.

Stackpole, Robert. 1939. "Pacific Is Unveiled on Fair Island." *San Francisco Chronicle,* February 17.

Turner, Frederick Jackson. 1920. *The Frontier in American History.* New York: Henry Holt.

Wang, Zhongwei, and Chao Song. 2008. *The World Exposition Reader.* Shanghai: Shanghai Scientific and Technological Publishing House.

5. A Local Global Utopia

The Japan Pavilion at the Golden Gate International Exposition

LYNNE HORIUCHI

A 1939 Golden Gate International Exposition brochure and visitor's guide, titled *The Japan Pavilion Welcomes World Visitors*, described the pavilion and its site to visitors in the romantic and overheated style of exposition rhetoric:

> Amidst an exotic Japanese setting of terraced gardens, with plants and shrubbery and many varieties of trees that shade the placid lagoons, Japan Pavilion, an original combination of the architecture of a Feudal Castle and a Samurai house of the 17th Century, stands in majestic splendor as one of the finest and most interesting sights of the Golden Gate International Exposition at Treasure Island. (1)

As an ephemeral Orientalist vision, this representation of the Japan Pavilion played out the utopian dream of the Golden Gate International Exposition (GGIE), out of step with the political realities of a world about to be engulfed in a global war (see Figures 5.1, 5.2, and 5.3).

With Japan invited as a host as well as a guest of the exposition, the Japan Pavilion presented—from the Japanese government's perspective—an opportunity to promote trade and brand their imperial colonial projects in China, Korea, and Southeast Asia for the US market. Just as the Japan Pavilion was being built and exhibited, Japan was carrying out a grand colonization program for the creation of

FIGURE 5.1   Southern elevation of the Japan Pavilion from across the lagoon, 1939. Kyosankai Nihonjin. The Bancroft Library, University of California, Berkeley.

FIGURE 5.2 Northern and western elevations of the Japan Pavilion, 1939. San Francisco History Center, San Francisco Public Library.

FIGURE 5.3 The Japan Pavilion Garden, 1939. Fang Family San Francisco Examiner Photograph Archive. The Bancroft Library, University of California, Berkeley

the Greater East Asia Co-Prosperity Sphere and forging political alliances with Axis governments between 1937 and 1940. Intently synchronized with GGIE themes, the Japan Pavilion had a highly visible site on which to project a version of its economic fascist ideologies and global vision for world commerce.[1] The narratives managed by the Japanese government in the Japan Pavilion sought to represent Japan as an "Oriental" nation of an equal, if not greater, power among modern nations interested in promoting world peace.

Over seven decades, under state control, Japan's population underwent major demographic changes that resulted in the interlocking of emigration with expansionism. By 1939, the Japanese government had normalized its incorporation of settler communities such as Japanese American communities into an extension of the Japanese empire (Azuma 2005). So it was not surprising that local San Francisco Bay Area and regional Japanese American communities participated in promoting the Japan Pavilion. Their commitments were expressed through the participation of their communities in performances, parades, events, sponsorship, and staffing at the Japan Pavilion. Their contributions to the Golden Gate International Exposition Kyosankai Nihonjin, a Japanese American community association, helped fund the construction and organize the programming of the Japan Pavilion. Taking pride in Japan's participation, the Kyosankai Nihonjin devised its own media representations of the Japan Pavilion through the publication of brochures in Japanese, one of which was sponsored by a Japanese American community recreational spa—the Gilroy Hot Springs located just south of San Jose. These publications appear to be officially associated with the GGIE with messages from the GGIE fair officials and the Japanese consul (Kyosankai Nihonjin 1939, 1940; Kyosankai Nihonjin and Gilroy Hot Springs 1939).

The trajectory of the physical existence of the Japan Pavilion, from its making to its destruction, reflects the state-driven urban reinventions described in this collection. The building and its grounds demonstrate the ways in which significant financial and cultural capital, both state and private, were invested in cooperative ways in spaces that were then demolished for urban change. As an example of world's fair architecture, the Japan Pavilion's extremely brief history encapsulates the ephemerality of these large developments. Its historical contexts raise complex questions about the representation of imperial power and national belonging as a prelude to World War II through Japanese representations of the Greater East Asia Co-Prosperity Sphere at the exposition, visions of American dominance in the Pacific, and the centrality of the San Francisco Bay Area to commerce and trade with Asian and Southeast Asian nations.

I argue in this essay that the pavilion's particular ephemerality and aesthetics were intricately interwoven in the prescient conditions of international conflict during the pavilion's brief existence from 1939 to 1940. The aesthetics of Japanese fascism were exhibited in the Pavilion's architecture, staffing, performances, and sponsorship. The demolition of the Japan Pavilion then functions as a sign of aesthetically related violence that must be understood within the context of competing imperial and colonizing nations and as a premonition of the bombing of Pearl Harbor on December 7, 1941, that resulted in the US involvement in World War II.

World fairs have provided architectural and art historians a culturally rich way to understand state-driven publicity and propaganda narratives for national visions of global ordering. For architecture, the world fairs have functioned as barometers of modern architecture and national identity alongside progressive exhibits of science and technology. If we frame the Japan Pavilion's interior architecture, art exhibits, silk demonstrations, themed exhibit halls, and programmed performances within the expansion of the Japanese empire, we may also see their gendered feminine qualities that soften and occlude the political codes of Japanese fascism. The fashioning of the Japan Pavilion might even be seen as part of a fascist myth of wholeness fortified by what Alan Tansman refers to as sublime "fascist moments"—a kind of apolitical cultural work that seduced the Japanese public "away from intellectual analysis into submission to a mystique of national and racial destiny" (Tansman 2009b, 18–19).[2] The Japanese American community through its participation contributed to the cosmopolitan conjoining of Japanese fascist and American imperial ideological systems while remaining vulnerable to discrimination and oppression in both Japan and America. The GGIE and Japan Pavilion expressed the ideological narratives of peace, harmony, faith, and commerce perfectly synchronized with the celebration of building bridges (Tansman 2009a).

My analysis here reflects a normal default starting point for architectural historians who deal primarily with materiality, space, spatial production and their interrelationships by focusing on single buildings. The analysis of its physical site reflects methodology adapted from art history to assess the art and aesthetics of individual objects, in this case a building. Architectural history often draws from its European classical traditions for its methodology and particularly the Vitruvian tradition for its qualities of *firmitas, utilitas,* and *venustas* (strength, functionality, and beauty), providing a certain neoclassical authority in the enlightenment and humanist tradition, although rarely engaging racial inequality, ephemerality, destruction, and war, which are the focus of this essay.[3]

Japanese Imperialism at the Golden Gate International Exposition

Delving into the production of the Japan Pavilion uncovers its various narratives of orientalism, imperialism, nationalism, gender, and performance in local and global contexts—not solely crafted by the American conveners of the fair. We may appreciate the beauty and craft of the building in the art historical tradition. Yet, though the Japan Pavilion was sited harmoniously within the exposition's ephemeral fantasy landscapes and narratives of trans-Pacific history, it was also an exercise in branding the Japanese empire in Asia and Southeast Asia, specifically the Greater East Asia Co-Prosperity Sphere, significantly playing out Japan's identity as a modern imperial nation.

The violence of war remained suppressed, just below the surface of the spectacular glamour and cosmopolitan ideals of the exposition, and was a major
frame for the aesthetics of the pavilion. While the exposition was planned and
held, Japan had engaged in major military actions to increase her colonial holdings. By 1937, Japanese imperial forces had occupied Nanking. On August 1,
1939, Japan officially launched the Greater East Asia Co-Prosperity Sphere and
claims to territories it would soon dominate militarily. By 1940 and Japan's alliance in the Tripartite Pact with European Axis nations, Japanese imperialism had
officially extended the government's ideologies to justify its imperial domination
of a pan-Asian sphere of influence. The Foreign Office announced the Tripartite
Alliance of Axis powers on September 27, 1940, reiterating a vision of global
peace:

> The Governments of Japan, Germany and Italy, considering it as a condition
> precedent of any lasting peace that all nations of the world be given each its own
> proper place, have decided to stand by and cooperate with one another in regard
> to their efforts in Greater East Asia and the regions of Europe respectively wherein
> it is their prime purpose to establish and maintain a new order of things. (quoted
> in Dower 1986, 281)

At GGIE, Japan was fulfilling her mission of becoming a first world power—
colonizing Asian nations and showcasing both her internal and external imperial
expansion: Hokkaido (1869), Okinawa (1870), Taiwan (1894), south Sakhalin
(1905), Kwantung Province (1905), the annexation of Korea or Chosen (1910), and
Manchukuo (1931). As a major emerging power among capitalist economies, the
Meiji Restoration's industrialization (1869–1911) had already integrated Japan into
international markets.

The Japan Pavilion and Representations
of Imperial Power at World's Fairs

The Japanese government had managed the representation of their national identity
at a number of past Euro American world's fairs whose ideological frameworks
had created world visions invested in European and American power, relegating
races and nations considered lower in stature to lesser exhibit spaces or demeaning exhibits (Gonzalez 2011; Wilson 2012; Cogdell 2004; Roskam 2014; Carpenter
and Totah 1989). The colonial expositions of the 1930s, such as the 1931 Exposition coloniale internationale de Paris, commodified world travel in one-day global
travelogues and tours and reified the colonial world order spatially (Çelik 1992;
Morton 2000; Rydell, Findling, and Pelle 2000).[4] Numerous non-European states
and nonwhite groups generally had to strategize to counter multidimensional and
racially demeaning processes and representations associated with world's fairs.
Not only did Euro American world's fairs display eugenics exhibits, they also often
used racialized scales of civilization replete with extreme stereotypes in popular

pseudo-ethnographic and more serious anthropological exhibits (Wilson 2012; Rydell, Findling, and Pelle 2000).

The Japan Pavilion was the inheritor of seven decades of the Japanese government's participation in their own domestic expositions, Euro American expositions and museum building dating from the Meiji era. Their participation in fair exhibitions was closely related to the national government's crafting of a modern national Japanese identity through visual narratives, art, and exhibitions. The government's efforts contributed to the creation of national museums, the museums' development of artistic consumer goods for burgeoning middle-class Japanese societies, and the export of Japanese aesthetics. The new domestic market for these goods produced many variants of hybrid Western and traditional Western art and architecture in the industrializing worlds of the Meiji, Taisho (1912–1926), and early Showa (1926–1989) imperial eras (Aso 2014; Tseng 2008).

The Japan Pavilion sat somewhat uncomfortably within these art and architectural historical traditions because of the history of bio-politically and racially charged exhibits in Euro American fairs in anthropology, ethnography, and eugenics that non-European governments constructing exhibits or buildings had to negotiate (Aso 2014; Roskam 2014). For Japan, the interwar colonial expositions, such as the 1931 Exposition coloniale internationale de Paris, may have served the Japanese government as models for fashioning the colonial fascist narratives exhibited at the Japan Pavilion—not as subjects or objects of colonizing, but as a modern Asian nation state fashioning colonial order with Tokyo as the metropole.

The Japan Pavilion conformed to contemporary prewar Japanese architectural and aesthetic conventions as well as to the standards of world expositions. In using international expositions to create Japanese national aesthetics, the Japanese government had carefully balanced paradigms for national representation, strategically locating Japan within the hierarchy of Western racial and cultural superiority with the West at the pinnacle. Using the trope of an ancient civilization, the state organized exhibits of Japanese religious icons and aristocratic aesthetics in their national pavilions and in other sections of the fairs. The teahouses and curio shops used Western Orientalism to draw in customers who then provided a flow of foreign currency for Japanese markets (Aso 2014; Tseng 2008).

The Japan Pavilion at the Golden Gate International Exposition

By 1937, the Japanese government was exercising increasing control over all types of cultural production—in literature, film, graphics, theater, and other sectors of art (Weisenfeld 2007; Tansman 2009a; Baskett 2009; Aso 2014). In the tradition of European world's fairs, Japan sought to advertise her colonizing commerce through

art and aesthetics with nearly complete control of the construction of and programming for the Japan Pavilion at the GGIE. Japan's participation in the GGIE was its
ultimate refinement of world's fair designs in which it had consistently invoked an
ancient civilization, claimed equal status with dominant modern nations, and used
Western Orientalism as a branding tool (Aso 2014).

With the Japanese government's $500,000 investment in the Japan Pavilion
and its prominent twenty-eight-acre site on a lagoon, Japan was the dominant and
largest foreign exhibit at the fair (Shanken 2014) (see Figures 5.1, 5.2, and 5.3). The
Japan Pavilion clearly occupied a central site a short distance from the Pacific Building and the Pacific Promenade near the intersection of the Court of Reflection—one
of the major axes of the GGIE plan and grid (see Figure 5.4). In 1938, Japanese
Consul Kanzo Shiozake had signed a contract with the president of the GGIE, Leland
Cutler, for the construction of the Japan Pavilion, with the provision that Japanese
carpenters, architects, engineers, and other building experts be brought, along with
the building material, from Japan. With this considerable expense, the Japanese
government was thus able to control the entire production of the Japan Pavilion.
The anchoring of the *Tatsuta Maru*, a Nippon Yusen Kaisha (NYK) luxury ocean
liner, off the south side of the Treasure Island Port of Trade Winds on October 13,
1938, became part of the GGIE spectacle. Built between 1927 and 1930 by the Mit-
subishi Shipbuilding and Engineering Company, the ocean liner showcased Japan's
industrial expertise while providing building materials from Japan and housing for
the Japanese carpenters building the Japan Pavilion. The major interaction between
GGIE planners or architects and the Japanese was over the siting of the building.

As a building, the Japan Pavilion is emblematic. It resonated with the spectacular mode of the GGIE and its exhibition buildings. The Japan Pavilion was, after all,
a building sited in an exposition that was described as a magical city, where the
GGIE's designers expressed an American imperialist Orientalism that romantically
conflated and eclectically mixed their visions of Asia, Indo-China, Latin America,
and Native America even as they arranged the plan for the participation of foreign
countries. GGIE fair planners recast American imperial power through the themes
of peace, harmony, and faith to serve commerce in the Pacific Rim, bringing together "the progress of the Pacific nations and the spirit of Western achievement"
(GGIE 1939, 4).

The shared utopian dreams of the GGIE literally bridged both American and Japanese narratives in which the focus of American international relations and global
commerce ostensibly moved from Europe and the Atlantic Ocean to the Pacific
Ocean (Azuma 2003). In a brochure published by the Golden Gate International Exposition Kyonsankai Nihonjin (1939, 1940), Consul Toshito Sato noted that in spite
of a national emergency and its recumbent national expenditures, Japan had taken
the lead among foreign nations in committing a large budget for its participation
in the exposition. The national emergency the consul referred to was Japan's ambitious imperial program in the second Sino-Japanese war—the Japanese invasion
of China and the establishment of Manchukuo or Manchuria as a Japanese puppet
state. Dovetailing with the American nationalist framing of GGIE utopian narratives,

Sato's narrative conformed to Japanese representations of the Greater East Asian Co-Prosperity sphere.

The pavilion occupied eighteen thousand square feet surrounded by a landscaped garden and was built on a ground area of fifty thousand square feet. The siting of the building and its design was coordinated through Arthur Brown Jr., chair of the GGIE Architectural Commission. Some of his sketches of the pavilion site document the planning for incorporating the building into the GGIE general plan. Although he probably did not serve as a consulting or associate architect, Arthur Brown Jr. did produce a detailed drawing of the east or back elevation of the pavilion and informal sketches of its footprint around the lagoon that appear to be some of the few extant plans of the building. A detail of one of his sketches for GGIE's ground plan show the footprint of the Japan Pavilion in relation to the lagoon and the Pacific Buildings (Figure 5.4).

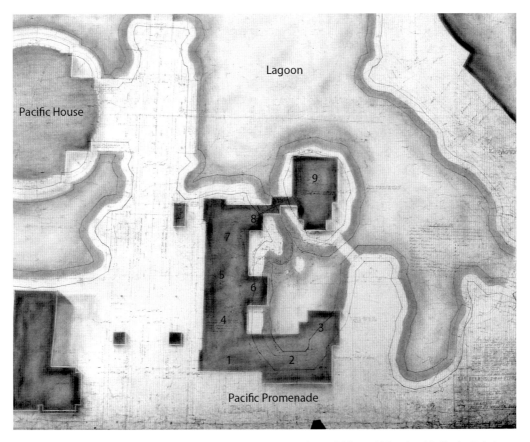

FIGURE 5.4 "Ground Plan," circa 1938. Arthur Brown Jr. Papers. The Bancroft Library, University of California, Berkeley . Approximate locations of exhibits in the Japan Pavilion footprint on a sketch drawn for the ground plan design by Arthur Brown Jr. and the Architecture Committee, circa 1938.
1–Pagoda Tower Entrance; 2–Silk Room; 3–Silk Making Demonstration; 4–Industrial Art Room; 5–Travel Hall; 6–Orient Calls Tea Room; 7–Transportation and Communication Room; 8–Outdoor Movie Hall; 9–Hall of Festivities

An Architectural Description of the Japan Pavilion

The stepped, graduated stories of the 125-foot pagoda, traditionally a separate architectural structure, dominate the entrance elevation accessed from one of the GGIE's major pedestrian streets, the Pacific Promenade (see Figure 5.4). The plain stucco walls with unadorned and deep window bays as well as the artisan-crafted traditional Japanese roof are associated with the imperial crown style of architecture (*teikan-heigō*) and its conservative hybrid of Western and traditional structures. It was an officially recognized nationalistic and eclectic style with "a Japanese-style castle-like rooftop with a Western-style geometrical structure" (Nakamori 2010, 23). Kenzo Tange's award-winning drawings for the Memorial to the Creation of the Greater East Asia Co-Prosperity Sphere in 1942 and a Japan-Thailand Friendship Hall in 1943 were designed as modern westernized alternatives to this style.

The pavilion design has been attributed to architects Yoshizo Utida and Tatunae Toki, who retained contact addresses in San Francisco. A GGIE interoffice memo issued by the Department of Foreign Participation also listed Gentoku Shimamoto as a contact in a list of foreign architects. It is not clear whether the Japanese architects came specifically for designing the pavilion or whether they were long-term residents in the United States.[5]

The building was ingeniously wrapped around the pavilion's garden and a lagoon inlet. A number of the exhibit halls seem to be approximately double height, although the pavilion appears to have two stories of exhibit halls opening in some places onto verandas that looked out at over the garden and lagoon (see Figures 5.1, 5.3, and 5.5). The verandas ran parallel to the exhibits on the west, south, and east exteriors of the building facing the lagoon, just as rooms and corridors in a traditional Japanese house would look onto an interior garden, providing views from all angles of the inlet and garden. The lower veranda functioned as a corridor connecting the exhibits halls while the upper veranda appears to have been accessed by a single door. The path of the wooden bridge over a small inlet on the approach to the Hall of Festivities, a separate building, turned right and left at 90 degree angles, offering different angles for viewing the garden. An arched bridge returned visitors to the Pacific Promenade. Landscape architects Takeshi Tamura and Nagao Sakurai designed a traditional tea garden with a pond and landscaped with stones and trees from Japan (Shanken 2014; *Japan Pavilion Welcomes* 1939).

To American viewers guided by GGIE publications, the pavilion appears to be emulating the estate of a medieval Japanese samurai residence and a Shinto shrine. But a closer look at its architecture reveals its modern hybrid architectural style that would have been quite at home with a similar tile roof, sheathed exterior stucco walls with nontraditional fenestration next to the Tokyo National Museum built in Ueno Park designed by Jin Watanabe and completed in 1937 (Ōshima 2009).

By Japanese standards, the pavilion design might have been a refinement of the Japanese government's cultural program of exhibiting ancient Japanese art and architecture to represent modern imperial Japan and its colonial nationalism at a world's fair. Despite a strong modernist avant-garde architectural movement in

Japan in the 1920s and 1930s, the Japan Pavilion's hybrid Westernized architectural style was clearly more conservative, approximating the imperial crown style of the Tokyo National Museum.

Because the imperial crown style was an accepted official genre by 1939, the Japanese carpenters brought from Japan would have recognized the pavilion as a constructed "Western space" or *Yōma*. In fact, Japanese carpenters with little direction from foreign architectural specialists had constructed the majority of what was considered Western architecture during Meiji period Japan (1868–1911) reflecting the idea of a "Western Orient" or *tōyō* (Ōshima 2009, 73–75). The pavilion's architectural style was a synthesis of lifestyles—Japanese *wa* and Western *yō*. *Yō*, a concept associated with ocean, foreign, and European that did not necessarily connote the West directly, but rather a Japanese interpretation of lands beyond the ocean (Ōshima 2009, 73–74).

By the 1930s, the synthesis in half-Japanese and half-Western domestic spaces and vernacular architecture had become widely accepted as one of a number of alternatives for a modern Japanese lifestyle. The carpenters' traditional wood framing had also been transformed under the influence of Western wood-frame technology, and as Ken Ōshima notes, "the importation of Western technology and materials could be seen in large public buildings and upon close inspection, in small wood-frame houses" (2009, 76). Such Western techniques as balloon framing had been introduced into Japan around 1875, yet the sensibility of Japanese carpenters' methods of building influenced both Japanese and European modernist syntheses of design and construction. Thus, the Japan Pavilion, though not progressive in the modernist sense, may be seen as an interesting successor and synthesis of modern European and Japanese styles of architecture.

The overall programming of the pavilion conformed to precedents using Japanese traditional architecture developed at the World's Columbian Fair of 1893, the 1909 Alaskan-Yukon-Pacific Expositions held in Portland and Seattle, and the Pan-Pacific International Expositions of 1915 held at San Francisco and San Diego. For these fairs, the Japanese government had used reduced-scale replicas of the Kinkaku-ji Temple or the Golden Pavilion of Kyoto and other clearly Orientalist archetypes such as tea houses and elaborate gardens. The GGIE trope of an ancient Japanese civilization expressed through an "original combination of the architecture of a Feudal Castle and a Samurai house of the 17th Century" aligned with the assortment of Mayan, Malay, and Khmer tropes incorporated into the fantastic architecture of the fair, nostalgically recalling Pacific Rim civilizations from the distant past.

Although the promotion of the Japan Pavilion as a trope of an ancient civilization heightened its appeal, the interiors were thoroughly modern, with spaces designed for a prominent contemporary world's fair that would attract 4.5 million visitors. The exhibits contained examples of the modern production of commercial art products normally sold to Western nations—silk, pottery, and art goods. There were also map displays of Japan's commercial interests that mirrored imperial expansion and photographic displays of its modern industries. Exhibit cases extended along the walls in unbroken lines illuminated by indirect ceiling lighting.

The programming or use of space was also based on the past commercial success of Orientalist enterprises such as the tea house and curio shops, some of which were run and staffed by Japanese immigrants or their college-age Japanese American children (Issei and Nisei respectively, as the generations were commonly referred to within the Japanese American community). The programming for the interior spaces included exhibits, demonstrations, photomurals, embroidered hangings, a performance area, a movie house and a Japanese garden built around the lagoon inlet. The garden was laid out in an Edo-era "*Kaiyu* style," or "circular style" (Kyosankai Nihonjin 1939, 13). Young English-speaking Japanese American women in Japanese kimono chosen for their educational background served as guides. The main exhibit spaces were the Silk Room, the Industrial Art Room, the Travel Hall that included a Tourist Information Office, the Transportation and Communication Room, an outdoor movie theater, and the Hall of Festivities—a separate building. Green tea and "green tea ice cream" were served with cookies at the "Orient Calls" Tea Room adjoining the Travel Hall that afforded the best views of the garden (*Japan Pavilion Welcomes* 1939) (see Figures 5.1, 5.3, and 5.4).

Mapping the Progress of the Empire

Mapping and place-naming to commemorate the Japanese empire was a major theme of the exhibits. Japan's official name for their colonized Korean state was Chosen, and for their colonized Manchurian regime, Manchukuo. In the Travel Hall, in addition to an elaborate map showing travel routes from the United States to Japan, Chosen, Manchukuo, and China, elaborate embroidered hangings illustrated Mt. Fuji and Miyajima, Mt. Kogo in Chosen, and the mausoleum of a Mancho emperor at Mukden, Manchukuo (*Japan Pavilion Welcomes* 1939, 5–6). The latter was probably a reference to the 1931 Mukden or Manchurian Incident that had provided Japan with a justification for the invasion of Manchuria. The Transportation and Communication Hall exhibited a network, illuminated on plate glass, of communication lines and steamship routes radiating from Japan to all parts of the world. The illumination was designed to alternately display the steamship routes with lines in colored electrical lights and then the international wireless telegraph and telephone services with two lines of different colors. In the same hall, a Telephoto Apparatus demonstrated the transmission of photographs between Tokyo and San Francisco along a global circle (*Japan Pavilion Welcomes* 1939).

Without detailed plans, it is a challenge to definitively identify the location of all the rooms and the traffic flow through the building, yet a reasonably accurate description may be reconstructed from brochures and photographs of the exterior and interior of the pavilion; there were also some minor changes in the exhibits between 1939 and 1940 (see Figure 5.4).[6] Just to the left of the simulated pagoda tower was an entrance into an exhibit room with a double-height

ceiling with a display of a modern
Japanese living room on the left and
the silk-making demonstration or the
Silk Room on the right, accessed by
a small circular ramp. The displays
in the Silk Room also displayed models of silkworm eggs and the growth
of the worms, moths, and cocoons
as part of a scientific display of the
production of silk. A separate room
housed a demonstration of the art of
modern industrialized silk weaving
by four young women selected from
two thousand sericulture workers,
one of whom was a Japanese American Kibei, that is, born in the United
States but educated in Japan (Ina
2005).

FIGURE 5.5   Travel Hall fountain and map, 1939. Kyosankai Nihonjin.
The Bancroft Library, University of California, Berkeley.

The Travel Hall occupied part of
the main axis of the building from which the "Orient Calls" Tea House extended
over the lagoon inlet. The Transportation and Communication Hall at the furthest
end from the entrance used large photomurals to illustrate Japan's technological
progress and displayed enlarged images of postage stamps. Just where the wooden
pathway led from this room an outdoor movie house was located. Exhibits of Japanese paintings, sculpture, bronze works, and flower arrangements were scheduled
in the Hall of Festivities as well as activities such as Hinamatsuri or Doll's Festival
for Girls' Day and Tango-no-sekku or Boys Festival, many of these organized by the
Japanese American community (*Japan Pavilion Welcomes* 1939).

Although the Japanese government used standard modes of exhibiting at world
fairs, an underlying ideological and political message at the Japan Pavilion drew
from the development of Japanese fascist aesthetics. Precedents for the Japan Pavilion may be found in colonial museums developed in Taiwan, Hokkaido, Sakhalin
(Karafuto), Korea (Chosen), and Guandong (Kantō) that were built for the promotion of Japanese fascism. The pavilion might also have been considered a model
for the planning under way in 1939 for the Greater East Asia Museum (Daitōa
Hakubutsukan) that would have provided the Tokyo metropole with an institution
for bringing together a network of colonial aesthetic interests (Aso 2014).

Gendered Japanese Imperialism at the Japan Pavilion

In the 1939 Travel Hall exhibit, gendered Japanese orientalism came graphically
into play in the promotion of Japanese fascist aesthetics with major roles for
women. In front of the map of travel routes connecting the Japanese empire with

America were three statuettes of young women in the middle of a small fountain standing with their backs to each other and their hands clasped behind them and revolving on cylindrical plate above a square base (Figures 5.6 and 5.7). A Japanese–English visitor's guide explained that the three girls in traditional dress represented Japan, Korea, and Manchukuo with their joined hands symbolizing "cooperation and peace between the three Asiatic races" (Kyosankai Nihonjin 1939, 5). On each side of the fountain sat a *komainu* or Korean dog, a legendary animal found on both sides of the entrance to Shinto Shrines in Japan and a beast to keep evil spirits away from the holy places. This representation of Japan as a dominant colonizing power through the soft power of the three feminine figures seen to dance on an equal plane with each other in the fountain reconfigures the critique of orientalism established through Edward Said's 1979 seminal work. By using gendered orientalism to represent their colonized nations and their own state, the Japanese government removed itself subtly and softly from Euro American perceptions of Asian states as subdominant or as threatening in any way, displacing Said's oppositional binary of the West and the Other.

These fascist aesthetics of the Greater East Asia Co-Prosperity Sphere appear as a subtle subtext in nearly perfect synchronicity with the utopian themes

FIGURE 5.6.   Travel Hall fountain and statues, 1939. Kyosankai Nihonjin. San Francisco History Center, San Francisco Public Library.

of the GGIE. In mode and code, they were multifaceted types of orientalism: the modern Japanese nation of the "Orient" orientalizing representations of the Japan Pavilion and its exhibits and performances—thus participating in the production of the "Orient" for a Western audience. Defining Japanese orientalism with a lowercase "o," Jennifer Robertson notes that the recognition of multiple Euro American Orientalisms has not translated into genuine awareness of non-European countries as more than a singular formation and one side of Said's binary. The Japanese government's shaping of these representations of Chosen and Manchukuo might be considered ethno-orientalisms of the non-West and even an orientalism with a lowercase "o" of its own Japanese culture in contrast to the binary products of Western Orientalism. Of such types of ethno-orientalisms found in the Japan Pavilion, Robertson observes that "Japan, which arguably was not colonized by Euro-American powers but was itself a colonizer, complicates the critique of Orientalism and the oppositional construction of an internally coherent third world" (1998, 98). The Japan Pavilion's ethno-orientalisms with a lowercase "o," as much as Said's "Orientalism," reflected the aesthetic embodiment of colonial expansion and its racial hierarchies that were key to Japan's imperial expansion. Japan colonized Western colonial outposts rather than invading independent countries; their colonial aspirations robed in peace and harmony with equal status for the colonized challenged American and European imperialism in ways that initially appealed to many Asians (Tansman 2009a). The soft promotion of the fascist aesthetics in the Japan Pavilion evoked empathy for Manchukuo and Chosen through the gendered beauty of women in traditional dress, occluding and obscuring the violence of war. Western Orientalism with a capital "O" was concurrently and prominently displayed at the GGIE in its populist American narratives through which American national cultural identity was constructed and dramatized with exotic representations of the Orient that the Japan Pavilion subtly sustained rather than countered.

The Gender Politics of the Grand Cherry Show Takarazuka Girls

Jennifer Robertson's analysis of Japanese orientalism evolved out of her monographic study of the Takarazuka Revue (Revue), an all-female and thoroughly modern theatrical company, reversing bans in place since 1629 preventing women from performing in public. The Takarazuka Revue, in fact, played at the GGIE's Japan Pavilion in late April of 1939 and 1940 as well as at the San Francisco War Memorial Opera House and other California venues. Like other popular wartime Japanese mass media and entertainment and cultural forums, the Revue played to a large spectrum of the Japanese population, activating a cosmopolitan familiarity with a discourse of otherness for Europeans and Asians alike (Robertson 1998).

Founded in 1913, an entrepreneur and department store owner, Ichizo Kobayashi, developed the troupe's home, named Paradaisu (Paradise), at a hot springs resort at the end of the Hankyu suburban rail line. Competing with an all-boys theater group sponsored by the Mitsukoshi Dry Goods Store, Kobayashi launched the Revue on the opening of the Paradise Theater in 1924. More than representative of the new middle class of the newly industrialized society of Taisho-era Japan, the Revue was and is one of the most popular of Japanese theater groups and has played for mass audiences for more than a century. Kobayashi was also a powerful politician, serving as minister of commerce and industry from July 1940 through April 1941. He managed the troupe's public personae representing modern women in Japan and the Revue's participation in the cultural life of Japanese colonization and militarization (Robertson 1998). Kobayashi figured prominently in the GGIE playbill for the Grand Cherry Show Takarazuka Girls, and the troupe was described as having "received a thorough training in music, art of playing and dance, European as well as Japanese" (Takarazuka Revue Company 1940, 17) (see Figure 5.7).

The Takarazuka Revue's Japanese orientalism played an ambiguous role in fascist narratives wherever the Japanese government chose to send them. The all-female gendering accentuated the apolitical character of fascist narratives, while the Takaruzukienne's spectacular performances, modeled after Parisienne entertainment, promoted the national culture of Asia's most powerful modern nation. As feminine representatives of modern Japan, their dazzling orientalized programs were designed to attract American tourists and trade. Like the Travel Hall exhibit, the Revue provided a feminized visual ideological framing of the Japanese empire in a popular cultural medium with a hybrid program of modern and traditional cultural forms, softly promoting assimilation. As part of the Japanese government's management of colonial settlers, their spectacles espoused the assimilation of Japanese identity to Japanese American communities.

By 1939, the Japanese government had firmly established assimilation policies for settler communities as well as for colonized populations (Robertson 1998). Colonial policy for both populations involved the state's management of the children's education. In Japan's Southeast Asian and East Asian colonies, the use of Japanese for everyday transactions was required along with maintenance of Japanese culture through commemoration of Shinto practices and the emperor. Assimilation into Japanese culture was a dominant policy in the homeland and abroad for Japanese emigrants and the colonized alike; Western, traditional Japanese, and hybrid modes were included in the cultural practice of assimilation (Laguerre 2000). The Takarazuka Revue promoted Japanese cultural identity to the Japanese American settler audience who made up a significant portion of the audience when the Revue was on tour in the United States.

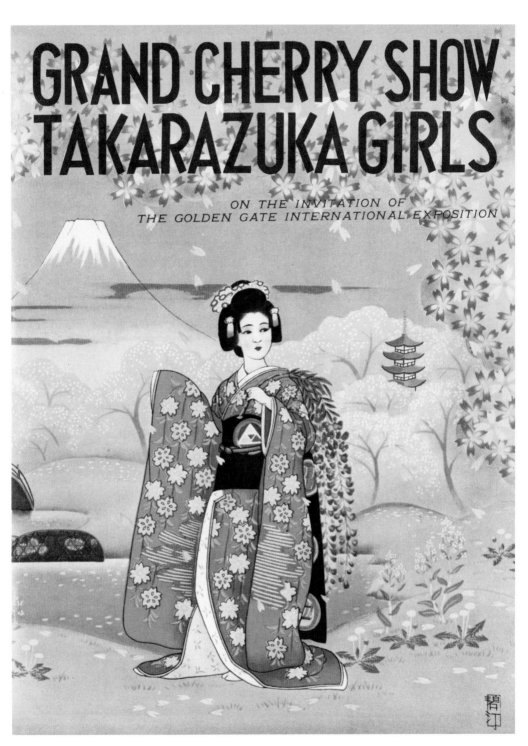

FIGURE 5.7 Program cover for the 1940 Takarazuka Revue GGIE performance, *The Grand Cherry Show Takarazuka Girls at the Golden Gate International Exposition*. © TAKARAZUKA REVUE COMPANY.

Local Issei-Nisei Bridges across the Pacific

The least visible performances in creating the Japan Pavilion may have been the contributions of Japanese immigrants residing in America as colonial settlers and who imagined themselves as pioneers on the outer edges of the Japanese empire, yet oppressed by both American and Japanese imperial racial hierarchies (Azuma 2005). The distinct generations of the Issei immigrants and their American-born children, the Nisei, had been configured by US controls over immigration of Asian nationals drawn to a halt by the US Immigration Act of 1924 and the elegibility of Asians in general to naturalize as American citizens based on their race. The Nisei, like Chizuko Iiyama one of the Japanese American female guides working at the Japan Pavilion, were relatively young, most of them barely adults. Although the celebration of the two new bridges in the San Francisco Bay provided an ideal event for Japan to promote the Greater East Asian Co-Prosperity sphere, the core of support for building the Japan Pavilion came from local Japanese American communities. The Issei organized the Kyosankai Nihonjin cooperative association that worked with the Japanese consulate. Functioning as a tightly organized ethnic group contributing to the building of the pavilion, it facilitated Japan Day at the GGIE and coordinated demonstrations of the Japanese arts of doll making and flower arrangement, the participation of the Konkyo Temple performing Shinto rites at the consecration, floats, parades, and the presence of Japanese American women representing Japan, much like other immigrant groups promoting the GGIE exhibits of their homelands (see Figures 5.8 and 5.9). They appear to have raised considerable capital to help fund the building of the Japan Pavilion, celebrated through their brochures, of which at least one was printed by the Gilroy Hot Springs (Kyosankai Nihonjin 1939, 1940; Kyosankai Nihonjin and the Gilroy Hot Springs 1939).

The Japanese government chose to have English-speaking Japanese American guides at the Japan Pavilion, whom the visiting public assumed were Japanese. For the coming-of-age Nisei, working at the GGIE was a privilege. The fair enthralled them like an exhilarating world tour. Like the extravagant entertainment of the Takarazuka Revue, the GGIE as a whole was known for the color and the thematic exoticism of its painted stucco architecture, the Gayway, and its nighttime displays of colored lights. As for other visitors, the GGIE seems to have enchanted the younger Nisei generation, delivering on its claims as the Magic City.

Chizuko Iiyama, who worked as one of the guides in the Japan Pavilion during her summer breaks from the University of California, provided insightful firsthand observations about the Nisei's enthusiastic responses to invitations to participate in the fair:

> The first day I thought it was totally different, totally magical. . . . From our house, my father's three-story hotel on the hill, we could see it. It was so lovely. . . . Something we had never seen before. I worked in the Japanese exhibit, not in the Japanese store. We were considered privileged . . . just to get on the ferry, to go there on the ferryboat

FIGURE 5.8 Celebrating Japan Day, May 1, 1939, near the entrance of the Japan Pavilion. Fang Family San Francisco Examiner Photograph Archive. The Bancroft Library, University of California, Berkeley.

was like magic. We lived on Clay Street in San Francisco. . . . we would take the Clay Street cable car all the way down straight to the ferry building. We were very poor so we didn't get around that much. We were so lucky. You are sixteen years old and suddenly you have the world. (Iiyama 2012)

Of her experience in representing Japan, she noted the ambivalence that her American citizenship and upbringing brought to her role hosting at the Japan Pavilion:

One of the reasons they hired me was because I was going to UC Berkeley. I was sixteen and a freshman at UC Berkeley. I worked in the Japanese exhibit, not in the Japanese store. . . . We had to wear kimonos to work. People thought we were Japanese. I know my mother was very critical because I didn't even walk like a Japanese. . . . she said, "You're walking so we can even see the split in the kimono," and she had to admonish me . . . to . . . walk in a more dignified manner and not to rush from one place to another. I was criticized by my mother for my inability to look like a real Japanese lady in Japanese dress—anybody could see you're not Japanese. (Iiyama 2012)

The kimono was, in fact, rarely worn by most Nisei women and most likely only for formal or ritual events within the Japanese American community.

Chizuko Iiyama's observations included a description of the interior architecture and exhibits; to her eyes, the exhibits stressed the ancient character of Japanese culture rather than its modern identity:

I remember being in awe at some of the simplicity of the Japanese. . . . So when we saw this very beautifully simple architecture with the rooms inside that would not be that cluttered like ours, where there were seven children in the house, I was struck by the simplicity; it was so spare . . . we were surprised because our vision of Japan was the vision that my parents talked about [turn of the century often rural Japan]. . . .

FIGURE 5.9   Japanese American Nisei women from San Francisco, Oakland, San Jose, Fresno, Sacramento, and Walnut Grove representing Japan in the GGIE Japan Day celebration on the birthday of the Japanese emperor, April 18, 1939. Tamiki Shiotsuki from San Francisco was named Miss Japan. San Francisco History Center, San Francisco Public Library.

They [her parents] had magazines and we saw them. And they [the exhibits] didn't look like modern Japan, they looked like the ancient Japan. Even the museums at that time had ancient Japan. I think for a long time we were a little bit critical of the Oakland Museum because they really only showed the old Japan . . . that you saw in the books about Japan. The ancient history, the ancient houses. (Iiyama 2012)

She noted the influence of the Japanese American community in directing the events with prominent Issei or first-generation immigrants instrumental in having Nisei selected to participate, unaware of the Japanese government's facilitation of Nisei participation as bridge of understanding as part of a larger policy of colonial education and the assimilation of Japanese identity.

As a metaphorical device, the concept of bridges played an important part in the dissemination of Japanese culture. At the GGIE, Japanese bridge metaphors intertwined with the world's fair formal themes and the creation of the two grand bridges. Toshiko Sato, the Japanese consul in 1939, expressed the utopian hope that the GGIE "would cause to dawn the real 'Pacific Era' based on peace and friendship among all participating nations" (Kyosankai Nihonjin 1939, 4).

As Sato must have known, the Pacific Era and education of the Nisei in Japan as a bridge of understanding between the United States and Japan were among the Issei generation's cosmopolitan utopian ideals for the Pacific Era. The Pacific Era was conceptualized at the turn of the nineteenth century by Japanese liberals addressing the positioning of Japan as an emergent Asian nation successfully modernizing to achieve equal status with Occidental powers. Eiichiro Azuma describes this intellectual project: "Sharing compatible moral precepts and cultural qualities, Japanese and white Americans were to be partners in the new era of hemispheric reconciliation and cooperation" (2003, 45). The Japanese government had concomitantly initiated in the mid-1920s with prominent Issei an educational program in Japan for the Nisei to increase their opportunities to prosper in the face of anti-Japanese sentiment in the United States. The ideal of the Nisei as a cosmopolitan bridge formed a positive impression for Japanese immigrants of international cooperation in contrast to their minority experience (Azuma 2003). Japanese interest in the local settlers was in part fostered by the privileging of their racial, blood, and ancestral ties over their citizenship status. So, the Nisei were considered state subjects. As Azuma observes, "American Nisei were expected to be but the first of the overseas 'vanguards' for the cause of their racial homeland" (2003, 48). The Issei believed that the Nisei could play a part through this new more civilized cooperative power because the Issei's homeland was destined to become the center of the world power shifting from the Atlantic to the Pacific.

Even as they collaborated with the Japanese government to establish an educational program for the Nisei in Japan, the Issei also saw the advantages in their Nisei children's American citizenship. For the Issei, the educational program was an opportunity they imagined might improve their children's chances of success in life, even as they imagined their offspring negotiating discrimination in the United States and Japan. The program, promoted with an international and cosmopolitan sensibility, glamorized a future role for the Nisei in a Pacific Era and beyond the pale of the American nation (Azuma 2005).

The Japanese American community itself was quite diverse in political ideologies vis-à-vis Japan, and the Nisei were generally pro-American, sometimes vociferously, like the Japanese American Citizens League of older Nisei cohorts. The Nisei rarely imagined themselves as promoters of Japanese fascist military expansion, though they found the idea of cosmopolitan commercial exchange at the GGIE and the related orientalism of the Japan Pavilion generally appealing.

After the outbreak of World War II in Europe in the late 1930s, the US government had significantly increased its efforts to coordinate counterintelligence. Unbeknownst to the Japanese American community, the US Navy had been spying on them, very likely for the entire time the Japan Pavilion was open, because President Franklin D. Roosevelt had initiated efforts to curb Japanese espionage as early as 1936 (Robinson 2001). In September 1939, Roosevelt ordered the Army G-2 division, the Office of Naval Intelligence (ONI), and the Federal Bureau of Investigation to coordinate efforts to monitor West Coast Japanese and Japanese Americans on the Pacific coast. The ONI was responsible for collecting information on Japanese American communities, and the FBI followed "individual subversives" (Robinson 2009, 47).

Stamped on the inside cover of one of the GGIE Nihonjin Kyosankai brochures published by the Gilroy Hot Springs may be found: District Intelligence Office, Twelfth Naval District, 717 Market Street, San Francisco, California. This particular publication was a kind of directory of Japanese American community members who belonged to the Kyosankai Nihonjin, similar to the Japanese American annual directories; it provided full biographies of associates with their photos as well as information not only about their trips to Japan but also trips taken by their family members (Kyosankai Nihonjin and the Gilroy Hot Springs 1939).

These people were no doubt among the first enemy aliens to be picked up by the FBI after the Pearl Harbor attack of December 7, 1941. The entire Japanese American community was moved to concentration camps following President Roosevelt's Executive Order 9066 of February 1942 empowering the US Army to remove them. Chizuko Iiyama was imprisoned in Tanforan Assembly Center in San Mateo County and then moved to Topaz Relocation Center, a euphemism for the government's semipermanent prison cities.

Nation building represented at a world's fair was a global tradition, largely configured by Euro American expositions that often promoted imperial projects in which the Japan Pavilion was but another addition. A confluence of diverse cultural forces of historic importance in Japan's modernization came together in the Japan Pavilion. In examining the nationalist narratives of the Japan Pavilion at the GGIE in its architecture, programming, and exhibit narratives, we might be tempted to regard these displays as a more positive lineage of aesthetics and politics in ways that are particular to Japanese fascism that favored traditional, conservative, and gendered modes of visual representation. The Japanese government had orientalized and feminized its national identity at home and abroad through the promotion and exhibition of oriental goods and the programming of architecture and performances to spur consumer relations and promote commerce.

Yet the aesthetics of Japanese fascism gathered their ideological power in the types of culture displayed at the Japan Pavilion, mirroring what Alan Tansman describes as the fascist moment in all its complexity that "provides the possibility of conversion by positing and taking advantage of an 'expressive vacuum' and filling it with the misleading promise of a new way of being." The fascist moment projected a "false auratic appeal" as in a cult attraction. Speaking to the fascist moment in literature, Tansman further notes that "the writer can be fascistic unawares, helping to produce the atmosphere needed for fascism to flourish, even while being shaped by that atmosphere" (Tansman 2009a, 19). In this sense, the Magic City synchronically served the Japan Pavilion's fascist aesthetic. Although the texts Tansman analyzes are literary, his concept may be applied to a reading of how the Japanese government sought to create a fascist moment in the Japan Pavilion at the GGIE in the many variants discussed in this essay (Tansman 2009a, 2009b; Dower 1986).

The global to the local came full circle in the Japan Pavilion with Japanese fascist narratives on the eve of World War II. With the participation of Japanese American communities in the programming, the Japan Pavilion connected the local to the global but within the very particular contexts of access to citizenship and generational differences; the Issei or Japanese immigrant experience with Japanese fascism contrasted with that of their American-born children. Though the Japanese American communities' participation was never explicitly political, Issei and Nisei participation in the exposition was most likely under the surveillance of the ONI and the FBI as part of the investigation of Japanese American communities begun in 1939. Only a few of the operatives in the surveillance project could have emphatically and sensitively keyed into the Issei's cultural, ethnic, and political relationship to Japanese fascism exhibited at GGIE or assessed accurately the Japanese American communities' threat to the security of the United States (Robinson 2001; Dower 1986; Azuma 2005).[7]

The destruction of the Japan Pavilion marks the beginning of another era for San Francisco's Treasure Island. In preparation for the construction of Naval Station Treasure Island, the US Army Corps of Engineers dismantled the exposition in late 1940, salvaging most materials and reducing the island to a flat bare surface. In April 1941, the Corps detonated a bomb in the Japan Pavilion to destroy it, and when that failed, set it on fire (Figure 5.10). Although barely within the sight of cars crossing the new San Francisco–Oakland Bay Bridge, the Japan Pavilion's brief two-year existence and its demolition was an arbiter of the totalizing violent force of war and the material destruction of World War II. As the US military prepared for conflict in the Pacific, they transformed Treasure Island into a major military base—an extreme case of recycling of space from tabula rasa. With the bombing of Pearl Harbor, the soft power of the racial colonial order

FIGURE 5.10 Destruction of the Japan Pavilion, April 8, 1941. Fang Family San Francisco Examiner Photograph Archive. The Bancroft Library, University of California, Berkeley.

mapped out in the Japan Pavilion, which had occluded and suppressed the violence of war, then exploded into a global conflagration that would result in the incarceration 120,000 Japanese and Japanese Americans and modify the national boundaries and identities of large geographical areas of East Asia, Southeast Asia, South Asia, and Europe.

Notes

Versions of this essay were presented at the Association for Asian American Studies in 2015, at the International Association for the Study of Traditional Environments in 2010 and 2014, and at the Association for Asian Studies in 2014. I wish to thank two institutions in particular: the Institute of Urban and Regional Development at the University of California at Berkeley for my stay as a visiting scholar, and the MacDowell Colony, where fellow residents inspired changes to the essay. I especially wish to thank Sean McPherson, Anoma Pieris, Andy Shanken, Richard A. Walker (DW), Greig Crysler, Elizabeth Deakin, Tanu Sankalia, Alice Tseng, Greg Levine, Mariko Takagi-Kitayama, Roger Daniels, Chizuko Omori, Chizuko Iiyama, anonymous reviewers, and a number of other contributors to this volume for their insights on earlier drafts. I am grateful for superb assistance from the staff at the Bancroft Library, especially Theresa Salazar, Crystal Miles, Jack von Euw, Susan Snyder, and Peter Hanff, and at the San Francisco Public Library, especially Jeff Thomas and Tami Suzuki. I am indebted to Chizuko Iiyama for her interview and to Laura Iiyama for her assistance.

1 For an in-depth analysis of the interlinking of colonizing practices and the racial ideologies of Japan, Germany, Italy and America in World War II, see Dower 1986.

2 Facism may be generally defined as an ideology for molding and controlling the masses to nationalize them, setting the stage for the devotion and sacrifice of the individual to the state, nation, or ancestral lineage. The binding or *il fascio* of a populace into a strong unified state was explicitly political in Italy and Germany; the fascist moment in Japan, as Tansman defines it, is "an aesthetically cathartic epiphany susceptible to being politically channeled into the creation of a fascist mood" (2009b, 19).

3 For an exception to this trend, see Craig Wilkins for a discussion of Locke's concepts of private property as a foundational structure for enlightenment privileging of white people and the exclusion of people of color from the humanities as an enlightenment project. In this discussion, Wilkins established the use of space and architecture as a racially encoded practice.

4 An increasing amount of literature is being produced about strategies of non-Western countries and racialized groups exhibiting at Euro American world's fairs that is useful for creating diverse readings of the sites. For example, to develop the concept of Pan-Americanism, Pan American republics left the world's fair model behind and turned to an organization and structure dedicated to Pan-Americanism (Gonzalez 2011, 59–60, 65). African Americans negotiated the implacable racism leveraged against their efforts to exhibit at world fairs (Wilson 2012, 50, 78–81). Chinese nationals of different political alliances raised formative questions about the representation of a modern Chinese national identity in Chinese architecture at the Chicago's 1933 World's Fair. At the GGIE, the Chinese American community mounted an effort to provide a separate area in the Gayway devoted to the representation of China (Roskam 2014; Carpenter and Totah 1989).

5 Arthur Brown Jr. Papers, Box 52. The Bancroft Library.

6 The fountain statue in the Travel Hall was replaced in the 1940 exhibit with a bejeweled million-dollar flower basket with traditional Japanese dolls playing shuttlecock one side and battledore on the other (Kyosankai Nihonjin 1940).

7 The US government's conclusions that Japanese American communities were a threat to US security were based largely on the racialization of them by blood, identifying "people of Japanese ancestry" as potential spies under the authorization of Presidential Executive Order 9066. Washington ignored the recommendations of ONI intelligence officer Kenneth Ringle, who advised his superiors that Japanese American communities were loyal. In a separate confidential report to FDR, Curtis B. Munson, who had access to both ONI and FBI information, reported that the majority of the Issei were either actively or passively loyal and the Nisei were 90 to 98 percent loyal (Robinson 2009).

References

Aso, Noriko. 2014. *Public Properties: Museums in Imperial Japan*. Durham, NC: Duke University Press.

Azuma, Eiichiro. 2003. "'The Pacific Era Has Arrived': Transnational Education among Japanese Americans, 1932–1941." *History of Education Quarterly* 43, no. 1 (Spring): 39–72.

———. 2005. *Between Two Empires: Race, History, and Transnationalism in Japanese America*. New York: Oxford University Press.

Baskett, Michael. 2009. "All Beautiful Fascists?: Axis Film Culture in Imperial Japan." In *The Aesthetics of Japanese Fascism*. Berkeley: University of California Press.

Brown, Arthur, Jr. Papers. BANC MSS 18/142c. The Bancroft Library, University of California, Berkeley.

Carpenter, Patricia F., and Paul Totah. 1989. *The San Francisco Fair: Treasure Island, 1939–1940*. San Francisco: Scottwall Associates.

Çelik, Zeynep. 1992. *Displaying the Orient Architecture of Islam at Nineteenth-Century World's Fair*. Berkeley: University of California Press.

Cogdell, Christina. 2004. *Eugenic Design: Streamlining America in the 1930s*. Philadelphia: University of Pennsylvania Press.

Dower, John W. 1986. *War without Mercy: Race and Power in the Pacific War*. New York: Pantheon Books.

Fang Family San Francisco Examiner Photograph Archive Photographic Print Files. Circa 1874–2000 (bulk 1911–2000). BANC PIC 2006.029—PIC, Box 080. The Bancroft Library, University of California, Berkeley.

Golden Gate International Exposition (GGIE). 1939. *1939 World's Fair Progress on San Francisco Bay*. Bulletin no. 1. San Francisco: San Francisco Bay Exposition.

Gonzalez, Robert Alexander. 2011. *Designing Pan-America: U.S. Architectural Visions for the Western Hemisphere*. Robert Fullington Series in Architecture. Austin: University of Texas Press.

Iiyama, Chizuko. Interview by the author, December 6, 2012.

Ina, Satsuki, Stephen Holsapple, Emery Clay, and Lawson Fusao Inada. 2005. *From a Silk Cocoon*. Documentary. San Francisco: Center for Asian American Media.

The Japan Pavilion Welcomes World Visitors to Treasure Island. 1939. The Bancroft Library, University of California, Berkeley.

Kyosankai Nihonjin and the Gilroy Hot Springs. 1939. *Kinmon Bankoku Daihakurankai Kinenshi*. San Francisco: Shinsekai Asahi Shinbunsha/New World Sun.

Kyosankai Nihonjin and the Golden Gate International Exposition (Kyosankai Nihonjin). 1939. *Kigen Nisen-Roppyakunen Kinmon Bankoku Daihaku Kinen: Golden Gate International Exposition*. San Francisco: Kyosankai Nihonjin.

———. 1940. *Kigen Nisen-Roppyakunen Kinmon Bankoku Daihaku Kinen: Golden Gate International Exposition*. San Francisco: Kyosankai Nihonjin.

Laguerre, Michel S. 2000. *The Global Ethnopolis: Chinatown, Japantown, and Manilatown in American Society*. New York: Macmillan.

Morton, P. A. 2000. *Hybrid Modernities: Architecture and Representation at the 1931 Colonial Exposition, Paris*. Cambridge, MA: MIT Press.

Nakamori, Yasufumi. 2010. *Katsura: Picturing Modernism in Japanese Architecture*. Photographs by Ishimoto Yasuhiro. Houston, TX: Museum Fine Arts.

Ōshima, Ken Tadashi. 2009. *International Architecture in Interwar Japan: Constructing Kokusai Kenchiku*. Seattle: University of Washington Press.

Robertson, Jennifer Ellen. 1998. *Takarazuka: Sexual Politics and Popular Culture in Modern Japan*. Berkeley: University of California Press.

Robinson, Greg. 2001. *By Order of the President: FDR and the Internment of Japanese Americans*. Cambridge, MA: Harvard University Press.

———. 2009. *A Tragedy of Democracy: Japanese Confinement in North America*. New York: Columbia University Press.

Roskam, Cole. 2014. "Situating Chinese Architecture within 'A Century of Progress': The Chinese Pavilion, the Bendix Golden Temple, and the 1933 Chicago World's Fair." *Journal of the Society of Architectural Historians* 73, no. 3:347–371.

Rydell, Robert W., John E. Findling, and Kimberly D. Pelle. 2000. *Fair America: World's Fairs in the United States*. Washington, DC: Smithsonian Institution Press.

Said, Edward W. 1979. *Orientalism*. New York: Vintage Books.

Shanken, Andrew Michael. 2014. *Into the Void Pacific: Building the 1939 San Francisco World's Fair*. Berkeley: University of California Press.

Takarazuka Revue Company. 1940. *The Grand Cherry Show Takarazuka Girls at the Golden Gate International Exposition—Return Engagement and Farewell Performance*. Opera House, Sunday Evening, May 14.

Tansman, Alan. 2009a. *The Aesthetics of Japanese Fascism.* Berkeley: University of California Press.

———, ed. 2009b. *The Culture of Japanese Fascism.* Durham, NC: Duke University Press.

Tseng, Alice Yu-Ting. 2008. *The Imperial Museums of Meiji Japan: Architecture and the Art of the Nation.* Seattle: University of Washington Press.

Weisenfeld, Gennifer. 2007. "Publicity and Propaganda in 1930s Japan: Modernism as Method." In *La Société Japonaise devant la montée du militarisme: Culture populaire et contrôle social dans les années 1930,* ed. Jean-Jacques and Claude Hamon Tsuchidin, 47–70. Arles: Editions Philippe Picquier.

Wilkins, Craig. 2007. *The Aesthetics of Equity: Notes on Race, Space, Architecture, and Music.* Minneapolis: University of Minnesota Press.

Wilson, Mabel. 2012. *Negro Building: Black Americans in the World of Fairs and Museums.* Berkeley: University of California Press.

Part II

NAVAL STATION TREASURE ISLAND AND MILITARY OCCUPATION

6. Trial by the Bay

Treasure Island and Segregation in the Navy's Lake

JAVIER ARBONA

During the months of September and October 1944, Admiral C. H. Wright, commandant of the Twelfth Naval District, placed fifty black sailors on trial for mutiny at the Treasure Island US Naval Training and Distribution Center. Although this event is largely forgotten or its location confused, the Treasure Island naval base served as a setting where the Navy asserted its power to maintain Jim Crow segregation—frequently misunderstood as a Southern system alone—at the same time that the United States and its allies battled totalitarianism abroad.

The fifty men were survivors of a catastrophic munitions detonation at the Port Chicago naval magazine, approximately thirty-five miles northeast of Oakland, on the south shore of the Suisun Bay, connected to the enormous San Francisco Bay estuary system. After the blast, they refused to continue working under the same segregated and dangerous conditions. In this essay I explain why this trial was no exception for Treasure Island and the Bay Area—and why its convenient forgetting, along with its disappearance of its evidence from the physical space of Treasure Island, serves the same conditions that gave rise to it.

On the night of July 17, 1944, the Port Chicago explosion went off aboard two docked ships, killing 320 civilian and military personnel working at the base. The explosion jolted awake residents all over the Bay Area, blissfully unaware of the dangerous conditions at local naval facilities; this ignorance included white clerical workers at Port Chicago. Many believed at first that Japan was attacking (see, for example, Magleby 2010, 13). But black personnel had anticipated the dangers of the Navy's plantation-like installations. Also revealing the combined dimensions of labor and race oppression in the Navy, the branch ignored union warnings of untrained, inexperienced labor at Navy depots. Slightly better than the Navy, the Army hired unionized and trained civil services, predominantly—if not exclusively—white, at its Bay Area installations, in contrast (Allen 2006, 42; Meeker 2010, 18–21).

White officers overseeing work conditions at the Bay Area's two naval ammunition depots, Port Chicago and Mare Island, imposed arbitrary orders and punishments while placing bets on ship loading speeds. For the population of the Bay Area, the explosion was the greatest catastrophe since the 1906 earthquake. For segregated personnel, however, it was the only imaginable outcome for a long history of racial rule. The naval inquiry into the causes of the explosion was predictably inconclusive, but made racist references to the "poor quality of the personnel" (US Navy 1946).

Two-thirds, an estimated 202, of those who perished were segregated steve-dores. The killed or injured were either loading the two ships (the USS *E.A. Bryant* and the USS *Quinault Victory*) or resting in their barracks near the dock. Two weeks after the traumatic event, three units of Port Chicago survivors realized that they would not receive survivors' leave time and would soon be ordered to load more explosives at the neighboring Mare Island depot north of Richmond.

On August 9—less than three weeks after the blast—an estimated 330 Port Chicago survivors disobeyed the order to board a ferry to the ammunition depot and staged a work stoppage outside their reassigned barracks in Vallejo (Allen 2006; Wollenberg 1979) (Figure 6.1). The wildcat strike was not the first time the sailors had resisted segregated conditions; it was simply the largest such resistance (Campbell 2012; Arbona 2015; Sikes 1995).

After three days of confinement (without charges), imprisoned aboard a barge on the Napa river, Admiral Wright spoke to the group in person. He threatened, "[I] want to remind you men that mutinous conduct in time of war carries the death sentence, and the hazards of facing a firing squad are far greater than the hazards of handling ammunition" (quoted in Allen 2006, 85). Eventually, the

FIGURE 6.1 Segregated barracks after the Port Chicago explosion on July 17, 1944. Photo: US Navy official photo. National Park Service, Port Chicago Naval Magazine National Memorial.

Navy whittled the group down to fifty "ringleaders," some seemingly chosen at random.

As meticulously documented by Robert Allen, the Port Chicago Fifty were subjected to a kangaroo court somewhere at the Treasure Island installations. The trial was open to the media and carefully tracked by the National Association for the Advancement of Colored People (NAACP) and its chief counsel, Thurgood Marshall. Nevertheless, the legacies of criminalization trailed the survivor strikers, who wouldn't qualify for jobs or loans if their status were revealed in public; most refrained from speaking much more about their cases for decades, even to close family. Thus, the carceral geography of the trial on Treasure Island, as an important site of the "long Civil Rights" struggle (Hall 2005), has been continually denied a tangible place in the Bay Area, partly through the ongoing criminalization, up to the present day, of the insurrection.

The precise location of the barracks remains unknown but could have been on the adjoining Yerba Buena Island, which was also a territorial part of the Treasure Island naval base. The barracks themselves might have been demolished after World War II. I was not able to find any notation of building numbers in the court-martial proceedings to cross-reference with existing maps. The process was a show trial designed to dispel mounting accusations of racism. Instead, the verdict in the proceedings—all fifty were found guilty and given lengthy sentences that were commuted after the war—paradoxically strengthened the case for the integration of the armed forces under Harry Truman's Executive Order 9981 on July 26, 1948 (Wollenberg 1979; Elinson and Yogi 2009). But the court-martial permanently ruined the careers and futures of the fifty, not to mention the rest of the striking sailors, who were summarily tarred and dismissed without benefits (Allen 2006; Arbona 2013).

In what follows, I provide a *longue durée* to the endogenous racism of the Navy in the bay. In recounting this spatial history, I show that the trial of the Port Chicago Fifty on Treasure Island was no special circumstance. On the contrary, the events at the Treasure Island naval base complex were a culmination of a long-standing racial ideology. I show how the continual urban growth from the first arrival of US seamen in the 1840s to the buildup for World War II inscribed white supremacy onto the emergent city.

I argue that three elements joined together in the urbanization of the Bay Area: one, white supremacy; two, American imperialism imbued with expansionism and ravenous accumulation; and, three, the infallibility of divine providence. These elements help situate the logic of the Port Chicago Fifty trial in a documented history of oppression, rather than in the Navy's allegation of wartime exception. Although the trial led to reforms of the military (which had been insistently demanded at the start of the war), I also suggest that these conditions of oppression, and historical amnesia, persist in the Bay Area under a new era of urban development on Treasure Island. Indeed, these conditions not only persist but also facilitate these continuing and rapid changes of the urban landscape.

Whiteness, Profiteering, and the City

"In the Bay Area," writes Roger Lotchin, "the entanglement of the city and the sword dates from the foundation of the Presidio in 1776, the year of San Francisco's birth" (2002, 42). Taking Lotchin's statement a degree further, the American invasion of Mexican Alta California, finalized with the signing of the Treaty of Guadalupe Hidalgo in 1848, came less than a century after Spanish colonization of California in 1769. US conquest of the West achieved an unparalleled marriage between racial dominance and jingoist military profiteering. Together, this alliance was hardened within the rapid urbanization of the San Francisco Bay Area after the Gold Rush (Brechin 2006, 280–330).

San Francisco's natural resources were to make it the new Rome on the Pacific, as imagined by the rich and powerful "thought shapers" like the De Youngs, Hearsts, and Stanfords—the ruling patriarchs of the city (Brechin 2006, 1998). These thought shapers also envisioned a pairing between white "Anglo-Saxon" superiority and imperial power, as Bishop George Berkeley augured in his poem "On the Prospect of Planting Arts and Learning in America," which proclaimed, "Westward the course of empire takes its way" ([1752] 2013, 1060–1061). Crowning this empire would come to be the urban seat of San Francisco, where "mining, mechanization, metallurgy, money, and the military all found their headquarters in the city so rapidly growing by the Golden Gate" (Brechin 2006, 124).

Once the Gold Rush was under way, San Francisco was immediately fashioned as destined to rule an expansive hinterland, much as Rome had in times past. At great costs to the natural environment of vast regions, what Gray Brechin describes as a "vortex" that consumed people and resources, San Francisco lived up to its rulers' fantasies (2006, xxix). In the mid-nineteenth century, the city first amassed its wealth with distant sources of gold, silver, and timber, as well as wheat crops and mercury mines closer to home. Decentralized manufacturing, including explosives and chemicals, and unbridled real estate speculation quickly followed, spreading south down the stretch of the peninsula and jumping over the bay to Contra Costa (present-day Alameda and Contra Costa Counties) from the central place often referred to simply as "the City" (Walker 2004). Periodically, the federal government would dredge waterways clogged by the debris from hydraulic mining in the Sierras, starting with the San Francisco channel in 1868 (Chin, Wong, and Carson 2004, 5). Military expansion on the federal dole entered the picture soon thereafter, highlighted by the construction of an armored cruiser, the *Charleston,* entirely fabricated at the Union Iron Works shipyard in 1886 (Brechin 2006, 127) and followed by several more ships for the Spanish-American War.

This entire urban and militarized vision of the greater Bay Area made possible through the control of news, printed media, and higher education (with the first University of California campus at Berkeley, named after the bishop himself) combined resource extraction and the subjugation of indigenous people and migrant workers, setting the stage for events at ammunition depots later. In addition, a spirit of foreign adventurism throughout the Pacific and the Americas forged ahead in a hungry search for more resources, lands, and people—assumed to be "primitive" races—as potential laboring classes (Almaguer 1994).

One exemplary moment that illustrates this unholy mixture between militarism, exploitation, and racism was when Naval Commodore Matthew Perry set his desires on having his own profiteering commercial steamship enterprise. In his public orations he would cite the Bishop Berkeley line about the westward course of empire as his justification for seizing Pacific islands and establishing the "Saxon race" on the shores of Asia (Brechin 2006, 7, 331).

Bay Area power, ciphered in urban development, thus brought together three elements: white supremacy, American imperialism imbued with expansionism and ravenous accumulation, and the infallibility of divine providence. Expansionism, backed by military aggression, was coupled with the deployment of symbolic monuments and statues in the landscape throughout San Francisco, directly or indirectly lionizing the military. For example, one such monument was inaugurated in 1903 and is still one of the most visited sites in San Francisco today. Named after Commodore George Dewey, this naval monument is the centerpiece of Union Square; the square itself is named after the Union in the Civil War. The monument celebrates the sinking of the Spanish fleet in Manila Bay and was designed by sculptor Robert I. Aitken and architect Newton J. Tharp (Cerny 2007, 24). Another commemorative sculpture from 1903 is the winged *Pegasus* standing at the intersection of Dolores and Market Streets by Douglas Tilden and dedicated to the California volunteers of the same war (Brechin 2006,121–122). Pacific expansionism conveyed through sculptural, architectural fantasies would later attain its most hyperbolic expressions through the 1915 Panama-Pacific International Exposition and the 1939 Golden Gate International Exposition on Treasure Island (Moore 2013; Markwyn 2014; Shanken 2014).

Later, the buildup to fighting World War II in the Pacific brought to partial fruition what was long desired for the imperial and racial aspirations of San Francisco's white male builders, including a disastrous and uneven process of spatial segregation in California cities and the removal of the Japanese from their homes, who were sent off to remote concentration camps (Nash 1985; Wyatt 1998). The geographical transformation of this vast estuary system into a constellation of seemingly permanent bases during World War II and in the decades after represented the completion of a naval construction program that started on the barren Mare Island off the shores of a new town, Vallejo, in the northeastern reaches of the bay on the eve of the Civil War, as I narrate in the following section. This network of bases would be, in part, the carceral archipelago where rebellious black sailors would find themselves entrapped, targeted, imprisoned, and tried.

Other fortifications came earlier, but San Francisco's hydrological advantage was a natural fit for a naval bastion, even before the state's annexation in 1848. Yet it was the gold nuggets and the economic boom that followed their discovery that made the region attractive to greedy merchants and naval officers alike, seeing an opportunity to enrich themselves.

Anchoring in the San Francisco Bay at Mare Island

The Pacific Squadron, predecessor to the Pacific Fleet, ostensibly protected fueling stations and US merchant ships with commercial interests as far away as Chile, Hawaii, Alaska, and China. But the squadron was also present to suppress Native American insurrections in northern California and Oregon territory (Smith 1987; Johnson 1980). Coincidentally, the Pacific Squadron is sometimes known in current publications as the "old navy" or the "old Yankee navy." This phrase is more commonly seen in the current era plastered on American and Canadian shopping malls and retail districts to advertise the Old Navy chain of clothing stores. Old Navy, the chain, was founded in San Francisco by a modern clan of thought shapers—the Fisher family—best known as the owners of The Gap clothing empire, no doubt partly building their wealth on the backs of Pacific labor as the families of old did. The company claims on their website that the name was taken from a Paris café.

Led by Commodore Thomas ap Catesby Jones, the Pacific Squadron was manned by a rowdy—and in fact, racially mixed—crew of poorly compensated drifters and outlaws as well as skilled seamen, sodden with alcohol and frequently suffering from sexually transmitted diseases (McConaghy 2006). Jones and his squadron are infamous for a mistaken invasion of Monterey in 1842 that likely delayed US acquisition of California (Haas 1997).

Jones was under the mistaken impression, based on poor intelligence gathering, that a US war with Mexico was already under way. He also feared, at the time, an opportunistic colonization of Alta California by French ships that had reportedly sailed out of Valparaiso (Smith 1987). For this two-day aggression, Jones was relieved of his duties; he regained his leadership position during the Gold Rush six years later, however.

Jones gradually based his ships in San Francisco against direct orders from Washington, DC (Guice 1965). Presaging the important link to the federal dollar, he pressed the government for more ships and facility construction, even though Navy Secretary William B. Preston wanted Jones and his sailors out on patrol and away from the lure of gold that led to a heightened number of desertions.

Jones himself was likely involved in gold and land speculation in Benicia, which explains his telling obsession with bringing a shipyard to this inland location along the Carquinez Strait, a far distance from the Golden Gate and the Pacific. He was court-martialed in 1850 for misuse of government funds, disobeying orders, and draconian treatment of junior officers, among other charges. He denied the charges but was still suspended for five years, sealing his fate once and for all to never become the commander of the future Bay Area naval shipyard he dreamed of (Johnson 1980). Throughout naval history, high-up officers in the Navy (such as Jones) often faced disciplinary charges for malfeasance and neglect of duties yet still managed to continue their military careers after a slap on the wrist. Yet black sailors, like the Port Chicago strikers, disproportionately faced racialized disciplinary charges that affected their entire lives. For another example, Chester Nimitz was court-martialed in 1908 for running the USS *Decatur* aground and yet went on to become none other than fleet admiral and commander-in-chief of the Pacific Fleet in World War II (Sandler 2003, 757).

In spite of corruption and dubious reasoning, Jones' vision for a naval base came to fruition in 1852 when Commodore John D. Sloat led a study to identify a site for a naval yard and munitions depot. Isla de la Yegua (Mare) was chosen. It was similarly an odd decision—not close to the Gate either. Brechin notes that Mare Island, with its silted channel, was not a first choice for the shipyard, and that it was settled upon for the naval yard due to the finagling of Captain John Frisbie, who happened to have real estate interests in the Vallejo area (2006, 124). Yet a soon-to-be secretary of the Navy, William A. Graham, who later represented North Carolina in the Confederate Senate, agreed on Mare Island: "A new empire has, as by magic, sprung into existence, a navy yard is very much needed in California" (quoted in Chandler 2003, 229).

By 1854, a purchase was completed. Commander David D. Farragut was selected to lead the new yard (Johnson 1980). Mare Island was a symbol of the increasing militarization of a Western land increasingly fractured by the disparities of plentiful riches and blooming social upheavals. With the construction of forts at the Golden Gate and on Alcatraz Island in the 1850s, military leaders sought to thwart any pirate invasions (Lewis 1979). But Mare Island was of a different character: a well-stocked naval shipyard and depot producing ammunitions that could be used offensively, rather than merely reactive defenses. Later, Port Chicago's expansion well into the Vietnam War would come to dwarf the Mare Island depot in land area (only a portion of the larger Vallejo base), displacing the original town of Port Chicago itself.

Mare Island's location did prove to be rather far from where the Pacific Squadron was needed. The heightened role of the squadron was displayed when Commander Farragut haphazardly scrambled vessels into the Puget Sound area to take down a Native American insurgent attack on the town of Seattle in 1856, killing several dozen Indians (Johnson 1980; McConaghy 2006). After the Puget Sound massacre, a vessel from Mare Island took part in a similar domestic operation against a different enemy, threatening to take out the 1856 Vigilance Committee militia that had seized power in San Francisco (Florcken 1935).

The Civil War brought new rationales for construction and armaments in the Bay Area. Military commanders reported apprehension about three kinds of dangers: first, a Confederate strike on gold or other shipments that were vital to the Union; second, a British or French invasion to take advantage of the national schism; and, third, a secessionist act by their own military personnel stationed in California. Although the federal government made some concessions to fortifying the Bay Area during this period (mainly with additional troops, weapons, and makeshift batteries), by the time of the surrender of the Confederate South, San Francisco could hardly be considered impregnable by standard military logics.

Nonetheless, the advance preparation for war led to the procurement of San Francisco's first warship, the *Comanche*. The Donahue brothers' Union Iron Works in the south of Market Street area assembled the ship from prefabricated steel parts sent from the East Coast around the Horn (in contrast to the *Charleston*, which was manufactured entirely in San Francisco). The project foreshadowed what would go on to be a Union Iron Works staple and a Bay Area boom industry. Production, of course, came to an apex during World War II with shipyards in Vallejo, Richmond, Sausalito, and San Francisco. Launched on November 14, 1864, the vessel languished unused at a Mare Island wharf until 1899 (Gilbert 1954).

As the Civil War came to a close, the Donohues sold the foundry to their superintendent, Irving Murray Scott, who brought in his brother, Henry, to oversee operations. Put briefly, the Scott brothers rode a mining equipment boom to become some of the wealthiest and most influential industrialists in the city, as Brechin has extensively covered (2006).

Nevertheless, the industrialization of the bay created paradoxical obstacles for the very same people who most profited from its rapid growth. For instance, mine tailings silted much of the bay, threatening the productivity of ports that the Scotts had invested in. But as the volume of silver from the Comstock Lode declined (Brechin 1998), the federal government stepped in with its largess to dredge the bay (foreshadowing much more federal involvement in the future), just in time for the Scott brothers to move more fully into military shipbuilding, approximately twenty years after the Civil War.

The Scotts boasted to their employees in 1887 that they had found the proverbial keys to the federal coffers. They had another important key in their repertoire after moving into publishing. The *Overland Monthly* was a mouthpiece they used to fan the flames of the Spanish-American War, whipping up fears of a Philippine "counter-insurgency." More than 4,200 Americans died in the war and perhaps up to one million locals. For decades, the *Overland* played up fears of a "yellow peril." Meanwhile, the Scotts were simultaneously busy selling armaments to Japan and preaching the "subjugation of inferior races" (Brechin 2006, 126–170).

The case of the Union Iron Works is but one example, certainly an intriguing one, of the much larger post–Civil War industrialization—and decentralization—of the Bay Area, which has been captured in writing by Richard Walker (2004). This process is important to mention here, ever so briefly, because the build-out of the northeastern interior of the Bay Area (present-day Contra Costa County) precedes naval expansion into the region during World War II and after. Where wheat growers and manufacturers of steel, explosives, timber, and other goods laid down infrastructures during the early twentieth century, the Navy followed. For example, the Scotts' foundry in San Francisco would later change hands and eventually end up in 1939 as a Navy property (Lotchin 1979). And it was the industrial skeleton of ports, canals, and railways in Contra Costa, combined with the declining utility and capacity of Mare Island that pushed the Navy to develop another ammunition depot at the dock of a town called Port Chicago in 1942. The naval magazine came to be at the site of a former lumber and boat yard with a deep-water harbor and rail connection (McLeod 2007; Vance 1964).

The Sword and the Progressive Era

California became much more intimate with the sword during the Progressive Era. As Mike Davis says, "by stoking anti-Japanese hysteria in California to a fever pitch and producing the first 'war scares' with Japan in 1906 and 1913, the Progressives contributed to the geopolitical tensions in the Pacific that would eventually realign U.S. naval deployments. Indeed, the creation of a Pacific Fleet to protect California from the 'yellow peril' was a principal Progressive demand" (2003, 43–44). By 1907, the Asiatic and Pacific Squadrons were combined into one command to form the Pacific Fleet (US Navy 2012).

The new belligerence on the Pacific toward Japan was displayed, in addition to the new combined squad, through Theodore Roosevelt's show of force in a sea-going parade around the world—the Great White Fleet. The armada's triumphal march on the high seas was not only tinged with racial hysteria toward the East; it also marked an important turning point at home, in more ways than one.

Influenced by the eugenicist racial ideas of the time, the Navy desired a truly white force, not only in name, but also as a racial representation within the ranks—a racial vision that attained its highest symbolic expression with the Port Chicago trial at Treasure Island. They segregated the force, reflecting the Jim Crow system outside the military. On the ships, African Americans were relegated to messman or machine room duties; Filipino stewards, although not eligible for US citizenship, served the white officers on deck. In addition, the new ships were large and steam-powered, requiring more sailors than ever before. But the new recruits could work a ship with virtually no seafaring experience. The Navy set about filling its ranks with young white men from the South and Midwest, establishing the roots for a racially homogenous and exclusionist institution for decades to come (Nalty 1989, 78–86).

The opening of the Panama Canal in 1914 also added a new rationale for a Western buildup. Meanwhile, San Francisco was losing its dominant role among Pacific cities by World War I, and Mare Island was fast becoming obsolete, albeit headquartering the Twelfth Naval District officers until 1945. Military assets, which were accruing to Los Angeles, San Diego, and Seattle, were seen by San Francisco's elites as a vital linchpin for urban development. The Chamber of Commerce, working in concert with naval officers, spearheaded efforts to draw more military investments (Lotchin 2002, 1979). Yet it would take almost up to the dawn of World War II to see the plums fall on the San Francisco Bay region.

On the eve of the Japanese attack on Pearl Harbor, the bay still had relatively few naval installations. This was so despite the previous hundred years of near-constant—but also self-interested—pleas from the business establishment and officers for more facilities and federal dollars. Scattered naval facilities by then included Mare Island as the oldest continuous presence of the Navy in the area and the recently purchased Hunters Point shipyards, which had belonged to the Scotts. In addition, the Navy had new installations and plans for expansion on Alameda Island in the East Bay, a dirigible base and airfield in Sunnyvale to the south of San Francisco, and a leased airstrip on Treasure Island (Lotchin 1979; Allen 2006, 37). Beyond the constrained ammunition depot on Mare Island, the closest other naval ammunitions facility was out in the remote desert town of Hawthorn, Nevada.

Fighting World War II at Home

Much the same way that San Francisco's earlier frenzies for minerals seemed to change the city overnight, a few short years would make a world of difference for the landscape of the Bay Area and the region's racial demographics, as historians and geographers have amply studied. Says Joshua Jelly-Shapiro, "The U.S. effort to defeat the Axis powers during the Second World War brought more profound changes to the Bay Area than to any other region" (2010, 57). An emergent class of infrastructure barons—names such as Bechtel, McCone, and Kaiser—invested in wartime manufacturing throughout California. Bay Area cities like Richmond, Vallejo, Pittsburg, Oakland, and Sausalito were almost instantly transformed into boomtowns of shipbuilding and industrial parts for the war; but they struggled to meet the demand for housing, which remained an especially segregated domain (Nash 1985, 88–106). The Bay Area's population grew by half (Jelly-Schapiro 2010). More than a quarter million African Americans migrated to California during the war, mostly from the South (Murch 2010). They went straight to the urban centers to work, and a majority of able-bodied white men in early adulthood were able to serve on the war front. As Quintard Taylor explains, thousands of African American men also served in the military, but mostly without the chance to fight (1999).

The long tail of the previous century of naval expansionism and racial domination suddenly culminated in a relatively rapid period of approximately eighteen months at most. The military swooped down on the bay, making it into a Navy town with its roots in a century of stop-and-start planning. It quickly acquired several names and slogans: the Navy's lake, the American Singapore, and the "arsenal of democracy," in Roosevelt's famous words. The Navy took over Treasure Island hardly without asking for anyone's opinion on the matter. They purchased 412 acres of land in Richmond for a fueling depot (Point Molate), in addition to five hundred acres of marshland in Oakland for another fueling facility. They removed one hundred families in the vicinity of Hunters Point for shipyard expansion. They built an isolated radio communications "listening post" on a drained marsh in Sonoma (Skaggs Island), complete with a new town to keep the location in isolation from the rest of the world in the case of an attack on the Bay Area. The Navy also reclaimed an old coaling station in Tiburon for construction of a depot that fabricated a seven-mile-long, six-thousand-ton antisubmarine net that spanned from Sausalito to San Francisco.

Port Chicago

Finally, they landed on Port Chicago. By simply invoking condemnation, the commanders at Mare Island took over cattle ranches and farmland connected to the Southern Pacific by a rail spur and a deep-water port to build the naval ammunition magazine (Keibel 2009). Following the recommendations of a secret report drawn up by Captain Milton S. Davis in the months before Pearl Harbor and delivered just two days after the Japanese attack, the Navy started work on building the facility in February 1942 (Allen 2006, 39–41). With such expansion and the need for manpower, the Navy grudgingly accepted African American sailors into their ranks in 1942, but only as a servant class, and at select locations, as munitions handlers and despite dire personnel needs on all fronts (Sherwood 2007; Davis 2003, 47–49; Wollenberg 1979, 64) (Figure 6.2). With a segregated training facility in Illinois on Lake Michigan, called Great Lakes, Navy Secretary Frank Knox seeded the racial animosity toward black enlistees and insolent behaviors by white officers. As one Port Chicago sailor said of Secretary Knox,

> Negro sailors, we were called Negroes, Negro sailors were not accepted as real seamen. We were considered mess attendants or something of that nature. But they were finally going to allow us in the Navy. And we felt all the racism, the prejudices that was going on. Secretary of the Navy, Knox at that time, we had to square around for two days to clean up our barracks and put everything in tiptop order and be ready for the Secretary of the Navy to come visit our camp. And he came in and reviewed every camp except the black camp. He would not. And we read the next day in the paper that the Secretary of the Navy said that it was a disgrace that the United States had sunk so low as to allow Negroes into the Navy. So that didn't make us feel very proud or patriotic. (Edwards 1995, 64)

The pressures of a racially segregated Navy burst the valves on several occasions. In December of 1942, Vallejo police and Navy shore patrol fired on a group of unarmed black sailors who fought back against white mobs attacking them in the streets of the town. Several informal work stoppages took place at both ammunition depots (Mare Island and Port Chicago) manned by African American sailors, culminating with the work strike precipitated by the Port Chicago explosion (Arbona 2013, 2015). The unidentified remains of some of the men killed in the blast were buried in a segregated national cemetery (San Bruno). Altogether, these events can be seen as part of a much longer history, extending all the way back to the Native American genocide, and fixed in place by the combination of urban development, mineral accumulation, and racial purification.

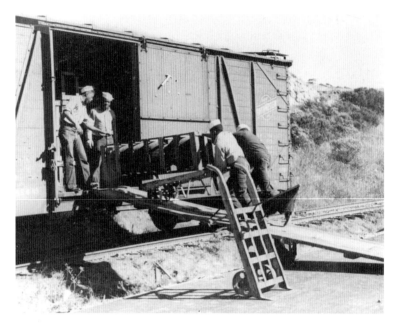

FIGURE 6.2 Loading ammunition onto a train car at the Port Chicago naval magazine. Date unknown.
Photo: US Navy official photo. National Park Service, Port Chicago Naval Magazine National Memorial.

The Treasure Island Trial of the Navy Blue
versus the Port Chicago Fifty

To conclude, I come back to the Port Chicago Fifty trial to reflect on the trial's spatial absence at Treasure Island. Rather than an isolated breakage of radical bravery
in the face of work pressures of the war period, I suggest that the court-martial
represents the inevitable fruition of the triple forces (frequently resisted in the face
of repression) of white supremacy, imperial expansion, and a faith in predestined
power anchored in the Bay Area as a Rome on the Pacific.

The trial was presided by Rear Admiral Hugo W. Osterhaus, a retired officer appointed by Admiral Wright of the Twelfth Naval District. Osterhaus led the tribunal
with six additional naval officers sitting along side him, inside what has often been
described as a cramped, makeshift barrack (see Figure 6.3). There was no jury. The
chief prosecutor against the Port Chicago stevedores was Lieutenant Commander
J. Frank Coakley. Notably, later in his career Coakley would go on to become the
Alameda County district attorney who prosecuted members of the Black Panthers and
East Bay antiwar protesters. This seemingly minor detail about Coakely reveals the
larger, continuing endurance of militarized white supremacy (imposing itself through
court and carceral power), even after the racial integration of the armed forces so
often suggested at sites like national parks as the final, happy resolution of Jim Crow
in the Bay Area. Court-appointed lawyers defended the fifty "mutineers." The NAACP
sent Thurgood Marshall to help the accused men, observe a portion of the trial, and

FIGURE 6.3 Port Chicago court-martial at Naval Station Treasure Island in October 1944. The sailors charged with mutiny sit in the back of the cramped barracks. Unknown source.

begin mounting an appeal. After the trial, Marshall filed to appeal the convictions but to no avail. Marshall said, "I can't understand, then, why, whenever more than one Negro disobeys an order, it is mutiny" (quoted in US Navy 1944). In 1994, the Navy secretary John Dalton again reviewed the case and declined to reverse the decision.

The same year that the Navy last upheld Jim Crow justice in the Port Chicago case, Congress and the National Park Service established a memorial at the site of the explosion (still an active military shipping facility, now owned by the Army), preserving an important site of African American and civil rights history. In 2010, Congress promoted the memorial to the status of a full unit in the national parks system to guarantee its preservation in perpetuity.

But we know little of the spaces of the mutiny trial. Because the former base that encompasses both Treasure Island and the connected Yerba Buena Island is set to pass over to the hands of the city of San Francisco for a profitable urban design transformation of vast proportions, the conditions of the sailors' detention and trial have seemingly been lost to demolitions over several decades of subsequent base transformations (see Stehlin, this volume). The condition of physical and historical erasure underpins the amnesia that surrounds this history of racial violence and enduring forms of domination as old as the urban development of San Francisco itself—ones that cannot be divorced from the continuing rabid development of this idealized blank slate.

Notes

I am greatly indebted to Tanu Sankalia and Lynne Horiuchi, who poured countless hours into improving this essay and who made key suggestions that helped my research more broadly. I would also like to thank Richard Walker and anonymous peer reviewers for their helpful suggestions. The National Park Service, Isabel Ziegler, and Sara Hay kindly helped with images.

References

Allen, Robert L. 2006. *The Port Chicago Mutiny: The Story of The Largest Mass Mutiny Trial in U.S. Naval History.* Berkeley, CA: Heyday Books.

Almaguer, Tomás. 1994. *Racial Fault Lines: The Historical Origins of White Supremacy in California.* Berkeley: University of California Press.

Arbona, Javier. 2013. "After the Blast: Building and Unbuilding Memories of Port Chicago." PhD diss., University of California, Berkeley.

———. 2015. "Anti-Memorials and World War II Heritage in the San Francisco Bay Area: Spaces of the 1942 Black Sailors' Uprising." *Landscape Journal* 34, no. 2:177–192.

Berkeley, Bishop George. (1752) 2013. "On the Prospect of Planting Arts and Learning in America." In *The English Literatures of America: 1500–1800,* ed. Myra Jehlen and Michael Warner. New York: Routledge.

Brechin, Gray. 1998. "Pecunary Emulation: The Role of Tycoons in Imperial City-Building." In *Reclaiming San Francisco: History, Politics, Culture,* edited by James Brook, Chris Carlsson, and Nancy Joyce Peters, 101–114. San Francisco: City Lights Books.

———. 2006. *Imperial San Francisco: Urban Power, Earthly Ruin,* 2nd ed. Berkeley: University of California Press.

Campbell, James. 2012. *The Color Of War: How One Battle Broke Japan and Another Changed America.* New York: Crown Publishers.

Cerny, Susan Dinkelspiel. 2007. *An Architectural Guidebook to San Francisco and the Bay Area.* Layton, UT: Gibbs Smith.

Chandler, Robert J. 2003. "An Uncertain Influence: The Role of the Federal Government in California, 1846–1880." *California History* 81, no. 3/4:224–71.

Chin, John L., Florence L. Wong, and Paul R. Carson. 2004. *Shifting Shoals and Shattered Rocks: How Man Has Transformed the Floor of West-Central San Francisco Bay.* Reston, VA: US Geological Survey.

Davis, Mike. 2003. "The Next Little Dollar: The Private Governments of San Diego." In *Under the Perfect Sun: The San Diego Tourists Never See,* ed. Kelly Mayhew, Jim Miller, and Mike Davis, 17–144. New York: New Press.

Edwards, Robert, Sr. 1995. "An Oral History of Port Chicago." Interview by Tracey E. Panek. National Park Service Eugene O'Neil National Historic Site, Danville, CA.

Elinson, Elaine, and Stan Yogi. 2009. *Wherever There's a Fight: How Runaway Slaves, Suffragists, Immigrants, Strikers, and Poets Shaped Civil Liberties in California.* Berkeley, CA: Heyday Books.

Florcken, Herbert G. 1935. "The Law and Order View of the San Francisco Vigilance Committee of 1856: Taken from the Correspondence of Governor J. Neely Johnson." *California Historical Society Quarterly* 14, no. 4:350–374.

Gilbert, Benjamin Franklin. 1954. "San Francisco Harbor Defense During the Civil War." *California Historical Society Quarterly* 33, no. 3:229–240.

Guice, C. Norman. 1965. "The 'Contentious Commodore' and San Francisco: Two 1850 Letters from Thomas ap Catesby Jones." *Pacific Historical Review* 34, no. 3:337–342.

Haas, Lisbeth. 1997. "War in California, 1846–1848." *California History* 76, no. 2/3:331–355.

Hall, Jacquelyn Dowd. 2005. "The Long Civil Rights Movement and the Political Uses of the Past." *Journal of American History* 91, no. 4:1233–1263.

Jelly-Schapiro, Joshua. 2010. "High Tide, Low Ebb." In *Infinite City: A San Francisco Atlas,* by Rebecca Solnit, 57–65. Berkeley: University of California Press.

Johnson, Robert Erwin. 1980. *Thence Round Cape Horn: The Story of United States Naval Forces on Pacific Station, 1818–1923.* New York: Arno Press.

Keibel, John. 2009. *Behind the Barbed Wire: History of Naval Weapons Station Concord.* Concord, CA: John A. Keibel.

Lewis, Emanuel Raymond. 1979. *Seacoast Fortifications of the United States: An Introductory History.* Annapolis, MD: Naval Institute Press.

Lotchin, Roger. 1979. "The City and the Sword: San Francisco and the Rise of the Metropolitan-Military Complex 1919–1941." *Journal of American History* 65, no. 4:996–1020.

———. 2002. *Fortress California, 1910–1961: From Warfare to Welfare.* Urbana: University of Illinois Press.

Magleby, Gloria. 2010. "Rosie the Riveter." World War II American Home Front Oral History Project. Interview by Javier Arbona. Regional Oral History Office. Berkeley: The Bancroft Library, University of California.

Markwyn, Abigail M. 2014. *Empress San Francisco: The Pacific Rim, the Great West, and California at the Panama-Pacific International Exposition.* Lincoln: University of Nebraska Press.

McConaghy, Lorraine. 2006. "The Old Navy in the Pacific West: Naval Discipline in Seattle, 1855–1856." *Pacific Northwest Quarterly* 98, no. 1:18–28.

McLeod, Dean L. 2007. *Port Chicago.* Images of America. Mount Pleasant, SC: Arcadia Publishing.

Meeker, Martin, ed. 2010. *The Oakland Army Base: An Oral History.* Berkeley, CA: The Bancroft Library, University of California.

Moore, Sarah J. 2013. *Empire on Display: San Francisco's Panama-Pacific International Exposition of 1915.* Norman: University of Oklahoma Press.

Murch, Donna Jean. 2010. *Living for the City: Migration, Education, and the Rise of the Black Panther Party in Oakland, California.* Chapel Hill: University of North Carolina Press.

Nalty, Bernard C. 1989. *Strength for the Fight: A History of Black Americans in the Military.* New York: Free Press.

Nash, Gerald D. 1985. *The American West Transformed: The Impact of the Second World War.* Bloomington: Indiana University Press.

Sandler, Stanley. 2003. *World War II in the Pacific: An Encyclopedia.* New York: Routledge.

Shanken, Andrew. 2014. *Into the Void Pacific: Building the 1939 San Francisco World's Fair.* Oakland: University of California Press.

Sherwood, John Darrell. 2007. *Black Sailor, White Navy: Racial Unrest in the Fleet during the Vietnam War Era.* New York: NYU Press.

Sikes, Spencer E. 1995. "An Oral History of Port Chicago." Interview by Tracey E. Panek. National Park Service Eugene O'Neil National Historic Site, Danville, CA.

Smith, Gene A. 1987. "The War that Wasn't: Thomas ap Catesby Jones's Seizure of Monterey." *California History* 66, no. 2:104–13.

Taylor, Quintard. 1999. *In Search of the Racial Frontier: African Americans in the American West, 1528–1990.* New York: W. W. Norton.

United States Navy (US Navy). 1944. "General Court Martial Convened at U.S. Naval Training and Distribution Center, San Francisco, California." Documents relating to Port Chicago mutiny trial, 1942–1944. BANC MSS 90/157c. Box 1, Box 2. The Bancroft Library. University of California, Berkeley.

———. 1946. "Port Chicago Naval Magazine Explosion on 17 July 1944: Court of Inquiry: Finding of Facts, Opinion and Recommendations." Box 7/12, Folder A17.25, Vol. 8. Record Group 181, 12th Naval District Commandant's Office, General Correspondence Series (Formerly classified). Pacific Sierra Region. US National Archives.

———. 2012. "Command History." Commander, U.S. Pacific Fleet. May 29. http://www.cpf.navy.mil/about/history/.

Vance, James E., Jr. 1964. *Geography and Urban Evolution in the San Francisco Bay Area.* Berkeley: Institute of Governmental Studies, University of California.

Walker, Richard. 2004. "Industry Builds Out the City: The Suburbanization of Manufacturing in the San Francisco Bay Area, 1850–1940." In *Manufacturing Suburbs: Building Work and Home on the Metropolitan Fringe,* ed. Robert D Lewis, 92–123. Philadelphia: Temple University.

Wollenberg, Charles. 1979. "Blacks vs. Navy Blue: The Mare Island Mutiny Court Martial." *California History* 58, no. 1:62–75.

Wyatt, David. 1998. *Five Fires: Race, Catastrophe, and the Shaping of California.* New York: Oxford University Press.

7. *Pandemonium* on the Bay

Naval Station Treasure Island and the Toxic Legacies
of Atomic Defense

LINDSEY DILLON

A man steps into his white, rubber-lined body suit, zipping it up to his chin. He pulls a protective hood over his head and tightens it against the straps of his gas mask. It is 1968. Flower children gather in San Francisco's Haight-Ashbury district, and an office-building boom shoots up skyscrapers in the financial district downtown. Across the Bay in Oakland, Huey Newton is convicted of manslaughter and J. Edgar Hoover declares the Black Panther Party "the greatest threat to the internal security of the country." Thousands of soldiers, headed for Vietnam, pass through the gates of Naval Station Treasure Island, in the middle of the San Francisco Bay, where the man in the white suit fastens his rubber booties and steps out onto the deck of the USS *Pandemonium*.[1]

A 173-foot mock patrol boat built from salvage and scrap parts, in 1968 the *Pandemonium* is anchored to the shallow sands of the northwest corner of Treasure Island. Wire cables run throughout the ship, connecting lead-shielded boxes, called pigs, containing radioactive cesium-137 are to a control room on board. A water tank nearby holds a diluted solution of radioactive bromine-82. At the command of the naval instructor in charge of the mock-atomic catastrophe on any particular day, the pigs are opened and 0.65 curies of cesium-137 are pulled up into the fresh air. Soldiers learning how to detect radiation will hunch over their devices and wander around the ship, taking measurements of gamma radiation. On other days the instructor might order the bromine solution poured across the length of the deck, spreading into its nooks and crannies.

The rubber-covered officer is enrolled in a six-week course titled Atomic, Biological, and Chemical Defense at the island's Damage Control School, and today he is learning how to decontaminate a warship. During yesterday's lecture, the course instructor sets the practice scenario: the ship has just survived a nuclear attack but is covered with the fallout of the bomb. The actual gamma radiation from the *Pandemonium's* cesium sources simulates the fallout. By 1968, decades of experience with nuclear bombs at the Bikini and Enewewok atolls in the Pacific Ocean had revealed, in no uncertain terms, that the threat of nuclear war to naval ships was not simply from the intensity of the bomb's blast, but the effects of its invisible, lingering radiation. Officers and enlisted men learned how to manage these and other disasters at training centers like the Damage Control School on San Francisco's Treasure Island (see Figure 7.1).

After the decontamination exercise on the *Pandemonium*, the student-officer hands his personal dosimeter—a badge containing radiation sensitive film—over to the school's radiological safety monitor. His daily exposure to radiation will be tallied and recorded in a logbook. The Navy's manual for running this practice exercise allows him to receive a maximum dose of three hundred millirems of radiation per week, calculated according to National Radiation Safety Committee standards of the time.[2] This threshold value, like the rubber suit, promises to keep him safe from the practice radiation. In 1971, the *Pandemonium* will be pulled like a parade boat to a new training facility on the northeast corner of the island. Military houses

FIGURE 7.1 Naval Station Treasure Island students learn techniques of radiological detection aboard the USS *Pandemonium*. San Francisco's Telegraph Hill is visible in the background. *The Masthead*, October 18, 1968. National Archives and Records Administration, San Bruno.

are built on top of the original Atomic, Biological, and Chemical Defense Exercise Area. The housing construction upturns and spreads radioactive radium-226 (which has a half-life of 1,601 years), polychlorinated biphenols, dioxins, arsenic, lead, and other contaminants in the surface soil across the site (US Navy 2008). When the naval station closes in 1997, civilians seek out homes on the island for the low rents and lovely views.

This essay examines the long-term toxic consequences of nuclear weapons, focusing on the environmental legacy of Cold War–era radiological safety and decontamination trainings on San Francisco's Treasure Island. It is based primarily on papers from the records of Naval Districts and Shore Establishments at the San Francisco branch of the National Archives, articles from the *US Naval Training Bulletin,* historical and recent newspaper articles, and technical reports on the island's current environmental hazards written by state environmental agencies and by engineering firms contracted by the US Navy. Exploring Naval Station Treasure Island's role within postwar US nuclearism reveals the slippage between simulated and actual environmental disaster in practices of national security. Writing about nuclear weapons testing in New Mexico, anthropologist Joseph Masco concludes that the goals of US nuclear weapons tests were simultaneously to advance weapons technology (building better bombs) and to study its environmental and biological effects, blurring any distinction between warfare and scientific research (2006). Similarly, at the same time that graduates from Treasure Island's Damage Control School learned methods of protecting naval personnel, ships, shore establishments, and even major cities against a potential future nuclear catastrophe, they practiced for war using real sources of radiation, contributing to today's environmental disaster on the island.

Situating the history of Treasure Island within the militarization of the San Francisco Bay Area and the broader Pacific Ocean provides a way of understanding the island's role within military nuclearism after World War II. I spend time exploring the relationship between San Francisco naval stations and the Marshall Islands because radiological defense trainings on Treasure Island grew directly out of the disastrous aftermath of the military's first set of nuclear test bombs in the Pacific Ocean, known as Operation Crossroads. Radioactive ships, returned from the Marshall Islands for decontamination at the Hunters Point Naval Shipyard in southeast San Francisco, were also berthed at Treasure Island and constitute one source of the island's radiological hazards today. Subsequently, graduates from radiological training courses on Treasure Island participated in the US nuclear weapons testing program in the Marshall Islands as radiation safety officers. These social and material connections compel the essay's analytical orientation, through which I keep in mind Marshallese people and the ways they were excluded from practices of radiological defense and national security, even after the Marshall Islands became a US trust territory in 1947. At the end of the essay, I describe an accidental radium spill in a Treasure Island classroom in 1950 that exposed San Francisco residents to radiation as a particularly dramatic example of when practicing for atomic war became an actual attack on the city.

Atomic (After)lives

At the analytical level, Rob Nixon's concept of slow violence informs this essay. Slow violence builds on the idea of structural violence—or physical suffering as the effects of structural social relations, like racism—but with an important twist. Slow violence emphasizes change and movement over time and space, broadening the common conception of violence as a discrete, immediate act. As Nixon writes, it is "a violence of delayed destruction that is dispersed across time and space, an attritional violence that is typically not viewed as violence at all" (2011, 2). Slow violence occurs at speeds and scales that are difficult to recognize—at the cellular level, for example, or over the course of generations. Importantly, Nixon explores this concept in relation to the socioeconomic effects of environmental disasters. The concept of slow violence is analytically useful in broadening the notion of military violence to include the dispersed and slow-moving effects of radiation—in which there is often a long time lag between exposure and detectable injury. I also engage with slow violence as a way of analyzing the use of radiation on Treasure Island within broader social and geographical relations of US nuclearism, across time and space—binding San Francisco to the Marshall Islands, for example, and 1968 radiation safety officers-in-training to future residents of the Treasure Island. Identifying the effects of the military's use of radiation as a form of violence also raises questions of responsibility and justice in the context of redeveloping Treasure Island today.

Treasure Island's historical and geographical entanglements define its place in the histories and geographies of US militarism, beginning with the establishment of a naval training school on Yerba Buena Island just after the Spanish-American War in 1898 and on the eve of the US invasion of the Philippines. Immediately after the United States began testing nuclear weapons in the Marshall Islands in 1946, the Navy set up a training program in radiological safety on Treasure Island, as part of the island's larger Damage Control School. Naval officers who enrolled in radiological defense courses on the island benefitted from the extensive expertise in nuclear science and toxicological warfare at institutions across the Bay Area (see Brechin 2006). Trainees took field trips to the University of California at Berkeley's Radiation Lab and the Naval Radiological Defense Laboratory (NRDL) on San Francisco's Hunters Point Naval Shipyard. They also visited Oakland's Naval Biological Laboratory to learn about advances in chemical and biological weapons.[3]

At the same time that students on Treasure Island practiced safety and decontamination procedures on mock ships like the USS *Pandemonium*, the military applied these methods as part of actual nuclear weapons explosions in the Marshall Islands and the Nevada test site. In the Pacific Ocean, the military relocated Marshallese communities from their homes in order to produce an outdoor laboratory for the US experimental nuclear weapons program. Radiation from the bomb's fallout did not obey imagined borders of the bomb's scientists or the radiation monitor's threshold values, and Marshallese people have subsequently suffered from increases in thyroid disorders, cancers and leukemia, cataracts, and other radiation-related illnesses (Guyer 2001; Pollock 2002; Johnston and Barker 2008). The Marshallese also became US test subjects through experimental research. After the Operation Castle tests of 1954, US scientists conducted research on Marshallese people who had been exposed to large doses of radioactive fallout. NRDL scientists collaborated on these experiments, bringing samples of Marshallese urine and hair—along with radioactive coconuts, grass, and seawater—to the laboratory at San Francisco naval shipyard for radiochemical analysis. For the Marshallese who were forced to live with the bomb's fallout, these explosions were not tests, but real catastrophes. Their experiences reveal some of the violent effects of national security as a set of practices through which some people in certain places are rendered more insecure and vulnerable to US weapons.

Today the US Navy is involved in a second decontamination project on Treasure Island—an island-wide environmental remediation project, part of a larger process of "shutting down the Cold War" (Sorenson 1998). In 1993, the Department of Defense's Base Realignment and Closure (BRAC) commission designated Naval Station Treasure Island "excess" military property, and the Navy arranged to transfer the island over to the city of San Francisco for urban reuse. Other military bases designated for disposal by the BRAC commission in the Bay Area include San Francisco's Presidio and the Hunters Point Naval Shipyard, Vallejo's Mare Island, the Alameda Air Force Base, Oakland's Army Base and Naval Supply Center, and Moffett Field in Sunnyvale. US military bases are some of the most contaminated spaces in the country, and transferring them often requires extensive environmental remediation work, including the removal of contaminated soils. This essay seeks to excavate the social history of pollution on the island along with its other toxic sediments.

Environmental remediation on Treasure Island is not as extensive as the Navy's projects at industrial shipyards like Mare Island or Hunters Point because Treasure Island was primarily used for naval training exercises and as a receiving station—a stopping point for crewmembers coming to and from sea. Even still, Treasure Island is contaminated with some of the twentieth century's most toxic wartime industrial chemicals. Along with trainings in radiological defense, the Damage Control School also offered firefighting courses on the northeast corner of the island, leaving dioxins and furans, petroleum hydrocarbons, volatile organic compounds, and polycyclic aromatic hydrocarbons (US Navy 2008). As of early 2014, a former storage yard near the middle of the island continued to store lead, dioxin, PAH, PCB, TPH, and radium-226. Adjacent to this storage yard was a tear gas training area, also used for storing hazardous materials, containing PCB, TPH, dioxins, pesticides, and arsenic. The locations and extent of toxic waste on Treasure Island, at least according to the Navy's assessment of the problem, is further detailed in its 2012 Site Management Plan (US Navy 2012). Although the focus of this essay is the island's historical geography of radiation, its environmental health concerns are broader in scope.

The Navy on the Island, 1898–1945

Treasure Island is a man-made landmass, constructed between 1936 and 1937 for the Golden Gate International Exposition and handed over to the US Navy in 1940 on the eve of World War II. It is connected to a natural island, called Yerba Buena, which became a military installation in 1867. In that year, the US Army set up barracks and a mess hall, a lighthouse and 125 officers. In 1871, the Army unit moved to the city's Presidio base, near the Golden Gate Bridge, and in the 1880s a fire destroyed Yerba Buena's original buildings. In 1891, the Army returned to the island and built industrial factories to assemble submarine mines, or torpedoes, to defend San Francisco Bay.[4]

In the late fall of 1898, the US Navy established a naval training school on Yerba Buena Island—what became the Damage Control School after World War II (US Navy 1962). By June 1899, nearly four hundred Navy apprentices had trained aboard USS *Pensacola*, docked at the island as a practice boat, similar to the radioactive *Pandemonium* sixty years later. In 1899, Yerba Buena Island was the fourth naval training station in the United States, and the only training center on the West Coast (see Figure 7.2). The Spanish-American War had just ended, the United States annexing Puerto Rico and the Philippines, both formerly Spanish territories (Brechin 2006). Navy apprentices training aboard the USS *Pensacola* in the summer of 1899 would likely have been preparing to cross the Pacific, furthering US imperial ambitions in the Philippines. San Francisco was also emerging as a center of war shipbuilding on the West Coast. Shipbuilding industries concentrated along the city's southeast waterfront, at Potrero Hill and Hunters Point (Brechin 2006).

Yerba Buena is not the only militarized island in San Francisco Bay. The federal government claimed Alcatraz Island in 1850, and by the end of that decade Alcatraz was a strategic defense installation. The United States had also just begun trading with Japan, and it hoped to acquire the Hawaiian Islands (Johnson 1996). North of Alcatraz, Angel Island housed a quarantine station, marine hospital, fumigation building,

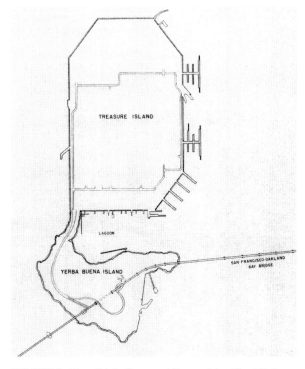

FIGURE 7.2   Map of Yerba Buena and Treasure Island Naval Stations. 12th Naval District Airbase Real Estate Acquisition Files, 1942–1958. National Archives and Records Administration, San Bruno.

and a detention barrack in 1898, the year the Navy began training crewmembers on Yerba Buena (Shah 2001). In the early twentieth century, in the context of racism directed against Chinese and Japanese in California and a series of plagues in San Francisco, US immigration officers would target Asian immigrants as a health threat to white Americans and subject them to strict medical examinations on Angel Island (Lai, Lim, and Young 1980; Shah 2001). The treatment of Asian immigrants on Angel Island is another example of the racial boundaries of national security—a dynamic this essay examines through nuclear weapons testing in the Marshall Islands.

Yerba Buena Island remained the only naval training center on the West Coast until 1923, when the Navy moved the school and most of its West Coast operations to San Diego. After 1923 and until World War II, Yerba Buena served as a receiving station for sailors coming to and from the military's operations in the Pacific. The Army Corps of Engineers constructed the approximately four-hundred-acre Treasure Island from the shoals of Yerba Buena for the 1939–1940 Golden Gate International Exposition. When the exposition closed in late 1940, Treasure Island was joined with Yerba Buena Island as naval property, and the Navy continued using the islands together for its training programs and as a receiving station. In 1941, as the United States prepared to enter World War II, the Navy also acquired the Hunters Point Shipyard in San Francisco and built up both Treasure Island and Hunters Point at a rapid pace, mobilizing for war. The Navy had operated another shipyard at Mare Island, in Vallejo, since 1854, and also maintained a large supply center across the Bay in Oakland. Gaining the official title of US Naval Station in 1946, Yerba Buena and Treasure Island formed one site within the broader militarization of the San Francisco Bay Area.

During World War II, instruction in "damage control" was part of the Treasure Island's operational training school, which provided basic instruction to naval crewmembers. Wartime operational training courses brought together the crew of a destroyer ship and trained them within six months. At the time, 80 to 90 percent of crewmembers-in-training had never been to sea. Mock warships—simulating disasters—were part of damage control practices. On Treasure Island, crewmembers practiced damage control aboard a training floater, called the USS *Buttercup*, which was designed to flood with water, catch on fire, and to suffer ruptured pipes and electric power failures (*Naval Training Bulletin* 1949, 1951). In one exercise called "A Closed Hatch Can Save a Ship," the *Buttercup* became pitch black, filled with smoke, and inundated with water. A phonograph played battle recordings while student-sailors practiced plugging holes on the sides of the "attacked" mock ship (*The Masthead* 1945). Later, radiological defense training on the USS *Pandemonium* extended this established practice of using mock ships to simulate disasters, in the context of new threats posed by nuclear weapons.

The Navy's presence on Yerba Buena and Treasure Island developed in relation to other military sites in the San Francisco Bay and in the context of US militarism directed across the Pacific Ocean. After World War II, this military geography would continue to develop in the context of US nuclear weapons tests, linking people and places through the social and ecological relations of military nuclearism.

Operation Crossroads and the San Francisco Bay Area

In 1946, nuclear weapons represented both the United States' postwar global dominance and a new threat to its national security. Most immediately, nuclear weapons called into question the vulnerability of the Navy's fleet to the atom bomb, which had been dropped on Hiroshima and Nagasaki by the new jet aircraft. These and other concerns motivated a joint Army-Navy task force to assemble 242 ships, 156 airplanes, 42,000 personnel, and 5,664 animals in the Marshall Island's Bikini lagoon in the summer of 1946 to test the material, biological, and environmental effects of two nuclear bombs (Weisgall 1994; Hacker 1994). The project was known as Operation Crossroads and marked the beginning of the US nuclear weapons testing program, which lasted until 1992.

Naval Station Treasure Island's weekly newspaper, *The Masthead,* covered the preparations for Operation Crossroads and its aftermath with special interest. Its pages during the late 1940s reveal anxieties about the effects of the bomb on both the Navy as an institution and the lives and bodies of naval crewmembers (1946c). At the same time, the paper dutifully reported reassuring comments made by top military officials, declaring to its readership that the bomb and its fallout could become part of a controlled military operation. One article in March 1946 is representative of the paper's ambiguous position. The article quotes Fleet Admiral Chester Nimitz, the Navy's top commander, who downplayed the effects of nuclear bombs on naval ships. According to Nimitz, "a fleet under way and properly deployed constitutes a very difficult target for this new and costly weapon" (*The Masthead* 1946a). Yet the very next paragraph of the article mentions that the US Fish and Wildlife Service would send its chief fishery biologist to Bikini to study the effects of the radiation on marine life. The article conveys a conflicting message—on the one hand, under normal conditions (ships "properly deployed"), a nuclear bomb would not constitute an insurmountable weapon. At the same time, the article registers the bomb as a historically new threat to biological life and thus, by implication, human crewmembers aboard Navy ships. On rare occasions, internal fissures in the Navy surface in *The Masthead.* In June 1946, only days before Operation Crossroad's first nuclear test, the paper ran a story titled "Bikini-Bound Enlisted Men Worry; Deny Volunteering for Atom Tests" (1946b). As the paper reports, "Interviewed aboard their ship, the seamen estimated that only a handful of the vast majority actually wanted to leave, and that most of them had been assigned to the task." That this story found its way into an official

"I Think He Calls It the Bikini Blowup!"

FIGURE 7.3   "The Bikini Blowup." *The Masthead*, June 13, 1946.
National Archives and Records Administration, San Bruno.

naval newspaper—apparently contradicting the assurances of top military officials—suggests the depth of uncertainty and unease about the effect of nuclear weapons.

A cartoon from *The Masthead* in June 1946, two weeks before the first Crossroads test bomb, playfully illustrates these anxieties. In the cartoon, a bartender serves up a new drink—the Bikini Blowup—to a crewmember at the bar, causing the man to visibly explode from the drink's intensity (see Figure 7.3). The atomic symbol, drawn over the center of the man's body, suggests the potential biological effects of this historically new "drink" as the bartender skeptically registers the bottle's ingredients—his eyebrows raised—as if he could not have anticipated its effects. The illustration renders as comedy how once-familiar practices (ordering a drink at the bar) had become potentially dangerous, and points to historically new concerns about the effects of nuclearism on everyday life.

In the months leading up to Operation Crossroads, which took place in July 1946, readers of *The Masthead* would have been aware that the future of the Navy as an institution hinged on the outcome of the test bombs. Headlines such as "All Because of Atom Bomb: Congressional Committee Cuts Navy Budget by One Billon" on May 25 and "Atom Bomb Blast May Determine Future Naval Plans and Tactics" on June 15 would have suggested unwelcome changes in the careers and lives of many of the island's crewmembers. An article from June 22, a few weeks before the first bomb at Bikini, describes how the Army would bring tanks, armored cars, trucks, and radar equipment to test the ability of these materials to withstand the nuclear weapons—perhaps evoking concerns about the vulnerabilities of military equipment with which crew members were familiar.

Readers would have also scanned *The Masthead* for information about the threat nuclear weapons posed for their own bodies. When the paper reported that "radio-active [*sic*] poison, sticking to ships like salt deposited from sea water, is expected to be a serious hazard in this summer's second atomic bomb test," they may have wondered about the effects of this new "poison" on the ship's human crew (1946c). Treasure Islanders knew from reading *The Masthead* that the Navy had brought clothes and food to Bikini to test the effects of radiation on materials crewmembers wore or ingested. "Whether food properly canned and packaged becomes inedible when atom-bombed is one of the questions expected to be answered after the smoke is cleared," an article reported on June 1, 1946. Treasure Islanders also knew that, in addition to ships, tanks, and food, the military task force would bring animals to test the biomedical effects of radiation. During the two nuclear explosions, the animals were strategically placed on twenty-two target ships, simulating a human crew during battle (Weisgall 1994). After the first bomb in the Operation Crossroads experiment, Treasure Islanders might have been relieved to read that medical personnel at Bikini believed the "majority of the crew members actually would have lived through the blast with no particular illness" in an article on July 27 titled "Crews Could Have Survived Blast Is Opinion of Crossroads Medics." Yet the same article also mentions that 108 mice had been shipped to the National Cancer Institute for further testing. During the months that the *The Masthead* reported on the clothes, food, and animals marshaled as stand-ins for the future atomic soldier (Masco 2006), the US military was busy removing 170 Bikinians from their home and taking them to the island of Rongerik, 130 miles away (Miller 1986).

A year after Operation Crossroads, in 1947, the United Nations designated the Marshall Islands a US trust territory. The United States continued to use the area as an outdoor laboratory for its experimental weapons program until 1958, ultimately exploding a total of sixty-seven bombs (Johnston and Barker 2008). Barbara Rose Johnston suggests the notion of a "radiogenic community" to describe the many groups of people whose lives have been deeply affected by the military's release of radiation (2007). Radiogenic communities are overly peopled with indigenous groups, like the Marshallese, and political minorities within nation-states, although term could be extended to the ecological life of the planet. The illnesses suffered by the Marshallese today, as well as their loss of land and traditional diets and livelihoods, is one example of Nixon's concept of slow violence—a form of destruction that is, like fallout, dispersed across time and space.

The first bomb detonated in Operation Crossroads, called Shot Able, was dropped by an airplane and missed its target by half a mile, disappointing over one hundred journalists the military had invited to witness and report on the event. Shot Baker, the second bomb, was detonated from ninety feet under the ocean, and produced a dome-shaped plume of radioactive water and coral that fell down on the target fleet with unexploded fission products in significantly larger quantities than had been predicted (Bradley 1948; Hacker 1987). Scientists and military commanders at Bikini were unprepared to deal with the pervasive fallout and worried about the shortage of radiological safety monitors (Bradley 1948; Defense Nuclear Agency 1984). Many of the target ships were eventually taken back to the Hunters Point Shipyard in San Francisco.

The Naval Radiological Defense Laboratory, which operated at Hunters Point until 1969, grew out of the attempts to simultaneously decontaminate ships used in Crossroads *and* prepare for future nuclear weapons tests. In the fall of 1946, radioactive ships docked at Hunters Point—returned from the Marshall Islands—were converted into floating labs. A handful of scientists conducted experiments with methods of removing radiation from the large surfaces, water piping, and ventilation systems of the contaminated ships—all historically new problems of national security. At the same time, the lab oversaw the operational task of granting clearance to other radioactive vessels, either for disposal (by sinking the ships in the ocean) or for future use. The work went quickly, despite the fact that NRDL scientists were still puzzled by the problem of decontamination on its experimental ships. By December 1946, the lab had cleared forty-three of the radioactive ships from Bikini (Defense Nuclear Agency 1984). Several of these ships were berthed at Naval Station Treasure Island while waiting for their final clearance. This material connection to Operation Crossroads constitutes one potential source of radiation on the island today (US Navy 2006). In this sense, the slow violence of Operation Crossroads extends in time and space from the Marshall Islands to Treasure Island, calling into question whether the nuclear experiment ever really ended, or whether and how it continues to unfold.

Through the biomedical effects of US nuclear weapons tests, the lives of Marshallese people became bound with others who would suffer from the US nuclear weapons program—downwind of the Nevada test site, for example, or downstream from the Hanford plutonium facility. The fate of Marshall Islanders were also bound with developments on Treasure Island, as graduates from its radiological defense training programs worked as safety monitors during future weapons tests. These duties included issuing dosimeters and protective clothing to soldiers and scientists working in radioactive areas, taking readings of radiation in the field, and disposing of contaminated gear afterward (Hacker 1994).

The pages of *The Masthead* show little concern for the effects of nuclear weapons on the bodies and environments of people living in the Marshall Islands, suggesting that Treasure Islanders would not have recognized the intimate connections newly forged through nuclear weapons explosions. In part, the newspaper channeled the military's discourse of controllable disaster, or the idea that proper procedures could manage and contain the effects of the radiation. Treasure Island graduates participated in this discourse of controllable disaster through their work as radiation monitors, appearing to regulate the boundaries between radiological safety and harm.

A cartoon in *The Masthead* from 1948 is indicative of the military's racialized relationship with Marshall Islanders, suggesting that they may not have been considered part of the population deserving of safety and protection by its radiation monitors. The 1948 cartoon appeared in the same moment that the United States had designated the Enewewok Atoll as its Pacific proving ground—an outdoor laboratory where scientists could test (or "prove") theoretical advances in nuclear weapons technology. The designation required further evacuations of Marshallese people. *The Masthead* ran several cartoons of Marshall Islanders during the late 1940s indicating the new relationships between the indigenous group and the US military. In the cartoon shown in Figure 7.4, Marshallese people are depicted as black, animal-like figures—racialized through the color of their skin and less-than-human physiognomy, and through their relation with the cartoon's white male naval officer. The officer stands over the seated Marshallese, directing them to row in the direction of a modern naval ship. The relations among the figures and the directionality of the Marshallese rowboat appears to justify the US occupation of the Marshall Islands and its weapons testing program as bearers of modernity.

'Stroke . . . stroke . . . stroke . . .'

FIGURE 7.4 "U.S.-Marshall Island Relations." *The Masthead*, April 9, 1948. National Archives and Records Administration, San Bruno.

Damage Control in the Atomic Age

In 1946, Operation Crossroads was the most photographed event in history. For the military, the events were simultaneously a display of its postwar power and a revelation of its new vulnerabilities, requiring new practices of national defense. An article titled "Radiological Defense Training in the Navy" in the *Naval Training Bulletin* from 1950 reflects that "the atom bomb dropped on Hiroshima did more than just reveal to the world the enormous destructive power of this new weapon," but also "gave a clue to the nature and enormous extent of the new training burden thrown on the Armed Services if they were to cope successfully with this new agency of warfare" (1950, 13). In November 1946, a hastily assembled training course in radiological safety was held in Washington, DC. Safety officers were desperately needed to oversee the ongoing decontamination work in the Marshall Islands, and the military anticipated the need for more monitors, as it prepared for future weapons tests (Defense Nuclear Agency 1984). In 1947, a six-week course in radiological safety was established at Treasure Island, to be offered on an ongoing basis. The course covered nuclear physics, the use of radiation detection instruments, hazard evaluation, and remedial measures (*The Masthead* 1948; *US Naval Training Bulletin* 1950). The proximity of Treasure Island to the Marshall Islands (where the military planned to stage future rounds of nuclear weapons tests) and to NRDL at the Hunters Point Shipyard (at the time, rapidly growing as the Navy's applied radiation lab) made it an ideal location for this new training program.

A survey of the *Naval Training Bulletin* from the late 1940s and 1950s reveals how military bases around the country began offering similar courses, such as at the Damage Control School at the Philadelphia naval shipyard, the Edgewood Army Base in Maryland, and the Keesler Air Force Base in Mississippi. In 1958, the Damage Control School at Treasure Island began training medical officers as well, in a course on defense against atomic, biological, and chemical warfare (*The Masthead,* June 6). The first month-long course, in January 1958, covered "medical problems by nuclear propulsion, missile fuels, atomic fallout and hospital isotope programs" (*The Masthead,* January 10). The course was subsequently offered twice yearly and included lectures by NRDL scientists from Hunters Point, Oak Knoll and the US Naval Biological Hospitals in Oakland, and UC Berkeley's Radiation Lab (*The Masthead* 1958a, 1958b, 1959).

The culmination of the medical training course was a special practice exercise: the Mock A-Bomb (see Figure 7.5). This practice attack was a large, staged event, which was also used by the Navy on Treasure Island to practice passive defense in the event of nuclear war. Nearly a thousand people from the island participated in the simulation, including 150 marines who pretended to suffer from radiation-induced casualties. Hospital corpsmen demonstrated first aid techniques in front of the medical students, accompanied by explanations of proper treatment in different cases of radiation injury. The mock bomb did not use fissionable materials, but neither was it harmless. For visual accuracy, with mushroom crown and all, it was designed using thirty pounds of TNT, three hundred gallons of napalm, five smoke grenades, and four hundred feet of cord containing explosives, and detonated in the San Francisco Bay (*The Masthead,* June 5, 1959).

The science and practice of radiological safety taught to naval officers on Treasure Island and at other military bases allowed for this systemic application of radioisotopes and toxic chemicals (*The Masthead* 1948). These courses and their graduates also provided the illusion that radiation could be safely controlled through proper procedures: by monitoring radiation with detection instruments and measuring individual dose levels with personal film badges, or with the physical barriers, like rubber suits around people and lead boxes around radiation sources. This illusion of control is challenged by accidents like the 1950 radium spill on Treasure Island, explored in the next section. It is also challenged by the existing threat of radiation on the island today.

"Can Your City Control an 'Atomic Accident'?"

In January 1950, a glass capsule containing 40.3 milligrams of radium sulfate broke open on the floor of a student laboratory in Building 223, on the eastern side of Treasure Island.[5] The event is described in detail in a 1953 article published in the industry trade journal *Nucleonics* by three NRDL scientists (Skow, Vandivert, and Holden 1953). The article is based on the authors' presentation to the American Industrial Hygiene Association conference in San Francisco, also in 1953. Later that year, in December 1953, President Eisenhower delivered his *Atomic Power for Peace* speech before the UN General Assembly. Eisenhower sought to mitigate fears of the destructiveness of atomic power, and the growing US stockpile of nuclear weapons, with its promises for "the peaceful pursuits of mankind" (Mazuzan and Walker 1984). In 1954, Eisenhower amended the original 1946 Atomic Energy Act to encourage private development of nuclear technology. The publication in *Nucleonics* would have reached out to an emerging private-sector readership, now grappling with problems that radiation accidents posed to the smooth running of industrial operations—including a disruption to human labor through radiation injuries. In the article, the NRDL scientists meticulously describe their decontamination methods.

SERENADE TO A MUSHROOM —Suddenly exploding in a geyser of smoke and fire, Treasure Island's mock atomic bomb set off here January 21, catches one naval observer (foreground) unprepared for the eruption. Purpose of the blast was to provide more realistic training for some 45 Armed Forces medical officers observing atomic, biological, and chemical defense methods here.

FIGURE 7.5 Mock A-Bomb in San Francisco Bay. *The Masthead*, June 5, 1959. National Archives and Records Administration, San Bruno.

Sections titled "Bodies," "Clothing," "Building Decontamination," and "Waste Disposal" detail ingredients of chemical solutions and types of radiation detection instruments used. "A tank-type vacuum cleaner," they write, "equipped with a high-efficiency backup filter, was used to remove the loosely held radium from the floors. It was estimated that about 35 percent of the spilled radium was recovered by vacuum cleaning." The radium accident in San Francisco, much like the ships from Operation Crossroads, was transformed by the Navy into an opportunity to develop better decontamination proce-dures in the context of the growing presence of radiation in everyday life.

Radium sulfate is a dry, powdery substance and spreads easily. According to the article's description of the event, the student-officers on Treasure Island continued to work in the classroom laboratory for an hour, until their Geiger counter readings showed radiation levels off-scale. An ad hoc decontamination center was established at the island's chemical warfare school, and soldiers were sent home. Scientists from the NRDL were called into manage the scene, and later to track down the soldiers who had returned home, into the city. Three days after the spill, a survey group wearing rubber suits and rescue breathing apparatus entered Building 223 to determine the extent of the health hazard. In 1953, the maximum permissible concentration—or the threshold value for "safe" exposure—for alpha radiation from radium was 0.33 counts per cubic foot (or dpm/ft^3). In Building 223, three days after the radium spill, the concentration of airborne alpha radiation activity was measured at a thousand cubic feet. In some areas of the classroom, levels of radiation were beyond the measuring capacity of the scientist's detection instruments, providing some perspective of the potential injuries to the safety school's students.

Yet the authors of the article downplay the potential human toll—maintaining their focus on the decontamination procedures, which they also determine to have been completely effective. However, an article from the *Los Angeles Times* on May 11, 1958, titled "Can Your City Control an 'Atomic Accident'?" and intended for a wider audience, speculates about the dangers the accident might have posed for an urban population (Robinson 1958, K10). The *Los Angeles Times* article is based on interviews with NRDL scientists, including the lab's scientific director, Paul Tompkins, and takes as its subject matter not the decontamination procedures but the threat to the city. After the spill, thirty-five students from the classroom had crossed the Bay Bridge, returning to their homes in San Francisco and bringing traces of radium sulfate with them. In the words of one Navy officer quoted in the article, "It was like letting an epidemic loose on the town." According to Tompkins, some of the soldiers were carrying so much radioactive powder on them that "we could trace their footsteps with Geiger counters. We could tell whether they went into the living room and kissed their wives, or walked into the kitchen for a glass of water."

The sensationalism the journalist creates around the radium spill—as evidenced by his choice of observers and quotes—is used to suggest the necessity for civil defense organizations against radiation. Specifically, the journalist favors the notion of nuclear fire departments set up in major US cities. It would have been an idea supported by the Damage Control School on Treasure Island, which ran a firefighting school that included trainings in chemical and radioactive fires. Rather than pose the broader question of whether industrial and military radiation ought to become part of urban life in the first place, the journalist takes for granted what he sees as the realities of the atomic age. "Just as boiler explosions and other accidents were part of the price of progress in the Industrial Revolution," the journalist concludes, "atomic mishaps are the normal hazards of the advancing Nuclear Era." The journalist's analysis of the radium spill in 1958 is one indication of the normalization of radiation in everyday life (Robinson 1958, K10).

As I began to write this essay in December 2013, the issue of radiation on Treasure Island had resurfaced in the San Francisco Bay Area news media. The recent news articles reported ongoing revelations of the extent of radiation and documented fears of long-time residents who had lived on the island for years without knowledge of its toxic history.

The Department of Defense requires that the Navy produce a document called a historical radiological assessment (HRA), which guides the process of managing and remediating radiation on all military sites. The word "management" is key: the Navy cannot return the island to its pre-militarized state—it can only reduce the concentration of toxic chemicals to quantities within current risk thresholds. As part of this remedial work, truckloads of contaminated earth from Treasure Island are relocated to hazardous waste facilities in other parts of the country, displacing the problem of toxic waste management onto other communities.

The primary purpose of HRA is to designate areas of a military base as "impacted" or "nonimpacted" with potential radiation. These categories guide the remediation process, including safety measures and where the toxic earth is relocated to—not all waste facilities are equipped to receive radioactive material (US Navy 2006). The Navy published Treasure Island's HRA in 2006, but the extent of radiation on the island was subsequently revealed to be much greater than acknowledged in the original assessment. In 2012, the Navy published an updated version of its HRA, in part returning to the environmental legacy of the USS *Pandemonium*. The original, 2006 assessment had identified both USS *Pandemonium* sites as radiologically nonimpacted. In the 2012 update, the Navy reclassified both sites as impacted, based on new findings (US Navy 2012).

These findings include the discovery, in 2008, of radium shards at the original *Pandemonium* location, with the highest concentration of radium found near a residential street, Westside Drive (US Navy 2008). Other pieces of radium were found near a children's playground on the island (Smith and Mieszkowski 2013b). The Navy initially assured Treasure Island residents that the pieces of radium were buried under enough dirt that they posed no risk to people, but state health officials could not guarantee that the area was safe. In the spring of 2013, two independent laboratory analyses funded by the Center for Investigative Reporting found levels of cesium-137—the same radionuclide used on the USS *Pandemonium*—up to three times higher than the Navy initially reported (Smith and Mieszkowski 2013a). Cesium-137 is an intensely radioactive isotope with a half-life of thirty years, meaning that it persists in the environment for a long time. Because of its chemical nature, it also moves through the landscape easily, making it difficult to remove (Walker 2009; Johnston 2007). In December 2013, residents of twenty-four housing units on the northern side of the island, which had been built on top of an old military waste disposal site, were asked to vacate their homes. New evidence revealed the old waste site, and current residential neighborhood, has a more dangerous toxic history than previously determined (Wildermuth 2013).

The Navy's attempts to manage its environmental legacy on Treasure Island is part of the historical geography of US nuclearism and the social and ecological relations of

national security. In practicing for a future atomic disaster, the US Navy produced today's polluted environment in San Francisco, which I argue constitutes a form of slow
violence. The temporalities of slow violence pose particular problems of recognition
and representation. Radiation, for example, is invisible, and its biological effects do
not manifest for decades, and sometimes span generations. It is often impossible to
link any one source of radiation with a particular person's cancer, yet this is often the
burden of proof legally required to hold a company or the government accountable.

Today the city of San Francisco has plans to redevelop the island, transforming
the military base into an urban landscape of high-rise condominiums, office spaces,
hotels, and waterfront parks. Environmental engineering firms contracted by the
Navy have reduced the amount of radiation and toxic chemicals in Treasure Island's
soils, appearing to produce a clean slate for urban development. As part of this
process, samples of these polluted sediments are sent to laboratories for analytical
testing to determine their material composition. Along with these technical methods, this essay sought to excavate and analyze some of the social and ecological
relations of the US military's presence on Treasure Island, so that these histories are
not buried under the landscape of new development.

Notes

I would like to thank Robert Glass at the National Archives–San Francisco, who was an immense help in the
research for this essay. I would also like to thank the California Studies Association for the opportunity to
present a part of this research, and Lynne Horiuchi and Tanu Sankalia for putting together this wonderful
collection of essays.

1   The following description is based on a news article, "Pandemonium Teaches Contamination,"
    from the Naval Station Treasure Island newspaper (*The Masthead* 1968) and from US Navy
    records in the National Archives, "Safety and Operating Regulations, Radioactive Sources for
    U.S. Naval Schools Command, Treasure Island" (1958). The only aspect of this narrative not
    explicitly in those documents is that the course instructor made up a "practice scenario,"
    although this is likely given the nature of the exercise.

2   A *rem* measures the amount of radiation absorbed by a body. Today, the Department of Energy,
    as noted on its Oakridge webpage, "Emergency Public Information—About Radiation," maintains
    a 100-millirem a year limit for public from exposure to radiation as a result of its operations. Still,
    according to the National Academy of Sciences' most recent Board on Radiation Effects Research
    Committee on the biological effects of ionizing radiation (BEIR VII), there is no demonstrated
    threshold of exposure below which ionizing radiation is not potentially harmful (Johnston 2007).

3   See *The Masthead* 1958a. Scientists from the Naval Radiological Defense Laboratory (NRDL)
    on the Hunters Point Shipyard gave lectures on radiological safety to nonmedical officers
    and enlisted men enrolled in the Damage Control School on Treasure Island. The NRDL also
    worked with the Naval Schools Command on Treasure Island to build a radiological shelter, for
    training purposes, in the former Building 283 (US Navy 1957).

4   This early history of Yerba Buena Island was compiled by PAR Environmental Services (1997)
    for the Navy as part of the base disposal and reuse process.

5   The year 1950 was not a good one for San Francisco. The city was also "attacked" by the
    military in an experiment testing the vulnerability of the city to biological warfare. During the
    week of September 20 to September 27, 1950, the Army sprayed the San Francisco Bay Area
    with two organisms, *Bacillus globigii* and *Serratia marcescens,* thought to be nonpathogenic.
    Data on airborne dispersal patterns was collected with sampling stations, placed throughout
    the city, which indicated that nearly everyone in San Francisco had inhaled millions of the
    organisms each day of the test sprays. *Serratia marcescens* was later determined to have

adverse health effects on people with particular immune vulnerabilities. The 1950 experiment resulted in the hospitalization of at least eleven people and the death of one man (see Cole 1990; Guillemin 2005; US Army 2008). The Naval Biological Laboratory in Oakland and UC Berkeley collaborated on *Serratia marcescens* studies in the 1960s.

References

Bradley, David. 1948. *No Place to Hide*. Boston, MA: Little, Brown.

Brechin, Gray. 2006. *Imperial San Francisco: Urban Power, Earthly Ruin*. Berkeley: University of California Press.

Cole, Leonard. 1990. *Clouds of Secrecy: The Army's Germ Warfare Tests over Populated Areas*. Lanham, MD: Rowman & Littlefield.

Defense Nuclear Agency. 1984. "Operation Crossroads 1946: United States Atmospheric Nuclear Weapons Tests, Nuclear Test Personnel Review." Washington, DC: US Department of Defense.

Guillemin, Jeanne. 2005. *Biological Weapons: From the Invention of State-sponsored Programs to Contemporary Bioterrorism*. New York: Columbia University Press.

Guyer, Ruth Levy. 2001. "Radioactivity and Rights: Clashes at Bikini Atoll." *American Journal of Public Health* 91, no. 9:1371–1376.

Hacker, Barton. 1987. *The Dragon's Tail: Radiation Safety in the Manhattan Project, 1942–1946*. Berkeley: University of California Press.

———. 1994. *Elements of Controversy: The Atomic Energy Commission and Radiation Safety in Nuclear Weapons Testing 1947–1974*. Berkeley: University of California Press.

Johnson, Troy. 1996. *The Occupation of Alcatraz Island: Indian Self-Determination and the Rise of Indian Activism*. Champaign: University of Illinois Press.

Johnston, Barbara Rose, ed. 2007. *Half-Lives & Half-Truths: Confronting the Radioactive Legacies of the Cold War*. School for Advanced Research, Resident Scholars Series.

Johnston, Barbara Rose, and Holly M. Barker. 2008. *The Consequential Damages of Nuclear War: The Rongelap Report*. Walnut Creek: Left Coast Press.

Lai, H. Mark, Genny Lim, and Judy Yung eds. 1980. *Island: Poetry and History of Chinese Immigrants on Angel Island, 1910–1940*. San Francisco: HOC DOI (History of Chinese Detained on Island) Project Study Center.

Masco, Joseph. 2006. *Nuclear Borderlands: The Manhattan Project in Post-Cold War New Mexico*. Princeton, NJ: Princeton University Press.

The Masthead. 1945. "Students Baptized with Disaster in Mock Damage Control Drills." November 3.

———. 1946a. "Atomic Bomb Fans Warned by CNO." March 9.

———. 1946b. "Bikini-Bound Enlisted Men Worry; Deny Volunteering for Atom Tests." June 22.

———. 1946c. "Radioactive Poison May Prove Dangerous for Atom Bomb Ships." June 22.

———. 1946d. "Crews Could Have Survived Blast Is Opinion of Crossroads Medics." July 27.

———. 1948. "Sixth Class in Radiological Safety." January 30.

———. 1958a. "Medical Group Here for Atomic Training." January 10.

———. 1958b. "High Ranking Medical Officers Meet Here for Special Course." June 6.

———. 1959. "Mock A-Bomb Blast in 'Operation Medic'." June 5.

———. 1968. "*Pandemonium* Teaches Contamination." October 18.

Mazuzan, George, and J. Samuel Walker. 1984. *Controlling the Atom: The Beginnings of Nuclear Regulation, 1946–1962*. Berkeley: University of California Press.

Miller, Richard. 1986. *Under the Cloud: The Decades of Nuclear Testing*. New York: The Free Press.

Nixon, Rob. 2011. *Slow Violence and the Environmentalism of the Poor*. Boston, MA: Harvard University Press.

Par Environmental Services. 1997. "Archeological Inventory and Assessment of Naval Station Treasure Island Disposal and Reuse Project, San Francisco County, CA, Final Report." Box 23,

Cultural Resources Files, 1969–2000. Records of Naval Districts and Shore Establishments, Record Group 181. National Archives Branch Depository, San Francisco.

Pollock, Nancy J. 2002. "Health Transitions, Fast and Nasty: The Case of Marshallese Exposure to Nuclear Radiation." *Pacific Health Dialog* 9, no. 2:275–282.

Robinson, Donald. 1958. "Can Your City Control 'atomic Accident'?" *Los Angeles Times,* May 11.

Skow, R. K., V. V. Vandivert, and F. R. Holden. 1953. "Hazard Evaluation and Control after a Spill of 40 mg of Radium." *Nucleonics* 11, no. 8:45–47.

Shah, Nayan. 2001. *Contagious Divides: Epidemics and Race in San Francisco's Chinatown.* Berkeley: University of California Press.

Smith, Matt, and Katharine Mieszkowski. 2013a. "Nuclear byproduct levels on Treasure Island Higher than Navy disclosed." *Reveal,* April 12. https://www.revealnews.org/article/nuclear-byproduct-levels-on-treasure-island-higher-than-navy-disclosed/.

———. 2013b. "Radioactive Poisoning May Still Be Risk on Treasure Island, Memo Says." *Reveal,* November 13. https://www.revealnews.org/article/radioactive-poisoning-may-still-be-risk-on-treasure-island-memo-says/.

Sorenson, David. 1998. *Shutting Down the Cold War: The Politics of Military Base Closure.* New York: St. Martin's Press.

United States Army (US Army). 2008. "Medical Aspects of Biological Warfare." Walter Reed Army Medical Center Borden Institute. http://www.cs.amedd.army.mil/borden/.

US Naval Training Bulletin. 1949. "Training Command, U.S. Pacific Fleet." January.

———. 1950. "Radiological Defense Training in the Navy." December.

———. 1951. "Training in the San Francisco Area." June.

United States Navy (US Navy). 1954. "Summary of all work completed on Project 4.1 as of May 7, 1954." Box 2. US Naval Radiological Defense Laboratory, General Correspondence 1954–55. Records of Naval Districts and Shore Establishments, Record Group 181. National Archives Branch Depository, San Francisco.

———. 1957. "Letter of Appreciation for Construction of Radiological Shelter (Training)." Building Design and Construction. File 1 of 2, Box 10. Commanding Officers Subject Files, 1957. Records of Naval Districts and Shore Establishments, Record Group 181. National Archives Branch Depository, San Francisco.

———. 1958. "Safety and Operating Regulations, Radioactive Sources for U.S. Naval Schools Command, Treasure Island." Airbase and Real Estate Acquisition Files, 1942–1958. Records of Naval Districts and Shore Establishments, Record Group 181. National Archives Branch Depository, San Francisco.

———. 1962. "Command History." Naval Station Treasure Island, San Francisco, California – Public Affairs Office; Command Histories, 195–1991. Records of Naval Districts and Shore Establishments, Record Group 181. National Archives Branch Depository, San Francisco.

———. 2006. *Final Treasure Island Naval Station Historical Radiological Assessment, Former Naval Station Treasure Island.* San Diego: Department of the Navy, Base Realignment and Closure Program Management Office West. https://assets.documentcloud.org/documents/809298/radiologicalassessment-2006.pdf.

———. 2008. *Final Sampling and Analysis Plan, Groundwater Monitoring Program, IR Sites 12 and 6, Naval Station Treasure Island.* San Francisco: Department of the Navy, Department of Toxic Substances Control.

———. 2012. "Summary of Navy's *Draft Historical Radiological Assessment Supplemental Technical Memorandum.*" San Francisco: Treasure Island Development Authority. http://www.sftreasureisland.org/modules/showdocument.aspx?documentid=1311.

Walker, J. Samuel. 2009. *The Road to Yucca Mountain: The Development of Radioactive Waste Policy in the U.S.* Berkeley: University of California Press.

Weisgall, Jonathan. 1994. *Operation Crossroads: The Atomic Tests at Bikini Atoll.* Annapolis, MD: Naval Institute Press.

Wildermuth, John. 2013. "Navy Cleanup Forces Dozens to Move on Treasure Island." *San Francisco Chronicle,* December 2.

8. Visions for Reuse

The Legacy of the Bay Area's Military Installations

MARK L. GILLEM

As a cool bay breeze swept across Treasure Island, forgotten aluminum cans rattled against a chain link fence. Regularly spaced along the fence were warning signs painted with the universal yellow background and black icon: a black center circle of the sign at the focal point of three black pie-shaped wedges whose wider ends implied the circumference of an outer circle. From Chernobyl to Treasure Island, the frighteningly familiar sign warned of radioactive danger lurking in the background. For Treasure Island, the radioactive waste is just part of the slowly decaying history of the US military's presence on the island and across the entire Bay Area (Figure 8.1). This presence peaked during the mobilization for World War II in the early 1940s and remained robust through the wartime period and into the Cold War, then the drawdowns started in earnest in the late 1980s, after the collapse of the Soviet Union.

The Bay Area was once a military juggernaut: home to numerous Army, Navy, and Air Force installations. At the height of the Cold War, the Bay Area supported one of the largest military communities in the country across fifteen major installations (Figure 8.2). Changing strategies, new weapon systems, progressive political interests, and the economics of supporting military personnel in one of the country's most expensive real estate markets all contributed to the decanting of the Bay Area's military landscape.

With few exceptions, what remains is not a legacy of successful redevelopment but a landscape of abandonment and despair. Hollywood producers would find it easy to film the latest zombie blockbuster in the burned-out and used-up landscapes. Boarded-up buildings, weed-choked streets, and overgrown parks make many of these former bases look like scenes from the apocalypse that never happened. These same places, though, were once

FIGURE 8.1 Fenced-off area with radioactive contamination at Treasure Island, 2014. Photo: Mark Gillem.

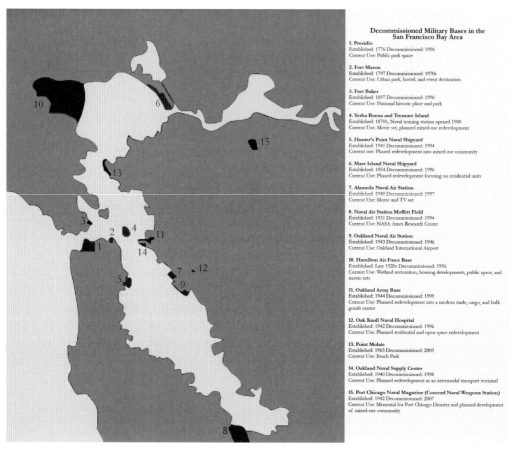

Decommissioned Military Bases in the
San Francisco Bay Area

1. Presidio
Established: 1776 Decommissioned: 1996
Current Use: Public park space

2. Fort Mason
Established: 1797 Decommissioned: 1970s
Current Use: Urban park, hostel, and event destination

3. Fort Baker
Established: 1897 Decommissioned: 1996
Current Use: National historic place and park

4. Yerba Buena and Treasure Island
Established: 1870's, Naval training station opened 1900
Current Use: Movie set, planned mixed-use redevelopment

5. Hunter's Point Naval Shipyard
Established: 1941 Decommissioned: 1994
Current use: Phased redevelopment into mixed-use community

6. Mare Island Naval Shipyard
Established: 1854 Decommissioned: 1996
Current Use: Phased redevelopment focusing on residential units

7. Alameda Naval Air Station
Established: 1940 Decommissioned: 1997
Current Use: Movie and TV set

8. Naval Air Station Moffett Field
Established: 1931 Decommissioned: 1994
Current Use: NASA Ames Research Center

9. Oakland Naval Air Station
Established: 1943 Decommissioned: 1946
Current Use: Oakland International Airport

10. Hamilton Air Force Base
Established: Late 1920s Decommissioned: 1996
Current Use: Wetland restoration, housing developments, public space, and movie sets

11. Oakland Army Base
Established: 1944 Decommissioned: 1999
Current Use: Planned redevelopment into a modern trade, cargo, and bulk goods center

12. Oak Knoll Naval Hospital
Established: 1942 Decommissioned: 1996
Current Use: Planned residential and open space redevelopment

13. Point Molate
Established: 1965 Decommissioned: 2003
Current Use: Beach Park

14. Oakland Naval Supply Center
Established: 1940 Decommissioned: 1998
Current Use: Planned redevelopment as an intermodal transport terminal

15. Port Chicago Naval Magazine (Concord Naval Weapons Station)
Established: 1942 Decommissioned: 2007
Current Use: Memorial for Port Chicago Disaster and planned development of mixed-use community

FIGURE 8.2   Bay Area's military landscape. Source: Mark Gillem.

thriving communities on the front lines of the military-industrial complex. Taken together, they make up a unique West Coast military history based initially on defense
of a major continental harbor and later on power projection for a nation engaged in
numerous hot and cold wars fought in and around the Pacific Ocean.

The geography of the San Francisco Bay that made the area so attractive
for the Spanish Empire through the eighteenth century also made it attractive
to the US military in the nineteenth and twentieth centuries. The protected
harbors and warm waters, the deep ports and numerous channels, and the
Mediterranean climate worked together to create an ideal platform from which
to project military power across the Pacific. The Bay Area was also a great place
to work and to live, which is no small advantage when trying to recruit and re-
tain a strong and stable enlisted and officer corps. But geography is not always
destiny. The locational assets eventually became a liability when nonmilitary
uses (attracted by those same assets) began their irreversible encroachment on
the area's military landscape.

Given that the Bay Area currently has no military installation around its shoreline, the twenty-first century is an anomaly in the area's military legacy. More than five thousand years ago, Native Americans from the Ohlone tribe recognized the advantages of the protected harbor and formed rudimentary defenses. Much later, when the Spanish first settled in the region, they established missions and presidios to advance and defend their interests, including San Francisco's Presidio, which Juan Bautista de Anza first established in 1776 (Chatfield-Taylor 1988). Then, in 1850, after the US government took possession of California and prospectors found gold in the Sierra Nevada foothills, a military commission took responsibility for enhancing existing bases such as Fort Mason to ensure adequate defensive coverage of the bay (Figure 8.3) and developing other bases around the Bay Area to preserve law and order and to protect the gold (Benton-Short 1998).

The commission enhanced the Presidio, established defensive positions on Alcatraz and Angel Island, opened Mare Island as a shipyard, and created an arsenal in what is now Concord. As Amy Hoke and Eliot Foulds note, "The booming Gold Rush economy of San Francisco understandably led to squatters, land disputes, and rapid development. The need for coastal fortifications to protect the rich new state led the federal government to stake its own land claims" (2004, 29). These claims were for strategically important landscapes all around the bay.

Although existing bases in the San Francisco Bay Area changed little during the 1930s, military planners for World War II used the area's military infrastructure to prepare for and support the Pacific theater of operations. To support World War II, between 1940 and 1945, the military rapidly expanded existing bases and new bases came on line as fast as possible. Not to be outdone, private companies set up massive shipbuilding yards as well, including Bechtel's 210-acre Marinship yard in Sausalito (1942–1945) and Kaiser's 880-acre Richmond Shipyards (1942–1945). At Marinship, Charles Wollenberg shows that industrial production techniques allowed unskilled laborers to produce complex ships in record time. But racial strife and conflicts associated with increasing participation of women and African Americans in the workforce marred the legacy of these military landscapes (1990).

Although the private shipyards closed at the end of World War II, most of the military bases remained active in support of later wars,

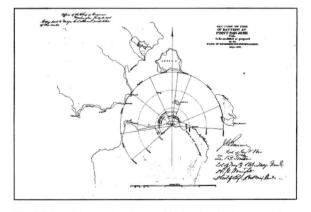

FIGURE 8.3 Diagram showing Fort Mason circa 1876, representing fire battery sectors and range of artillery fire. Note the full coverage of the entry into the bay. Point San Jose renamed Fort Mason in 1882. National Park Service.

including the Korean War, the Vietnam War, and the Cold War. Then, largely in response to the slow demise and eventual fall of the Soviet Union in 1991, the Department of Defense (DOD), through the Base Realignment and Closure (BRAC) process, managed a series of base closures that occurred in 1988, 1991, 1993, 1995, and 2005. Across the United States, the DOD closed a total of 140 major installations and realigned another fifty-five (Gross 1990). The DOD spared no region but the ax fell hardest on the Bay Area. Over this period, with the exception of Camp Parks in Dublin, all of the Bay Area's remaining bases shut down. With the post–Cold War drawdown in troop strength, the DOD needed fewer installations and the resulting Peace Dividend could theoretically be used for other purposes. The Bay Area was an attractive target for closures given its high cost of living, encroachment around many of its installations, and even the Left-leaning political inclinations of the area's residents and its congressional delegation. Left behind is a legacy of either long-term success (for the few bases that had a clear vision and purpose) or short-term failure (for those bases too contaminated to remediate quickly or those bases that failed to identify a clear purpose).

In this essay, the focus is on the history and future of the Bay Area's closed bases and four key lessons they offer in terms of reuse. Given that another round of BRAC may occur in the not-too-distant future as a result of the drawdown from the Iraq and Afghanistan conflicts, these lessons may indeed be timely for communities faced with similar circumstances. First, from a negative perspective, some of the bases illustrate the pitfalls of dealing with contamination. Second, many of these same bases as well as others in the Bay Area demonstrate the challenges of working with the unknowns that inevitably accompany vague reuse plans that privilege the Holy Grail to many planners and architects—the mixed-use _____ (fill in the blank with a marketable word like "center," "village," "district," or "neighborhood."). Third, on a more positive note, two bases demonstrate the benefits of simple plans that are consistent with former uses on the land, even if the plans inevitably take time to mature. Fourth, three bases illustrate the power of conversion to primarily parkland. This is one area where agreement has been widespread. Apart from these four lessons, one finding is clear. Namely, compelling visions drive successful reuse.

The Former Bases

Each of the four lessons, and the importance of a clear vision, give structure to this overview of Bay Area military bases and apply in some measure to the reuse of Treasure Island.

The Pitfalls of Contamination

Naval Station Treasure Island, NSTI

(1846–1997, 525 acres). Imagine a largely open, four-hundred-plus-acre development site surrounded by water with million-dollar views to downtown San Francisco, the Golden Gate Bridge, the Marin Headlands, and the Oakland Hills. Located in the middle of San Francisco Bay with primary vehicular access by the Bay Bridge, Naval Station Treasure Island and Yerba Buena Island provide this opportunity. The Works Progress Administration built Treasure Island with bay fill in the 1930s to serve as an airfield for the Bay Area, which is one reason the San Francisco International Airport is coded SFO, short for San Francisco–Oakland. Instead of serving as the region's airport, however, Treasure Island supported the 1939 Golden Gate International Exposition—the West Coast's answer to the World's Columbian Exposition held in Chicago in 1893. After the expo, the Navy moved in and used the island as the center of naval activities on the Pacific Coast (*San Francisco News* 1942). The island served as a point of departure for sailors bound for the Pacific theater of war, an administrative center for numerous headquarters, and a support center with housing and other community facilities. With its designation as a Training and Distribution Center, NSTI hosted numerous training schools and served as an embarkation point where more than 4.5 million soldiers passed through the island in less than five years. But with the Cold War drawdown, like many other Bay Area bases, the military no longer needed NSTI and the Navy's departure launched a long process of rethinking the use and purpose of the island.

The planned transfer hit numerous snags. Lindsey Dillon (this volume) describes the legacy of environmental contamination, which complicated reuse efforts at NSTI. As with many closed bases, a key sticking point in the transfer negotiations revolved around who would pay for all of the environmental remediation. Although BRAC legislation made the Navy responsible for remediation of known contamination, what about the unknown—like the recent discovery of radioactive soil in the old housing areas? In addition, how can the appraisers determine a fair price for the land transfer given the known and unknown contamination (Dodge 2013)? Then came valuing the damage and subsidence of the island following the 1989 Loma Prieta earthquake (Elliot 1996).

Despite these hurdles, in 2011, the Treasure Island Development Authority completed a comprehensive master plan, the *Treasure Island and Yerba Buena Island Design for Development*. An impressive array of leading design firms collaborated on the project and a peer review team provided input. The title is instructive in that it assumes development will happen and as a result design needs to be prioritized in the process. This is a refreshing change from traditional land use plans and zoning codes that have little to do with physical design. The 2011 plan is a solid example for a form-based code because it tries to codify a desired physical form using regulating plans and illustrative plans as well as standards for open spaces, streets, landscapes, and buildings. What is missing, however, is a discussion of the role community participants played in the process beyond one passing reference in the plan. Who were these community participants? How were they involved? Did they represent other stakeholders? How were the inevitable disagreements adjudicated? In the end, a plan with broad-based support may more likely weather the vagaries of public opinion, market forces, and political guidance.

San Francisco Naval Shipyard at Hunters Point

(1941–1994, 638 acres). Another San Francisco base that has seen numerous plans for conversion into a major mixed-use district delayed by contamination issues is the massive San Francisco Naval Shipyard at Hunters Point. Like NSTI, reuse plans have stalled out amid debates about remediation, land values, and appropriate reuse. Located near south San Francisco on the waterfront, Hunters Point was a major shipyard and home to the Pacific Reserve Fleet and the Navy's Radiological Defense Laboratory. In 2011, the Discovery Channel's *Forgotten Planet* series focused its lens on the abandoned landscape of the shipyard and realized that the deteriorating buildings and crumbling roadways on the base made for compelling imagery (Noble, Hense, and Verklan 2011). Like other abandoned installations, Hunters Point looked like a ghost town. The cameras went around, above, under, and inside the remaining buildings to tell a story of industrial decline. The collapsing office desk with a few moldy files and the lone ceramic plate resting uneasily in the mess hall's rusted-out, industrial-grade dishwasher were the few traces of humanity left. The slow death of Hunters Point did not actually begin until well into the Cold War. Opened in 1941 after extensive construction that turned the circa 1870 commercial shipyard into a military zone (just a few months before the attack on Pearl Harbor), and closed in 1994 due to radioactive contamination, the shipyard served a vital role in the defense of the United States.

The reopening in 1941 was quite timely. After the attack on Pearl Harbor, local resident Carl Noble recalls in an interview broadcast on the Discovery Channel that "the reaction was shock and outrage but also panic because we believed the Pacific Fleet had been sunk at Pearl Harbor and we had no defense here" (2011). When the realization sunk in that the fleet had survived but was badly damaged, the mission of Hunters Point crystallized. Initially, the seventeen thousand workers at the shipyard built and repaired the capital ships of the Pacific Fleet and supported the staging functions of the installation. At one point during World War II, according to Noble and his colleagues, the San Francisco Bay area was the largest shipyard in the world and Hunters Point was at the center of activity. The workers could assemble a massive Liberty-class ship in two weeks and had the capacity to launch three new ships every day, which was faster than the enemy could destroy them. Like most installations, Hunters

Point operated as a little city—replete with family housing, a library, cafeterias, offices, industrial areas, parks, a theater, and even a regular bus service. The shipyard also played a key role in ending the war. The cruiser USS *Indianapolis* docked at Hunters Point so that unsuspecting workers could load unmarked crates bound for the South Pacific. Inside these lead-lined wooden boxes were the deadly ingredients for Little Boy—the 9,700-pound atomic bomb dropped on Hiroshima on August 6, 1945. A year later, the lasting effects of Little Boy reverberated back at Hunters Point. The installation could not escape the consequences of the nuclear age. Operation Crossroads brought ninety surface ships to the remote Bikini atoll then subjected them to not one but two nuclear blasts to study the effects of radiation on warships. The telltale mushroom clouds rose thousands of feet into the sky then gave way to a radioactive fireball of immense proportions. The ships did not stand a chance. Fourteen of the surviving ships were slowly towed back to the West Coast, and a few stayed at Hunters Point for in-depth analysis. As a result of winning a sales contest for paper delivery boys, the young Carl Noble saw the ships firsthand. In his Discovery Channel interview, he asked, "Have you ever seen a can with sardines when you peel back the lid?" He continued the interview by explaining what he saw, "It was like that. The flight deck of an aircraft carrier was peeled back from the force of the nuclear explosions" (2011).

To study the detonation's effects, the Navy established the U.S. Naval Radiological Defense Lab at Hunters Point (see Dillon, this volume). At the time, scientists knew little about the effects of radiation on ships or on people, so they conducted studies and experiments on site until 1969. The Navy eventually abandoned the place in 1974 and leased the area to a commercial ship repair company until 1989, when the radiation experts realized that the site was still hazardous. The entire place shut down in 1994, and cleanup continues. But the contaminated sites and lack of a clear vision hampered this intent. The closure of Hunters Point was part of the so-called Peace Dividend, but the only current peace at the point came from abandonment, not redevelopment. Grand plans remain for reuse of the base as a mixed-use district but will be slow to come to fruition. Like NSTI, developers will need to address nuclear contamination, which is likely more of an issue at Hunters Point, before private development and its risk-averse backers transform the former shipyard into a mixed-use district.

Point Molate

(1942–1995, 413 acres). Contamination is not unique to shipyards and Navy bases. Like so many gas stations across the United States, with their leaking tanks and ever-widening plumes from fuel spills, the future of Alameda County's Point Molate has been clouded by the legacy of contamination that resulted from its role as a major refueling point for Navy ships. Given its direct access to the bay, Point Molate was an ideal fueling facility. Because its adjacent neighbor was one of the

West Coast's largest private oil refineries, this use made eminent sense. But due to changing mission needs, the DOD no longer needed the base for refueling operations in the 1990s, so it made the closure list. By the time Point Molate closed, the Navy controlled the land and sold 218 acres to the City of Richmond for $1 and also provided the city with $28.5 million of cleanup funds (City of Richmond, n.d.). The city then commissioned a forty-five-member committee that eventually developed a plan for the site that called for mixed-use development, preservation of the historic district with its Rhineland-style castle as a winery and commercial center, and the use of 191 acres as a shoreline park.

Like many former military sites biding time until the remediation concludes, Point Molate's future was regularly in flux. Without a clear vision to guide redevelopment, the plans fell victim to the political winds of the day, including, at one point, plans for a $1 billion Las Vegas–scale casino. This particular plan, however, did not emerge from a community-based process. It came from behind closed doors. The city's Public Works director, Rich McCoy, even made a trip with the developer to Las Vegas to experience firsthand the benefits of casino gambling and came back impressed. In response to the request for proposals for developing the site (which did not mention a casino), a developer with ties to the casino industry known as Upstream Point Molate submitted a plan that also conveniently left out the casino component and kept the citizens in the dark as long as possible (Simerman 2010).

With its promise of seventeen thousand jobs and $20 million in annual tax revenue, the idea of a casino did have some traction in Richmond, which at the time suffered from an unemployment rate of nearly 20 percent (Shih 2010). In an ultimately unsuccessful attempt to gain passage of the plan, the developer effectively bought off opponents. Because the project depended on a federally recognized Native American tribe for land use approvals, the development team, which included former Secretary of Defense Richard Cohen, found a small band of Native Americans (112 members) from distant Mendocino County to meet his criteria. But Contra Costa County's own hired expert called this association duplicitous and intellectually bankrupt (Simerman 2010). Yet the promise of $12 million a year into the county's coffers swung county leaders around to support the project. Likewise, the developer promised environmental groups $48 million if they would drop litigation, which they did (2010). This strategy is not uncommon in the annals of base reuse. At Point Molate, after publication of the proposal, tension and anger built up over all the shenanigans until a legally required ballot measure in support of the casino failed. The public finally had a chance to weigh in and was not impressed. Nathanial Bates lost to the incumbent and a plan for preservation and parks has now slowly moved forward. The gamble for the casino came up empty, and redevelopment plans remain in flux but still include a component of mixed use, which, like the fog of war, is hard to see through and constantly shifting. Mixed use solutions rely on "market conditions" and how well any given configuration of uses "pencils out" to the interested development teams.

The Fog of Mixed Use

Mare Island Naval Shipyard

(1854–1996, 4,351 acres). This sizable island was home to a naval shipyard that at one point serviced the nation's nuclear submarine fleet as well as a military hospital and supporting functions. In 1850, President Fillmore declared the island a government reservation, which led to the construction of what would become the Navy's largest shipyard west of the Mississippi (McCloud 1996). Between 1854 and 1970, the shipyard produced an astonishing 512 ships (Cooper 2002), including the battleship USS *California*. The shipyard was also the "largest single industrial plant west of the Mississippi, representing $100 million in investment" (Thoreson 1939, 1). Despite all of these records, the Navy determined that the shipyard was excess to its needs and closed the site in 1996.

The Lennar Corporation, which is also developing Hunters Point and is part of the Treasure Island development team, has the right to develop a portion of the island into a mixed-use district of 1,400 homes and commercial space. Although some of the site's historic buildings have been renovated and repurposed, the goal of a thriving mixed-use district remains elusive. Nearly twenty years after closure, the proposed housing is still in the planning stages and the bulk of the site's industrial space has yet to find profitable tenants.

Concord Naval Weapons Station

(1944–2007, 12,800 acres). Like that at Mare Island, redevelopment at the Concord Naval Weapons Station is largely on hold. Separated by rolling hills and a state highway, this base actually had two areas—the Tidal Area (7,630 acres) that fronts Suisun Bay, referred to as Port Chicago, and the Inland Area (5,170 acres) within the City of Concord in San Francisco's East Bay. For many years, the Navy stored powerful munitions of all types and sizes in the Inland Area and shipped them out through the Tidal Area. The latter was the site of the deadly 1944 Port Chicago explosion that killed 320 men, including two hundred African Americans, while they were loading a Navy ship with ammunition (Allen 2006). The incident highlighted the racial injustices found in the nation's military force during World War II (see Arbona, this volume). Segregation was the norm, and at Port Chicago supervisors frequently assigned the most dangerous duties to the African American units. The US Army now operates the Tidal Area, and the Inland Area—vacated by the Navy in 2007—is still up for grabs. But redevelopment must follow the community's vision for the site, which emerged out of a participatory process that included numerous public workshops and resulted in a vision to create a series of clustered, mixed-use villages with more than 12,000 homes, 6.2 million square feet of commercial space, and 2,800 acres of parks and open space all connected by public transit (DOD 2009) (Figure 8.4).

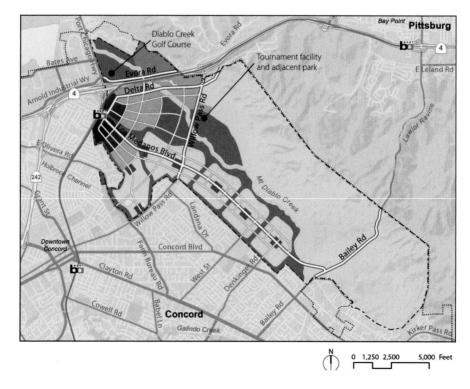

FIGURE 8.4   Plan for reuse of Concord Naval Weapons Station, 2008, calls for "clustered, mixed-use villages" on the southwest portion of the site. The northwest portion will remain open space. Courtesy of the City of Concord.

In a rare moment of introspection regarding a BRAC process, the community identified key lessons learned including the primacy through the process of transparency as well as consistency throughout the process (DOD 2009). But this desire for a mixed-use district slowed redevelopment considerably. If all goes according to plan, proponents do not expect completion until 2030.

Alameda Naval Air Station

(1931–1997, 1,526 acres). Another Bay Area installation that pinned its hopes on becoming a mixed-use mecca is the Alameda Naval Air Station. Located near the heart of the Bay Area on a beautiful waterfront site mostly reclaimed from the bay through extensive fill operations starting in the 1890s, Alameda Naval Air Station started life as a small city-owned airfield and then transitioned to an Army Air Corps facility in 1931 (Global Security, n.d.). The site continued to grow in support of World War II, at which point the Navy took command and used the air station as a home to a variety of air units that roamed the Pacific theater, including aircraft carrier based units and seaplanes (Rhodes 1955). By the time of closure, the air station employed eighteen thousand people, making it the largest single employer in Alameda.

After years of bickering about responsibility for environmental cleanup, the Navy finally agreed to transfer the land to the City of Alameda for free and complete the cleanup in 2011 (Alameda Naval Air Museum, n.d.). Opposition to closure was intense but to no avail. Given the inevitability of closure, not one but two community groups formed to develop a reuse vision for the site. The City of Alameda established the Alameda Base Reuse Advisory Group, and Congressman Ron Dellums commissioned the East Bay Conversion and Reinvestment Commission with a goal of "outlining how a community should effectively close a base" (Global Security, n.d.). Given that most of the land still sits vacant nearly twenty years after closure, Dellums' ambitious target has been missed by a wide margin. Part of the problem was that there was never a clear vision for reuse. Plans were prepared. Speeches were made. Hopes were raised. But in the end, the lack of clarity and purpose undermined the collective efforts of competing agencies and organizations.

Plans for Alameda Point (the new name of the site) have languished. The Navy certainly deserves some of the blame. It took the agency fourteen years to turn over title to Alameda because of constant "dickering over price" (Jones 2011a). After the reuse plans changed from a primary focus on residential use to a more balanced approach with industrial and commercial development, the Navy decided to hand over the land for nothing according to William Carsillo, the Navy's real estate consultant on the project (2011b). In the meantime, the vacant airstrip and abandoned and decaying buildings have served as backdrops for several Hollywood movies, including the *Matrix Reloaded*. In fact, using old bases for movies has been a fairly common occurrence in the Bay Area (Ackley 1997).

Oak Knoll Naval Hospital

(1942–1996, 334 acres). Amid cries of joy (from the developer) and tears of sorrow (from former staff), the 597-bed, eleven-story tower that was Oak Knoll Naval Hospital imploded on April 8, 2011. Eight hundred pounds of dynamite brought down the hospital, which was built in 1965, in just ten seconds to make room for a new mixed-use development (Jones 2011a). But the hospital was not the only building in the way of the ambitious plan. More than 130 buildings built by the Navy to heal soldiers returning from the Pacific occupied the hillside site, including staff homes, a shopping center, a library, and a chapel (California State Military Museum 2008). The City of Oakland led the effort to develop the original reuse plan, but the Navy rejected Oakland's plans and sold 167 acres of the site to a partnership between SunCal and Lehman Brothers for $100 million (Jones 2012). The developer's plans included rehabilitation of a historic structure, fifty acres of parks and open space (including restoration of Rifle Creek, which runs through the heart of the site), a new mixed-use village center, and up to 960 homes in a variety of configurations from large-lot detached homes to small row houses (Torres 2014). The economic collapse in 2008 led to the bankruptcy

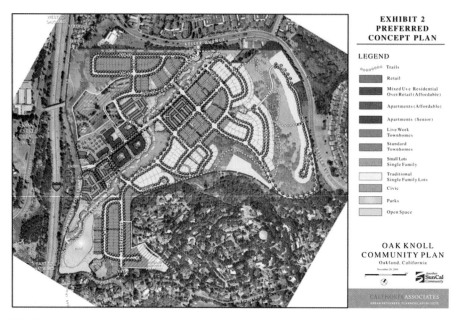

FIGURE 8.5   Oak Knoll master plan, 2006. Courtesy of Calthorpe Associates.

of Lehman Brothers, and SunCal abandoned the property to bankruptcy court. After a period of neglect, SunCal bought the property a second time for roughly $76 million (2014). Calthorpe Associates, an award-winning urban design firm, facilitated a public process and produced a plan following a simple vision, "to create a new community while taking advantage of the natural beauty of the varied topography and terrain of the area in which it is located" (City of Oakland 2007, 8) (Figure 8.5).

Moffett Field

(1930–1994, 1,000 acres). A massive blimp hangar marks Moffett Field and is a landmark for the entire South Bay (Figure 8.6). It can be seen from miles around and is a reminder of the area's military origins. Google recently acquired the rights from NASA and the GSA to renovate and use historic Hangar 1 for its private fleet of aircraft. The hangar's original purpose was to support the Navy's largest airship base on the West Coast, which was built on land in Sunnyvale purchased by the community (at a cost of $467,000) and sold for $1 to the military for use as a military base (Lardinois 2014).

Located in the South Bay, Moffett Field served a variety of air units, including dirigibles, fighters, bombers, and research planes. The field and its massive hangar could support the largest airship of the 1930s—the USS *Macon*, a 785-foot lighter-than-air dirigible. After a spectacular crash in 1935, the Navy transferred Moffett Field to the new Army Air Corps (predecessor to the US Air Force) but then retook control after the Pearl Harbor attack in 1941. The field consisted of a seven-thousand-foot runway, 1.14 million square yards of apron space, housing for nearly three thousand soldiers and airmen, and the Ames Aeronautical Laboratory, which eventually became part of NASA (Barista 2003). In 1995, the field closed and was transferred to NASA as a federal airfield now used for research purposes and public-private partnerships such as the Google venture.

NASA developed a master plan that intends to convert the field into the NASA Research Park, "a shared-use research and development campus in the heart of California's Silicon Valley" (Barista 2003, 1). The master plan calls for redevelopment of 234 acres to support new technologies in association with academia, industry, nonprofits, and government agencies. Carnegie Mellon University, for instance, signed a fifteen-year lease for its High Dependability Computing Consortium as well as space for classes in robotics and information technology (Barista 2003). The plan also calls for construction of homes for five thousand employees and students on a ninety-six-acre parcel, which will be a first for NASA and important given the chronic housing shortfall in the area. The plan also converted the historic hangar into a museum showcasing NASA accomplishments, but that plan has been superseded by Google's plan to reuse the hangar for its own purposes (Lardinois 2014). The change was lauded by the GSA director, Dan Tangherlini,

FIGURE 8.6   Hangar 1 at Moffett Field, 1933. Photo: US Navy. Courtesy of Moffett Field Museum.

who noted that "NASA's partnership with the private sector will allow the agency to restore this treasure for more efficient use" (Lardinois 2014, 1). This proposed reuse of Hangar 1 was not universally admired. John M. Simpson, project director for Consumer Watchdog, noted that Google's flight operations routinely get tax cuts on the jet fuel it purchases at a discount from the government, and now letting them use the historic hangar is "like giving the keys to your car to the guy who has been siphoning gas from your tank. It is unfairly rewarding unethical and wrongful behavior. . . . These Google guys seem to think they can do whatever they want and get away with it—and it's beginning to look like that is true" (Lardinois 2014, 1).

In each of these cases, the reliance on a complex mixed-use solution lengthened the process of reuse considerably. When reuse plans rely on private developers for their implementation of not only the infrastructure but also the actual buildings, the work must necessarily wait for the moment these same developers think is right for development. The wait may be much longer than the affected communities initially envision. Ultimately the approach may be the right one for these former bases, but the long timeline for redevelopment dampened the initial promises of politicians and developers. All of these plans are complex real estate transactions that are neither simple to execute nor easy to fund. If time is of no concern, a reactive approach may be reasonable. If, however, communities want to avoid years of delay and regular reassessments of the use mix, simpler solutions may be in order.

Simple and Consistent Plans

Hamilton Air Force Base

(1930–1988, closed as an Air Force Base in 1976, 2,184 acres). This former Air Force base is a case study in simple solutions. With the high housing costs of Marin County, the reuse plans for Hamilton Air Force Base were straightforward: build as much infill housing as possible and preserve a few key historic structures. For many years, the base served as a headquarters for numerous Air Force commands and at one point supported two squadrons of fighter-interceptors and could support multiple bomber squadrons (Chappell 1998). By 1940, it was described as "looking more like a modern residential suburb of Spanish California homes than the Army's pursuit base for northern California" (2). This clarity of the original plan is in part what helped expedite reuse planning. Rather than start from a blank slate, reuse planners just doubled down on what Hamilton was best known for—its lovely housing and great location.

The durable concrete structures with their solid walls and red tile roofs did obscure the fact that it was a military base. By World War II, with its hangars, office buildings, barracks, dining halls, warehouses, schools, hospital, and family housing, Hamilton supported a military population of twenty thousand (Newman 2001), which made it one of the largest air bases in the United States. Its two runways, including an eight-thousand-foot main runway, could support most aircraft in the military's inventory. But after the Cold War ended, the DOD no longer needed the base. Now, when viewed from ten thousand feet, it seems as if the base's massive airfield never existed. In the spring of 2014, engineers breached dykes built in the 1930s to separate the bay from the base to flood the airfield and munitions storage area so the land could revert to bay marshland. Developers converted the remaining original buildings to a variety of uses, including "senior housing, a homeless shelter, and an arts center" (2). Additionally, nine original hangars with their elegant bow trusses and art deco details as well as the control tower have been renovated and converted into a business park. The bulk of the base returned to open space in the form of the tidal wetlands and estuaries, and a tight-knit collection of nearly one thousand new homes filled the gaps between the existing historic buildings.

Oakland Army Base

(1941–1999, 430 acres). The Oakland Army Base is another example of a clear and simple reuse plan that is consistent with former uses on the site. The base was an industrial site and it will continue to be an industrial site. Built between 1941 and 1946 to expand the cargo capacity of San Francisco's Fort Mason, the Oakland Army Base managed cargo transfer into the Pacific from the western United States. Its waterfront location at the western edge of Oakland and its ready access to railheads and loading docks made it a premier cargo handling facility for the military. During World War II's four most active years, 8.5 million tons of cargo passed through the base. During the Korean War's three years, 7.2 million tons of cargo transited the base. During Vietnam, it was the largest military port complex in the world (California State Military Museum 2016). Many competing ideas for reuse surfaced after closure, which eliminated more than seven thousand jobs, but the enduring strategy was to use most of the land for expansion of the Port of Oakland. Even with this clear mission, it still took nearly fourteen years from the closure before developers broke ground on a $1.2 billion reconstruction of the site in support of a cargo and logistics center that may eventually support 1,800 permanent workers (Tavares 2013). The use as an industrial area has been largely free of controversy and is consistent with the former use of the site. But the net job loss is a significant concern for Oakland, given an unemployment rate that has approached 45 percent in West Oakland. Although many scholars argue that base closures result in a net economic gain (Gross 1990; Price 1994), it has certainly not been the case for Oakland, which lost not only the Army Base but also Alameda Naval Air Station and Oak Knoll Naval Medical facility for a combined job loss of nearly thirty thousand.

When existing uses are disparate enough that a clear and simple reuse plan based on previous uses may not be possible, another approach exists that can expedite reuse. The trio of bases that eventually became part of the Golden Gate National Recreation Area illustrate the power of converting old bases to parks and associated uses.

The Power of Parkland

The Presidio

(1776–1994, 1,480 acres). The Presidio, located at the base of the Golden Gate, served military purposes since its founding by the Spanish in 1776. For the Spanish Empire, the original purpose was to "meet the Russian threat," but Eric Blind notes, "ambitious bureaucrats and eager missionaries pressured the Viceroy (Antonio) Bucareli to quickly expand into the San Francisco Bay area" and the Presidio was needed to defend their interests, including six missions, two civil communities, and numerous ranches and farming outposts (2004, 1). This serves as an early example of the military-industrial complex at work. The Mexican Army took over the area and held the Presidio between 1822 and 1846. In 1846, the US Army captured the Presidio and operated it as a major military base until its closure in 1994. For the Army, the Presidio served primarily as an administrative headquarters as well as the home to the Letterman Army Hospital. On December 7, 1941, after the Japanese attack on Pearl Harbor, military leaders designated the Presidio as the Western Defense Command center and it served as a staging area in support of operations in the Pacific theater (Benton-Short 1998).

Even though it was an active base at the time, in 1972, as part of the enabling legislation that established the Golden Gate National Recreation Area, all 1,480 acres of the Presidio fell entirely within the boundaries of the new urban park. The 1989 BRAC round called for the closure of the Presidio, and the Army agreed to transfer the land and nearly 900 buildings to the National Park Service in 1994 (National Recreation and Park Association 1997). At the time of listing for closure, the Presidio, which is now a National Historic Landmark, was—with its 5,300 employees—the third largest employer in San Francisco (Price 1994). The Presidio was a literal "city within a city" that had "more than 800 buildings, including an officers' club, a bowling alley, a commissary, a research hospital, warehouses, residences, a movie theater, horse stables, a museum, and a golf course" (Benton-Short 1998, 4) (Figure 8.7).

Like many communities forced to accept base closure, some in the local area reacted with "outrage, accompanied by denial, primarily based on economic factors" (Benton-Short 1998, 87). But others met the announcement with "elation, because the Presidio would finally be transformed into the long-anticipated park within the Golden Gate National Recreation Area" (Benton-Short 1998, 87). To address the economic concerns, Congress created the Presidio Trust in 1996, a federal corporation charged with managing the Presidio so that it would be fiscally self-sustaining (a milestone achieved in 2013). So far, the effort is going well. Randolph Delehanty reports that about "2,700 people now live in some 1,100 units of former military housing. Approximately 4,000 people work for a mix of some 200 for-profit and nonprofit organizations in rehabilitated Army buildings" (2013, 45). Since assuming management of the Presidio in 1998, the Trust and its

FIGURE 8.7   Northwestern tip of the Presidio abuts the Golden Gate Bridge and welcomes commuters from Marin County into a park-like setting with Spanish-colonial architecture and ample greenery. Courtesy of Sasaki Associates.

partners have transformed nearly half of the Army's buildings and funneled over $416 million into preservation and development projects (Presidio Trust 2012). The Presidio offers many lessons in base reuse planning but perhaps the most important one is the necessity of having a clear, community-based vision to guide redevelopment.

Fort Mason

(1797–1976, 68.5 acres). Located just east of the Presidio, Fort Mason served many purposes until its closure in 1976. Through the nineteenth century, Fort Mason served primarily as a coastal defense site defending what President Grover Cleveland considered the second most important harbor in the United States (after New York). During the Great Depression, Fort Mason benefited from several Works Progress Administration projects that positioned the base for a significant role in World War II. Throughout the war, the base functioned as a transport and administrative headquarters as well as an industrial base due to its three large docks and extensive warehouses. Like Naval Station Treasure Island, Fort Mason served as a point of embarkation. During the war, 1.5 million soldiers transited through Fort Mason en route to the Pacific theater (Rafkin 2012). Combined, both bases supported the transit of six million soldiers, sailors, Marines, and airmen. This was movement of men and material on an historic scale. Following the war, the "dominance of airpower and air transportation rendered the once state-of-the-art shipping facilities at Fort Mason obsolete. By the 1960s, Fort Mason had become a satellite facility to the more spacious Oakland Army Base" (Rafkin 2012, 4). The 1972 law authorizing the Golden Gate National Recreation Area (GGNRA) allowed Fort Mason to become one of the first pieces in this plan for the country's first urban national park.

Fort Baker

(1850–2002, 335 acres). Located across from the Presidio and Fort Mason in Marin County, Fort Baker served primarily as a headquarters garrison for units defending the Bay Area first with massive batteries and then with Nike guided missiles. With technology that led to iron-clad naval ships and armor-piercing artillery in the late nineteenth century, and the onset of the Spanish-American War in 1898, the coastal protection provided by Fort Baker was critical in the defense of the Bay Area prior to World War I. This strategically important site compelled President Millard Fillmore in 1850 to assign the land to defensive purposes (National Park Service 2005) (Figure 8.8).

With the onset of World War II and the arrival of Japanese submarines prowling outside the Golden Gate, Fort Baker remained a useful installation (National Park Service 2005). But, as the Pacific War moved west, the need for the type of coastal defense provided by Fort Baker disappeared. Starting in 1967 and ending in 2002, the Army transferred portions of Fort Baker to the National Park Service, fulfilling a vision of Fort Baker becoming a key part of the GGNRA's 2,279 acres of former military land in Marin County. With the GGNRA's other sites, according to the National Park Service, it is the "country's largest collection of military installations and fortifications dating from 1776 through the Cold War."

FIGURE 8.8 Fort Baker, showing the parade ground defined by officer housing on the left and enlisted barracks on the right, circa 1925. Industrial area is at center right. National Park Service.

The Primacy of the Vision

In these examples, an underlying strategy that helped advance some base reuse plans over others centered on the primacy of a clear planning vision tied to the former use of the base and its socio-cultural context. When it comes to planning for base reuse, the biblical saying that "Where there is no vision, the people shall perish" could easily be modified to "Where there is no vision, the plans shall perish." At least in the Bay Area, an obvious conclusion is that communities with clear visions for the reuse of their shuttered bases often found success in redevelopment. Hamilton's clear vision as a residential neighborhood and the Presidio's vision for reuse as a park are perhaps the best examples.

At the Presidio, the aptly titled "Grand Vision" set the stage for successful re-purposing from an Army post to a new type of national park. This Grand Vision, however, was more about purpose and less about buildings. In fact, as Lisa Benton-Short notes, the transformation was in a change of meaning and purpose (from post to park) rather than dramatic changes in the landscape, infrastructure, or buildings (1998). The participation of the public was instrumental in the creation of this vision. Although the outcome was a product (a master plan), the process was equally if not more important. Planners encouraged participants in the process to envision the Presidio as it could be and encouraged them to define the role and meaning of an urban national park (Benton-Short 1998). There were clearly challenges, including the cost of maintaining this new type of park. But creative solutions emerged from the collaborative process, including the idea of eventual self-funding through the Presidio Trust, a federal corporation charged with securing income from the Presidio's many assets and covering expenses for its upkeep. But remarkably, "no group or individual filed a lawsuit challenging the Presidio Plan (which is) a testament to the strong sense of community enthusiasm for the vision and concepts that had emerged during the planning process" (Benton-Short 1998, 111). The process brought the public into the discussion through a series of public workshops where participants outlined their ideas for the post's redevelopment. This outcome supports Michaela Dodge's argument that engagement with local communities in the United States will be "one of the keys to a successful evaluation and implementation of any future military installation decision" (2013, 4).

A primary goal of the vision for the Golden Gate National Recreation Area, which includes the Presidio, Fort Mason, and Fort Baker, was to bring the "park to the people" (Fort Mason Center 2014; Hoke and Foulds 2004). As Benton-Short argues, this concept, which was a unifying theme in the Presidio's visioning process, can be seen as an act of social justice that benefited significantly more people than just converting the site to housing or commercial development (1998). Congress also supported the concept with federal legislation that called for transferring unneeded DOD land in San Francisco to the Department of Interior for national park purposes (Benton-Short 1998). In the Presidio, this meant that the six-hundred-acre Presidio Forest would be open to the public. At Fort Mason, this meant that acres of asphalt and vacant land would be converted not to active recreation areas (which benefit the few who can reserve play times) but to landscaped open spaces like the Great Meadow with "great expanses of lawn and meandering walkways" (Hoke and Foulds 2004). In fact, during the more than four hundred workshops and meetings that were part of the visioning process for Fort Mason, the "findings revealed the diverse park constituents had surprisingly similar requests. Specific recreation amenities such as baseball fields and basketball courts were far less crucial than access to open space" (Hoke and Foulds 2004, 157). This is an important lesson for Naval Station Treasure Island planners. Rather then build open spaces based on the needs of specific uses, they could have considered more flexible approaches to create simple, easily accessible parks that can be used for multiple purposes.

Finally, the best visions, as represented by the Presidio, are oftentimes evolutionary, not revolutionary. The idea of the Presidio as a park did not materialize out of thin air in the 1990s (the Park Service released its Grand Vision in 1993). As Benton-Short notes, it evolved from the urban park movement of the late 1800s that led to landscape improvements across the post, the history of the open post (almost anyone could access the Presidio during its heyday as an Army post), the increased access with the opening of the Golden Gate Bridge and coastal scenic drives, and federal legislation in the 1970s that protected the Presidio from future development even if the Army left (1998).

Hunters Point, the shuttered shipyard offers a cautionary note. Unlike the Presidio, there was never a clear vision for the reuse of this massive industrial site. At various stages, alternatives called for a dizzying array of combinations that at some point included a new football stadium for the San Francisco 49ers, up to 4,275 residential units, 245 acres of parks, up to five million square feet of research and development space, 125,000 square feet of retail space, and a three-hundred-slip marina. Without a clear vision to follow, these various schemes floundered for years. In fact, the 49ers, a team that waited patiently for decades to win five Super Bowls under Joe Montana and Steve Young, finally gave up on the city and moved to Santa Clara into a gleaming new stadium next to an amusement park.

Alameda Naval Air Station's transformation is another sad tale. As Carolyn Jones notes, "Alameda's gone through two developers, a few high-ranking city officials, and a bevy of lawsuits in its efforts to create a utopian mash of housing, retail, offices, and parks at Alameda Point" (2011b, 2). Likewise, the plans for a massive casino at Point Molate in Richmond flamed out when the citizens finally weighed in using the ballot box. They rejected the plan created behind closed doors by politicians, developers, and a former secretary of defense.

When it comes to developing planning visions for reusing retired military installations, developers like SunCal's Pat Keliher (SunCal is an Orange County developer that tried to redevelop several Bay Area bases) argue that "developers need more flexibility to adapt to market conditions" (SunCal 2011, 2). But that flexibility may undermine a community's vision for the site. David Price argues that "to achieve sustainability in communities, cities and regions it is essential that the planning process address the factors of citizen involvement and sense of place" (1994, 10). Of course, when there is no clear vision, all bets are off and, consequently, as this essay shows, most development is likely off as well.

Following the end of the Cold War, the Bay Area rapidly transformed itself from a military juggernaut to a haven for high-tech industries. Apple, HP, Google, and Adobe replaced the Army, Navy, Air Force, and Marines as significant employers in the area. Military bases across the region closed down amid high hopes for a more peaceful world and optimism about transformations that could convert each installation's infrastructure and locational advantages into a jackpot of jobs and revenue for the host communities. Nearly two decades after that last round of Base Realignment and Closure concluded by gutting the Bay Area of its military landscape, these hopes remain largely unfulfilled. The agonizingly slow process of transformation has left most of the shuttered bases in an eerie state of limbo. Without a clear vision supported by a broad community consensus and built through a transparent and democratic process, the redevelopment of many of these former bases may remain a distant dream. Repurposing military installations is a slow and tedious process. As Jones argues,

> Each of these reuse projects has its own tale of failure. Some, like Mare Island, are casualties of the recession. Others are mired in toxic sludge, left over from decades of heavy industrial use. Some, like Point Molate, are victims of shifting political climates. Most are some combination thereof. (2011b, 2)

Although this discussion privileges planning, certainly other factors are at work in the base reuse equation, from local politics to global economic conditions. Nevertheless, the role of a clear and simple vision anchored to the specifics of each base's complex context and supported by a proactive plan cannot be underestimated. Moreover, though the geographic advantages of sites as compelling as Treasure Island, Alameda Point, and Hunters Point would seem to warrant rapid redevelopment, the reality has been a bit more nuanced. When compelling geography, consistency with previous uses, and clarity of vision work together, base reuse plans tend to succeed. For example, the Oakland Army base was contiguous with the Port of Oakland, along rail networks, and adjacent to highways, so it was quite logical to expand into the port. The Presidio was already part of the GGNRA in 1972 and could therefore be converted to parks and open space. Certain installations did have a locational logic based on adjacencies where new uses could be more fluidly established. As this volume shows, what is unique about Treasure Island is its location at the center of the Bay Area, its adjacency to the Bay Bridge, and its potential to be a new city that in many ways could mirror the compact, gridded morphology of San Francisco. But the tendency to view the site as a tabula rasa has added layers of complexity and inconsistency that have undermined redevelopment proposals.

The four lessons from the Bay Area's legacy of military bases apply directly to Treasure Island's future. First, the island's well-known contamination presents substantial hurdles for any future development and especially for the creation of safe neighborhoods and useable parks. The best strategy is to approach the situation with honest transparency and a sizable contingency. Current and future residents need to know the context within which they are living, and development teams need to have the funding and flexibility to remediate the land in an effective and efficient manner. Arguments about liability could derail the entire plan. Second, the fog of mixed use should not blind planners and developers to a romantic notion of a new urbanist community set in the middle of the bay. Although the principles of horizontal and vertical mixed use districts are sound, the complexities they add to financing, permitting, and leasing are profound. As it stands, the Treasure Island Master Plan envisions a large mixed-use district on the island's southern edge. Developers should be prepared for this district to evolve much more slowly than the more straightforward residential districts. Third, planners may want to reconsider the 362-page master plan (see TIDA 2011) and look for ways to streamline the document and the planning process. Successful base reuse programs leveraged simple and consistent plans. Fourth, the power of parkland cannot be underestimated. For Treasure Island, this means staying true to the open space morphology in the master plan. The planned network of seven neighborhood parks, three linear parks, open "wilds," urban agricultural land, and a sizable sports park reflect an appropriate prioritization of varied and useable open spaces. However, as costs inevitably increase and schedules slip, developers will be tempted to cut back on these non-revenue-generating spaces. Although the plan dedicates a big chunk of the island to open space, the location and use appears secondary to the goal of commercial development, the quantity of which has only grown because of rising project costs owing to environmental remediation, seismic instability and imminent sea-level rise (see Stehlin, this volume). Finally, the importance of a clear and compelling vision that can drive appropriate development is a must for any successful base reuse. For Treasure Island, one of the most important findings from previous reuse and conversions is that the vision for redevelopment needs to be specific and clear yet flexible enough to accommodate an unknown future. The 2011 Treasure Island plan has such a vision. It is broad yet specific and is written in a way that helps readers envision the actual space. However, it does slip into planning jargon in some spots with references to "world-class neighborhoods and "innovative design." These terms are not well defined and leave too much room for interpretation. Nevertheless, the vision and the plan's supporting principles establish a strong foundation that can guide a new future for the worn-out island.

Following a long legacy of major investment in fifteen military bases, before and after World War II, the US government faced major base closures at the end of the Cold War. The process of closure and redevelopment has been uneven at best, ranging from success stories, such as the Presidio, to unsuccessful and prolonged efforts such as Naval Station Treasure Island. One of the key ingredients of successful reuse is a collective vision. Bases that have had a thoughtful, community-oriented process (such as the Presidio) have succeeded in reimagining themselves, whereas others have failed. Although Naval Station Treasure Island has its own context, it must be seen as a part of a larger phenomenon of military base closure and reuse. The planning goals for Naval Station Treasure Island and the accompanying master plan promise a gleaming new city in place of a worn-out military base. Planners hope its glass and steel towers, trendy cafes, and manicured parks will attract a new type of warrior—the Silicon Valley type with a tablet rather than an M16. Only time will tell whether this vision will actually materialize in the real world.

References

Ackley, Laura. 1997. "Islands in the Limelight." *Variety,* June 30.

Alameda Naval Air Museum. n.d. "History of Naval Aviation Depot Alameda." http://alamedanavalairmuseum.org/history/nadep-history/.

Allen, Robert L. 2006. The Port Chicago Mutiny. Berkeley, CA: Heyday Books.

Barista, Dave. 2003. "NASA has big plans for historic Moffett Field." *Building Design & Construction,* March. http://www.bdcnetwork.com/nasa-has-big-plans-historic-moffett-field.

Benton-Short, Lisa M. 1998. *The Presidio: From Army Post to National Park.* Boston, MA: Northeastern University.

Blind, Eric. 2004. "El Presidio De San Francisco: At the Edge of Empire." *Historical Archaeology* 38, no. 3:135–149.

California State Military Museum. 2008. "Historic California Posts, Stations, and Airfields: Naval Regional Medical Center." http://www/military,useum.org/navhosppakland.html.

———. 2016. "Oakland Army Base." Museum.org, February 16. http://www.militarymuseum.org/OaklandArmyBase.html.

Chappell, Gordon. 1998. "Hamilton Air Force Base." *Historic California Posts, Camps, Stations and Airfields.* http://www.militarymuseum.org/HamiltonAFB.html.

Chatfield-Taylor, Joan. 1988. "San Francisco's Military Base with Scenery." *New York Times,* October 16.

City of Concord. 2014. "Concord Selects Four Firms to Compete for CNWS Master Developer." News Release, June 30. http://www.ci.concord.ca.us/about/citynews/releases/2014/06_13_2014.asp.

City of Oakland. 2007. "Oak Knoll Mixed Use Community Plan Project Environmental Checklist." http://www.oakknollcoalition.org/documents/.

City of Richmond, California. n.d. "Point Molate." http://www.ci.richmond.ca.us/270/Point-Molate.

Cooper, David C. 2002. "Army Reserve Engineers Help Convert Base." *Army Reserve Magazine,* April.

Delehanty, Randolph. 2013. *Crown Jewels: Five Great National Parks around the World and the Challenges They Face.* Washington, DC: American Alliance of Museums Press.

Dodge, Michaela. 2013. "Beyond BRAC: Global Defense Infrastructure for the 21st Century." *States News Service,* May 3.

Elliot, Jeff. 1996. "Treasure Island Is 'Oil-Soaked Sponge,' Suit Claims." *Albion Monitor,* March 10.

Fort Mason Center. 2014. "Fort Mason Center, San Francisco." *Fort Mason Center for Arts and Culture.* https://fortmason.org/about/.

Global Security. n.d. "Alameda Point." http://www.globalsecurity.org/military/facility/alameda.htm.

Gross, Jane. 1990. "Base Closings Seen as Opportunity inside Problem." *New York Times,* February 4. http://www.nytimes.com/1990/02/04/us/base-closings-seen-as-opportunity-inside-problem.html.

Hoke, Amy, and H. Eliot Foulds. 2004. *Cultural Landscape Report for Fort Mason, Golden Gate National Recreation Area.* Brookline, MA: Olmsted Center for Landscape Preservation.

Jones, Carolyn. 2011a. "Oakland Naval Hospital Demolished with a Bang." *SFGate,* April 8. http://www.sfgate.com/bayarea/article/Oakland-Naval-Hospital-demolished-with-a-bang-2376304.php.

———. 2011b. "Ex-Navy Bases in Bay Area Remain Stuck in Limbo." *SFGate,* April 18. http://www.sfgate.com/news/article/Ex-Navy-bases-in-Bay-Area-remain-stuck-in-limbo-2375035.php.

———. 2012. "Judge's Ruling Makes Oak Knoll's Future a Mystery." *SFGate,* March 10. http://www.sfgate.com/bayarea/article/Judge-s-ruling-makes-Oak-Knoll-s-future-a-mystery-3407501.php.

Lardinois, Frederic. 2014. "Google Wins Right to Lease Moffett Field, Will Restore Hangar One." *TechCrunch,* February 10. https://techcrunch.com/2014/02/10/google-wins-right-to-lease-moffett-field-will-restore-hangar-one/.

McCloud, John. 1996. "Real Estate: A California City Is Attracting Short-Term Leases to a Naval Shipyard while It Works on a Long-Term Plan." *New York Times,* January 31. http://www.nytimes.com/1996/01/31/business/real-estate-california-city-attracting-short-term-leases-naval-shipyard-while-it.html.

National Park Service. 2005. *Cultural Landscape Report for Fort Baker, Golden Gate National Recreation Area: Fort Baker, Barry and Cronkhite Historic District, Marin County, California.* San Francisco: US Department of the Interior.

National Recreation and Park Association. 1997. "The Presidio—From Post to Park." Vol. 32, no. 12 (December).

Newman, Morris. 2001. "Hundreds of Homes Rise at Ex-Air Base in Bay Area." *New York Times,* February 11. http://www.nytimes.com/2001/02/11/realestate/hundreds-of-homes-rise-at-ex-air-base-in-bay-area.html.

Noble, Carl, James Hense, and Laura Verklan. 2011. "Balestrino/Hunters Point." *Forgotten Planet.* Discovery Channel.

Presidio Trust. 1987. "National Parks: Significant Progress Made in Preserving the Presidio and Attaining Financial Self-Sufficiency." Report No. GAO-02–87. Washington, DC: General Accounting Office. http://www.gao.gov/assets/240/232796.pdf.

———. 2012. "Performance and Accountability Report." San Francisco: Presidio Trust.

Price, David T. 1994. "Planning and the Sense of Place." Thesis, University of Oregon.

Rafkin, Louise. 2012. "Youth Hostel: Fort Mason, San Francisco." *New York Times,* March 18.

Rhodes, George. 1955. "Vast Ring of Bases Keeps Up Constant Vigil against Attack." *S.F. Call-Bulletin*, October 10. *Virtual Museum of the City of San Francisco.* http://www.sfmuseum.org/hist8/bases.html.

San Francisco News. 1942. "Treasure Island Accord" March 19, 1942. Virtual Museum of the City of San Francisco. http://www.sfmuseum.org/hist9/tilease.html.

San Francisco Redevelopment Agency. 1996. *Naval Station Treasure Island Reuse Plan.* City and County of San Francisco.

Shih, Gerry. 2010. "Race for Richmond Mayor Focuses on Jobs, Casino and Class." *New York Times,* September 9. http://www.nytimes.com/2010/09/10/us/10bcrichmond.html.

Simerman, John. 2010. "The Play on Point Molate." *Contra Costa Times,* October 23.

SunCal. 2011. "Former Oak Knoll U.S. Naval Medical Center in Oakland Imploded Using 800 Pounds of Dynamite." *PR Newswire,* April 8. http://www.prnewswire.com/news-releases/former-oak-knoll-us-naval-medical-center-in-oakland-imploded-using-800-pounds-of-dynamite-119494559.html.

Tavares, Steven. 2013. "First Phase of Massive $1.2 Billion Oakland Army Base Project Begins." *East Bay Citizen,* November 3. http://oaklandlocal.com/2013/11/first-phase-of-massive-1-2-billion-oakland-army-base-project-begins-east-bay-citizen/.

Thoreson, L. L. 1939. "Mare Island Where the Pacific Fleet Is Maintained." *Magazine of the Pacific,* June.

Torres, Blanca. 2014. "SunCal Revives Plans for Oakland's Oak Knoll, Buys 167-acre Development Site for the Second Time." *San Francisco Business Times,* May 14.

Treasure Island Development Authority (TIDA). 2011. "Treasure Island and Yerba Buena Island Design for Development." San Francisco: TIDA.

US Department of Defense (DOD). 2009. "Base Realignment and Closure Community Profile." San Francisco: Office of Economic Adjustment.

White, Lisa. 2014. "Concord Naval Weapons Station development plans moving ahead." *Contra Costa Times,* March 5.

Wollenberg, Charles. *Marinship at War: Shipbuilding and Social Change in Wartime Sausalito.* Berkeley, CA: Western Heritage Press, 1990.

THE TREASURE ISLAND–YERBA BUENA ISLAND DEVELOPMENT PROJECT

9. Visions of an Island Ecotopia

TANU SANKALIA

On June 7, 2011, the City and County of San Francisco Board of Supervisors approved a new redevelopment project for Treasure Island (TI) and Yerba Buena Island (YBI) (SFBOS 2011).[1] The news of the approval was welcomed in the local press (Kane 2011), possibly foreshadowing a fourth reinvention of the island following its previous three avatars as airport site, fairground, and naval base. The timing of the approval was contemporaneous with a steadily growing heated public debate surrounding housing demand in San Francisco—a good reason for why the project was approved—and meant that Treasure Island and Yerba Buena Island could be concretely counted as sites for new multifamily homes that would ease some of the pressure on the city's ability to deliver more residential units. Yet, the approval clearly did not signify just another prosaic redevelopment project that would add to the housing stock, but backed the lofty goal of creating "San Francisco's newest and greenest neighborhood"—a veritable new island city of nineteen thousand residents.

The Treasure Island–Yerba Buena Island Development Project (TIDP) is an ambitious proposal for a sweeping reinvention of the islands (Figure 9.1).[2] Its most striking physical feature is the unusual mix of open space and built form: about one hundred acres of densely clustered mid-to-high-rise LEED-certified condo towers laid out on a cleverly skewed grid introduced to counter the chilling ocean winds that sweep the island from the northwest, and three hundred acres of open space—spread across both islands—that contain man-made wetlands, urban farmland, sports fields, and a variety of trails (TIDA 2011a) (Figure 9.2). The project requires massive infrastructure improvements, including new streets, public utilities, community services, the island's own wastewater treatment plant, and berms to guard against sea-level rise. A new intermodal ferry-bus terminal is also proposed, which will complement transportation strategies that discourage car ownership and incentivize transit use (TICD 2011a, 53–62). Other than an existing forty-acre US Department of Labor Job Corps training facility—located in the middle of Treasure Island, which will continue as is—and a few extant historic structures from the Golden Gate International Exposition (GGIE) along with the Coast Guard Station and historic Navy mansions on Yerba Buena Island that will be retained, the majority of land on Treasure Island and Yerba Buena Island (440 acres in all) will be redeveloped.

FIGURE 9.1   Model of the Treasure Island–Yerba Buena Island Development Project. Treasure Island Community Development/Treasure Island Development Authority, 2005–2011. Courtesy of Treasure Island Community Development.

In its current incarnation, the TIDP has won widespread acclaim as a model for future cities. In the lead up to its approval in 2011, the project received strong support from urban policy groups such as San Francisco Planning and Urban Research (SPUR 2011), and urban design critics and experts described it as a triumph in "green" design (Biello 2008; Ward 2008), "enviably sustainable" (Scott 2007), utopian "eco-urbanism" (Jost 2010; King 2010), and, indeed, "ecotopia" (Burres 2008). Building on this initial wave of critical approval, an exhibition held between March 24 and June 23, 2012, at the History Center of the San Francisco Public Library christened the latest vision of TI-YBI as "Magic City 2.0, A Legacy of Big Ideas," celebrating its inclusion among sixteen other Climate Positive communities worldwide in the Clinton Climate Initiative (SFPL 2012).[3] Thus backed by numerous awards and resounding public endorsement,[4] the TIDP can be seen as a persuasive precedent for the redevelopment of decommissioned US military bases and a powerful signifier of a global trend toward large-scale, capital-intensive, sustainable urban developments (see Kim 2013).[5]

Despite the TIDP's positive reception, its planning and design process was contentious and drawn out. After two decades of planning and review (as of 2015), and soon after the environmental impact report (EIR) was approved by San Francisco's supervisors in June 2011, the project was challenged by a California

Environmental Quality Act lawsuit initiated by a group ironically named Citizens for a Sustainable Treasure Island. The lawsuit—subsequently dismissed in an appeals court in June 2014 and by the California Supreme Court in October 2014—claimed that the TIDP will create immitigable traffic congestion on the San Francisco–Oakland Bay Bridge, will not provide adequate amounts of affordable housing (in the context of overall residential development on the island), and will unsatisfactorily deal with extant toxic soils—a legacy of the island's use by the US Navy (Schrieber 2011). Groups such as Arc Ecology (arcecology.org), the Sierra Club, and the SF Public Press (Schlesinger 2010; Hawkes and Yeung 2010) presented strong criticism against the project, citing environmental issues similar to those forwarded by the lawsuit. Charges of cronyism were leveled against former Mayor Willie Brown (1996–2004) in the local press for awarding redevelopment contracts on Treasure Island to close associates (Finnie 2003; Hawkes and Yeung 2010). In the early planning stages of the project, during the late 1990s, an independent review conducted by a San Francisco civil grand jury found the planning and implementation process to be "hampered by concern about the concentration of power, jurisdictional squabbling, political infighting, and poor public relations" (SF Superior Court 1998, 1).

In this essay, I first trace the two-decade-long planning history of the TIDP. Since 1993, following the federal mandate to begin the process of transfer of Treasure Island from the US Navy to the city, the island been through five different scenarios for development, ranging from modest urban design solutions to its most recent grand vision. As I document the project through these transformations, I want to show how Treasure Island, as a disconnected island site with a specific history, was considered exceptional to the norm and therefore subjected to special planning

FIGURE 9.2   Illustrative plan of the Treasure Island–Yerba Buena Island Development Project. Treasure Island Community Development/Treasure Island Development Authority, 2005–2011. Courtesy of Treasure Island Community Development.

processes and state control. Further, I hope to demonstrate that it is within this structure of exceptionalism, and other political economic contingencies, that the project took a turn toward sustainability and the use of spectacular form. Crucial in this regard is how government agencies, planners, developers, urban designers, architects, nonprofit organizations, environmental activists, the popular press, and other urban actors have shaped and contested the proposed Treasure Island development and transformed the project from its unassuming beginnings to a vision for a spectacular island ecotopia.

In this process, two striking significations, or meanings, that the project now embodies form the basis of my discussion. First is the project's ambitious claim of sustainable development. As the development team turned to sustainability to buttress a megaproject such as the TIDP, the unsustainable history of the island—its unstable, low-lying, and contaminated ground—was largely ignored, or, at the least, they believed that it could be overcome by technological means. Moreover, the efforts of certain urban actors who championed sustainable development ideas in the first place were relegated to the margins. The project's creators and promoters presented sustainability as entirely obvious and natural to the design process, which enabled them to ratchet up the quantity of development on the island (see Stehlin, this volume). As a consequence, I argue that not only does sustainability operate as a questionable signifier of techno-environmental progress and a widely accepted justification for capital-intensive development, it also ends up undermining the historical role that local grassroots groups have played in shaping the practice of sustainability.

Second is the project's promise of delivering a sustainable green city or ecotopia. The idea of ecotopia, as Ernest Callenbach so vividly describes in his seminal 1975 novel, was, from its Greek roots, "home place"—far from perfect, not futuristic or science fiction, but a call for fundamental social change. It was, he explained in 2004, to offer a real, hopeful, alternative to "our present corporatist, militarist, ultracompetitive, oil-obsessed course . . . [in] . . . speeded-up, stressed-out, consumption-driven lives ([1975] 2014, 170–171). But the TIDP is far from that because it isn't a radical alternative to present-day systems of property development. In fact, Treasure Island's history (man-made island, world's fair site, military base), its separation from San Francisco, and the absence of a vocal local community point to that strange and removed spatial offspring of society—heterotopia or "other place" (Foucault and Miskowiec 1986). Whereas utopias are imagined places—inconceivable because of the inherent contradiction in the term itself (ideal place, *eu-topia*, and a nonplace, *ou-topia*, from the Greek)—heterotopias are actual places that mirror a society's ambitions. It is in this sense that the TIDP mirrors the utopian ideals of San Francisco, of creating a picture-perfect sustainable high-rise city, but within the structure of a heterotopia—a detached, other place—where the messy and imperfect social and historical processes that constitute the host city are ostensibly kept at bay or magically transcended. Free of such social and historical constraints, city planning and urban design become formal representations—utopias of form—that end up serving as instruments to further capital accumulation.

Planning and Designing the TIDP

1993–2000

In 1993, Naval Station Treasure Island (NSTI) was marked for closure in accordance with the federal Base Realignment and Closure (BRAC) process of 1990.[6] Following BRAC directives, the city was appointed as the Local Reuse Authority (LRA) charged with producing a reuse plan for the island, negotiating land transfer with the Navy, managing leases of existing properties, and providing homeless housing assistance in accordance with the Federal Base Closure Community Redevelopment and Homeless Assistance Act of 1994 (SF Planning 2010). The city's Office of Military Base Conversion (OMBC), a joint effort of the San Francisco Planning Department, the Redevelopment Agency, and the Port of San Francisco, took up reuse planning for the island. The following year, then San Francisco mayor Frank Jordan appointed a twenty-two-member NSTI Citizens Reuse Committee (CRC) to provide oversight, study reuse plans, and offer policy recommendations to the OMBC and to the San Francisco Planning Commission and Board of Supervisors. After a two-year planning process, on July 22, 1996, the San Francisco Board of Supervisors approved a draft *NSTI Reuse Plan* prepared by the ROMA Design Group (1996) for the OMBC with input from the CRC. This first, new vision for Treasure Island explored the public, recreational, and entertainment potential of the site, proposing a theme park, sports fields, 1,300 hotel rooms, about 2,500 residential units, a ferry terminal, research and development facilities, and film production studios (ROMA Design Group 1996) (Figure 9.3). The plan followed much of the existing grid of streets, kept the Job Corps training site, and retained the three remaining GGIE buildings required by the National Historic Preservation Act.

Only months later, from September 15 to September 20, 1996, the city invited the Urban Land Institute (ULI) to shepherd TI's development beyond its study and planning phase toward specific strategies for "development, marketing and implementation" (Urban Land Institute 1996, 10). The ULI panel's *Strategy for Implementation and Development* made a significant departure from the 1996 *NSTI Reuse Plan*. Its proposal was to transform Treasure Island into a space for recreational uses, "a playground that would benefit all of the city's citizens and visitors" (13). The plan proposed an eighteen-hole public golf course, sports facility, theme park, conference center, and hotels (Figure 9.4). The justification for this turnaround seemed uncharacteristically ideological—the belief that the highest and best use of land could transcend merely economic considerations—and material, in that the ULI identified several significant constraints for new development on the island. Prominent were the geotechnical hazards of building on landfill that were expensive to mitigate, outdated ramps for vehicular access to and from the SFOBB in addition to projected future vehicular congestion from new development, and legal issues associated with the Tidelands Trust, administered by the California

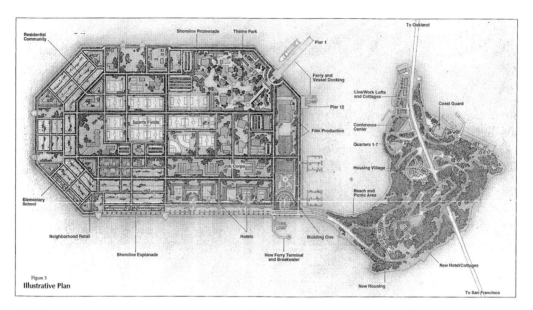

FIGURE 9.3   Naval Station Treasure Island reuse plan, 1996. Office of Military Base Conversion, Planning Department, City and County of San Francisco, and the San Francisco Redevelopment Agency.

State Lands Commission, which prohibits privatizing commercial and residential development on fill lands. Moreover, the presence of incompatible interim land uses, such as the Job Corps training site and the San Francisco Fire Department's in-service training facility, were identified as "leaving less than a 'clean slate' with which to attract future developers and operators" (11). Curiously, the panel noted that there were no serious "toxic remediation issues" for development to contend with, and clearly did not "endorse the long term use and continuation of housing on Treasure Island" (11, 14). Moreover, these plans were created with little awareness of the emerging ideas and technologies of sustainability as noted by the redevelopment officer who worked on the 1996 *NSTI Reuse Plan* and ULI study.[7]

The prospects of private commercial development on Treasure Island were kept alive despite the ULI panel's rhetoric of turning the island over to public use. The ULI panel recommended the formation of a single-purpose entity, Treasure Island Development Corporation, renamed the Treasure Island Development Authority (TIDA), which could partner with a master developer in reenvisioning the island, negotiate land transfer from the US Navy to the city, and manage the land in the interim—that is, until plans for redevelopment were drawn up. At this time, Hong Kong billionaire Li Kai-Shing is reported to have provided further promise by exploring plans to turn Treasure Island into a "paradise resort" with a golf course, luxury hotel, and theme park—evidently in keeping with the ULI proposal (Matier and Ross 1997).

On May 2, 1997, the San Francisco Board of Supervisors established TIDA, governed by a seven-member board whose appointment and removal was entirely under control of the San Francisco mayor (SF Superior Court 1998). The formation of TIDA was necessary for two interconnected reasons. Treasure Island was subject to the Tidelands Trust, which prohibits private ownership, encourages public use, and restricts nonmaritime land uses—such as housing and nonmaritime offices—on fill lands (CSLC 2014). However, to redevelop the island, the plan would have to be administered by a redevelopment agency in order to use tax increment bond financing that could fund such a project (SF Superior Court 1998). Lands under the Tidelands Trust, according to the Burton Act, could only be conveyed to the Port of San Francisco, which was a trustee of the California State Lands Commission but did not have taxing authority. Thus the California State Legislature approved the Treasure Island Conversion Act of 1997 to allow the creation of TIDA, incorporated with redevelopment powers in February 1998, by amending the Burton Act to make TIDA a trustee of the Tidelands Trust and to ostensibly avoid dual-agency control of Treasure Island–Port and Redevelopment (SF Superior Court 1998).

The US Navy officially closed NSTI in 1997. Its relationship with the city had been largely fraught as the Navy tried to eke out the maximum possible price for what it thought was a prime site with great views and few potential contamination issues (at the time), and the city tried to pursue a no-cost land transfer. According to BRAC directives, however, a no-cost land transfer could occur only if the base was to be converted to public recreational use and open space (Urban Land Institute 1996). This directive had been further complicated by President Clinton's

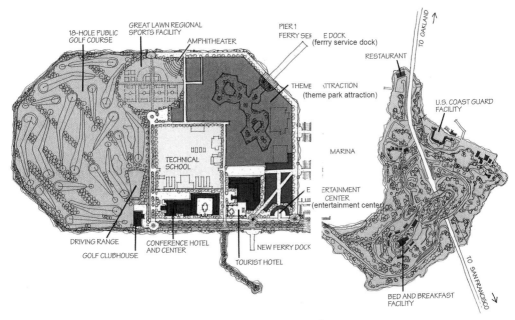

ILLUSTRATIVE REUSE PLAN

FIGURE 9.4   Illustrative reuse plan, 1997. Urban Land Institute, "Strategy for Implementation and Development."

announcement in 1993 of a strategy that would put economic recovery through the redevelopment of military bases at the forefront, to address the loss of jobs, which would in turn appease members of Congress in whose jurisdictions bases were being closed (Cornwell 1993; Urban Land Institute 1996). In keeping with this strategy, the city seemed committed to housing and commercial development on Treasure Island, and armed with TIDA it could once again begin the process of reenvisioning the island.

2000–2011

Between 1997 and 2000, TIDA began to lay the groundwork for future redevelopment by initiating the modernization of the Clipper Cove marina, located between Treasure Island and Yerba Buena Island (Hawkes and Yeung 2010). Nonetheless, it was in October 2000 that TIDA began in earnest to pursue the redevelopment of Treasure Island by issuing a request for qualifications (RFQ). Teams of qualified developers and architects were invited to submit their credentials, one of which would be selected after a competitive selection process as master developer, to partner with TIDA and begin reenvisioning the future of Treasure Island. It was expected that the RFQ respondents would be narrowed down to a short list of teams that would then receive the request for proposals (RFP). Representatives from about 150 firms, architects and developers, attended the pre-bid informational meeting held in December (Hawkes and Yeung 2010). In an introduction to the RFQ, then mayor Willie Brown lent his "full and enthusiastic support" for the project, inviting bidders to "create a vision that captures the spirit of 'The Magic City' . . . [and] to integrate Treasure Island into the urban fabric of San Francisco" (TIDA 2000, 3).

In February 2001, TIDA received only two RFQ submissions, one from the Navillus Group and the other from Treasure Island Community Development LLC (TICD)—a developer consortium consisting of Kenwood Investments, Lennar Communities, Desert Troon, Interland, architectural firm Simon Martin-Vegue Winkelstein and Morris (SMWM, now Perkins and Will), landscape architects Conger Moss and Guillard (CMG), and various other consultants.[8] TICD was selected as the only team deemed qualified to receive the RFP on the basis of its experience and strong financial footing. However, it was alleged that Darius Anderson's and Ron Burkle's—principals at Kenwood—strong ties to Mayor Brown had clinched the deal (Finnie 2003; Hawkes and Yeung 2010).

Following a "focused" RFP issued by TIDA in April 2002, TICD was selected for exclusive negotiations. The team proposed three development scenarios between 2002 and 2010 (TICD 2002). The first plan from July 2002, submitted by Interland, Lennar Corporation, and Kenwood Investments, and designed by SMWM and CMG with other consultants as part of the RFP process, was essentially an update of the 1996 *NSTI Reuse Plan*. With 2,800 units of housing and six hundred hotel rooms, minus the theme park, the plan was suburban in density but contained notable elements not seen earlier—a serpentine bio-swale with wetlands (Figure 9.5). Over

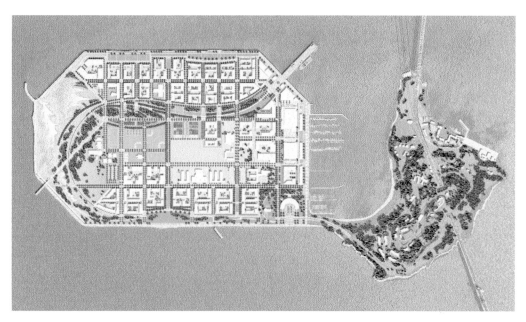

FIGURE 9.5   Illustrative plan, 2002 proposal for development. Treasure Island Community Development/Treasure Island Development Authority. Courtesy of Treasure Island Community Development.

the next two years, the plan ran into a number of the issues earlier identified by the ULI study: limitations of the Tidelands Trust, seismically unstable soils, and emerging information on soil contamination (Figure 9.6). These constraints, which have played a defining role in the current form of the plan, mandated greater setbacks and open space, and further limited development to a smaller portion of Treasure Island made possible through a clever "land swap." Counting TI and YBI as a single redevelopment project, some of the Tidelands Trust limitations were shifted onto Yerba Buena Island, which is a natural island and not fill land, thus allowing for residential and commercial development on portions of Treasure Island (also see Stehlin, this volume).

The second iteration of the plan, proposed in October 2004 by SMWM, had the same program as the earlier version but consolidated buildings and increased open space (Figure 9.7). The plan was to serve a population of about seven thousand residents and included a ferry terminal located at the eastern edge of the island facing Oakland. Despite the plan's sustainable intentions of providing wetlands, "green" buildings, and midscale, neighborhood-centered development, John King, the urban design critic of the *San Francisco Chronicle*, wrote, "It is not the stuff dreams are made of . . . . But sometimes bold is what is called for—perhaps right here and perhaps right now" (2005a).

To characterize the plan as not bold seemed paradoxical. The idea of even attempting to build on an island constructed out of dredged bay mud, known to be contaminated and prone to seismic liquefaction, was in itself a bold and perhaps

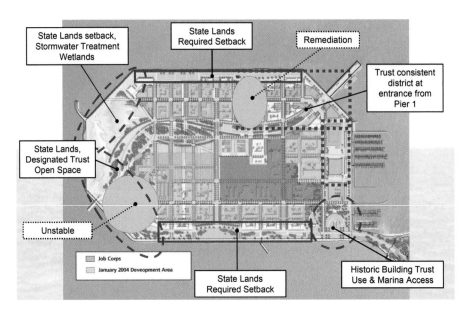

FIGURE 9.6 Changes to 2002 proposal for development required by California State Lands Commission mandated setbacks, seismic considerations and emerging information on soil contamination. Treasure Island Community Development/Treasure Island Development Authority, 2004. Courtesy of Treasure Island Community Development.

foolhardy proposition. In fact, a 2005 Navy Department memo issued by the deputy assistant secretary of installations and facilities concluded that the "No Action alternative is the environmentally preferred alternative," but admitted that it would not meet Congress' goal of economic recovery promised to local jurisdictions going through base closure and reuse (Navy Department 2005). Despite the Navy memo, by 2005, TICD was in need of a boost to dream up a bolder, more ambitious plan. The TICD team brought in Chris Meany of Wilson Meany—developers of the successful Ferry Building Marketplace in San Francisco—and the internationally renowned global architecture and urban design firm Skidmore Owings and Merrill (SOM) to deliver a new architectural image for the project. The design brief for the newly assembled team, according to Kevin Conger of CMG, who were still part of the development team, was to come up with a vision that was "Not Beaux Arts, not New Urbanist or historicist, and not another Mission District!"[9]

In November 2005, TICD unveiled its third and final vision for Treasure Island—fifth in all—following the *1996 Reuse Plan* and the ULI study (see Figure 9.1). At first glance, its unusual distribution of built form and open space seemed original, but on closer examination revealed to have been partly an outcome of the environmental and legal constraints imposed on the project (see Figure 9.5). The plan's influential leadership team comprised Chris Meany (Wilson Meany), Anthony Flanagan (president of Lennar Urban), and Craig Hartman (design partner at SOM), as well as the TIDA executive director, Jared Blumenfeld, who was intent on an increased focus on sustainability. Arup, the global engineering firm, was also brought in to work on a discrete sustainability plan, which was first completed in 2006 and then updated in 2011 (TICD 2011b). From an initial proposal of 5,500 units in 2005, the 2011 agreement calls for eight thousand units, of which 25 percent are expected to be below market rate. In addition, proposed commercial and retail square footage was also significantly increased, and now stands at one hundred thousand square feet of new office space, approximately 207,000 square feet of new retail space, three hundred thousand square feet of adaptive reuse commercial-retail space, and five hundred hotel rooms (TIDA 2011b).

The steady increase in the size of the project, it was reported, was for good reasons (King 2010). TIDA planners claimed the island needed more people for it to thrive; urban activist groups were in agreement, arguing for greater densities on the island that would support mass transit and prevent suburban-style development (King 2010). In turn, the project's developers proposed that Treasure Island needed about nineteen thousand residents to support a large grocery store or supermarket (King 2010). But the steady creep in residential and commercial space, despite other reasons offered by constituent groups, was arguably dictated by the significant increase in the cost of the project in light of emerging information on expensive toxic cleanup requirements, the need for high seismic stability and structural shoring, and the need to protect Treasure Island against imminent sea-level rise (see Stehlin, this volume).

The transformation of the TIDP from a low-visual-impact development to a grand scheme with high-rise towers was made palatable to city residents and leaders precisely because of the plan's turn to sustainability and its use of spectacular

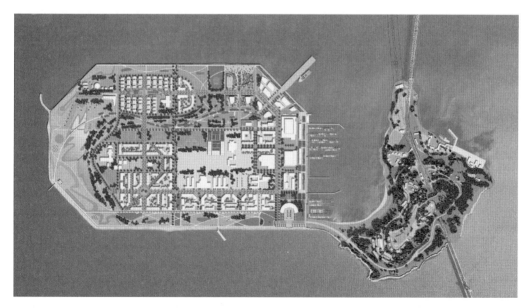

FIGURE 9.7 Revised proposal for development following mandated setbacks, seismic issues, and soil contamination considerations. Treasure Island Community Development/Treasure Island Development Authority, 2004. Courtesy of Treasure Island Community Development.

FIGURE 9.8   TIDP promotional material showing the transformation of Treasure Island to an idyllic future landscape of recreation and entertainment, 2005. Courtesy of Treasure Island Community Development.

form; in other words, what was perceived as its "integration of environmentalism" and its "startling new image" (King 2005b, 2010). Accompanying the lush renderings of high-tech buildings and sustainable landscapes, promotional literature from the TIDP illustrated an island completely transformed. One such illustration shows several dots on a Treasure Island map—which were once contaminated sites and settings of postmilitary dereliction—now depicted as idyllic future landscapes of recreation and entertainment (Figure 9.8). Following the publication of the SOM led plan in 2005, the design of the TIDP has changed little, though the project's numbers have increased significantly. Nonetheless, it is this award-winning design— well received in magazines such as *Scientific American, Popular Mechanics, Wired,* and *Landscape Architecture*—that now stands at a symbol of twenty-first century sustainable development in the San Francisco Bay Area.

Sustainability and the Treasure Island Development Project

The TIDP's validation as an eco-city is consistent with a global groundswell in capital-intensive, large-scale property developments. Consider, for example, Masdar City outside Abu Dhabi, Dongtan zero-carbon eco-city in China, Lingang New City in China, or the Nordhavnen project on Copenhagen's northern harbor, among others. The rise in these eco-cities is synonymous with the growing use of sustainability by planning and urban design firms for whom creating sustainable cities, sustainable environments, sustainable places, sustainable neighborhoods, and sustainable buildings is as much a prerequisite ideological mooring as it is a practical skillset in the competitive marketplace.

In recent years, the output of literature on sustainable design has been so vast that it almost impossible to venture a reasonable survey. Nonetheless, I want to point out some works published by planning and urban design practitioners who strongly believe in design as a solution to the mounting environmental challenges facing our cities in the era of climate change. Agreement is considerable in design circles, especially in discussions that converge around the Congress for the New Urbanism, that urban compactness can reduce auto dependency and green design can promote efficient building performance, which can then work together to reduce carbon emissions (Congress for the New Urbanism 1990; Farr 2008; Coyle 2011). Indeed, nothing is controversial about these claims, and, accordingly, John Kriken, senior SOM urban design partner and active TIDP participant, and his colleagues believe that sustainability should be an entirely commonsensical and axiomatic principle for twenty-first-century city building (2010). Peter Calthorpe, on the other hand, proposes a far more ambitious approach, one involving "whole systems design" that goes beyond merely climate efficient buildings to ultimately achieve a "green urbanism" (2010). Tigren Haas, along somewhat similar lines, advocates "holistic regional design" accompanied by management strategies of "maintenance and governance'" as the path for future city building (2012).

Design expertise, though uncontroversial, perhaps ignores the reality that sustainable urban futures are both socially and economically shifting and perennially contested. Planning's noble goal of achieving "green, fair, profitable, and sustainable development" remains inherently contradictory because of the tension among the competing goals of social justice, economic growth, and environmental protection, which invariably produce conflicts related to the use of resources, the rights of private property, and the need for development (Campbell 1996, 298). Similarly, architecture's uncritical certainty in the ability of sustainable design to shape environmental and social transformation by framing the problem in "purely scientific or quantitative terms," and to then suggest that there are "no barriers, save our awareness, to implementation," appears simplistic (Guy 2005, 5). Yet, sustainability often prefigures urban development—as an apolitical, clean, and safe technocratic solution—sidelining issues of class, race, access, and local agency (Checker 2011). In many cases, the result is a homogeneous and elite social sphere that is seen as the steward of sustainability, producing, in turn, a "specific class-based idea of the city" (Gissen 2009, 24). As Lizbeth Cohen bluntly puts it, "sustainable urbanism cannot mean green cities for the white wealthy" where racial and economic integration is overlooked and sustainability is reduced to mere infrastructure improvement (2010, 135).

Our present understanding of the term "sustainability"—defined as a balance between environment and development that meets present-day needs without compromising those of the future—arguably finds its origins in the Brundtland report (World Commission on Environment and Development 1987). Environment is understood here as where we live, and development as how we alter that abode. Consequently, the term "sustainable design" has come to include broader economic and social goals, whereas "green" denotes technologies that are considered nonpolluting, resource sensitive, and unharmful (Parr 2010). However, since the publication of the Brundtland report, consensus has been scant on the ideas, practices, and effects of sustainability in the social, economic, or environmental spheres of human life, and even more so about what constitutes green urban design and architecture. The debates surrounding sustainable development since the 1980s have only reinforced that the concept remains contradictory, at once susceptible to serve the vested interests of corporations and the free market, and yet suggestive of an alternative way of life (Springett 2013).

Although sustainability is a powerful concept in city building, it is inseparable from popular culture. This is amply evident in our active embrace of recycling, composting, solar and wind energy, urban agriculture, hybrid vehicles, compact fluorescent lamps, and so on (Parr 2010). In other words, sustainability is at once an instrument of design and a powerful cultural signifier of techno-environmental progress that enables the popular dissemination and consumption of megaprojects such as the TIDP. Pertinent, in this regard, is Roland Barthes' analysis of mass media, which proclaims everyday objects—such as compact fluorescent lamps or hybrid vehicles—to possess magical properties, elements of "goodness," or "what goes without saying" (1972). These proclamations, or language—the combination of a form and concept (hybrid vehicles and goodness, for instance)—is what Barthes equates with myth, which he argues is a type of depoliticized speech, textual and imagistic, that is contingently produced, denies history, claims value (goodness), and pretends to be entirely natural.

Thus, it is not sustainability itself but its deployment as a specific language—entirely natural, obvious and emerging from authority—that tends toward myth. As Barthes puts it, myth "hides nothing and flaunts nothing: [but] distorts; myth is neither a lie nor a confession: it is an inflexion" (1972, 129). It is this instability of mythic speech, and its propensity to distort, that supports Adrian Parr's claim that sustainability has been "hijacked" (2010). Parr argues that multinational corporations and prominent institutions such as Wal-Mart, BP, the White House, the US military, Hollywood, among others, have all embraced the cause of sustainability and manipulated it to continue socially and politically exploitative practices that further their self-interests aligned with capitalist values.

At Treasure Island, ideas of green urbanism were scarcely on the agenda in its early stages of planning in the mid-1990s. Arguably, this was because the awareness of sustainability entered mainstream architecture and urban design in the United States after the formation of the US Green Building Council in 1993 and LEED (Leadership in Energy and Environmental Design) in 1998; at the same time, alternative ideas of eco-urbanism were not entirely alien to the Bay Area during the late 1980s, nor for that matter was the idea of ecotopia (see Register 1987; Callenbach [1975] 2014). Almost two decades later, the cornerstone of the TIDP is its self-evident claim to being a model sustainable community. In a talk given in June 2013 as part of the lecture series titled "Little Island, Big Ideas," organized by the Treasure Island Museum Association, Jay Wallace of TICD declared that the project's primary focus was "sustainable development," and that its core principles included "leadership in sustainability, establishing a regional destination, a unique San Francisco neighborhood, and creating community benefits."

Central in this turn toward sustainability, as I have documented, has been the role of the planning and architecture firm SOM. Craig Hartman, design principal at SOM's San Francisco offices, well known for the elegant designs of the San Francisco International Airport and Oakland Cathedral of Christ the Light, is considered the chief architect of the 2005 plan and is recognized in interviews and articles as a specialist in environmentally sustainable master planning—an expertise he was not traditionally known for. Writing in *San Francisco Magazine,* Pamela Feinsilber christened Treasure Island as "Mr. Hartman's neighborhood," asserting that "Hartman [had] laid out a future in which companies such as his [SOM] will design not just great looking green buildings but whole neighborhoods that are so technologically advanced and well-planned, they can actually begin to repair the damage we've done to the planet" (2010).

Even Arnold Schwarzenegger, California's Humvee-driving former governor (2003–2011), was unable to resist sustainability's allure of providing political capital. On December 2, 2009, the former governor visited Treasure Island to unveil his own California Climate Initiative (Buchanan 2009) (Figure 9.9). Pointing at a map produced by the San Francisco Bay Conservation and Development Commission (BCDC), Schwarzenegger proclaimed, "Within a century, Treasure Island, this place where we are right now, could be totally under water" (Foreign Mail Service 2009). The map estimated fifty-five inches of sea-level rise in the San Francisco Bay Area by the end of the century, which could potentially affect the lives of 270,000 residents and result in damage to property worth $62 billion including other cumulative impacts to "public health, economic security and quality of life" (SFBCDC 2011, 3).[10]

It seems perverse to pack a sinking island with new development and then demonstrate how it can be saved. This irony perhaps escaped the governor. In fact, the recommendations of the California Climate Adaptation Strategy report, which Schwarzenegger was following, called for restricting development "in areas vulnerable to climate change impacts" (Buchanan 2009). Nonetheless, as it appears, the governor too had hijacked sustainability with his California Climate Initiative, proposing a positivist technological fix to overcome the adverse ecological transformations predicted for the San Francisco Bay Area. As Schwarzenegger noted, "It is technology in the end that will save us," perhaps indirectly alluding to the TIDP's ability to surmount climate change, which was affirmed only a year earlier when the project was given the Governor's Environmental and Economic Leadership Award (Foreign Mail Service 2009).

At the forefront of the discourse on sustainability surrounding the TIDP are dominant political and economic groups such as members of the development team,

FIGURE 9.9 Former California governor Arnold Schwarzenegger, at Treasure Island on December 2, 2009, speaking in front of a map showing what areas might be affected by global warming in San Francisco, his hand completely covering Treasure Island. Schwarzenegger released California's Climate Adaptation Strategy final report and a new Google Earth–based application, CalAdapt, that displays the risks of global warming. Photo: REUTERS/Kim White.

TICD, architects from SOM, and even the former California governor. But missing are grassroots organizations and less powerful urban actors who have played an active part in shaping sustainability in the TIDP. This equation undermines the role of nondominant groups who do not subscribe to the idea of sustainability as a techno-scientific complement of capitalist development, and neglects to take into account a wide range of social groups who can suggest alternatives to purely technocratic solutions that address social and environmental transformation.

The opposite scenario, however, is not without precedent. In the Pacific Northwest, urban sustainability encompassed a wide spectrum of contestations over open space, public gardens, neighborhoods, and access to local markets and food, and was indeed defined by this process of grassroots activism and environmental politics. These historic struggles led to new subject formations and reconceptions of urban life that reveal sustainability to ultimately be a praxis based on "intimate local knowledge" (Sanders 2010, 15). In the San Francisco Bay Area, the efforts of women activists in the decades between the 1920s and 1940s, largely ignored in most accounts of environmental history, paved the way to what is now an eminently livable greensward enjoyed by the millions who inhabit the region (Walker 2007).

Environmentalism and sustainability are thus historically produced and locally constituted by a broad spectrum of social groups spanning gender, class, and race.

Local activism has been critical to the planning of the TIDP. Since the mid-1990s, San Francisco environmental activists the late Eve Bach and Ruth Gravanis, Public Trust advocates and frequent attendees of TIDA Board and CAB (Treasure Island/Yerba Buena Island Citizens Advisory Board) meetings, may have been crucial to some of the sustainable ideas that have shaped the TIDP, but their work has remained outside the popular dissemination and consumption of the plan. During the early planning stages of Treasure Island, Bach and Gravanis worked closely with then supervisor Mark Leno to mandate the inclusion of wetlands for storm water treatment as a programmatic component after seeing their absence in both the 1996 *NSTI Reuse Plan* and TICD's initial response to the RFQ.

The two were also instrumental in bringing together several nonprofit groups to initiate discussions about the TIDP. In the early 2000s, as Gravanis pointed out, presentations and discussion of the TIDP were conducted in "highly controlled meetings" where members of the public were given only three minutes to speak.[11] To make their views heard, on November 17, 2004, Gravanis and others organized an alternative community workshop, at the offices of the Sierra Club in San Francisco, to discuss the TIDP. According to the meeting agenda and subsequent report, the workshop was attended by about thirty people representing groups such as Arc Ecology, Bluewater Network, San Francisco Bicycle Coalition, San Francisco League of Conservation Voters, San Francisco Tomorrow, Sierra Club, Transportation for a Livable City, Treasure Island Wetlands Project, and Walk San Francisco. Discussion at the meeting on issues of transit and walkability compelled planners and administrators to take their own rhetoric of transit-oriented development more seriously, and may have spurred the decision to relocate the ferry terminal to the western edge of the island toward San Francisco from its intial location on the eastern side.

The manner in which sustainability has been shaped and given shape to the TIDP presents an intriguing dialectic. Definitions of sustainability and its socioeconomic benefits remain controversial and largely disputed. On the one hand, we encounter the distinctive language and images of green technologies—contingently summoned from the top by the developers and planners of the project—in tune with global corporate models of sustainable development based in the extraction of profit. On the other, groups and individuals with a historical commitment to local environmental activism—conservation of the bay, preservation of greensward, and provision of wetlands, among others—have carved out subjective agency by contesting and shaping sustainability from below. Sustainable design, as a techno-environmental tool, has been widely criticized by scholars for its role in city building, particularly the manner in which it is conceived and promoted by planners and architects who advertise its environmental benefits but seem unaware of its adverse social and economic outcomes. Sustainability is also produced and contested in popular culture where it operates—as I have shown with regards to the TIDP—as a powerful, yet unstable signifier that can be easily appropriated to serve political economic interests.

Heterotopia and Utopias of Spatial Form

As a disconnected and peripheral place, Treasure Island sits outside the conscious-
ness of most San Franciscans. It is off their radar, so to say, and, with regard to
the new development, as a former development director from the Mayor's Office of
Economics and Workforce Development put it, "there is less screaming."[12] In other
words, Treasure Island, having no historic claims to being a neighborhood of San
Francisco, has no significant constituency other than a few thousand people who
live on the island in low-income, Navy-era housing. Moreover, because of its long
history as a naval base, it was never subject to San Francisco's general plan requirements or zoning laws. As a specialized island site with single-purpose entity control
(TIDA), Treasure Island is a space of exclusion. Despite attempts to address it as a
inextricable part of San Francisco, as a distinct "neighborhood" reintegrated into
its "fabric"—as ex-mayor Willie Brown stated in the original RFQ document put out
by TIDA, and as later qualified on the TICD website—its sheer physical disconnectedness and separation by planning law cannot be easily overcome (TIDA 2000).

As an exception from the prevailing urban structure, TI can be seen as a heterotopia, or "other place" (Foucault and Miskowiec 1986). Here a society's utopian
ambitions are at work in specialized delimited spaces such as prisons, hospitals,
and schools, for instance, where reformation, cure, and education, respectively, become the overt utopian goals of a society. The TIDP, similarly, appears to be hetero-
topic test bed of environmental, architectural, and engineering experimentation,
where urban change can be contained and facilitated by creating "miniature cities"
governed by their own codes, controls, and interactions (Shane 2005, 10). But this
experimentation—separated as it is from the lived spaces, traditions, and histories of the host city—only ends up serving, at one level, the techno-environmental
ambitions of administrators and planners, and, in turn, the interests of property
development. Moreover, it continues in the face of the obvious risks associated with
sea-level rise, seismic instability, and toxic soils, despite the extent to which it may
be claimed that these risks are being addressed.

For Michel Foucault, utopias were not real spaces but nonetheless purported
to present society in its perfect form, whereas heterotopias were actualized, constructed spaces—consider, for example, "all inclusive resorts"—that mirrored the
utopian conceits of the larger society around them (1986). Heterotopias are built for
a single purpose (as Treasure Island was), have different functions over time—airport, fairground, naval base, for instance—and result in a variety of incompatible
uses that we now see on the island. Notably, heterotopias are enclaves; they have
a point of entry, gates, and walls—much like the TIDP will have with a narrow
causeway linking it to the Bay Bridge—and still function within the urban system
as sites of freedom or illusion (Foucault 1986; Shane 2005). The TIDP mirrors San
Francisco's utopian ideals of creating a new sustainable, high-rise city, and projects
the city's desire to be at the forefront of ecotopian urbanism.

The focus on sustainable urban form in the TIDP, which has been a signifier
of ecotopia, is quite far from the social and political experimentation imagined in

Ernest Callenbach's eponymous 1975 novel. But in the TIDP, it is its image as a perfect place—unique distribution of buildings and open space, distinctive architectural and landscape elements—that has been widely admired in the press as a vision of an island ecotopia (see Figure 9.1) (see Scott 2007; Biello 2008; Burres 2008; Ward 2008; Jost 2010; King 2010).

Such a characterization of ecotopia thus remains inextricably tethered to formal visions. Arguably, this has not changed much since the sixteenth- and seventeenth-century utopias of Thomas More and Francis Bacon, which were conceived around spatial order. These utopias posited visions of better places, emptied of exploitation and disruption, located in vaguely defined distant locales where usually an ocean separated imagination and reality (Polledri and Brechin 1990; Harvey 2000). Although Treasure Island is separated from San Francisco only by the western span of the Bay Bridge and a ten-minute ferry ride, it is still an island where its geographical (spatial) disconnectedness limits the city's volatile social and historical influences on the project, and spatial form freezes a particular (temporal) formal vision of the future. In other words, the "screaming," or the undesirable political and social influences of San Francisco are seen to have a limited bearing on Treasure Island's future, but its formal image, with little contestation and much admiration, can effectively set in place a future city.

But if the optimistic reception of the TIDP as ecotopia is based largely on a formal and not social vision, it brings into question the role of architectural and urban form in utopian place making. Manfredo Tafuri links the utopian impulse in formal visions to the development of modern architecture in the mid-nineteenth century just as it sought to detach from traditional morphologies and yet provide political economic stability (1976). However, modern architecture was rapidly subsumed into capitalist production of the nineteenth-century city leading to the demise of utopian social thought. The agency of architects and planners in shaping social change was repressed by a "realism" committed to evolving capitalist production, a surrender to the "politics of things," in other words, the law of profit (Tafuri 1976, 48). As Tafuri writes, "Architecture, artistic and urban ideology was left with the utopia of form" (48). The architect, and urban designer—much like we see with SOM and its design leaders in the TIDP—Tafuri argues, emerged as the mouthpiece for an instrumental vision of the future, an active agent of a vision where "architecture [is] obliged to return to *pure architecture,* to form without utopia; in best cases to sublime uselessness" (ix).

In this essay, I provide an account of the TIDP's transformation from a low-impact development to a grand vision for the future. After the federal government's decision to close down NSTI in 1993 and turn the island over to the City of San Francisco, early studies for base conversion, such as the *1996 Reuse Plan* and the ULI study, which proposed public uses and underscored the risks of residential development, were largely disregarded by local leaders for a vision to turn the island into a mixed-used residential enclave. Planning for the island's future was made possible by the formation of TIDA—a special agency expressly formed for the redevelopment of Treasure Island and Yerba Buena Island—which was approved by the San Francisco Board of Supervisors in 1997 and placed under direct control of the San Francisco mayor. To allow for changes in land use on the island, TIDA administrators had to find innovative and, arguably, dubious ways to bend state regulations that disallowed residential and nonmaritime commercial development on man-made reclaimed sites.

From initial proposals of low- to mid-rise development, the final version of the TIDP is a grand vision for a mini-city of about nineteen thousand new residents. The steady increase in the overall size of the project was necessary because of its price tag, which had to account for environmental remediation of toxic soil, seismic shoring of unstable landfill, and massive infrastructure to cope with sea-level rise. Considering Treasure Island's unsustainable and precarious condition, the new vision was made palatable to lawmakers and the public at large, ironically, by a turn to sustainability. The administrators, developers, planners, and architects of the TIDP promoted sustainable development as their main focus, which has been central to the project's dissemination and popular consumption. Although the project has been hailed as an ecotopian vision of the future, and its layout singled out for its inventive approach to site planning, what I have tried to demonstrate is that the plan was in fact an outcome of the raft of constraints—toxic soils, seismic stability, and mandated setbacks—that slowly emerged during the lengthy planning process and that ultimately dictated its current form.

Sustainability (and sustainable design), as I have shown in my discussion spanning the writings of architects, planners, social scientists, and cultural theorists, remains a hotly contested and problematic concept. Although it promises an alternative way of life and is a powerful cultural symbol of progressive values, it is equally susceptible to being appropriated by individuals, states, and corporations to serve their self-interests. Thus the manner in which sustainability operates in the TIDP, brought in by the project team to buttress capital-intensive property development, disavows a long history of local green praxes in the San Francisco Bay Area and drowns out the voices of nondominant groups involved in the project who have shaped sustainability from below.

As a disconnected site, Treasure Island appears to be a heterotopia or "other place" that has its own unique history and set of rules. Such exclusive sites, detached from the historical and social context of the city, make possible large-scale formal experimentation, which is far removed from the larger social and economic goals that constitute the notion of ecotopia. Its urban form and representations, lacking the social agency and historical exigencies that inform normative development in the city, do the bidding of property capital and are actively disseminated by the architects who create them. The TIDP thus appears as an empty signifier of sustainability—a hollow experimental form that serves the interests of property development. City planning and urban design would be better served by seriously considering how socially equitable development forms the basis of urban form, and how sustainability is inclusively shaped by disparate voices, especially those from below, to collectively shape urban futures.

Notes

The International Association for the Study of Traditional Environments (IASTE) conferences in Beirut (2010) and Portland, Oregon (2012), and the Society for American City and Regional Planning History (SACRPH) Conference in Toronto (2013) gave me the opportunity to test critical ideas on utopia and sustainability. Thanks to Lynne Horiuchi, Pedro Lange, and Devyani Jain for comments on earlier versions of the essay. I am grateful to Jack Sylvan for first providing me with an overview of the TIDP's planning process, which helped kick-start my research. Patrick Vaucheret, Chris Guillard, Kevin Conger, and Amy Neches all provided input on the design of the TIDP, as did Michael Jacinto and Rick Cooper on the EIR. The comments of the anonymous reviewers helped in improving the first draft. A special thanks to Ruth Gravanis for talking to me at length about the project, and for providing detailed comments and suggestions that significantly improved the essay.

1   The Yerba Buena and Treasure Island Development Project (TIDP) consists of the redevelopment of Naval Station Treasure Island, located on Treasure Island and Yerba Buena Island, which are connected by a narrow causeway. A portion of the 409-acre Treasure Island, minus the Department of Labor's Job Corps training site, and a part of the 147-acre Yerba Buena Island, minus the fifty-seven-acre US Coast Guard and Caltrans holdings, make up the entire proposed development project of about 440 acres.

2   Even though the entire project includes redevelopment of portions of both islands, a major portion of the project is located on the 409-acre Treasure Island, which is the focus of this essay. However, when I do refer to Treasure Island and its programmatic outlay, I refer to both islands.

3   The Clinton Climate Initiative is a program developed under the Bill, Hillary, and Chelsea Clinton Foundation that "focus[es] on helping cities reduce their carbon emissions." The Climate Positive Development Program is geared to creating models for "large scale urban communities to reduce greenhouse gasses and serve as urban laboratories for cities seeking to grow in ways that are environmentally sustainable and economically viable." See more at http://www.clintonfoundation.org/our-work/clinton-climate-initiative.

4   A list of awards that the TIDP has been awarded, particularly the Design for Development (D4D) document, can be found on Skidmore Owings and Merrill's website (http://www.som.com/projects/treasure_island_master_plan).

5   For large-scale, capital-intensive, sustainable projects, see, for example, Masdar City outside Abu Dhabi (http://masdarcity.ae/en/), Arup's Dongtan zero-carbon eco-city in China, Lingang New City in China (http://www.china.org.cn/english/2006/Mar/164148.htm), or the Nordhavnen project on Copenhagen's northern harbor (http://www.nordhavnen.dk/)

6   In 1990, Congress passed the Defense Base Realignment and Closure (BRAC) Act as a framework for the closure of military bases and installations around the country. The first round of base closures was initiated in 1988; subsequent rounds followed in 1991, 1993, 1995, and 2005. Treasure Island was part of several military bases closed in the San Francisco Bay Area; others include the Presidio in San Francisco, Moffet Field, Hunterspoint Shipyard, and the Naval Air Station Alameda. See http://www.brac.gov.

7   Author's field notes, February 20, 2014.

8   Because the composition of Treasure Island Community Development, the master developer of the projects, has changed so much over the years, it would be unwieldy to keep updating the list. I have therefore chosen to list its members who are significant to my narrative and at key historic moments.

9   Author's field notes, August 21, 2010.

10 The SF Public Press published a map in July 2015 showing a number of projects in the San Francisco Bay that are threatened by sea-level rise. See http://sfpublicpress.org/news/searise/2015-07/interactive-map-a-baywide-building-boom-threatened-by-rising-waters.

11 Author's field notes, August 20, 2010.

12 Ibid., June 23, 2010.

References

Barthes, Roland. 1972. *Mythologies*. New York: Hill and Wang.

Biello, David. 2008. "Eco-Cities: Urban Planning for the Future." *Scientific American*. http://www.scientificamerican.com/article/eco-cities-urban-planning.

Buchanan, Wyatt. 2009. "Governor: Back up Plan on Global Warming Needed." *San Francisco Chronicle*, December 3. http://www.sfgate.com/green/article/Governor-Backup-plan-on-global-warming-needed-3207887.php#photo-2349618.

Bures, Frank. 2008. "Ecotopias Aren't Just for Hippies Anymore—and They're Sprouting Up Worldwide." *Wired Magazine* 16, no. 2 (January). https://www.wired.com/2008/01/st-infoporn-7/.

California State Lands Commission (CSLC). 2014. "The Public Trust Doctrine." http://www.slc.ca.gov/About/Public_Trust.html.

Callenbach, Ernest. (1975) 2014. *Ecotopia: The Notebooks and Reports of William Weston*, 40th anniversary edition. Berkeley, CA: Heydey Books.

Calthorpe, Peter. 2010. *Urbanism in the Age of Climate Change*. Washington, DC: Island Press. http://site.ebrary.com/id/10437867.

Campbell, Scott. 1996. "Green Cities, Growing Cities, Just Cities?" *Journal of the American Planning Association* 62, no. 3 (September): 296–312.

Checker, Melissa. 2011. "Wiped Out by the 'Greenwave': Environmental Gentrification and the Paradoxical Politics of Urban Sustainability." *City & Society* 23, no. 2 (December): 210–229.

Cohen, Lizabeth. 2010. "Black and White in Green Cities." In *Ecological Urbanism*, ed. Mohsen Mostafavi and Gareth Doherty, 134–135. Baden: Lars Müller Publishers.

Congress for the New Urbanism. 1990. *Congress for the New Urbanism, CNU*. Chicago and Washington, DC: Congress for the New Urbanism. http://www.cnu.org,

Cornwell, Rupert, 1993. "US to Close 129 Military Bases: Clinton Vows Dollars 5bn Aid to Local Communities." *The Independent*, July 3. http://www.independent.co.uk/news/world/us-to-close-129-military-bases-clinton-vows-dollars-5bn-aid-to-local-communities-1482642.html.

Coyle, Stephen. 2011. *Sustainable and Resilient Communities: A Comprehensive Action Plan for Towns, Cities, and Regions*. Hoboken, NJ: John Wiley & Sons.

Farr, Douglas. 2008. *Sustainable Urbanism: Urban Design with Nature*. Hoboken, NJ: John Wiley & Sons.

Feinsilber, Pamela. 2010. "Mr. Hartman's Neighborhood." *San Francisco Magazine*, April 23. http://www.modernluxury.com/san-francisco/story/mr-hartmans-neighborhood.

Finnie, Chuck. 2003. "Treasure Island Project Expected to Go to Mayor's Cronies / Huge Development Lacked Competition, according to Critics." *San Francisco Chronicle*, April 6. http://www.sfgate.com/bayarea/article/Treasure-Island-project-expected-to-go-to-mayor-s-2623789.php#page-1.

Foreign Mail Service. 2009. "Arnold Schwarzenegger Unveils Dramatic Climate Change Map which Shows Flooded San Francisco of the Future." *Daily Mail*, December 9. http://www.dailymail.co.uk/news/article-1232884/Arnold-Schwarzenegger-unveils-dramatic-climate-change-map-shows-flooded-San-Francisco-future.html.

Foucault, Michel. 1986. "Of Other Spaces." Translated by Jay Miskowiec. *Diacritics* 16, no. 1 (Spring): 22–27.

Gissen, David. 2009. *Subnature: Architecture's Other Environments*. New York: Princeton Architectural Press.

Guy, Simon. 2005. *Sustainable Architectures*. London: Routledge.

Haas, Tigran. 2012. *Sustainable Urbanism and Beyond: Rethinking Cities for the Future*. New York: Rizzoli.

Harvey, David. 2000. *Spaces of Hope*. Berkeley: University of California Press.

Hawkes, Alicia, and Bernice Yeung. 2010. "Through Two Mayors, Connected Island Developers Cultivated Profitable Deal." *SF Public Press*, July 1. http://sfpublicpress.org/news/2010-06/through-two-mayors-connected-island-developers-cultivated-profitable-deal.

Jost, Daniel. 2010. "America's Ecocity." *Landscape Architecture* 100, no. 4 (April): 1–10.

Jung In Kim. 2013. "Making Cities Global: The New City Development of Songdo, Yujiapu and Lingang." *Planning Perspectives* 29, no. 3 (December): 329–356.

Kane, Will. 2011. "S.F. Approves Treasure Island Plan." *San Francisco Chronicle,* June 7. http://www.sfgate.com/bayarea/article/S-F-approves-Treasure-Island-plan-2368950.php.

King, John. 2005a. "If a Green Utopia on Treasure Island Sounds Far-Fetched, Dreamers Have a Plan." *San Francisco Chronicle,* June 2. http://www.sfgate.com/entertainment/article/If-a-green-utopia-on-Treasure-Island-sounds-2666119.php.

———. 2005b. "Towers, Farm Seen for Treasure Island: Self-Sustaining Neighborhood of 5,500 Residences Proposed." *San Francisco Chronicle,* November 8. http://www.sfgate.com/bayarea/place/article/Towers-farm-seen-for-Treasure-Island-2596465.php.

———. 2010. "Treasure Island Plan a Trove Full of Promise." *San Francisco Chronicle,* April 12. http://www.sfgate.com/bayarea/place/article/Treasure-Island-plan-a-trove-full-of-promise-3267672.php.

Kriken, John Lund, Philip Enquist, and Richard Rapaport. 2010. *City Building: Nine Planning Principles for the Twenty-First Century.* New York: Princeton Architectural Press.

Matier, Phillip, and Andrew Ross. 1997. "Treasure Island Luxury Resort-S.F., Businessman in Talks." *San Francisco Chronicle,* March 28. http://www.sfgate.com/bayarea/matier-ross/article/Treasure-Island-Luxury-Resort-S-F-2848299.php.

Parr, Adrian. 2009. *Hijacking Sustainability,* Cambridge, MA: MIT Press.

Polledri, Paolo, and Gray A. Brechin. 1990. *Visionary San Francisco.* San Francisco: San Francisco Museum of Modern Art.

Register, Richard. 1987. *Ecocity Berkeley: Building Cities for a Healthy Future.* Berkeley, CA: North Atlantic Books.

ROMA Design Group. 1996. *Naval Station Treasure Island Reuse Plan.* San Francisco: Office of Military Base Conversion, Planning Department, City and County of San Francisco, and the San Francisco Redevelopment Agency.

San Francisco Bay Conservation Development Commission (SFBCDC). 2011. "Living with a Rising Bay: Vulnerability and Adaptation in San Francisco Bay and on Its Shoreline." October 6. http://www.bcdc.ca.gov/BPA/LivingWithRisingBay.pdf.

San Francisco Board of Supervisors (SFBOS). 2011. "Board of Supervisors City and County of San Francisco: Meeting Minutes." http://www.sfbos.org/ftp/uploadedfiles/bdsupvrs/bosagendas/minutes/2011/m060711.pdf.

San Francisco Planning and Urban Research (SPUR). 2011. "Treasure Island Moves Forward to Planning Commission." http://www.spur.org/news/2011-03-02/treasure-island-moves-forward-planning-commission.

San Francisco Planning Department (SF Planning). 2010. "Planning Commission Final Motion." April 8. http://sf-planning.org/ftp/files/Commission/CPCmotions/18071.pdf.

San Francisco Public Library (SFPL). 2012. "Past Exhibition 2012." San Francisco Public Library. http://sfpl.org/index.php?pg = 2000546301.

San Francisco Superior Court (SF Superior Court). 1998. "1997–1998 Report on Treasure Island." http://www.sfcourts.org/Modules/ShowDocument.aspx?documentid = 2254.

Sanders, Jeffrey C. 2010. *Seattle and the Roots of Urban Sustainability Inventing Ecotopia.* Pittsburgh, PA: University of Pittsburgh Press.

Schlesinger, Victoria. 2010. "Treasure Island Building Plans Draw Fire." *San Francisco Public Press,* November 29. http://sfpublicpress.org/news/2010-11/treasure-island-building-plans-draw-fire.

Schrieber, Dan. 2011. "San Francisco's Treasure Island Plan's Face Lawsuit." *San Francisco Examiner,* May 11. http://www.sfexaminer.com/sanfrancisco/treasure-island-redevelopment-challenged-in-new-appeal/Content?oid = 2174775.

Scott, Craig. 2007. "Green Gold: Treasure Island Set to Become Enviably Sustainable." *Architect's Newspaper,* May 2. http://archpaper.com/news/articles.asp?id = 1334.

Shane, David Grahame. 2005. *Recombinant Urbanism: Conceptual Modeling in Architecture, Urban Design and City Theory.* Chichester, UK: Wiley-Academy.

Springett, Delyse. 2013. "Editorial: Critical Perspectives on Sustainable Development." *Sustainable Development* 21, no. 3 (March): 73–82.

Tafuri, Manfredo. 1976. *Architecture and Utopia: Design and Capitalist Development.* Cambridge, MA: MIT Press.

Treasure Island Community Development (TICD). 2002. "Response to Request for Proposals, Naval Station Treasure Island." July 2. San Francisco: TICD.

———. 2011a. *Treasure Island Transportation Implementation Plan.* June 11. San Francisco: TICD. http://sftreasureisland.org/modules/showdocument.aspx?documentid = 1077.

———. 2011b. "Treasure Island/Yerba Buena Island Sustainability Plan." June 28. San Francisco: TICD. http://sftreasureisland.org/sites/default/files/Documents/Master_Develpment_Submittals/Final_Docs_July_2011/Treasure_Island_SP_2012.02.02_digital_version_.pdf.

Treasure Island Development Authority (TIDA). 2000. "The Redevelopment of Treasure Island, Review: Request for Qualifications." San Francisco: TIDA. Copy in author's possession.

———. 2011a. *The Treasure Island and Yerba Buena Island Design for Development—D4D.* San Francisco: TIDA.

———. 2011b. "Disposition and Development Agreement." San Francisco: TIDA. http://www.sftreasureisland.org/modules/showdocument.aspx?documentid = 1110.

US Department of the Navy (Navy Department). 2005. "Record of Decision for the Disposal and Reuse of Naval Station Treasure Island, California." Washington, DC: US Department of Defense. http://www.sftreasureisland.org/Modules/ShowDocument.aspx?documentid = 74.

Urban Land Institute. 1996. "Treasure Island Naval Station, San Francisco, CA: An Evaluation of Reuse Opportunities and a Strategy for Development and Implementation." Washington, DC: Urban Land Institute. http://sf.uli.org/wp-content/uploads/sites/47/2011/06/San-Francisco-CA-1999.pdf.

Walker, Richard. 2007. *The Country in the City: The Greening of the San Francisco Bay Area.* Seattle: University of Washington Press.

Ward, Logan. 2009. "Why Treasure Island Is the Super Green City of the Future." *Popular Mechanics,* October 1. http://www.popularmechanics.com/science/environment/4239381.

World Commission on Environment and Development. 1987. *Our Common Future.* Oxford: Oxford University.

10. Magic City 2.0

Articulations of Soil, Law, and Capital
on Treasure Island

JOHN STEHLIN

If you could start from scratch, absolute scratch, what would you build?

JARED BLUMENFELD, SAN FRANCISCO
DEPARTMENT OF ENVIRONMENT

Few landscapes are as obviously constructed as Treasure Island, a stretched oc-tagon of landfill jutting awkwardly out from Yerba Buena Island in the middle of the San Francisco Bay. The island is constructed in a dual sense, however, as a technical object in continual flux and as a political mirror for San Francisco's developmental ambitions. The most recent plan echoes an increasingly dom-inant commonsense regarding sustainable urbanism, calling for a futuristic, carbon-neutral eco-city of nineteen thousand new residents (see Sankalia, this volume). Its signature feature is the construction of a dense, walkable urban form connected by frequent ferry to San Francisco, surrounded by verdant open space, an organic farming education center, and nutrient-cycling artificial wet-lands. Treasure Island can host this fusion of intensive urbanization and high-tech eco-futurism, according to prevailing discourse, *because* it can act as a blank slate on which to push design boundaries and generate an experimental urban form for a postcarbon future. Getting ecological urbanism "right," in this fram-ing, depends on the availability of a tabula rasa, a radical break from the material histories that have produced it. This essay pushes against this framing, reading the island's materiality back into the structure of the plan, in spite of the depar-ture it purports to make. It also moves beyond a "greenwashing" narrative that reduces Treasure Island to a screen for San Francisco's development machine. Treasure Island is a site on which a fantasy of a green urban future plays out through techno-fetishist design and the ideology of a start "from scratch," but is in fact subject to very material "enabling constraints" (Butler 1997) on the possi-ble futures Treasure Island holds.

Since 1997, the "empty" island, with its cheap housing built for military fami-lies and almost devoid of services, has acquired many temporary uses, such as the Treasure Island Music Festival, various sporting events, a flea market, and several wineries. But as housing costs in San Francisco continue to rise, the island has seen an influx of low-income residents (US Census Bureau 2015). Many new residents since base closure are formerly homeless, rehoused through the Treasure Island Homeless Development Initiative (TIHDI), a program federally mandated for shuttered military bases. The specter of radioactive pollution from the Navy's tenure (see Dillon, this volume) haunts current residents, who are formally temporary and frequently relocated when areas that had been deemed safe by the Navy are reopened for further remediation. Much of the public discussion of the island focuses on this toxic legacy, a growing social justice issue as the temporary tenure of some residents has stretched to nearly two decades. At the same time, in built-out San Francisco, the irresistibility of unbuilt land acquired through "accumulation by demilitarization" (following Harvey 2003) makes its redevelopment a foregone conclusion.

Less well documented, however, is how the materiality of the island's construction from dredged soil itself shapes the current plan. In what follows, I argue that it does so in three ways. First, the poorly consolidated soils making up Treasure Island are vulnerable to seismic destabilization, making any foreseeable development plan contingent on offsetting the high costs of seismic retrofitting by attracting capital investment. Second, as coastal landfill, Treasure Island is legally required to be used in the public trust and is administered by the California State Lands Commission (CSLC). This designation strictly precludes residential uses. Thus, the balance of open space and intensive urbanization for which the redevelopment plan has been hailed is in fact the result of legal maneuvers to circumnavigate this legal framework and free up as much land as possible for residential development. Finally, the initial "conjuring" of the island as a projection of San Francisco's regional ambitions continues to resonate in this current "utopic cycle" (following Sheridan 1999, 3). In the days of the Expo, the raising of the island from the bay floor played as key a role to its image of futurity as the pavilions and demonstrations it assembled. Plans for the eco-city of the future reference the technical prowess that initially formed the island, celebrating the engineering challenges it presents as part of assembling a spectacular site where the fantasy of a sustainable future generates value in the present. Through attention to "past processes whose traces are not always evident in the landscape" (Lefebvre 1977, 341), I hope to show that Treasure Island is anything but a blank slate.

Accumulation by Demilitarization

The closure of Naval Station Treasure Island (NSTI), initiated in 1993 on the end of the Cold War, the devolution of federal power, and the neoliberalization of the state's economic role, constituted "accumulation by demilitarization," to borrow from Harvey (2003): a privatization of state space, in this case military land. The transfer of the island to civilian ownership—and essentially to the private sector, though formally owned by the City of San Francisco—opened a large swath of land to profitable redevelopment. Unlike the closure of military bases in econom-ically depressed regions such as the Southeast, NSTI's realignment has freed land adjacent to one of the West's most dynamic property markets. As the *Los Angeles Times* put it, redeveloping former military land on the booming California coast is a "cottage industry" for the project's builder, Lennar Urban, a wing of Lennar Homes, which at the time of the 2008 financial crisis was the second largest homebuilder in the United States (Pasco 2005).

Although "accumulation by demilitarization" opens up "empty land" in ad-vantageous locations, the land it opens is laden with challenges and obstacles. These do not block efforts to renew accumulation, however: Treasure Island's toxic, seismically vulnerable soils generate opportunities for innovation. As Karl Marx well understood, the limits placed upon processes of capital accumula-tion do not halt them, but in fact force technical and political changes to spur new rounds of accumulation (Marx [1852] 1992; Harvey 2007). The not-at-all-empty materiality of the island itself thus decisively shapes the possibilities for how to profitably develop it, not because of its essential properties, but because of the way that state-facilitated capitalist development works through material constraints rather than erasing them, recombining the material into new profit-able configurations.

Emptying Treasure Island: From Grandeur to Dereliction

In many ways, Treasure Island was built to commemorate the start of the gasoline age. It was built within the context of a broad, state-led move toward regional in-tegration and modernization, particularly with respect to the infrastructure of the automobile and airplane. The US Navy arrested this arc, taking control of the island in February of 1941 and transforming it into a base of operations in anticipation of war in the Pacific. NSTI served as a routing center, a node in the network of military bases stretching throughout the Bay Area region from Santa Cruz to Point Reyes. But its absorption into the region's military geography (see Arbona, this volume) and subsequent slow deterioration after World War II essentially foreclosed the pos-sibility of it keeping pace with the world it had commemorated. Not itself a primary site of shipbuilding, munitions production and storage, or troop quartering, NSTI's role as an administrative and circulatory command center, processing thousands of troops daily, meant that it saw little of the residential clustering common to bases with large permanent populations, and far less of the heavy pollution that saturated other sites such as Hunters Point.

Nevertheless, an early 1990s study in anticipation of base closure identified twenty-nine sites on the island contaminated with PCBs, diesel fuel, pesticides, petroleum, lead, and various other compounds, and eleven thousand feet of buried, aging fuel lines lie leaking (ROMA Design Group 1995a, vol. 1; 1996, 21). Most alarmingly, postwar radioactive materials training has left accumulated deposits of radium and cesium-137 (Hice and Schierling 1995, 68; Benkowski 2006, 7; see also Dillon, this volume). Locations that the Navy had declared safe, particularly in the island's low-lying northwest corner, have been reopened for remediation, and the families living atop the questionable soils have been relocated (Russell 2007). In addition to documenting pollution on the land, a suit brought by Arc Ecology and others named more than four hundred thousand separate violations of clean water laws, events that stand to increase as climate change–related sea-level rise could bring deeper toxins closer to the surface (Holding 1996; Schlesinger 2010). Since 1997, the Navy has spent more than $100 million on cleanup, and in 2009, after seemingly endless negotiations with the City of San Francisco over the terms of transfer, the parties settled a $105 million deal, which includes a possible $50 million to be paid to the Navy if the redevelopment is successful (Coté 2009).

Treasure Island is currently home to an estimated 2,300 temporary residents living in remaining naval housing, mainly on the island's northwest corner, as well as some privately built market-rate houses. Accessed at the midpoint of the no-toriously traffic-plagued Bay Bridge by car or a single hourly bus line, the island remains cut off from the rest of San Francisco, forcing residents to leave the island for even the most basic needs. Services such as schools and a grocery store, pres-ent during the period of Navy use, have since been removed, leaving only a pair of convenience stores in their stead (though in June 2013, perhaps recognizing market potential, a small, full-service grocery store did open). Current uses of the space include film production, an annual music festival, and various sporting events. Per-haps most poignantly, it is noteworthy as a destination from which to gaze back upon San Francisco itself. The only permanent uses are a federal job training cen-ter and TIHDI, both mandated by the Base Realignment and Closure Act of 1990 (P.L. 101-510). Its residents considered temporary and movable, Treasure Island has been construed as a space arrested in a holding pattern, both materially and discursively emptied of durable content and awaiting development. Meanwhile, booming, space-hungry San Francisco is undergoing an affordability crisis with little parallel in recent history.

A Blank Slate for an Ecotopia by the Bay: The Treasure Island-Yerba Buena Island Development Project

Framing the island as a tabula rasa is the basis on which planners, investors, and pro-gressive organizations all interpret its possibility. After fitful planning efforts throughout the 1990s, the Treasure Island Development Authority (TIDA), a state agency formed to oversee the transfer, finally introduced the current master plan in 2005. The plan's moving parts represent the contingent articulation of San Francisco's growth machine with a rising discourse of sustainable urbanism that has gained traction over the past two decades and is hegemonic within California (Hawkes and Yeung 2010; Russell 2005). The planning of "San Francisco's newest neighborhood" is handled as one large site overseen by a mayoral appointee (for a more detailed analysis, see also Sankalia, this volume), in a process that typifies the neoliberal public-private partnership model and its evasion of democratic planning processes (Harvey 2000, 1989).

In a virtually uncompetitive selection process, Treasure Island Community Development LLC (TICD), a joint venture of Lennar Urban, boutique developer Wilson Meany, and two private equity firms, submitted the winning proposal.[1] Expected to eclipse $6 billion in cost, the project features a hundred-acre pocket of dense, mixed-use urbanization at the southwest corner of the island with eight thousand housing units, two thousand of which are below market rate,[2] complete with a tourist-oriented commercial and hotel district (Ward 2009). This new urbanization will connect by ferry service to San Francisco with strict parking maximums designed to create disincentives to car ownership in favor of pedestrian-, bicycle-, and transit-based mobility (TICD/TIDA 2007; TICD 2011, 56; Hawkes and Yeung 2010). Three hundred or more acres of open space surround this "town center," including a twenty-acre organic agricultural education center, a wastewater-cycling artificial wetlands, parklands, and walkways. LEED-certified buildings, including a glass condo tower of between forty and sixty stories, boast "world-class" views of San Francisco to attract affluent buyers. Even the street grid will be realigned to block the bay's notorious winds to reduce energy used for heating (Ward 2009).

In 2008, the project received the Governor's Environmental and Economic Leadership Award; at the ceremony, Mayor Gavin Newsom called the project "a model of how communities can grow sustainably and prosper economically" (San Francisco Office of the Mayor 2008). Meanwhile, bringing in the expertise of various stakeholders, from bicycle advocates to environmental activists, built the credibility of the design as a wholesale departure from previous efforts and a mirror of the green future. The result, advocates hope, will be a self-sustaining, carbon-neutral ecological utopia in the bay, one that will serve as a model for other localities that intend to adopt aspects of its organizational logic in order to forward a more sustainable urban agenda.

The notion of the island as a tabula rasa shapes the discourse surrounding its redevelopment. Thus, even as he acknowledges the obstacles, TIDA board member John Eberling argues,

> There are no NIMBYs. It's nobody's backyard. Instead, people have addressed a series of policy issues they care about. The military's withdrawal from the Bay Area has left all these huge opportunities around. Hunters Point, Concord. These are all huge opportunities. And they come with a tremendous collection of problems. (Simerman 2010)

TIHDI head Sherry Williams sounded a similar note when we spoke in an interview: "Since there is no existing neighborhood, there is no need to deal with NIMBY-ism about the formerly homeless. It is a unique opportunity to build in the homeless from the ground up."[3] These statements imply that an existing community would act as an obstacle to both comprehensive ecological design and poverty alleviation, raising the obvious question of how the project could become a model for comprehensive sustainable and socially just development elsewhere. Meanwhile, the "tremendous collection of problems" that issue from the island's material legacies can be overcome with the application of technical expertise. Aspects of the island laid down in its very construction, however, have shaped the plan in ways as decisive as the perceived opportunity to design in sustainability from the beginning. I now turn to the technical, legal, and political-economic framework through which the island's materiality acts on the project.

Risk and Capital on Shifting Ground

The lasting effects of Treasure Island's construction hinge on the particularities of how its soils were made into a landmass to begin with. Establishing the island as solid ground is a process that has never been complete. Treasure Island as a whole is sinking. Its north end, where most of the remaining Navy housing is currently located, was never expected by the original builders to remain solid. It sits on the deepest part of the shoal and currently lies below sea level, where it is prone to flooding and upwelling that draws pollution to the surface. More importantly, the entire island is at high risk for liquefaction, the destabilization of saturated soil caused by major seismic activity, as demonstrated by the extensive boiling, lateral spreading, and flooding caused by the 1989 Loma Prieta earthquake (see Figure 10.1) (ROMA Design Group 1995b).

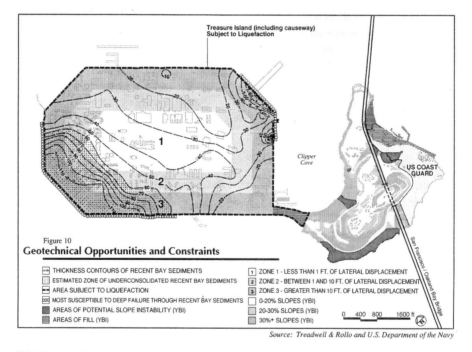

Source: Treadwell & Rollo and U.S. Department of the Navy

FIGURE 10.1 Geotech plan, Treasure Island Reuse Plan: Existing Conditions Report, 1996. Office of Military Base Conversion, Planning Department, City & County of San Francisco, and the San Francisco Redevelopment Agency. San Francisco History Center, San Francisco Public Library.

TABLE 2

ORDER OF MAGNITUDE COST ESTIMATES OF PHASED STABILIZATION APPROACHES

(PRELIMINARY: BASED ON JULY 1995 DOLLARS)

Improvement	Approach 1 Baseline	Approach 2 100 Acres	Approach 3 215 Acres	Approach 4 330 Acres
Causeway Stabilization				
Perimeter Strengthening	$ 3,778,720	$ 3,778,720	$ 3,778,720	$ 3,778,720
Subtotal	$ 3,778,720	$ 3,778,720	$ 3,778,720	$ 3,778,720
Shoreline Stabilization				
Perimeter Strengthening	$ 6,270,000	$ 13,794,000	$ 19,437,000	$ 23,512,500
Mitigation of Rotational Dike	—	$ 14,288,000	$ 17,328,000	$ 14,288,000
Subtotal	$ 6,270,000	$ 28,082,000	$ 36,765,000	$ 37,800,500
Roadway Stabilization				
Stone Columns	$ 4,075,500	—	—	—
Paving	$ 2,520,000	—	—	—
Subtotal	$ 6,595,500	—	—	—
Ground Improvement				
Fill	$ 1,181,800	$ 19,323,133	$ 40,274,357	$ 61,365,212
Dynamic Compaction	—	$ 17,390,825	$ 36,246,931	$ 55,228,691
Subtotal	$ 1,181,800	$ 36,713,958	$ 76,521,288	$ 116,593,903
Accelerated Settlement				
Surcharge Fill	—	$ 13,043,119	$ 27,185,198	$ 41,421,518
Wick Drains	—	$ 10,869,266	$ 22,654,332	$ 34,517,932
Subtotal	—	$ 23,912,385	$ 49,839,530	$ 75,939,450
TOTAL OPTION COST	**$ 17,826,020**	**$ 92,487,063**	**$ 166,904,538**	**$ 234,112,573**

Note: This chart is based on the same assumptions regarding unit costs as described more fully in Table 1, and associated footnotes. These estimates are based on order of magnitude costs for land and shoreline stabilization of portions of Treasure Island; they imply, but do not include, the costs of building and roadway demolition. In addition, roadway and utility replacements would be required, but are not included.

FIGURE 10.2   Geotech table, Treasure Island Reuse Plan: Existing Conditions Report, 1996. Office of Military Base Conversion, Planning Department, City & County of San Francisco, and the San Francisco Redevelopment Agency. San Francisco History Center, San Francisco Public Library.

By 1995, it was clear to planners that without geotechnical improvements only 120 acres in the center of the island would be developable space (ROMA Design Group 1995b, 19). An early stabilization approach study indicated that though $18 million in improvements would yield the capacity to use this 120-acre core covering the original shallow shoals, $234 million would be needed to render the bulk of the island safe for intensive construction (see Figure 10.2). Ironically, the most radically minimalist option—simply removing the seawalls and letting the island return to the bay floor—would violate federal clean water laws due to the extent of pollution in the soil. Base conversion law also mandates the redevelopment of former military lands, although provisions for low- or no-cost transfer are in place if the land will be used for parks and open space (Urban Land Institute 1996; US Congress 1990).

Even though an independent evaluation by the Urban Land Institute specifically recommended against housing (1996, 14), the need for remediation efforts was never substantively called into question in official plans. Fixing liquefaction simply requires the application of capital and technology to shift risky soils into a more solid combination. As Jack Sylvan from the mayor's office tellingly puts it, "It's about as risky a project as there is. It's massively front-loaded" (Simerman

2010). Here, positing seismic activity as a *risk* already advances the possibility of a technical rather than an ethico-political solution, and attests to the inevitability of the undertaking (Winner 1989; Beck 1992). Thus, instead of posing an insurmountable barrier, these challenges spurred the planning of a larger and more intensive project to offset the costs. As early planning documents make clear, the return on the capital required to cover geotechnical engineering could not be raised by low-rise residential uses alone, but only by combining dense housing with more outwardly directed accumulation strategies (ROMA Design Group 1995b, 39–40). In 2010, two thousand more units were added to the plan in accordance with this logic.

In other words, Treasure Island could never be just another average neighborhood of San Francisco. Long before its green turn, planners were convinced of the need to produce it as a spectacular space that could stimulate the requisite investment, mobilizing a nominally public interest in sustainability to generate private accumulation. In this way, planners were constrained both by the general requirement to return a profit in order to attract investment capital and the specific requirements made by the very mode of construction of the soils, in the context of this instrumental understanding of what is possible in urban redevelopment. This is the first paradox of the supposedly blank space of Treasure Island.

Trading Places: Abstract Space and the Treasure Island Trust Exchange

A second constraint concerns the fill landscape as a jurisdictional category. Although Treasure Island falls within the City of San Francisco, because it is constructed from landfill, on transfer from the Navy it becomes subject to regulation by the California State Lands Commission under the Tidelands Trust. The CSLC was founded to protect coastal areas from development and hold them in the public trust for the use of the citizens of California. Tidelands Trust lands were originally limited to maritime commerce, navigation, and fishing, but since the 1970s, the list of possible uses has expanded through case law to include recreational open space, swimming, hunting, scientific study, and ecological value (Ziemann 1973).

The Tidelands Trust specifically excludes residential real estate, a constraint that would jeopardize the main basis of the profitability of the island's redevelopment as determined by the ROMA studies. Planners had anticipated the need to negotiate with the commission to relax these strictures long before the current character of the plan took shape. Although when base realignment was first explored it was not yet clear whether Tidelands Trust constraints would apply, the commission had already indicated willingness to "negotiate flexibility" (ROMA Design Group 1995b, 40–41), perhaps recognizing the political and economic pressure for the development of newly acquired land.

To circumvent these strictures, representatives from the City of San Francisco successfully lobbied the state legislature for the passage of the Treasure Island Public

Trust Exchange Act in 1994, which lifted trust status from roughly one hundred acres of Treasure Island and in exchange assigned it to portions of Yerba Buena Island deemed of equal value. In the bill's language, "the existing configuration of trust and non-trust lands within the property is such that the purpose of the public trust cannot be fully realized. This measure is intended to allow for the exchange of lands to maximize public trust values for the benefit of the statewide public" (Senate Committee on Governmental Organization 2004). Left unexamined is that the existing configuration considered unable to realize the public trust is, paradoxically, the designation intended to preserve coastal areas for public uses. The majority of the hundred acres freed for private real estate development, roughly a quarter of the area of the island, will be devoted to real estate sales and a small portion of rental properties (for a discussion of the legal history of the Tidelands Trust in California and the dubious constitutionality of trust exchanges, see Martyn and Bohner 1978).

Trust exchanges have become the norm in the redevelopment of riparian lands, occurring throughout the bay on decommissioned military lands such as Hunters Point Naval Shipyard, Naval Air Station Alameda, and the Oakland Army Base. Between 1968 and 1978 alone, the state legislature authorized 150 trust exchanges involving an unknown amount of acreage. "Most of the coastal wetlands boundaries," Martyn and Bohner note, "have never been completely and accurately surveyed in metes and bounds. . . . [I]f the state does not know what it originally owned, and thus what it is giving away, one can question whether what it is giving away is equal to what it is receiving" (1978, 42–43). In this case, the flat, sea-level landfill of Treasure Island bears no resemblance, save the abstraction of surveyed area, to the rocky slopes of Yerba Buena Island. Treasure Island, however, is far better suited to intensive development.

Here, instead of an imaginary all-powerful force of capital, flowing without restraint across abstract space, we find a legal maneuver within the constraints of environmental regulation and material conditions to generate new sources of value. Ironically, given the artifactual quality of Treasure Island, environmental law spurred this jurisdictional transfer. Without the trust exchange, no land could have supported the residential development needed to make seismic retrofitting feasible. Furthermore, the balance of urban density and open space outlined by the plan—indeed, one of its main selling points as a space of eco-urbanist harmony—is not simply the result of enlightened land-use planning and cultural progress, but a response to the durability of these constraints and the opportunities they nevertheless present. Whether the public benefits from the maneuver depends on how one construes the public interest, but planning documents appear to interpret it as synonymous with whatever chain of events facilitates the island's development.

Even within the dichotomy of trust- and nontrust land that the Trust Exchange Act created, prospective uses are unevenly prioritized. Trust lands only permit commercial uses that are directed toward "publicly oriented uses"—meaning for the benefit of the citizens of California as a whole (ROMA Design Group 1996). Housing and retail intended to serve residents are legally confined to the acres transferred from Yerba Buena Island. The 2010 increase in the planned number of units, from

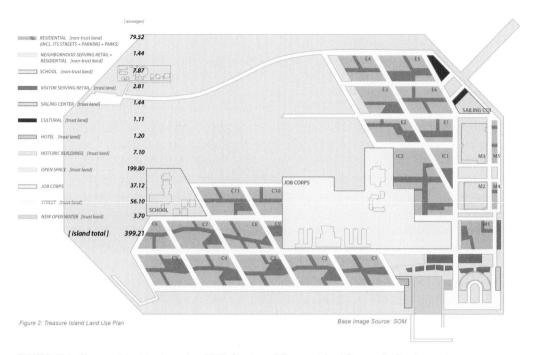

[acreages]

RESIDENTIAL [non-trust land]   79.52
(INCL. ITS STREETS + PARKING + PARKS)

NEIGHBORHOOD SERVING RETAIL +   1.44
RESIDENTIAL [non-trust land]

SCHOOL [non-trust land]   7.87

VISITOR SERVING RETAIL [trust land]   2.81

SAILING CENTER [trust land]   1.44

CULTURAL [trust land]   1.11

HOTEL [trust land]   1.20

HISTORIC BUILDINGS [trust land]   7.10

OPEN SPACE [trust land]   199.80

JOB CORPS   37.12

STREET [trust land]   56.10

NEW OPEN WATER [trust land]   3.70

[island total]   399.21

Figure 2: Treasure Island Land Use Plan   Base Image Source: SOM

FIGURE 10.3   Treasure Island land use plan, 2006. Courtesy of Treasure Island Community Development.

six thousand to eight thousand, expands the consumer pool to attract retailers, particularly a large grocery store (Dineen 2010) but could bring housing into competition with neighborhood-serving retail. Ironically, such constraints do not apply to some of the most potentially lucrative land uses like the proposed hotel, "wellness center," sailing center, and various "visitor-serving" retail and entertainment uses, which occupy nearly twice the land area of retail-serving residents. These outwardly oriented uses occupy areas where public trust status has not been lifted (Figures 10.3 and 10.4).

Indeed, high-value land uses intended to serve visitors form a large portion of the expected revenue from the project (TICD 2011). Because the trust exchange imposed the requirement to both generate profit and "serve" the citizens of California, the development's claimed energy neutrality depends on tourism from the wider carbon-intensive world. Furthermore, this speaks powerfully to the neoliberal underpinnings of this framing of sustainability, implying that the kind of public interests to be enhanced are those that support the engine of accumulation. This contortion of the Tidelands Trust, the expansion of which specifically named the value of keeping coastal areas in their "natural state," materially underpins the green design for which the plan is celebrated (Ziemann 1973). Paradoxically, instead of limiting development, its manipulation encouraged it. As one critic said of a similar trust exchange in San Diego: "The public lost a jewel that defines what the California Coastal Act was created to protect" (CSLC 2003, 30).

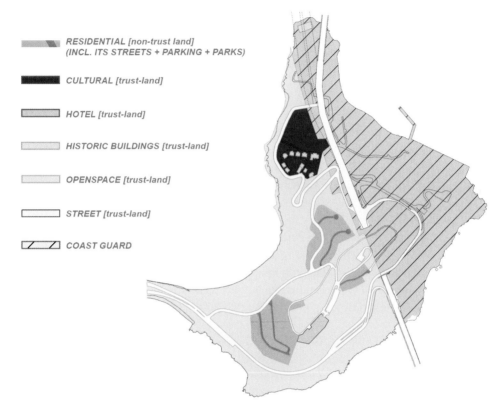

RESIDENTIAL [non-trust land]
(INCL. ITS STREETS + PARKING + PARKS)

CULTURAL [trust-land]

HOTEL [trust-land]

HISTORIC BUILDINGS [trust-land]

OPENSPACE [trust-land]

STREET [trust-land]

COAST GUARD

FIGURE 10.4   Yerba Buena Island land use plan showing Tidelands Trust Areas, 2006. Courtesy of Treasure Island Community Development.

Magic City 2.0: An Expo for the Postcarbon Future

The ways these material and legal strictures have shaped the island's devel-opment fall away in the triumphalist account of the opportunity to build an ecological future "from scratch" in the present. Moreover, this technological celebration harkens back to the narrative of the island's construction itself. The island's construction is not in itself unusual in San Francisco Bay history, where constantly shifting boundaries between land and ocean correspond to periods of intensive urbanization, industrial growth, and transport revolutions (Chin et al. 2004). But a qualitatively different imaginary accompanied the writing on Treasure Island at the time of its manufacture. In contemporary and more recent accounts alike, the island "literally ris[es] from the bay," "takes shape," and "blossoms" from the bay itself. In photographs, dredges and other heavy machinery operated by engineers "work," build," and "fill" (Pipes 2007, 12–21). This erasure of labor by a highly technical account of engineering and sheer mechanical power frames the island's construction as the inevitable result of merging natural materials with high technology and expertise. Triumphant accounts at the time proclaimed, "To the average person it appeared that Aladdin rubbed his 'Magic Lamp' and 'lo there arose before him, out of the waters' depths and through the mists, a City, glowing in magnificent splendor and beauty," mobilizing awe over technological progress that was capable of conjuring an island from nothing (Bottorff 1942). The grandeur of the Expo was not simply an escapist paradise but a representational space showcasing the technological future built into its very construction (Lefebvre 2004, 44).

The utopian celebration of the development plan as a fresh start seems directly tied to the island's role as a space within which to realize grand, carefully choreographed visions of a bright future. These visions largely reflect the ideological preoccupations of San Francisco's evolving growth machine. Plans floated before the current one included a golf course, sports complex, theme park, casino, and even an Expo '99 to commemorate sixty years since the Golden Gate International Exposition, all of which predated the noted seismic assessments (Expo '99 1995, 44; Urban Land Institute 1996). Such plans had a global patrimony; the 1990s air was thick with excitement over themed urban space, and planning documents from this period cite themed island parks in Stockholm and Singapore as viable precedents (ROMA Design Group 1996, 44). A 1993 Sustainable Communities workshop at the University of California at Berkeley articulated aspirations for developing Treasure Island most clearly: "Globalization is here. The Bay Area is the gateway to the expanding Pacific Rim trading network and to the global economy. Just as soldiers left the Bay Area for the Pacific theatre of war, so trade will dock here to make the peace" (Blakely 1993, 4).

Nearly two decades later, the TICD plan in a sense still proposes a theme park. The holism articulated by the plan responds as much to the need to assemble a complete experience of a commodified version of sustainability as to a newfound attention to ecological urbanism. Put another way, the project captures place-based monopoly rents through a commodified appeal to ecological urbanism while enrolling environmental advocates into a capitalist redevelopment project. Moreover, it depends on a fetishized conceptualization of sustainability in which the decisive relationships are between technical objects, not social groups or classes (see Marx [1852] 1992, 163). This vision of urban sustainability fundamentally requires a blank slate on which to operate. Moreover, it requires a vast landscape of global capital to secure investment, the underpinnings of which are hardly ecologically positive.

These aspects of ecological future-world and themed commodity blur together in the utopian narrative that carries the day in media. Various reports on the current plan excitedly proclaim the project to be "a model for cities everywhere," an eco-"Xanadu" in the bay and the "super-green city of the future," "the world's hottest property, a showcase of sustainable design," while emphasizing the technological sophistication enabling this sustainable development (King 2005a, 2005b; Ward 2009). Pipes links the new plan directly to the Expo, seeing the island as poised to be "transform[ed] entirely into a place as magical and important as it had been in the past," and *Popular Mechanics* reminds the reader that, like the development plan, the island is itself "an engineering feat" (Pipes 2007, 7; Ward 2009). As the Expo did with the postwar consumer utopia, the project's rhetoric makes an imagined future of ecological and social harmony spatially tangible through the workings of capital. Hence, the reworking of soil and space provide the backstory and the material grounds for Treasure Island's sustainable spectacle in the ecotopia to come.

Jason Hannigan argues that fantasy spaces constitute a powerful arena of municipal expenditure in urban development, as cities are disciplined by the need to attract real estate investment and tourist revenue (1998). He focuses on the entertainment spaces built by downtown redevelopment, but we can see in the Treasure Island plan a similar dynamic. Following Hannigan's concept of "empire's theater," Treasure Island's second act will be as "ecology's theater," where designers have created spaces to produce not subjects of empire but ecological subjects (18–21). The fantasy at work in this environmental dreamworld is that of direct engagement with ecological problems through correct design. This fantasy mobilizes progressive notions of environmentalism and a just way of life as the basis for a spatial commodity produced by the same real estate interests that in other times and places have harnessed notions of the "good life" to sell extensive and ecologically destructive suburban tract developments.[4]

Moreover, the Treasure Island planners and boosters are explicit in their claim that the arrangement of urban space in the plan not only is a prototype that can travel, but also represents the future of urban form itself. In the green present, consumer environmentalism is not escapism or postmodern hyperreality, but an interaction with the all-too-real threats of climate change, sea-level rise, and so on, mediated by a fantastic amount of knowledge about what patterns of consumption represent the responsible life. This is the serious turn of consumption, in which it has taken on all of the weight of politics itself (Barnett et al. 2005). The fantasy being assembled in space is the perfect spatial commodity that can serve as the example for all others, pointing the way for other cities by showing that ecological citizens vote with their feet and dollars.

The development of an ecotopia on Treasure Island is in some ways a response to an ecological crisis that requires a reimagination of urban space. But it may also postpone any direct engagement with the capitalist social relations that generate many of the conditions that mark the galloping crisis. It would be far too functionalist to assert that global capitalism facing catastrophe requires such escape valves. However, Treasure Island's selection for intensified investment in sustainable design has a flavor of Aiwha Ong's notion of spaces of "positive exception," where change is modeled at small scales, rather than carried out broadly, through arrangements amenable to existing power structures (2006). If Treasure Island is the model of ecological urbanism, its spread would focus on spatial design as against social and political processes (see Harvey 2000), rescaling the zone of ecological responsibility to the level of the enclave (Hodson and Marvin 2010). Just as the rehabilitation of Treasure Island acts as a proxy for the ecological leadership of the city and region as a whole, the site-specific public-private economic partnership embodied in TIDA fragments the political administration of ecological governance in ways that are productive of capitalist value (see N. Smith 2002, 438–439). Ecological urbanism is in this sense a way to generate differential rents, and they become proof of its viability (Walker 1974; Harvey 2007).

Thus, while planners tortuously orchestrated a hyper-ecological utopia over the past two decades, poor San Franciscans priced out of longstanding working-class neighborhoods in San Francisco and Oakland decamped to the sprawling exurbs of Antioch, Brentwood, and Oakley (Schafran 2013). Experiments in prefigurative ecotopias such as Treasure Island bring the "nonplace" of utopia into being precisely as an exception to normal life—one that allows its normalcy to persist. The packaged fantasy of the sustainable future, in this respect, permits us to tolerate the contradictions of the present.

The Treasure Island plan, which stalled between 2006 and 2010 in negotiations with the Navy over the terms of transfer and remediation, was cleared to advance by the Board of Supervisors in 2011, only to stall again during the investment freeze of the 2008 financial crisis and then again in 2012 with the withdrawal of Chinese investment capital (M. Smith and Mieszkowski 2012; Gammon 2013). With the demise of California's Redevelopment Agencies in 2012, Treasure Island was discharged by the city's successor agency and converted to an Infrastructure Financing District, which retains tax increment financing powers but does not carry the same affordable housing requirements. Accordingly, TIDA reduced the proposed percentage of affordable housing (Treasure Island Development Authority 2016).[5] Outcry over the contaminated legacy of military use, especially given that current housing is to remain in use long after construction begins, continues (Smith and Meiszkowski 2013; Smith 2012). Moreover, complaints have already begun about the expected increase in already choked bridge traffic.

Although these concerns have important political implications, the dominance of the pollution narrative and the uncertain financing landscape obscures how the plan itself has been fundamentally constrained by the material politics of the island's soils. Just as the site plan erases the labor of environmental activists in shaping a regional politics of sustainability (see Sankalia, this volume), the framing of the island as empty, and the plan as a reflection of astute ecological design alone, obscures the materiality of the undertaking and the island's history. The need to maneuver around the strictures of the Tidelands Trust, combined with the projected cost of seismic stabilization, go further toward accounting for the land-use plan and the profit structure, respectively, than explanations focusing on the emergent green economy or the ability to start again from scratch on Treasure Island.

But neither can these be considered outside the neoliberal logic of urban development, in which no project escapes the disciplining of fiscal responsibility exerted by the need to raise private capital or to finance redevelopment using future property tax increases (Hackworth 2007; Weber 2002). In this case, part of such fiscal responsibility has been the ability of the plan to mobilize markers of a global ecological citizenship in space itself, sustained by liberal environmentalism and capitalist development, as a secure revenue stream. Perhaps the most powerful legacy of the island's construction—a vision of a future consumer utopia unified under a wise, carbon-intensive capitalist American hegemony—has found new life in the holistic package of the "super-green city of the future" leading the way for the urban anthropocene. In this narrative, Treasure Island is the model for a green consumer public to come. But it has come to be so by virtue of the less spectacular and marketable constraints imposed by the unsteady soils of which it is made.

Notes

I would like to thank Lynne Horiuchi and Tanu Sankalia for their dogged persistence on this project, the Center for Middle Eastern Studies at Berkeley for generous funding of conference travel to present this research, and the anonymous reviewers for their incisive comments. Any errors are, as always, wholly my own.

Epigraph. Quoted in Logan Ward, "Why Treasure Island Is the Super-Green City of the Future," *Popular Mechanics*, October 30, 2009, http://www.popularmechanics.com/science/environment/a2442/4239381/.

1 Portions of the site development have since been subcontracted to a variety of architecture and planning firms in the Bay Area. I am grateful to Alison Ecker for pointing this out.

2 In a strong market like San Francisco's, "below market rate" is still open to people making up to 120 percent of area median income.

3 Sherry Williams, interview with the author, Treasure Island Homeless Development Initiative, October 23, 2009.

4 Indeed, Lennar Homes was a major player in the low-density suburban building boom that led up to the subprime housing crash of 2008.

5 In March 2016, TIDA recommended forming an Infrastructure and Revitalization Financing District, a new tool signed into law in 2014 specifically targeted to military base redevelopment, but less specific than previous tools in its requirements for affordable housing (Treasure Island Development Authority 2016b).

References

Barnett, Clive, Paul Cloke, Nick Clarke, and Alice Malpass. 2005. "Consuming Ethics: Articulating the Subjects and Spaces of Ethical Consumption." *Antipode* 37, no. 1:23–45.

Beck, Ulrich. 1992. *Risk Society: Towards a New Modernity*. Newbury Park, CA: Sage.

Benkowski, Paul. 2006. "Treasure Island, Navy's Plunder." *Nukewatch Pathfinder*. http://www.nukewatch.com/quarterly/2006fall/Page 7.pdf.

Blakely, Edward. 1993. "Sustainable Communities Workshop: A Case Study of Base Conversion: Treasure Island." Working Paper No. 601. Berkeley: University of California, Institute of Urban and Regional Development.

Bottorff, H. 1942. "Closing Report, San Francisco Bay Exposition, Sponsor for the Golden Gate International Exposition." San Francisco: Bottorff.

Butler, Judith. 1997. *Excitable Speech: A Politics of the Performative*. New York: Routledge.

California State Lands Commission (CSLC). 2003. "Open Session Minutes." December 9, 2003. Sacramento: California State Capitol. http://archives.slc.ca.gov/Meeting_Summaries/2003_Documents/12-09-03/Items/Minutes.pdf.

Chin, John, Florence Wong, Paul Carlson, and David Cacchione. 2004. "Shifting Shoals and Shattered Rocks: How Man Has Transformed the Floor of West-Central San Francisco Bay." Menlo Park, CA: US Geological Survey.

Coté, John. 2009. "Treasure Island Utopia Gets Reality Check." *San Francisco Chronicle,* December 28. http://www.sfgate.com/news/article/Treasure-Island-utopia-gets-reality-check-3204750.php.

Dineen, J. K. 2010. "Treasure Island Boosts Housing; 2,000 More Units Key to Funding $6B Plan." *San Francisco Business Times,* February 1. http://www.bizjournals.com/sanfrancisco/stories/2010/02/01/story4.html.

Expo '99 Treasure Island Committee. 1995. "Expo '99 Treasure Island: Project Feasibility Assessment." San Francisco.

Gammon, Robert. 2013. "Friday Must Reads: San Francisco's China Deal Unravels; Treasure Island Toxics Are Much Worse than Previously Disclosed." *East Bay Express,* April 12. http://www.eastbayexpress.com/SevenDays/archives/2013/04/12/friday-must-reads-san-franciscos-china-deal-unravels-treasure-island-toxics-are-much-worse-than-previously-disclosed.

Hackworth, Jason. 2007. *The Neoliberal City: Governance, Ideology, and Development in American Urbanism.* Ithaca, NY: Cornell University Press.

Hannigan, John. 1998. *Fantasy City: Pleasure and Profit in the Postmodern Metropolis.* New York: Routledge.

Harvey, David. 1989. "From Managerialism to Entrepreneurialism: The Transformation in Urban Governance." *Geografiska Annaler* 71, no. 1:3–17.

———. 2000. *Spaces of Hope.* Berkeley: University of California Press.

———. 2003. *The New Imperialism.* Oxford: Oxford University Press.

———. 2007. *The Limits to Capital,* updated ed. London: Verso.

Hawkes, Allison, and Bernice Yeung. 2010. "Through Two Mayors, Connected Island Developers Cultivated Profitable Deal." *SF Public Press,* November 9. http://www.sfweekly.com/2005-11-09/news/the-deal-with-treasure-island/.

Hice, Eric, and Daniel Schierling. 1995. "Historical Study of Yerba Buena Island, Treasure Island, and Their Buildings." Oakland, CA: Mare Island Naval Shipyard, BRAC Environmental Division.

Hodson, Mike, and Simon Marvin. 2010. "Urbanism in the Anthropocene: Ecological Urbanism or Premium Ecological Enclaves?" *City* 14, no. 3:298–313.

Holding, Reynolds. 1996. "Treasure Island Pollution Suit: Fuel Leaks Fouled Bay, Too, Environmentalists Claim." *San Francisco Chronicle,* March 6. http://www.sfgate.com/green/article/Treasure-Island-Pollution-Suit-Fuel-leaks-2991103.php.

King, John. 2005a. "Towers, Farm Seen for Treasure Island: Self-Sustaining Neighborhood of 5,500 Residences Proposed." *San Francisco Chronicle,* November 8. http://www.sfgate.com/bayarea/place/article/Towers-farm-seen-for-Treasure-Island-2596465.php.

———. 2005b. "It's Got High-Rises, It's Got Organic Gardens and It Just Might Be a Model for Cities Everywhere." *San Francisco Chronicle,* December 15. http://www.sfgate.com/bayarea/article/It-s-got-high-rises-it-s-got-organic-gardens-and-2588194.php.

Lefebvre, Henri. 1977. "Reflections on the Politics of Space." In *Radical Geography: Alternative Viewpoints on Contemporary Social Issues,* ed. Richard Peet. Chicago: Maaroufa Press.

———. 2004. *The Production of Space / Henri Lefebvre ; Translated by Donald Nicholson-Smith.* Malden, MA: Blackwell.

Martyn, Lynda, and Hal Bohner. 1978. "The Loss of Public Tidelands to Private Parties through Unconstitutional Land Trades." *University of San Francisco Law Review* 13:39–61.

Marx, Karl. (1852) 1992. *Capital.* Vol. 1, *A Critique of Political Economy.* Translated by Ben Fowkes. New York: Penguin Classics.

Ong, Aihwa. 2006. *Neoliberalism as Exception: Mutations in Citizenship and Sovereignty.* Durham, NC: Duke University Press.

Pasco, Jean O. 2005. "In Vallejo, a Lesson in Converting El Toro." *Los Angeles Times,* March 21. http://articles.latimes.com/2005/mar/21/local/me-vallejo21.

Pipes, Jason. 2007. *Treasure Island: San Francisco's Exposition Years.* Charlestown, SC: Arcadia.

ROMA Design Group. 1995a. "Treasure Island Reuse Plan: Existing Conditions Report." San Francisco: City & County of San Francisco, Office of Military Base Conversion, Planning Department and San Francisco Redevelopment Agency.

———. 1995b. "Treasure Island Reuse Plan: Issues and Opportunities." San Francisco: City & County of San Francisco, Office of Military Base Conversion, Planning Department and San Francisco Redevelopment Agency.

———. 1996. "Naval Station Treasure Island Reuse Plan." San Francisco: City & County of San Francisco, Office of Military Base Conversion, Planning Department.

Russell, Ron. 2005. "The Deal with Treasure Island." *SF Weekly,* November 9. http://www.sfweekly.com/2005-11-09/news/the-deal-with-treasure-island/.

———. 2007. "Dig This." *SF Weekly,* February 21. http://www.sfweekly.com/2007-02-21/news/dig-this/.

San Francisco Office of the Mayor. 2008. "San Francisco Receives Governor's Environmental & Economic Leadership Award for Treasure Island Redevelopment Plans." Press Release, December 4. http://sfmayor.org/ftp/archive/209.126.225.7/archives/PressRoom_NewsReleases_2008_94177/index.html.

Schafran, Alex. 2013. "Origins of an Urban Crisis: The Restructuring of the San Francisco Bay Area and the Geography of Foreclosure." *International Journal of Urban and Regional Research* 37, no. 2:663–688.

Schlesinger, Victoria. 2010. "Pollution: Experts Concerned about Treasure Island Cleanup as Seas Rise." *SF Public Press,* June. http://sfpublicpress.org/news/2010-06/pollution-experts-concerned-about-treasure-island-cleanup-as-seas-rise.

Senate Committee on Governmental Organization. 2004. "SB 1873 Treasure Island Public Trust Exchange Act Bill Analysis." Sacramento: State of California. ftp://leginfo.public.ca.gov/pub/03-04/bill/sen/sb_1851-1900/sb_1873_cfa_20040504_152933_sen_floor.html.

Sheridan, David. 1999. "Making Sense of Detroit." *Michigan Quarterly Review* 38, no. 3 (Summer): 320–353.

Simerman, John. 2010. "Treasure Island: A View of the Future." *San Jose Mercury News,* January 21. http://www.mercurynews.com/breaking-news/ci_14243461.

Smith, Matt. 2012. "Treasure Island Residents Seek Answers." *San Francisco Public Press,* September 20. http://sfpublicpress.org/news-notes/2012-09/treasure-island-residents-seek-answers-from-navy-on-radioactive-waste-cleanup/.

Smith, Matt, and Katharine Mieszkowski. 2012. "Treasure Island Development Plans Inch Forward." *KQED,* December 3. https://ww2.kqed.org/news/2012/12/03/treasure-island-development-plans-inch-forward/.

———. 2013. "Treasure Island Soil Tests Raise Concerns—San Francisco Chronicle." *San Francisco Chronicle,* April 21. http://www.sfchronicle.com/bayarea/article/Treasure-Island-soil-tests-raise-concerns-4450631.php.

Smith, Neil. 2002. "New Globalism, New Urbanism: Gentrification as Global Urban Strategy." *Antipode* 34, no. 3 (July): 427–450.

Treasure Island Community Development (TICD). 2011a. *Treasure Island Transportation Implementation Plan.* San Francisco: Treasure Island Community Development, LLC. http://sftreasureisland.org/sites/sftreasureisland.org/files/migrated/FileCenter/Documents/Master_Develpment_Submittals/2011_Entitlements_Presentations/04.21.11_TIDA_Joint_Hearing_Materials/Transportation_Implementation_Plan_FINAL.pdf.

Treasure Island Community Development and Treasure Island Development Authority (TICD/TIDA). 2007. "Development Plan and Term Sheet for the Redevelopment of Treasure Island." San Francisco: Treasure Island Community Development, LLC. http://www.sftreasureisland.org/Modules/ShowDocument.aspx?documentid=308.

Treasure Island Development Authority. 2016a. "Item 8: Housing Plan Overview and Update," January 13. http://sftreasureisland.org/sites/default/files/011316 Item 8_Housing Plan Overview.pdf.

———. 2016b. "Item 9: IFD/CFD Update." March 9. http://sftreasureisland.org/sites/default/files/030916/TIDA Board Item 9 IFD-CFD Update.pdf.

US Census Bureau. 2015. "5-Year American Community Survey, 2008–2012." Washington, DC: US Department of Commerce. http://www.census.gov/programs-surveys/acs/data/summary-file.2012.html.

US Congress. 1990. Defense Base Closure and Realignment Act of 1990 (P.L. 101-510). Washington, DC. http://www.brac.gov/docs/brac05legislation.pdf.

Urban Land Institute. 1996. "Treasure Island Naval Station, San Francisco, California: An Evaluation of Reuse Opportunities and a Strategy for Development and Implementation." Washington, DC: Urban Land Institute. http://sf.uli.org/wp-content/uploads/sites/47/2011/06/San-Francisco-CA-1999.pdf.

Walker, Richard. 1974. "Urban Ground Rent: Building a New Conceptual Framework." *Antipode* 6, no. 1 (April): 51–58.

Ward, Logan. 2009. "Why Treasure Island Is the Super-Green City of the Future." *Popular Mechanics,* October 30. http://www.popularmechanics.com/science/environment/4239381.

Weber, Rachel. 2002. "Extracting Value from the City: Neoliberalism and Urban Redevelopment." *Antipode* 34, no. 3 (July): 519–540.

Winner, Langdon. 1989. *The Whale and the Reactor: A Search for Limits in an Age of High Technology.* Chicago: University of Chicago Press.

Ziemann, Timothy H. 1973. "California's Tidelands Trust for Modifiable Public Purposes." *Loyola of Los Angeles Law Review* 6, no. 3 (1973): 485–525.

11. Groundwork

(De)Touring Treasure Island's Toxic History

C. GREIG CRYSLER

As is the case with many feats of engineering, Treasure Island is often described through the scale of the technical achievements involved in producing it. The island was created from below the waters of the bay using industrial dredging techniques, a spectacle of production that formed a complementary narrative to the completion of the two bridges nearby. Both used the latest in engineering to cross between land; here dredging was used to produce an exploitable terrain. The process of forming Treasure Island's four-hundred-acre surface took more than eighteen months. Twenty-five million cubic yards of fill was mechanically sucked and clawed away from the base and shoreline of the surrounding bay and deposited within a perimeter formed of boulders stacked on the Yerba Buena shoals (Pipes 2007; Reinhardt 1978; Shanken, this volume). In its completed form—after the dredging was finished and before anything was built on it—Treasure Island appeared as a concise materialization of the tabula rasa, the conceptual groundwork of modernist planning epistemology. Its detachment from the adjacent urban region by virtue of its location, combined with its unnatural geometric shape, and above all, its stage-like flatness, enabled it to merge seamlessly with the practices of total planning, which have always demanded a planar starting point free of the burdens of history. Whereas utopian projects such as Brasilia had to first claim the land and refigure it symbolically as the origins of a new wave of national development, Treasure Island emerged gradually from below the waterline (Holston 1989; Scott 1999; Stierli 2013). It was claimed in the imagination before it was completed in material form.

The ways in which the site has been assembled, seized, exchanged, and (re)valued over time contribute to its aura of abstraction, the complex physical conditions that define it receding behind the totalizing schemes that have repeatedly viewed it as inert potential. The language used to describe the island's successive fate underscores its status as a purified abstraction. Originally owned by the City and County of San Francisco (CCSF), Treasure Island was leased to the Navy on July 1, 1941, but with the onset of World War II, its strategic value increased, and in 1942 it was seized under the War Powers Act by the US government. After a court settlement, the island was traded by the CCSF for the parcel of land that became San Francisco International Airport in the south of the city (VMCSF 1942; TIMA 2003; Pellissier 2010). More recently, the island was transferred back to the city, following the

Base Realignment and Closure Act of 1993 (OMBC 1996). In 2014, it was conveyed to Treasure Island Community Development LLC, a real estate consortium including Lennar Corporation, which plans to turn what has become a military-industrial brownfield into a model green city (United States/TIDA 2014). In its final form, the $1.5 billion development will contain more than eight thousand housing units in an arrangement of buildings and parks that its boosters claim will be a global model of green urbanism.[1]

The island's production as a technical surface of transfer, seizure, and exchange has occurred alongside a second set of processes, at once haphazard and unpredictable, in which its fabricated geology became a receptacle for a history of deposits, many of them highly toxic. During its use as a naval station, the soil was contaminated through the production and disposal of military equipment and waste, through training exercises involving nuclear material, and through the "decontamination" of ships arriving at the base from test sites in the Pacific (Weston Solutions 2006, 6–18; TriEco-Tt 2012, 27; 2014a, 2; Dillon, this volume).

When the current plans for Treasure Island were first announced, the toxic and techno-utopian remained largely separate from each other, held apart by the lack of a full accounting of the site's history and a wall of public pronouncements that focused on the Island's dramatic potential as a green city. As part of its agreement to transfer the island to the city, the Navy is required to remediate the site according to federal regulations that operate in tandem with the Base Realignment and Closure Act of 1993.[2] The cleanup process has taken its own tangled course since the closure of the base in 1997. Scientific analyses produced by Navy subcontractors, much of it contradictory, gradually trickled into the public realm. The Navy's containment and dispersal activities have also become visible to visitors and residents of its former military housing, who have been left to correlate what they observe on a day-to-day basis with the Navy's highly technical reports, media investigations, and the "hot" discoveries of the residents themselves.[3] Slowly and surely the complex mixture of chemicals with radioactive and organic materials just below the surface have seeped back into the present in unstable combinations.[4]

The past has contaminated the future before it can be materially realized in the present. Since 2006, the year the Navy released its historical radiological assessment (HRA) of the island, two versions of spatial management have been under way at the same time: one concerned with the past, and the other with the future. On the one hand is the Navy's plan to "remediate" the island to current regulatory standards outlined in its report, based on detailed assessments of toxic conditions by waste management subcontractors. On the other is the comprehensive urban design document produced by the Treasure Island Development Authority (TIDA), the agency set up by the city to consult with stakeholders and the property developer in the production of a master plan (TIDA 2011). The implementation of the resulting document, with the apt subtitle "Design for Development" (or D4D, as it is better known), is predicated on the successful conclusion of the Navy's "restoration" actions, which are now represented as variants of sustainability practice.[5] Both planning logics are shaped by waste: the Navy's report comprises an elaborate plan for detection, subtraction, and displacement of toxic materials designed to enable a partial "unbuilding" of the site; TIDA's plans depend on the successful completion of the Navy's remedial strategies, after which, according to the D4D documents, a highly efficient environment that generates minimal waste will be built.[6]

The release of the Navy's HRA in 2006 immersed the island in an atmosphere of uncertainty that was intensified through the lack of definitive information, the intrinsic uncontainability of waste, and the residents' periodic discoveries of toxic substances.[7] Numerous town hall meetings were held and investigations were launched.[8] In July of 2014, the environmental impact report for the new development withstood a court challenge, and after investigations into health and safety concerns on the Island by the California and CCSF Departments of Public Health, the San Francisco Board of Supervisors approved the transfer of the island to the developer, marking the formal start of the construction process and bringing to a close, for now at least, official engagement with questions about the island's toxic past.

The bulldozers have arrived at Treasure Island to begin the first of four construction phases. The entire process, which will take more than fifteen years to complete, has started with the clearing away of some the island's ruins—and the construction of infrastructure. These changes mark the beginning of the site's reorganization around the twin planning logics of remediation and green urbanism. In the discussion that follows, I depart from these modernization narratives to dwell in the paradoxes of the present. Treasure Island is, for now at least, a destination of temporal mixing and contingency, a place in which traces of its toxic history are being uncovered even as buildings from its military and fairground past continue to be occupied with new, if temporary uses. I examine these remains and reuses alongside visions of the future contained in the D4D master plan, by strategically juxtaposing the unbuilt with what either no longer exists or is about to disappear.

This essay bypasses the certainties of master planning to investigate the entanglement of the site's past and future from the ground up. You might think of our route as a detour—an alternate path through the island's history—one that enters, rather than steers clear of, various zones of construction: of radiological history, financial value, risk, and the relationship between the public and the private, amongst others. Our siteseeing follows the island's datum line, examining the changing meanings, investment structures, policy initiatives, buildings, and utopian proposals that have been projected upon, altered, or removed from the site's planar surface, each time leaving traces in the soil that lies beneath. Each point on our route is a stage in the terrain's paradoxical history of conversion, in which the muck taken from the bay is first transformed into national soil, then becomes a toxic military-industrial sponge, a partly remediated development site waiting to be reused, and finally, the foundation for a green techno-utopia (Figure 11.1). The tour that follows is delivered in the almost-present, with explanatory asides and backward glances. I present an incomplete archive of the soil, and a time capsule of toxicity—at once a commemoration of the site's current uncertainties and an unsettling reminder of the contradictions embedded in it through strategies of displacement, burial, and forgetting.[9]

FIGURE 11.1   Stopping points on a (de)tour of Treasure Island. The map shows the location of images in Figures 11.2 to 11.9. Satellite image courtesy of Google Earth.

Perimeter

We begin our tour on the northwest side of the island, following a path between two sections of former military housing (Figure 11.2). On the left, the backyards are surrounded by chain-link fencing covered with green protective mesh punctuated with hazardous waste symbols; on the right, housing now occupied by civilian tenants, in a neighborhood where nearby buildings have been declared radiologically impacted. In the strange lexicon of terms the Navy has developed to categorize conditions on the island, "impacted" denotes ambiguity: it refers to locations whose safety is as yet indeterminate.[10] They are grey zones subject to further study and recommendations: their contents are cocooned in the time lag of toxic administration. The current inhabitants of Treasure Island, approximately two thousand people scattered across the island in former naval housing, live in close proximity to this uncertainty: it is their next-door neighbor, at once a specter of the past and possible contamination of their futures.

In their tentative sequestration, bounded by flimsy barriers and cut across by powerful bay winds, these "areas of interest" form their own sequence of exhibitionary display, a reverse history that begins with the abandoned domestic spaces of former military workers and their families, whose efforts sustained the atomic dreams of Cold War deterrence. The miniature island suburbia, crafted of cheap materials and organized around cul-de-sacs oblivious to their dramatic surroundings, appears banal today. In its careful, even absurd reproduction of the suburban periphery of the US city, the housing constitutes its own version of a ghostly model city, one that is encumbered not only with the historical knowledge of the limitations of suburban design, but also with the radioactivity that has leaked through the lax regulations, haste, and (sometimes willful) misunderstandings of prior moments. The combination of stucco and aluminum siding, of cheap windows and barren gardens, now carries the subtle threat of danger: residents have been told not to dig in the ground. Only potted plants are permitted.

A raised path crosses the horizon ahead, just beyond the backyards for the housing we pass between. A horizontal sliver of the bay is visible beyond, then the sky. As we clamber up, someone walking their dog ignores the warning signs and steps through a gap in the rusted, partly collapsed fencing. We watch as they continue on their way, following the shoreline walk, past partly demolished housing on their left (Figure 11.3). As they disappear out of view, they will pass alongside the first of

FIGURE 11.2   Path to the shoreline walk on Treasure Island. On the left, unoccupied housing is surrounded by protective fencing punctuated with nuclear contamination warning signs. On the right, market rate housing is occupied by current Treasure Island residents. Photo: Greig Crysler, 2014.

FIGURE 11.3   Looking southwest toward San Francisco, on the shoreline walkway of Treasure Island. To the left, partly demolished housing in the contaminated Site 12; in the distance is the original location of USS *Pandemonium*. The poorly maintained fence permits easy if risky trespass. Photo: Greig Crysler, 2014.

two locations for the USS *Pandemonium,* the mock battleship the Navy built out of scrap metal in drydock on the shoreline as part of its efforts to train personnel in the decontamination of ships.[11] Wells containing "sealed cesium-137 sources" were installed on the ship; using cables, the instructor would withdraw the sources and students would begin the detection process (Weston Solutions 2006, 6-12). As the program developed, short-lived isotopes were also used to contaminate the decks of the mock vessel, which were hosed down with water and detergent. The effluent was allowed to soak into the soil. The Navy stated in its 2006 report that the isotopes had a half-life of thirty-five hours, meaning that the area was not "impacted" (2006, 6-15). The original site of the *Pandemonium* was reclassified for further analysis in 2012 after a "more conservative interpretation of existing information in the HRA" (TriEco-Tt 2012, 26). The change in classification does not stem from concerns about toxic materials deposited in the site as a result of training exercises. The memorandum reveals that the site may have been contaminated during routine visits by the Radiological Services Office (RSO), which "used non-regulated radium devices as check sources" (26). Ra-226, used on the RSO's hazard gauges, has a half-life of 1,600 years, and is 2.7 million times more radioactive than the same molar amount of uranium. Unregulated use or disposal of the devices may have led to radioactive contamination, ironically necessitating the detection of prior forms of detection. The shift in classification underscores the incidental and fragmentary process of historical reconstruction and, by extension, its capacity for potentially endless revision as new details about previously unacknowledged threats are discovered. The island's risk is magnified by an incomplete and unrecoverable knowledge of the past, created by holes in official records, lack of prior regulation, and a predisposition to regard the ground as neutral container with endless absorptive capacities.

We turn away from the fencing that cordons off the shoreline route to the *Pandemonium* site and head in the opposite direction, passing in front of another long line of empty housing whose boarded-up windows face dramatic views of San Francisco. The appliances of the units have been moved outside, and now face the bay in abject clusters with the housing as their vacant backdrop (Figure 11.4). The composite image of buildings turned inside out, their rusting remains awaiting pickup and disposal, occurs on the outer edge of what was once a parking lot—a vast expanse of unpaved surface designed to accommodate twelve thousand cars visiting the Golden Gate International Exposition (GGIE) each day. It was turned into a munitions storage area after the Navy took over the site in 1942 and, later, into the housing we now face. All that remains visible of the parking lot is the flatness of its ground plane.

Although its function is entirely different today, the naval housing forms a silent, if spectacular, display of urban disposability (housing as refuse), one that recalls the architecture of the GGIE. By its very (un)nature, the site was suited to a provisional architecture of illusion, a quality that the exposition celebrated with its building technology of temporary permanence: while appearing eternal, it was revealed to fairgoers as a temporary stage set and promoted as such (San Francisco Bay Exposition 1939, 101–103; *Popular Mechanics* 1939, 6). The island's bounded, stage-like

FIGURE 11.4   Former naval housing facing San Francisco Bay. The appliances have been removed as part of the preparation for demolition. Photo: Greig Crysler, 2016.

surface amplified the exhibition's flat theatricality: it was an artificial world, one that could best be grasped in its totality from a clipper plane, from the city, and most spectacularly from the Bay Bridge, which provided a dramatic auto-entry ritual that began with glimpses from above and continued through a winding descent to a mass arrival point on the manufactured ground plane. All this was perceived through the mobile screen of a car's windshield.

The parking lot became one of the most dramatic displays on the GGIE site—and perhaps the one most overlooked by the exhibition's historians. It formed a massive, machinic boundary that visitors filtered through as the final part of the entry sequence. When it was filled to capacity, the array of cars formed a visual threshold to dramatic views of San Francisco, Alcatraz, and the Golden Gate Bridge just beyond (Figure 11.5).

Just past the abandoned housing, we turn inward from our shoreline walk, tracing the steps of fair goers from the car park to the entrance gate as we walk along Avenue B, turning left to walk along 9th Street to the intersection with Avenue C. Our path takes us just beyond the point where the GGIE's entry gate once stood, a monumental threshold to an ersatz proto-imperial dreamworld. The modeling of US power through a spectacular combination of national exhibition halls, displays of commodities and corporate power, and pleasure grounds was amplified by the geometrical flatness of the island setting. The exhibition's goal was to reconstruct the Pacific region as one of economic exchange, the Pacific Ocean becoming a denaturalized void across which trading would flow without interruption, under the apparently benign control of the

FIGURE 11.5   Specter of parking. During the GGIE, the northern end of Treasure Island was dedicated to a massive parking lot capable of holding twelve thousand cars at capacity. The parking area later housed a munitions warehouse, the first site of the USS *Pandemonium*, and the military housing that remains there now. Photo montage: Alberto Benejam.

United States. Pacifica was the name given to the combination of architectural styles drawn eclectically from nations bordering the aqueous terrain, a fable-like name that celebrated a new Oceanic civilization imagined through the lens of US hegemony (Reinhardt 1978; see Horiuchi, this volume). Both Pacifica and its subsequent iteration Pacific Rim reduce the Pacific Ocean to a flat abstraction: a neutral, blue plane across which forces emanating from distinctive coordination points would flow (Connery 1994). In this respect, the GGIE was a miniaturized version of a desired space of transnational assimilation, where the flatness of the island replicated the conceptual abstraction of the ocean that surrounded it. Both the land and the water are reduced to representations of frictionless abstract space, in which one model of the Pacific region is surrounded by another, operating at a planetary scale.

Cash Register

We continue along 9th Street, walking eastward on a route that roughly follows the axis of the La Plaza zone of the GGIE, arriving at the intersection with what was once Avenue F, roughly in the center of Treasure Island. To our left is Building 257, now shuttered and posted with warning signs about asbestos contamination. Across the street is a baseball field and, just beyond it, a giant mountain of dirt, perhaps four stories in height. In its gargantuan, unfinished presence, the mound stands as a reminder of the many forms of human and material displacement that now haunt the island. No signs explain what the huge pile is for or where its contents are from. It looms large without qualification, creating a backdrop at once banal and threatening in relation to the baseball games played on the grassy expanse just in front of it.[12]

As we face the mound at the edge of the playing field, we stand near the point where a monumental figure of money once rose above the GGIE: a recorder of dollars spent, it was a portly figure of consumption in a time of scarcity. The National Cash Register (NCR) Pavilion took the form of a giant two-story cash register, one whose interior displayed the latest machines for the tabulation and storage of cash; on the outside, the horizontal glass window above the machine's numeric buttons tallied the visitors to the fair and, by extension, the dollars spent on admission (Figure 11.6).

The NCR Pavilion was both an index of the exhibition's popularity and profitability, and a monumental cypher of the consumer society it both prefigured and attempted to jolt into being. It was placed on a picturesque diagonal, making it stand out as an object on the approach from the Court of the Pacific. The giant cash register sums up the political economic processes that created the site, and, as a point of recollection, marks the historical transformation of capital between the Great Depression and the present. Treasure Island was an artifact of state intervention in the 1930s. Like the 1939 World's Exposition in New York, the competing San Francisco fair created a cash infusion into a deeply depressed economy: it was one of the many infrastructure and building projects undertaken with the benefit of federal funding through its New Deal programs to create jobs and, through wage support and related consumption, to stimulate the economy (Rydell, Schiavo, and Bokovy 2010).

FIGURE 11.6   Specter of cash. A ghost of the NCR Pavilion from the 1939 GGIE appears in roughly its former location, as a commemorative afterimage to the age of cash. Photo montage: Alberto Benejam.

The construction of both the island and the newly completed San Francisco–Oakland Bay Bridge that connected it to the mainland were financed by the federal government, making the cash register into a surreal marker of public investment as much as a prefiguration of the consumer society that was to come. As a figure of financial exchange, the monumental cash register seems quaintly nostalgic from a contemporary vantage point, when credit has largely replaced cash and the economy is organized around the accumulation and management of debt. If there is a comparable structure that acts as a similar intersection point for economic processes on the island today, it would be the prosaic figures of the storage containers scattered in various locations—whether stacked up as modules of secure space to hold personal possessions that no longer have a home or as sealed receptacles filled with contaminated dirt from the island—awaiting shipment to one of the Navy's remote storage facilities.[13] Both forms of containment share a common basis in toxicity: one financial, the other, chemical and radiological.

Containment

From our position adjacent to the ghostly cash register, multiple forms of containment surround us: the naval housing located in the Halyburton Court cul-de-sac, to the northwest, is now an open-air storage site, evacuated of its human and material contents and ringed with protective fencing, through which blue storage containers for contaminated waste are visible. Farther beyond, at the north end of the island, an empty lot bounded with more protective fencing acts as one of several staging areas where caskets of toxic waste are stored while they await transport to a remote disposal site in Clive, Utah. Sites for extraction, containment, and shipping of toxic materials are matched by a parallel landscape of personal containment: self-storage businesses where everything from RVs and boats to the furniture and personal effects of individual households occupy rented modules of space. In some cases, the units are within former naval warehouses. At the eastern end of the island, tidy rows of modules are joined together in long, prefabricated alleys framing views of the East Bay. In our current position, opposite the giant mound of dirt, self-storage takes the form of a large parking lot, populated with dormant RVs, boats, and cars (Figure 11.7).

FIGURE 11.7   Storing the self. This self-storage business occupies the vacant lot opposite the former site of the National Cash Register Pavilion. Self-storage is a specter of transition: a rentable occupation of the ground plane that marks both the excess and deferral of consumption. Photo: Greig Crysler, 2014.

The self-storage containers on Treasure Island, when viewed as companion memorials to the NCR cash register, underscore the rise of indebtedness as a generic condition of US capitalism.[14] The containers are typically rented using credit cards, they store goods purchased with credit, and they have become holding tanks for the artifacts of the dispossessed (Mooallem 2009; Streitfeld 2008). The latter includes a large segment of the population that has either entered bankruptcy, is simply no longer able to afford housing, or—as is sometimes the case in the Bay Area—has been forced to downsize because of high housing costs.

Toxic Assets

The privatized redevelopment of Treasure Island—destined to be one of the most expensive of its kind in the world—could not have come into being without the financial resources of a corporation with immense assets of its own, and access to other sources of capital.[15] Lennar Corp, the lead entity in the corporate partnership known as Treasure Island Community Development, has (with some difficulty) managed to leverage the financing necessary to launch the eco-city through a combination of its own financial prowess, its extensive connections to other aspects of the property development industry, and favorable connections to policy makers (Phelan 2008; Smith 2013).[16] During a time in which cities across the United States have been forced to cut programs and engage in brutal versions of "austerity urbanism," Lennar has been the fortunate beneficiary of extensive public support (Hawkes and Young 2010). This includes direct subsidies, such as the agreement to build new and more generous ramps from the Bay Bridge to the island at no cost to the developer, an elaborate web of indirect subsidies extending from the federal government's initial building of the island and postclosure cleanup of the contaminated military base, and the remediation of Lennar's toxic assets in the wake of the last financial crisis. The last enabled Lennar to survive a housing crisis it helped create, allowing the development behemoth to live another day and initiate the massive Treasure Island project.

The giant cash register, invoked here as a specter of a prior model of state intervention, can also be rethought as a signpost dedicated to contemporary forms of cashing in, not only through federal bailout packages, but also through profits achieved by Lennar when it engages in the remediation of foreclosed properties into new sites of investment.[17] As one of the largest home-building companies in the country, Lennar benefited from the massive expansion of credit enabled by adjustable-rate mortgages and new financial instruments such as derivatives and collateralized debt obligations that gathered individual loans into large-scale investment frameworks and eventually plunged the entire system into crisis (Cook 2010).

When the housing market experienced a severe contraction in the wake of the collapse of the speculative investment bubble in 2008, the federal government stepped in with legislation that allowed home-building companies to claim their massive losses against profits they made before the crash (Labaton and Herzenhorn 2008; Corkery

2009; Erickson, Heitzman, and Zhang 2013).[18] In Lennar's case, the bailout resulted in a tax rebate estimated at the time to be as much as $1.5 billion dollars. The rebates were reinvested in Lennar's business operations, including its own mortgage subsidiary, aptly named Universal American Mortgage Corporation, which specializes in offering adjustable-rate mortgages to purchasers of Lennar's housing (Cook 2010).

By centralizing home building and lending in a single entity, Lennar created a unique ecology of surplus accumulation: profit when a housing unit is sold, profits again through the mortgage provided by a subsidiary, and yet again when the mortgage is bundled into a securitized debt obligation. Each step in this triplicate process adds money to Lennar's coffers while diminishing its risk should the mortgage holder default. Lennar has also used the reverse strategy, in which its mortgage subsidiary buys up "distressed properties" produced by the very conditions Lennar helped create. In what is now a common practice in the housing industry nationwide, Lennar has become a significant investor in foreclosed properties, acquiring large developments at significant reductions in market value and reselling them later at considerable profit (Barger 2014; Blake 2014; Mauer 2013).[19]

The financial bailouts offered to Lennar and other corporations in the wake of the credit crisis were recycled policy artifacts from the "national cash register" period of state intervention, and as such they sparked considerable controversy in the United States, where since at least the last major liquidity crisis of comparable magnitude in 1973, the country has headed decisively in the direction of deregulation and the embrace of free market ideologies. Indeed, precisely because the magnitude of the 2008 crisis was so severe and state intervention an unavoidable alternative for all but the far right of the Republican Party, the policy legacy of John Maynard Keynes was opened up for reexamination. For a brief time, President Obama was portrayed (often unfavorably) as a latter-day FDR, whose interventionist policies formed the backbone of the New Deal programs that were responsible for the creation of Treasure Island in the first place. The current eco-development therefore represents both a departure from the political economic context in which its earthen groundwork was created and a return to it by an elaborate route through toxic asset pools and debt remediation.[20]

Design for Development

As we enter our next site, I coordinate present conditions with a specter of the future rather than the past. My reference points are two zones in the master plan published by the Treasure Island Development Authority (TIDA 2011). I summon images that have been made ghostly through the abstracting processes of urban design and representation. The first set describes a park-like amenity that wraps around two sides of the new model city, including a zone referred to as The Wilds. The second set simultaneously cite and negate the Job Corps campus, which occupies a portion of the site at the center of D4D owned by the federal government and therefore is not available for redevelopment. I refer to it as the absent center of the plan.

We begin by projecting ourselves skyward into the elevated station point of the master plan, which, on the first page, offers a diagonal view high above the site (TIDA 2011, i). We now have enough altitude to grasp the new city's systematic procession of shoreline towers juxtaposed with the picturesque jumble of the San Francisco waterfront in the distance. As is so often the case for large development projects, the buildings here are represented as abstract volumes in pure white, removing any architectural detail, color, or signs of life. We ascend even higher to occupy the next level of abstraction, encoded in a satellite view of the site on the next page (2011, vi). We see the entire site in its island purity, surrounded by blue water that appears still and indigo deep, only the shape and density of the buildings providing a suggestion of the how the model city is organized.

As we descend downward through scales, we reach an enlarged site plan (Figure 11.8). Two interlocking L shapes define the organization of the redevelopment: the first, on the south and west sides of the site, contains various configurations of high-density housing, shops, and other amenities. A second L, wrapping around the north and east sides, defines a swath of parkland and recreational amenities (TIDA 2011, 4). The landscaped areas are rendered as a patchwork of green signifiers, ranging from the highly geometrical to the meandering, in various shades of saccharine green. One of these features, a long, rectangular space subdivided into irregular plots, is the Urban Agriculture Park, which D4D claims will offer "outstanding educational opportunities for residents" (90). Benches and walkways will provide opportunities to view a veritable encyclopedia of green technology in action, from wind turbines and solar panels to compost heaps and grey water reprocessing. Just beyond this, The Wilds provide stormwater reprocessing, while acting as a picturesque flood buffer:

> The Wilds are envisioned as being an ecologically valuable habitat area that recalls the once-predominant Bay Area shoreline ecosystems of dune swales and moist grassland. This constructed landscape will mimic a native landscape, supporting activities such as hiking, ecological education programs, habitat viewing and camping. Seasonal and/or perennial wetlands are planned as part of the stormwater treatment system. (84)

The description performs a process of textual abstraction that amplifies the graphic simplifications of the plan: first, The Wilds implies a return to a purified wilderness that never existed on the site, replacing its history as engineered, now-toxic soil with a new condition that is as fabricated as the one it seeks to replace. As we descend from our stratospheric viewpoint back to the ground at the intersection of 9th Street and Avenue F, the full extent of the master plan's project of historical burial becomes clear. The Wilds and the shoreline park that runs alongside it sit atop some of the most contaminated areas on the island.[21] The promised environmental mimicry is carried out in the name of community education but obscures both the existing history of the site and—in the massive removal and soil engineering program that will be required to produce the landscape—the welfare of the creatures who have somehow adapted to the landscape around them.

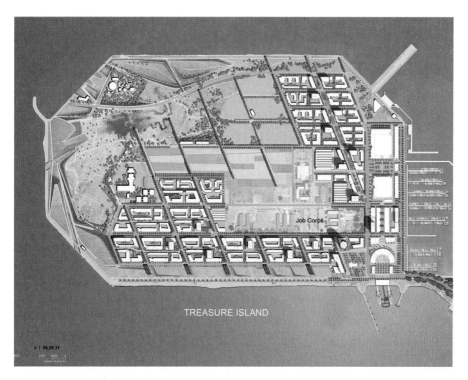

FIGURE 11.8 D4D master plan consistently represents the Job Corps campus (controlled by the federal government, and not part of the redevelopment) as a whited-out abstraction to emphasize the formal coherence of D4D, 2011. Courtesy of Treasure Island Community Development.

The Wilds effectively shift the terrain of education away from the site, which is now subsumed in the larger and far less threatening history of an ambiguously defined regional geography. Yet these landscapes not only are concerned with washing away reminders of the site's past; they also are flood protection devices, planned around selectively managed evidence of sea-level change. As such, both The Wilds and the wetlands could best be described as landscapes of risk: they provide a comforting image of restoration and accommodation, even as their partial disappearance is imagined as an integral part of their design.

Absent Center

D4D's juxtaposed logic of natural mimicry and simulated urbanism attempts to create a bounded plan: an epistemological eco-bubble whose formal coherence would be complete were it not for the stubborn intrusion of several historical remainders that have survived within it. In addition to the expanded version of the site's original wastewater treatment plant and a Coast Guard facility, a third condition, much larger and more awkwardly prominent, sits within the site plan: the space currently occupied by the campus for the Job Corps, a residential program designed to provide at-risk youth with intensive training for employment. It is the partial representation of this space, at once whited out through the master plan's homogenizing abstraction and present as a large and tangible social world organized on strikingly different principles from the new development's vision of community, that forms the next stop on our tour (Quandagno and Forbes 1995; Rawlins 1971).

The Job Corp's campus extends south along Avenue D, comprising an ad hoc jumble of former Navy facilities just to the south of where the NCR cash register once stood. A pragmatic mixture of low-budget modernism and military sheds, they are architecturally far removed from the coordinated aesthetic of their future surroundings, or the Pacifica style of the large exhibition halls that stood in the same location before the Navy arrived. The buildings are remnants from prior moments in the discourse of efficiency, when leakages of heat and radiation passed freely through black holes of knowledge, regulation, and porous materiality into the earth's atmosphere and surfaces (Figure 11.9). The buildings are not only archival statements of a prior "un-eco" military city with outdated cladding systems; they also shelter an institution that is segregated from the new development by its ownership. And in another sense, the Job Corps is under the perpetual threat of burial: almost since its inception, it has been attacked by antigovernment conservatives, who have decried it as part of the failed imperatives of the welfare state, a budget drain that must be blocked to avoid further wasteful spending (Anderson 1973).[22]

FIGURE 11.9   Un-eco-city. The Job Corps campus, at the center of the Treasure Island Development, will remain under federal management and is not part of the D4D plan. It will stand as an unintended exhibition of "inefficient" models of building technology and a partly superseded model of welfare. Photo: Greig Crysler, 2014.

The program was founded in 1962 as part of the Manpower Development Act, and expanded under the Johnson administration's War on Poverty, as an institutionalized effort to salvage the damaged lives of troubled and "failed" youth, both from themselves and their inner city environments, which were then embroiled in violent protests. In its current form, the Job Corps program at Treasure Island (one of 115 campuses across the country) has a residential population of more than eight hundred participants and eight large buildings. The Job Corps' regimented model of individual reform contrasts sharply with D4D's parallel staging of spectacular "ecological learning opportunities" that will supposedly enable visitors and residents to freely aggregate into a classless, green citizenry. It remains to be seen whether the temporary residents of Job Corps, many from impoverished backgrounds, will be able to participate in the spectacle of consumption placed just beyond their reach.

Despite the many striking differences between the Job Corps campus and the rest of the site, the contrasts are skillfully reduced through the graphic style of D4D: the Job Corps' messy, conflicting reality is mastered with white abstraction and made to disappear amidst the plan's white forms. It achieves the minimal status of number 20 in the key to the "illustrative plan" (TIDA 2011, 6). Beyond this, it is not mentioned in the plan's narrative: it remains an ambiguous zone of almost obsolete welfare planted at the very center of the development. For all the emphasis on the eco-city's production of community, D4D offers no explanation of what the Job Corps is, or how its institutional space will be connected to everyday life in the model city that surrounds it on all sides. Unlike the generic names evoking collective urban life given to other districts in the plan, the space occupied by Job Corps is designated only by its militaristic program name and then whited out.

Although the built landscape of the Job Corps disappears into the graphic ordering of the master plan drawings, the entire campus remains awkwardly embedded in the development because it is owned and managed by the federal government. It will continue to occupy the site's 1939 ground plane, and the rest of the island will be built up around it with new layers of protective gradient designed to accommodate sea-level change. The projected maximum of gradient change is based on mid-level estimates produced by averaging available predictions, some extending back over two decades, when climate change science was relatively new. The current plan is to raise the site gradient by thirty-six inches, largely through elaborate soil engineering concealed beneath the contours of the Wetlands, and the new ground levels of the eco-city's urban districts (Schlesinger 2010b). Recent discussions of climate change, particularly those following the partial collapse of an ice sheet in Antarctica in 2014 (far ahead of even liberal predictions), suggests that the pace and severity of sea-level rise may exceed current and widely divergent estimates (Rignot et al. 2014).

The master plan permits an additional foot of tolerance in the grade changes embedded in the plan. The sea wall surrounding the island will be converted into something akin to a dyke if necessary, an extraordinarily expensive option that occupants would be charged a tax for, should it become necessary.[23] Others have argued that the soil should be raised to a higher level as part of the current development, a proposal that would further encase the Job Corps campus in flood protection engineering and run the risk of causing the entire island to collapse under the weight of the additional soil.

Skidmore Owings and Merrill (SOM), the lead designers of TIDA's master plan, turned the possible flooding resulting from the new development's conservative estimates of sea-level change into the basis of a design opportunity elsewhere on the bay. Their successful entry to the 2009 Rising Tides Competition, called the BayArc, is designed to protect the Bay Area from sudden changes in sea level, whether from periodically extreme high tides or tsunamis. A giant water catcher, improbably tied to the Golden Gate Bridge, would be raised from the depths of the bay when the time comes, to save not only the metropolitan area but also its new icon, the Treasure Island redevelopment. A completed version of the pristine eco-city is shown in artists' renderings as a something akin to an aquatic hood ornament, safely installed on the other side of the proposed barrier (Naidoo 2009).

Historical Foils

In the final stop on our tour, we enter the textual space of the Navy's *2014 Technical Memorandum*, a lengthy two-part document issued to correct the findings of the *2006 Historical Radiological Assessment*. As outside observers to the seemingly arcane and highly specialized language of military-nuclear history, it is apparent from the outset that the report constitutes a self-referential display that is only partially (if at all) accessible to civilians who lack scientific training in the minutiae of nuclear waste management. Nevertheless, the report is based on familiar historiographic methods of positivist detection, and it begins gamely, by setting the scene, and thereafter also follows the logic of a tour, focusing the readers' attention by magnifying some locations and ignoring others. The array of confirmed chemical and nuclear hotspots—areas of interest or safe zones—become stopping points on the tour, resulting in a taxonomic system of immense complexity, one whose deeply coded meanings are available only to highly specialized experts. Although issued to the general public in a gesture of transparency, to the nonexpert who may be affected by what the report describes, it will remain for the most part utterly opaque.[24] The report describes the elaborate buildup of a toxic archive, mapped in relation to the soil and catalogued in as much detail as imperfect records and largely subcontracted institutional processes permit. Old black-and-white photographs, new and historical interviews, meeting minutes, maps, Geiger counter readings, chemical tests, newspaper articles, letters, emails, and prior reports are among the materials gathered here in the effort to reconstruct the history of Naval Station Treasure Island.

In its reliance on the abstract authority of aerial photography and maps, and its progression around the island's toxic hot spots in the clinical-diagnostic language of technical rationality, the report constitutes a reverse narrative of D4D: an apocalyptic rendering of modernization in reverse, one that, with each new iteration further intensifies, rather than settles, the island's toxic uncertainties. We might regard the site as a potentially infinite archival display, one whose traces extend in all directions: into the atmosphere (where incinerated toxic materials were discharged); deep into the ground where they seeped; through the currents of the bay (where they flowed in discharged wastewater); across the country on rail lines to disposal sites; and into bodies, both human and nonhuman, who have ingested or been exposed to the island's deadly materials.

The paradoxical combination of positivist history and multiplying uncertainty can be summarized by a visit to a small group of still indeterminate objects displayed on page 5 of the 2014 Supplemental Technical Memorandum. Small, shiny, and about the size of a dime, each has flattened edges that recall in miniature the artificial geometry of the island. Approximately seventy-five have been discovered to date, unearthed from their position just below grade through the movement of remediation equipment across what were once solid waste disposal areas (TriEco-Tt 2014a, 5). Others have been discovered on the sidewalks or grass adjacent to residents' housing. It was also the possible discovery of such objects that led to the reclassification of the USS *Pandemonium* site. While explaining how the disruption of the former dumpsites could lead to the accidental emergence of the disks, the 2014 memorandum reflects puzzlement about their origins. The best guess offered—without any strong evidence to support it—is that they were used as calibration foils for high-range "Radioactive Detection, Identification and Computation" sets (5). These fragments of prior forms of nuclear surveillance equipment have now become urgent objects of investigation. They are eternal reminders of waste's uncontainable properties. As such, they are foils to the certainties of linear history.

The plight of the foils, their murky origins, and their indeterminate numbers summarize the ambiguity surrounding the island's toxic history. Indeed, the entire island was misclassified in the 2006 HRA. It described Naval Station Treasure Island as a training facility. This foundational assumption was overturned when an article in a back issue of the naval magazine *The Masthead* was subsequently discovered describing Treasure Island as producing up to two hundred thousand pounds of salvage material a month (TriEco-Tt 2014a, 24). From this seemingly modest source, many assumptions about the island were revised once it became clear it was a significant site for repairs and radioactive damage control.

The residents, together with what remains of the independent media in the Bay Area, have been largely responsible for bringing the hazardous qualities of the island to light.[25] The residents have discovered radium foils in their yards; they have observed trucks with uncovered soil being moved from one hazardous waste location to another; they have witnessed soil from adjacent lots being dug up and stored in secure containers for removal; they have been warned not to dig into the soil or plant vegetation in their yards; they have watched as sections of Area 12 (first a parking lot, then a munitions bunker, then a dump, and finally a housing subdivision) have been emptied of occupants and cordoned off with protective fencing marked with hazardous waste warning signs. All of this has occurred amidst continuous statements from both the Navy and later the San Francisco and California Departments of Public Health that the housing they occupy is safe.[26] The contradictory qualities of their everyday experience have fueled skepticism and led to distrust of the official response, intensifying the intrinsic uncertainty of the island's waste.

Grounding Infinity

Before departing, there is one final site to see. We return to what was once the GGIE's grand entry route—the space in front of the curving Fine Arts Building that is now a parking lot. On this flat, stage-like surface, cars and crowds have circulated; just beyond, spectacles of power have risen and fallen, their remnants accumulating above and below the ground. The disintegrating remains of a time capsule lie buried in this vicinity. A redwood chest was lowered into the ground here by local dignitaries as part of the GGIE's groundbreaking in 1936 (Reinhardt 1978, 38).[27] The locked chest contained only one set of artifacts: copies of the architectural drawings for the GGIE, to remain submerged until an unknown moment of rediscovery. We can imagine how, over the years, earthly forces have eaten away at the timber capsule, dissolving its integrity, gradually consuming its message. The chest's location is approximate, and its contents are—for now at least—blocked from access by the thick layer of bitumen pitch, gravel, and sand we stand upon.

From the island's muddy emergence until now, the site's flat datum line has also defined the boundaries between the past and the present, the visible and the invisible, the toxic and the techno-utopian. It also acts as the baseline for investments, both symbolic and speculative, that have reshaped the land over time. Our detour has followed this line, revealing what is buried below it, viewing what remains above it, taking account of what is about to disappear, and imagining—through a sequence of specters—the momentary return of what has been demolished. We have also followed this line into the present, as it reappears in the two reports now guiding the island's redevelopment.

Although completed separately, and according to a formal division of responsibilities, the Navy's 2014 technical memorandum and the D4D master plan are interdependent, one based on the authority of the other. The memorandum manages the remediation of the past in order to allow D4D—an idealized vision of the future—to materialize. Both reports are efforts at containment: time capsules at an urban scale. Although claiming to overcome the escalating environmental, financial, and regulatory contradictions that surround them, their coherence and authority depend on continuous acts of extraction, removal, and burial of both hazardous materials and contentious facts. They are waste systems in motion: rhetorical frameworks for a cleanup operation that attempts to limit both the mental and material understandings of the site.

Yet the many ambiguities and silences in official records, the unavailability of personnel who have passed away or are unable to remember, and different cultural attitudes toward both waste and the soil have led to ongoing seepages and leaks of the past into the present. The Navy's assessments and subsequent memos in relation to the radiologic history of the site bring new meaning to the word "final." In 2006, when the Navy published the HRA, the word appears in boldface below the title. The report was significantly amended by two subsequent technical memoranda (the most recent from July 1, 2014), each constituting an internalized waste ecology of toxic history: entire sections of the original report are reused verbatim in ways that merge seamlessly with new information, thus conserving the authority of the document as a statement of truth within a framework of potentially endless revision.

The processes the Navy used suggest that a combination of scientific intelligence and technical competence can achieve a situation of secure containment, thereby restoring the soil to the status of an abstract Other: inert, docile, and ready for development. From the standpoint of the Navy, its successive assessments lead toward a definitive cataloguing of the site. Yet the very act of reiteration, combined with the continual citation of gaps in knowledge, suggests that the events to be reconstructed can never be fully known: their traces can never fully tracked down, and their threats never fully contained. The Navy's elaborate historical reporting on radiological dangers is constructed according to a familiar modernist teleology, in which past (toxic) events are arranged in a way that leads to the desired moment in the present, one of resolution and stasis.

The island is viewed by the Navy and the developers as a resource, but one whose value is not grounded in what can be extracted but, rather, in what remains after extraction has occurred. The contaminated earth generates surplus both through the process of its removal, and through the potential value of the "decontaminated" land left behind. This process of abstraction, enacted at both a material and symbolic level, lays the groundwork for the latest version of Treasure Island now being constructed according to the protocols of D4D. The redevelopment necessarily defines the ground plane as resolved, and hence a neutral starting point for a new (green) history: a third-order tabula rasa, after the GGIE and the naval base, on which a new enclave will be built. Despite the eco-city's skyward ambitions, the organizing logic is also one of burial: the new plan caps off the existing soil and its damaged history, while burying contradictory signs of contemporary life. The massing of cars formed a spectacular boundary to the imperial narrative of pan-Pacific production and consumption of the 1939 World's Fair, an automotive edge that has been interiorized and placed out of view in D4D. Cars come to rest in garages, allowing a pastoral image of green modernism, accompanied by a miniature farm and wetlands of artificial history, to predominate.[28]

D4D captures views of the city as a selling point and offers its skyline as a complimentary mirror in exchange: the new towers will, the feasibility report tells us, reflect the adjacent city in all its uniqueness. The rhetoric of D4D turns environmental risks into urban features, making the transitory feel concrete and the unpredictable seem manageable. Planetary processes such as high winds, toxic flows, rising sea levels, and shifting grounds are reframed as budget costs to be managed, giving unruly processes precise actuarial boundaries. Such logic ironically suggests that the global financial system is somehow more stable than the planetary ecology it must both maintain and exploit, a point that has been refuted to devastating effect by the events of 2008. The costs of fully responding to the site's worst-case scenarios would require the new development to either sink under its own weight or to become a sealed compound for millionaires, a future possibility that remains too contentious to imagine, for now at least.

Although the island's redevelopment is dependent on a myriad of incentives and the distinctive political maneuvering and resistances characteristic of Bay Area politics, its proponents claim it will stand as a universal model of exemplary urbanism to be easily replicated in other cities around the world (CCI 2009). Yet, as our detour suggests, when all its conceptual and physical acts of burial, displacement, filtering, and downcycling are accounted for, D4D is less a model for how to save the planet than an elaborate demonstration of sustainability's narrative of disavowal: a split discourse that "indexes nature and humanity's depletion only to convert them back into 'capital,' the very force that depleted them in the first place" (Medovoi 2010, 138).

If a model for the future has emerged, it is not to be found in the white abstraction of D4D, but rather in what can be seen and heard on the ground: the disparate, sometimes competing voices of residents, activists, journalists, and dissident professionals, whose "hot" discoveries, speculations, and rumor-trackings have helped unravel the presumption of a full and final cleanup. In the process, a different vision of the future has emerged, one shaped by permanent ambiguity that cannot be overcome by scientific prediction or resolved through the "politics of prophesy" (Evans and Reid 2014, 189–190; Amoore 2011).[29] The island's relation to its toxic past will never be definitively settled, but the process of bringing that uncertainty to light has laid the groundwork for a different kind of ecological politics, in which the finite limits of planetary life define the creative terrain of the future.

Notes

I would like to thank Kouros Alaghband for his research assistance and comments on an earlier version of this draft, and Wanda K. Liebermann and Maria Moreno Carranco for their reviews of earlier versions of the essay. I am also grateful to Alberto Benejam for his specter montages, included as figures in this essay. The approach to this chapter was influenced by my ongoing collaboration with Shiloh R. Krupar on our coauthored book project, *Waste Complex: Capital/Ecology/ Sovereignty*. I am indebted to the co-editors of this volume, Tanu Sankalia and Lynne Horiuchi, for their patience and excellent guidance. Responsibility for the essay as published is entirely my own.

1 The redevelopment was, for example, selected for inclusion in the Clinton Climate Initiative to demonstrate "models for sustainable urban growth with projects in 10 countries on six continents" (CCI 2009). Since the announcement of the selected projects in 2009, the Promethean, globe-girding rhetoric of CCI has been diffused by the spectacular failure of some of the "star" developments. The eco-city in Destiny, Florida, collapsed after a legal dispute between the cofounders; others, such as the Elephant and Castle mega-development in London and the Donlands development in Toronto, are mired in controversy about the scale, decision-making processes, public-private funding mix, and environmental impact of the supposedly green but avowedly pro-growth and developer-friendly projects.

2 The Navy's Installation Restoration Program encompasses the federal Base Realignment and Closure program, and operates in accordance with the Comprehensive Environmental

Response, Compensation, and Liability Act of 1980 (CERCLA) and the Superfund Amendments and Reauthorization Act of 1986 (SARA). The Navy also operates the Restoration Advisory Board (RAB), composed of members of the local community and representatives of the Navy, US Environmental Protection Agency, California Environmental Protection Agency, the City of San Francisco, and other public agencies. The RAB is intended to facilitate communication about contamination concerns between various governmental and naval agencies and citizens.

3 The debates around safety and health stemming from the toxic history of Treasure Island represent the intertwined forces of threat and insecurity that inform Ulrich Beck's definition of risk. As Beck notes, ambiguity is intrinsic to risk: it "opens up a world within and beyond the clear distinction between knowledge and non-knowing, truth and falsehood, good and evil" (2007, 4). Thus the endless deferral of certainty at Treasure Island "amalgamates knowing with non-knowing within the semantic horizons of probability" (5). Soil samples and Geiger counter readings appear to multiply and fracture truth, rather than contain it in a neat and reassuring parcel for collective consumption. As the many reports about Treasure Island produced by the Navy show, more research paradoxically results in greater uncertainty. Such conditions exemplify what Beck has called World Risk Society, where we "must make decisions concerning the world's future under the conditions of manufactured, self-inflicted insecurity. . . . the world can no longer control the dangers produced by modernity" (8).

4 Peter C. van Wyck argues that nuclear contamination violates the conventional economy of accumulation (containment) and expenditure (disposal) that is characteristic of waste epistemologies and practices. Nuclear waste, he notes, "can neither be completely accumulated (contained) nor spent (disposed). It tends to drift" (2005, 4). Thus the "nuclear threat asserts a problem; a problem that demands a solution even while admitting of no solution in particular" (7).

5 The Navy, working in collaboration with the Department of Defense (DOD), has launched a system-wide sustainability program, which applies institutionalized epistemologies of technical rationality to equate various forms of efficiency, disposal, and remediation with sustainability. As Andrew Ross notes, the goal is to ensure environmental compliance in the same way as the DOD seeks to ensure combat readiness," in the process marking the arrival of a military-industrial-environmental complex (1996, 10). The strategic discourse of "greening military sites" and their intersection with the impression management of toxic threats is examined in Kenneth Hansen's *The Greening of Pentagon Brownfields* (2004). The process is consistent with what Leerom Medovoi describes as the capitalist discourse of "sustainability as disavowal" (2010).

6 D4D presents the city of San Francisco as a happy, classless family of equal neighborhoods, each distinguished from the next by their unique "world-class" personalities. As the latest addition to the family, D4D seeks to be a docile but scientifically informed sibling: "It is oriented around a progressive design philosophy reflecting San Francisco's commitment to sustainability and reflects years of planning and design by many contributors. Its goal is to ensure that the islands enter San Francisco's family of world class neighborhoods, using an innovative design that embodies the City's most desirable characteristics" (TIDA 2011,7).

7 Following the release of its 2006 HRA, the Navy hired New World Environmental (NWE) to conduct routine tests for radiation on Treasure Island. In 2013, Don Wadsworth, a health physicist for NWE, "broke his silence" and stated that he had found elevated radiation readings across the island as early as 2007 (Nguyen, Wagner, and Carroll 2013). His remarks appeared to be confirmed by a 2013 report describing tests completed in 2013 at Bigelow Court that revealed the soil beneath ground floor slab at 1101 Bigelow Court had elevated radiation levels of 80,000 cpm and 30 uR/hr (NSTI 2013, 7). Wadsworth claimed that the 2013 readings indicated the Navy's slowness to publicly acknowledge the island's radiological threat. His assertions were reinforced by Robert McLean, another NWE worker who also found elevated radiation levels on the island. He was the first to discover one of the radium disks described in detail in the Navy's 2014 technical memorandum, and was later fired by his own account because he was not wearing proper protective gear at the time of his discovery (Smith and Mieszowski 2014). The Bigelow Court housing is adjacent to other occupied housing. TIDA argued that any radioactive material was effectively contained and, based on naval intelligence, posed no threat to residents (Smith 2013).

8   Although radiological evidence was found on the site starting in 2007, a memorandum to
    the original HRA was not issued until 2012, identifying new sites for investigation. It was
    in 2014 that the island's status as a construction, repair, and salvage site is referenced,
    seven years after the initial radioactive discoveries by naval subcontractors. The 2014 report
    acknowledges that naval ships were decontaminated and repaired at Treasure Island after
    atomic warfare exercises, a set of operations well beyond the island's previously assumed
    role as a rest stop and port of deployment for Navy operations. The new understanding of the
    history of the island suggested the possibility of greater levels of contamination. Meanwhile,
    roughly two thousand persons continued to inhabit former naval housing, much of it adjacent
    to areas where the first evidence of nuclear contamination was discovered in 2007 (Smith
    and Mieszkowski 2014).

9   This essay follows in the tracks of recent literature concerned with the intersection between
    toxic remainders, ecological politics, and the posthuman condition, including Shiloh Krupar's
    "Situated Spectacle: Cross-Sectional Soil Hermeneutics of the Shanghai 2010 World Expo"
    (2015, 152–189; see also Cooper 2010; Gabrys 2009; Gille 2007; Kennedy 2007; Krupar 2013;
    Scanlon 2005; van Wyck 2004, 2010).

10 Both the California Department of Public Health and the Navy define "radiologically
    impacted" as referring to a site that requires further investigation to determine its radiological
    status. Though the word "impacted" clearly suggests otherwise, in this context it does not
    mean that the site exhibits levels of radiation above those considered safe background levels.
    Indeed, the very ambiguity of the official meaning of the term (which both implies a threat
    and denies it until it is officially proven otherwise) has clearly played a role in magnifying the
    concerns of local residents. In a letter dated October 15, 2012, Amy Brownell, environmental
    engineer for the San Francisco Department of Public Health, wrote to the San Francisco
    Board of Supervisors to explain the meaning of the term, following a letter sent to Treasure
    Island residents notifying them the Navy would be undertaking tests of nine radiologically
    impacted areas on the Island: "Please note that the term 'radiologically impacted' does
    not mean that these areas are known to contain radiological materials or that a release of
    radiological materials is known to have occurred. It simply means that the Navy is required
    to conduct further investigations to determine whether any radiological contamination is
    present" (2012).

11 The USS *Pandemonium* was moved to the northeast side of Treasure Island in 1969, where
    it remained until it was demolished in 1996. The training ship was part of a new Damage
    Control School that opened in three buildings adjacent to mock battleship's site. The storage
    tanks for contaminated wastewater from training exercises on the *Pandemonium* are cited as
    an area of interest in the Navy's 2014 memorandum (TriEco-Tt 2014a, 52).

12 The mysterious mound of earth is composed of the dirt extracted during the fourth boring
    of the Caldecott Tunnel, a vehicular route through the Berkeley Hills between Oakland and
    Orinda, California, and completed in 2013. Starting in 2010, approximately 183,000 cubic
    meters of dirt and rock were removed and transported elsewhere. Of this, 280,000 cubic feet
    of "clean spoils" were taken to Treasure Island and deposited there in a huge mound (Lenhart
    2013). Before the extracted dirt was removed from the site, it was subject to "paleontological
    mitigation" in which experts subcontracted by Caltrans, the project's managing authority,
    examined the dirt for fossils and the deposits they are found in (Alden 2011; Cuff 2010).
    The dirt taken to Treasure Island will be spread across the site as part of the plan to raise the
    gradient in an effort to limit flooding from rising sea levels.

13 According to CalWatchdog, 705 containers of toxic soil had been shipped to the low-level
    radioactive waste storage facility in Clive, Utah, currently owned by EnergySolutions, by
    September 2010 (Pignataro 2010). It is one of four low-level storage facilities in the United
    States, all of which are in non-urban locations. Class A material sent from Treasure Island
    to the Clive facility will take up to one hundred years to decay to background levels. The
    Utah facility was operated by Envirocare Corporation until 2005, and had been the subject
    of controversy since its opening in 1988, with claims of irregular business practices and a
    questionable relationship between the company and state regulators highlighted in a detailed
    report by the League of Women Voters (2005). The facility was sold for $500 million to
    Lindsay Goldberg & Bessemer, a New York investment firm, and Creamer Investments of
    South Jordan, Utah. The sale allowed Envirocare to be reconstituted as EnergySolutions. The
    owners of Envirocare bought the British government radioactive waste cleanup company,

BNG America, and merged it with Envirocare and an Envirocare division, Scientech D&D, to create EnergySolutions. In this way, Envirocare underwent its own version of containment and disposal, as the original company is now invisibly stored within a new and larger corporate holding tank. The reformulated company has aggressively sought to expand its business, seeking, for example, to import nuclear waste to the facility from Italy, a proposal that was fought in the courts in Utah for more than three years. The 10th District Court of Utah ultimately ruled in 2010 that the Interstate Compact on Low-Level Radioactive Waste has authority over the Clive site, thereby establishing the legal basis to deny the shipments (*EnergySolutions LLC v State of Utah*, http://www.ca10.uscourts.gov/opinions/09/09-4122.pdf). In 2006, EnergySolutions was granted the naming rights for the stadium affiliated with the NBA Utah Jazz team, in Sault Lake City. In 2015, EnergySolutions acquired the Texas-based Waste Control Specialists (WCS), raising speculation that radioactive waste may redirected to WCS sites in Texas (Maffly 2016).

14 The shift to an economy organized around the production and governmentality of debt has been explored extensively by scholars since the 2008 credit crisis. Maurizio Lazzarato argues that indebtedness emerged together with neoliberalism as a primary disciplining mode of social organization that colonizes the future of late capitalism (2011); Andrew Ross argues that we now operate within the debt-saturated context of a "creditocracy," effectively ceding democratic decision-making and the design of public policy to banks and the managers of debt; other scholars, such as David Graeber, have reinterpreted debt as the misunderstood foundation of economic relations before and then within capitalism, in the process extending its organizing significance to the last five thousand years (Lazzarato 2011; Graeber 2011; Ross 2013).

15 The financing arrangements enabling the Treasure Island development to proceed became considerably more complicated after the 2008 credit crisis, despite the growing demand for housing in the Bay Area in recent years. Conventional investment sources proved difficult to attract to the development in the conservative lending environment that followed 2008. The financial crisis left pension and private equity funds with huge losses; California also ended its redevelopment agency after 2008, which eliminated another traditional source of infrastructure bonds. Initially the city and the developer were optimistic that investment funds from China would replace those no longer available from domestic sources. The China Development Bank initially appeared willing to invest in the project. The deal, which also involved the massive Chinese Railway Construction Corporation, fell apart because the Chinese investors demanded a greater return on their investment and more control over the project as a whole (Corkery 2009; McMahon and Whelan 2012).

16 Top city officials have migrated to appointments in Lennar and related companies in the property development industry. In 1997, Mayor Willie Brown appointed Kofi Bonner as his chief economic policy adviser. Bonner became the head of Lennar Urban in 2006, two years after Brown's second term ended. Brown is a minority partner in the San Francisco Bay Area Regional Center, which attracts overseas investment in US projects from individuals seeking to immigrate to the United States. The center is contributing to the cost of building the infrastructure on Hunters Point, the other major development by Lennar in San Francisco (Smith 2013; Walker 1997).

17 As Christopher Cook notes, "In 2007, two hours before the end of the fiscal year, Lennar sold 11,000 lots in 11 seven states to Morgan Stanley at 2/5ths of their book value of $1.3 billion. Lennar was able to apply the losses to taxes paid two years earlier or 20 years forward. Lennar expected to gain 800 million from the deal. In the period following the 2008 crash, Lennar laid off 44% of its workforce and lost $3.4 billion over three years. Revenues plummeted to 2.8 billion in 2008 and 2009, 82% below 2006. Though its lending subsidiary, Homebuilding American (now called Universal American), Lennar increased its use of subprime mortgages by 157% from 2005 to 2006, percentage of riskier loans increased to 22.6%." (2010).

18 The *New York Times* reported that in 2008, fifteen of the biggest homebuilders, including Lennar, formed a coalition and hired a lobbying firm, C2 Group, in addition to the larger National Association of Homebuilders to ensure that operating losses could be carried back over four years rather than the previous two. The tax relief enabled Lennar to dramatically reduce its 2009 losses from $731.4 million to $417 million (Labaton and Herszenhorn 2008).

19 In perhaps its most stunning maneuver, in 2007, Lennar sold its stake in a land venture
    known as LandSource to Calpers for $660 million. As McMahon and Whelan note, "The
    following year LandSource filed for bankruptcy amidst nationwide losses in real estate
    values, and Lennar bought back much of the land for pennies on the dollar. Lennar's
    former Chief Investment Officer, Emile Haddad, and the main actor behind the LandSource
    deal, launched a land development company with Lennar as the main investor, known as
    FivePoints Communities. FivePoints became the major developer for four big real estate
    projects in California, including Hunter's Point [sic] and Treasure Island" (2012). During
    the same period, real estate investors began purchasing large quantities of homes through
    foreclosures and short sales. Blackstone Group LP, the largest private equity real estate
    in the world today, entered the market aggressively after 2008, and by 2013 was spending
    $100 million a week on houses (Gittelsohn and Perlberg 2013).

20 The use of targeted forms of state intervention to mediate the 2008 credit crisis led
    to the popular characterization of the plans launched by the Obama administration as
    the "New New Deal." The phrase was provocatively brought to life on the November
    27, 2008, cover of *Time* magazine, which featured Obama montaged into the position
    of Franklin D. Roosevelt in a famous 1930s photograph showing FDR in a motorcade
    following his election (*Time* 2008). The chairman of the Federal Reserve, Ben Bernanke, a
    former professor of economics at Princeton University, is an expert on the role of federal
    monetary policy during the Great Depression. He reversed his long-held position against
    federal intervention to argue in favor of significant spending by the Federal Reserve,
    primarily through "quantitative easing," or the Reserve policy of buying treasury notes
    to suppress interest rates and encourage borrowing. Bernanke summarized the Federal
    Reserve's strategies in a 2012 speech to the Kansas City Federal Reserve, when he
    discussed a broad range of "policy tools" to stabilize the economy, from printing more
    money, to communication techniques designed to restore confidence and encourage
    investment (2012).

21 The Shoreline Park, which wraps around the northwestern, northern, and northeastern
    part of the island, encompasses the location of the first and second site of the USS
    Pandemonium, where radiological decontamination exercises were staged as part of Naval
    Station Treasure Island's status as home to the Atomic Warfare School, later renamed as
    the Nuclear, Biological, and Chemical Warfare School; it also contained a Damage Control
    School, which included firefighting and control of radioactive material. Treasure Island
    also was a berthing station for ships involved in test explosions (1946) in the Bikini Atoll,
    known as Operation Crossroads (also see Dillon, this volume). According to the HRA, these
    ships were decontaminated at Hunters Point and then berthed at Treasure Island (Weston
    Solutions 2006, 6; TriEco-Tt 2014b, 5). The park will also sit atop Site 12, where housing
    has been closed due to contamination. The outer edge of the park, along the north edge of
    the island, is the location of a former solid waste disposal area, which has been identified as
    contaminated.

22 The Job Corps has been a target of attack by those in favor of smaller government since
    its inception. A systematic study of the Job Corps was undertaken during the Clinton
    administration, initiated by then labor secretary Robert Reich in 1993, which ultimately
    viewed the program favorably. The study, which took five years to complete, evaluated the
    program's sixty-eight thousand participants (McConnell and Glazerman 2001). The methods
    of the study itself, however, were subsequently compared with those of the Tuskegee
    Program by lawyers for the rejected applicants, who filed a successful lawsuit against
    the Department of Labor. Mathematica, the policy research group hired by the federal
    government for $17.9 million to complete the study, arbitrarily excluded one of every twelve
    eligible applicants in order to establish a control group for comparison. As John Price, a
    former admissions counselor during the time of the study explains, "All applicants during the
    study's 'random intake phase'—from November 1994 to February 1996—were asked to sign
    waivers agreeing to participate in the study. But if they refused, they were simply rejected
    and told to reapply after March 1996" (1999).

23 That a private tax for disaster avoidance could be integrated into the future planning of
    the site underscores the development's status as a luxury enclave with a relatively small
    percentage of affordable housing units. As such, it embodies what Mike Hodson and Simon
    Marvin describe as the "divisible security" of the premium environmental enclave (2010).

24   The representational conventions of similar nuclear assessments and other related reports connected to the arbitration of medical claims are analyzed by the cultural geographer Shiloh Krupar in her book *The Hot Spotter's Report* (2013).

25   The reporting by independent, nonprofit media on Treasure Island's development controversies reveals the transformation of investigative reporting and its relation to a highly differentiated public sphere, in an era where print journalism is in rapid decline and digital modes of the production and reception predominate. Several nonprofit centers for reporting in San Francisco, notably the Center for Investigative Reporting, the *San Francisco Public Press, Bay View,* and the remaining weekly alternative paper, *East Bay Express,* have all published and recirculated articles by the same authors across multiple platforms. Bay Area journalists Ashley Bates, Christopher Cook, Matt Smith, Katherine Mieszkowski, and Victoria Schlesinger have drawn attention to the toxic history of Treasure Island by republishing articles across multiple platforms, revealing previously undisclosed issues, amplifying and conducting parallel research on toxic experiences of the island's residents, and, together with other independent journalists, constructing a counter-history operating in the gaps of the official narrative, thereby constructing a counter-history to the official "scientific" version offered in multiple iterations by the Navy. The practice of cross-publishing, often recycling entire portions of articles, sometimes with only minor changes in title and content, recall the reiteration characteristic of the Navy's updates to its baseline reports through successive memoranda. In the case of the independent journalists, the effect is (unlike the Navy's) to distribute rather than concentrate knowledge, to magnify contradictions rather than attempt to resolve them, and to expose inconsistencies, often synchronically and diachronically. As the development of Treasure Island has proceeded the two knowledge systems have merged into a single interacting information ecology, one fueled by the massive resources of the Navy, and the other produced on a shoestring and coming from below in ways that official agencies have often been unable to predict (see, for example, Schlesinger 2010a, 2010b, 2010c, 2010d; Bates 2012a, 2012b). In this way journalistic excess and repetition is channeled to redirect economies of attention and connect different constituencies of readers together in new political formations. The process of attention gathering has been discussed at length by Richard Lanham in *Economies of Attention: Style and Substance in the Age of Information* (2006).

26   A sequence of California Department of Public Health reports—written by John G. Fassell, chief, Radioactive Material Inspection, Compliance and Enforcement Section—were issued in September 2012. They investigated areas that reporters and local residents had raised concerns about in children entering the Shaw environmental storage area, concerns about possible contamination at the Treasure Island Childcare Center, the Boys and Girls Club, the Kendrex Winery, the first site of USS *Pandemonium,* as well as various backyards. All sites indicated background levels of radiation, which are considered equivalent to those occurring naturally and deemed safe (Fassell, interviews with the author, September 2012).

27   A time capsule was also buried at the New York World's Fair at Flushing Meadows, the other major exposition in the United States in 1939. The New York capsule was sponsored by (and named after) the Westinghouse Corporation. Unlike the GGIE's chest, the Westinghouse capsule doubled as a demonstration of scientific ingenuity:

> "The Time Capsule, a metal tube containing a record of our civilization, was buried fifty feet underground at the Westinghouse building . . . to remain there for 5,000 years . . . it contains thirty-five articles of common use and a microfilm record equivalent to 10,000,000 words of printed matter. . . . It is made of copper alloy called Cupaloy which can be tempered to the hardness of steel and yet has a resistance to corrosion equal to pure copper. The torpedo-shaped shell is lined with an envelope of heat-resistant glass set in waterproof wax" (*Science Magazine* 1941, 251).

28   For more on the relationship between "feeling modern" and urbanization of neoliberal capitalism, see Adrian Parr's arguments about the conversion of Chicago into a city that is officially "green" (2013, 111–30).

29   Ulrich Beck uses the term "non-knowledge" to characterize the fundamental paradox of the unpredictable global present: "World risk society is non-knowledge society in a very precise way. In contrast to the pre-modern era, it cannot be overcome by more and better knowledge, more and better science; rather, precisely the opposite holds: it is the product of more and better science" (2009, 115). For a discussion of the politics of prophesy in the liberal political imaginary, see Brad Evans and Julian Reid's *Resilient Life: The Art of Living Dangerously* (2014, 180–90).

References

Alden, Andrew. 2011. "New Fossils from the Caldecott Tunnel." *KQED Quest,* May 26. http://ww2.kqed.org/quest/2011/05/26/new-fossils-from-the-caldecott-tunnel/.

Amoore, Louise. 2013. *The Politics of Possibility. Risk and Security beyond Probability.* Durham, NC: Duke University Press.

Anderson, Palmer R. 1973. "Job Corps and Neighborhood Youth Corps." *Humboldt Journal of Social Relations* 1, no. 1 (Fall): 8–16.

Barger, Kenny. 2014. "Lennar Snags Lake Worth Site at Big Discount." *The Real Deal* (blog), July 7. http://therealdeal.com/miami/blog/2014/07/07/lennar-snags-lake-worth-site-at-big-discount/#sthash.ldekYQbM.dpuf.

Bates, Ashley. 2012a. "Treasure Island. A Radioactive Isle." *East Bay Express,* September 5. http://www.eastbayexpress.com/oakland/treasure-island-a-radioactive-isle/Content?oid = 3328952.

———. 2012b. "Contamination Destination." *East Bay Express,* October 31. http://www.eastbayexpress.com/oakland/contamination-destination/Content?oid = 3378809.

Beck, Ulrich. 2007. *World at Risk.* Cambridge: Polity Press.

Bernanke, Ben. 2012. "Monetary Policy since the Onset of the Crisis." *Board of Governors Federal Reserve System,* August 31. http://www.federalreserve.gov/newsevents/speech/bernanke20120831a.htm.

Blake, Scott. 2014. "Lennar Takes Niche Housing Route." *Miami Today,* February 26. http://www.miamitodaynews.com/2014/02/26/lennar-takes-niche-housing-route/.

Brownell, Amy D. 2012. Internal Department of Public Health letter dated October 15, 2012. San Francisco: San Francisco Department of Public Health.

Cairns, Stephen, and Jane M. Jacobs. 2013. *Buildings Must Die. A Perverse View of Architecture.* Cambridge, MA: MIT Press.

Clinton Climate Initiative (CCI). 2009. "Clinton Climate Initiative to Demonstrate Model for Sustainable Urban Growth with Projects in 10 Countries on Six Continents." Press Release, May 19. https://www.clintonfoundation.org/main/news-and-media/press-releases-and-statements/press-release-clinton-climate-initiative-to-demostrate-model-for-sustainable-urb.html.

Connery, Christopher L. 1994. "Pacific Rim Discourse. The U.S. Cold War Imaginary in the Late Cold War Years." *Boundary 2* 21, no. 1:30–56.

Cook, Christopher D. 2010. "Homebuilder Lennar Uses Federal Taxpayer Funds to Balance Its Books." *San Francisco Public Press,* July 6. http://sfpublicpress.org/news/2010-06/homebuilder-lennar-uses-federal-taxpayer-funds-to-balance-its-books.

Cooper, Tim. 2010. "Recycling Modernity: Waste and Environmental History." *History Compass* 8, no. 9 (September): 1114–1125.

Corkery, Michael. 2009. "Land Deal Helps Builders Stay Alive." *Wall Street Journal,* June 26. http://online.wsj.com/articles/SB124562564321835575.

Cuff, Denis. 2010. "Caldecott Tunnel 4th Bore Dig Unearths Fossils from Millions of Years Ago." *San Jose Mercury News,* July 18. http://www.mercurynews.com/ci_15548021.

Erickson, Merle, L., Shane M. Heitzman, and X. Frank Zhang. 2013. "Tax Motivated Loss Shifting." *Accounting Review* 88, no. 5 (September): 1657–1682.

Evans, Brad, and Julian Reid. 2014. *Resilient Life: The Art of Living Dangerously.* Cambridge: Polity Press.

Gabrys, Jennifer. 2009. "Sink: The Dirt of Systems." *Environment & Planning D: Society & Space* 27:666–681.

Gille, Zsuzsa. 2007. *From the Cult of Waste to the Trash Heap of History: The Politics of Waste in Socialist and Postsocialist Hungary.* Bloomington: Indiana University Press.

Gittelsohn, John, and Heather Perlberg. 2013. "Blackstone Rushes $2.5 Billion Purchase as Homes Rise." *Bloomberg News,* January 9. http://www.bloomberg.com/news/2013-01-09/blackstone-steps-up-home-buying-as-prices-jump-mortgages.html.

Hansen, Kenneth N. 2004. *The Greening of Pentagon Brownfields: Using Environmental Discourse to Redevelop Former Military Bases.* Lanham, MD: Lexington Books.

Hawkes, Alison, and Bernice Young. 2010. "Through Two Mayors, Connected Island Developers Cultivated Profitable Deal." *San Francisco Public Press,* July 1. http://sfpublicpress.org/news/2010-06/through-two-mayors-connected-island-developers-cultivated-profitable-deal.

Hodson, Mike, and Simon Marvin. 2010. "Urbanism in the Anthropocene: Ecological Urbanism or Premium Ecological Enclaves." *City: Analysis of Urban Trends, Culture, Theory and Political Action* 14, no. 3:298–313.

Holston, James. 1989. *The Modernist City: An Anthropological Critique of Brasilia.* Chicago: University of Chicago Press.

Kennedy, Greg. 2007. *An Ontology of Trash: The Disposable and Its Problematic Nature.* Albany: State University of New York Press.

Krupar, Shiloh R. 2013. *Hot Spotter's Report: Military Fables of Toxic Waste.* Minneapolis: University of Minnesota Press.

———. 2015. "Situated Spectacle: Cross-Sectional Soil Hermeneutics of the 2010 Shanghai World Expo." In *Spaces of Danger: Culture and Power in the Everyday,* ed. Heather Merrill and Lisa M. Hoffman, 152–187. Athens: University of Georgia Press.

Labaton, Stephen, and David M. Herszenhorn. 2008. "Big Tax Breaks for Businesses in Housing Bill." *New York Times,* April 16. http://www.nytimes.com/2008/04/16/business/16bailout.html.

Lanham, Richard. 2006. *Economies of Attention. Style and Substance in the Age of Information.* Chicago: University of Chicago Press.

League of Women Voters of Utah. 2005. "Political Decisions and Nuclear Waste Storage in Utah." January. Salt Lake City, UT: LWVU. https://user.xmission.com/~lwvut/Studies/Political%20Decisions%20and%20Nuclear%20Waste%20Storage%20in%20Utah.pdf.

Lenhart, Gloria. 2013. "New Caldecott Tunnel Opens." *Guidelines: Newsletter for San Francisco City Guides and Sponsors.* http://www.sfcityguides.org/public_guidelines.html.

Maffly, Brian. 2016. "With EnergySolutions' Acquisition of Waste-Disposal Competitor, Is Depleted Uranium Still Headed for Utah?" *Salt Lake Tribune,* January 20. http://www.sltrib.com/home/3203096-155/utahs-energysolutions-to-acquire-key-waste-disposal.

Mauer, Mark. 2013. "Lennar Homes Gets 39 Percent Discount on Foreclosed Davie Townhouse." *The Real Deal,* July 8. http://therealdeal.com/miami/blog/2013/07/08/lennar-homes-gets-39-percent-discount-on-foreclosed-davie-townhouse/#sthash.0AOmm8vr.dpuf.

McConnell, Sheena, and Steven Glazerman. 2011. "National Job Corps Study: The Benefits and Cost of Job Corps." *Mathematica Policy Research,* June 2011.

McMahon, Dinny, and Robbie Whelan. 2012. "China in Talks with US Homebuilder." *Wall Street Journal,* June 25. http://online.wsj.com/articles/SB10001424052702304458604577489062449154168.

Medovoi, Leerom. 2010. "A Contribution to the Critique of Political Ecology: Sustainability as Disavowal." *New Formations* 69 (Summer): 129–143. doi:10.3898/neWf.69.07.2010.

Mooallem, Jon. 2009. "The Self-Storage Self." *New York Times*, September 2. http://www.nytimes.com/2009/09/06/magazine/06self-storage-t.html.

Naidoo, Ridhika. 2009. "SOM: The Rising Tides Competition." *DesignBoom,* August 3, 2009. http://www.designboom.com/architecture/som-the-bayarc-rising-tides-competition/.

Naval Station Treasure Island (NSTI). 2013. "Site 12. NTCRA at Bigelow Court. BRAC Clean-up Team Meeting." November 20.

Nguyen, Vicky, Liz Wagner, and Jeremy Carroll. 2013. "Navy Subcontractor Breaks Silence about Treasure Island Radiation." *NBC News,* December 12. http://www.nbcbayarea.com/news/local/Navy-Subcontractor-Breaks-Silence-About-Radiation-Contamination-at-Treasure-Island--235499911.html.

Office of Military Base Conversion (OMBC). 1996. "Naval Station Treasure Island Reuse Plan, Draft Plan." San Francisco: City and County of San Francisco, Planning Department.

Parr, Adrian. 2013. *The Wrath of Capital: Neoliberalism and Climate Change Politics,* chapter 7. New York: Columbia University Press.

Pellissier, Hank. 2010. "Local Intelligence: Building 1." *New York Times,* August 21. http://www.nytimes.com/2010/08/22/us/22bcintel.html.

Phelan, Sarah. 2008. "Selling Our City to Lennar Corporation," *Race, Poverty and the Environment* 15, no. 1 (Spring): 33–35.

Piagnataro, Anthony. 2010. "Treasure Island's Toxic Problem." *Cal Watchdog,* October 11. http://calwatchdog.com/2010/10/11/treasure-islands-toxic-problem/.

Pipes, Jason. 2007. *Images of America. San Francisco's Treasure Island.* San Francisco: Arcadia Publishing.

Popular Mechanics. 1939. "Treasure Island of 1939." May. [Souvenir reprint.]

Quandagno, Jill, and Catherine Forbes. 1995. "The Welfare State and the Cultural Production of Gender: The Making of Good Girls and Boys." *Social Problems* 42, no. 2 (May): 171–190.

Rawlins, Lane V. 1971. "The Urban Center as a Training Facility." *Journal of Human Resources* 6, no. 2 (Spring): 221–235.

Reinhardt, Richard. 1978. *Treasure Island, 1939–1940: San Francisco's Exposition Years.* Mill Valley, CA: Squarebooks.

Rignot, Eric, J. Mouginot, Mathieu Morlinghem, Helene Seroussi, and Bernd Scheuchi. 2014. "Widespread, rapid grounding line retreat of Pine Island, Thwaites, Smith, and Kohler glaciers, West Antarctica, from 1992 to 2011." *Geophysical Research Letters* 41, no. 10 (May 28): 3502–3509.

Ross, Andrew. 1996. "The Future Is a Risky Business." In *Future Natural: Nature, Science, Culture,* ed. George Robertson, Melinda Mash, Lisa Tickner, Jon Bird, Barry Curtis, and Tim Putnam. London: Routledge.

Rydell, Robert, and Laura B. Schiavo, and Matthew Bokovy, eds. 2010. *Designing Tomorrow. America's World's Fairs of the 1930s.* New Haven, CT: Yale University Press.

San Francisco Bay Exposition. 1939. *Official Guide Book: 1939 Golden Gate International Exposition on San Francisco Bay.* Rev. ed. San Francisco: The Crocker Company.

Scanlan, John. 2005. *On Garbage.* London: Reaktion Books.

Schlesinger, Victoria. 2010a. "Pollution: Experts Concerned about Treasure Island Cleanup as Seas Rise." *SF Public Press,* June 29. http://sfpublicpress.org/news/2010-06/pollution-experts-concerned-about-treasure-island-cleanup-as-seas-rise.

———. 2010b. "Uncertain about Rising Seas, Developers Use Mid-Range Estimates to Build Up Island." *SF Public Press,* June 29. http://sfpublicpress.org/news/2010-06/uncertain-about-rising-seas-developers-using-mid-range-estimate-to-build-up-island.

———. 2010c. "Financial Upside for Developer Is Long-Term and Risky, City Says." *SF Public Press,* July 1. http://sfpublicpress.org/news/2010-06/financial-upside-for-developers-is-long-term-and-risky-city-says.

———. 2010d. "Treasure Island Building Plan Draws Fire," *SF Public Press,* November 29: http://sfpublicpress.org/news/2010-11/treasure-island-building-plans-draw-fire.

Science Magazine. 1941. "Westinghouse Time Capsule." Vol. 94, no. 2439 (September 12): 251.

Scott, James, C. 1999. "The High Modernist City: An Experiment and a Critique." In *Seeing Like a State: How Certain Schemes to Improve the Human Condition Have Failed.* New Haven, CT: Yale University Press.

Shine, William A. 1968. "Can We Learn from the Job Corps." *High School Journal* 52, no. 2 (November): 73–82.

Smith, Matt. 2013. "Chairman Willie: Chairman Willie Brown's Not So Secret Connection to the Hunters Point Connection." *SF Weekly News,* July 17.

Smith, Matt, and Katherine Mieszkowski. 2014. "Treasure Island Cleanup Exposes Navy's Mishandling of Its Nuclear Past." *Bulletin of the Atomic Scientists,* February 24. http://thebulletin.org/treasure-island-cleanup-exposes-navy%E2%80%99s-mishandling-its-nuclear-past.

Stierli, Martino. 2013. "Building No Place." *Journal of Architectural Education* 67, no. 1 (March): 8–16.

Streitfeld, David. 2008. "Losing a Home, Then Losing All out of Storage." *New York Times.* May 11. http://www.nytimes.com/2008/05/11/business/11storage.html.

Time. 2008. "The New New Deal." Vol. 172, no. 21, November 24. http://content.time.com/time/covers/0,16641,20081124,00.html.

Treasure Island Development Authority (TIDA). 2011. "Treasure Island and Yerba Buena Island Design for Development." San Francisco: TIDA.

Treasure Island Museum Association (TIMA). 2003. "About Treasure Island." April 16. http://www.treasureislandmuseum.org/island.html.

TriEco-Tt. 2012. *Historical Radiological Assessment, Supplemental Technical Memorandum* (HRASTM). Washington, DC: US Department of the Navy, Base Realignment and Closure Office.

———. 2014a. *Historical Radiological Assessment, Supplemental Technical Memorandum* (HRASTM-1). Part 1. Washington, DC: US Department of the Navy, Base Realignment and Closure Office.

———. 2014b. *Historical Radiological Assessment, Supplemental Technical Memorandum* (HRASTM-2). Part 2. Washington, DC: US Department of the Navy, Base Realignment and Closure Office.

United States of America and the Treasure Island Development Authority (United States/TIDA). 2014. "Economic Development Conveyance Memorandum of Agreement for the Conveyance of the Naval Station Treasure Island." July 2. San Francisco.

van Wyck, Peter C. 2005. *Signs of Danger: Waste, Trauma and Nuclear Threat.* Kingston, Ontario: McGill-Queens University Press.

———. 2010. *The Highway of the Atom.* Kingston, Ontario: McGill-Queen's University Press.

Virtual Museum of the City of San Francisco (VMCSF). 1942. "Treasure Island Goes to Navy." *San Francisco News,* April 17. http://www.sfmuseum.net/hist9/tiseizure.html.

Weston Solutions. 2006. *Treasure Island Naval Station: Historical Radiological Assessment* (HRA). Washington, DC: US Department of the Navy, Base Realignment and Closure Office.

Contributors

Javier Arbona is a Chancellor's Postdoctoral Fellow in the American Studies Department at the University of California, Davis. He earned his PhD in geography from the University of California, Berkeley. Arbona conducted research on World War II with the Oral History Office at the Bancroft Library at the University of California, Berkeley. He is at work on a book manuscript about the landscapes of black radicalism in the Bay Area's World War II home front.

C. Greig Crysler is an associate professor of architectural theory and criticism, and Arcus Chair of Gender, Sexuality and the Built Environment, in the Department of Architecture at the College of Environmental Design, University of California, Berkeley. His research focuses on the theories and practices of architecture, urbanism, and the built environment in the context of globalization, activism, and the politics of cultural identity. He is the author of *Writing Spaces: Discourses of Architecture, Urbanism, and the Built Environment, 1960–2000* (Routledge, 2003) and co-editor with Stephen Cairns and Hilde Heynen of the *Sage Handbook of Architectural Theory* (2012). He is currently completing a co-authored book with Shiloh Krupar titled *Waste Complex: Capital / Ecology / Sovereignty.*

Lindsey Dillon is an assistant professor of sociology at the University of California, Santa Cruz. Her work focuses on environmental justice, urban ecologies, and histories of race and racism in US cities. She received her PhD in geography from the University of California, Berkeley, where she studied environmental politics in San Francisco, focusing on the Hunters Point Naval Shipyard. Her current work includes research on biomonitoring technologies and urban sustainability.

Mark L. Gillem, PhD, FAIA, AICP, is a professor of architecture and landscape architecture at the University of Oregon and director of the university's Urban Design Lab. He also serves as the director of the International Association for the Study of Traditional Environments. He is the author of numerous publications on urban design and development in the United States and abroad. In addition, he is the founder and principal of the Urban Collaborative, a multidisciplinary urban design firm. His firm's urban designs and master plans have received numerous regional and national awards. He has a PhD in architecture and a master's of architecture from the University of California, Berkeley, and a bachelor's of architecture with highest distinction from the University of Kansas. He is a licensed architect and certified planner and a member of the American Institute of Architects College of Fellows.

Lynne Horiuchi is an architectural historian who received her PhD in 2005 from the University of California, Santa Barbara. She has taught at the University of North

Carolina in the College of Architecture. Her work is cross-disciplinary, examining concepts of imprisonment, race, space, mobility, everyday racism, and civil justice. She is currently writing a book on the production of the prison camps built for Japanese Americans, *Dislocations and Relocations: Building Prison Cities for Japanese and Japanese Americans during World War II* (University of Washington Press, forthcoming). She has published widely in journals and collections on racial covenants, urban development, racialized sites, spatial jurisdictions, national belonging, and artistic representation in prison camps. She was named a National Endowment of the Arts Fellow at MacDowell Colony and has won numerous notable awards that include National Endowment for the Humanities grants.

Tanu Sankalia is an associate professor in the Department of Art + Architecture and program director of the interdisciplinary program in Urban Studies at the University of San Francisco, where he has been teaching since 2006. He was trained in architecture and urban design at the School of Architecture, Ahmedabad, India, and the University of California, Berkeley. He is currently engaged in a wide range of research projects, including work on public space and citizenship in Mumbai, comparative readings of cities in the Global South with a focus on Latin America and South Asia, and a book manuscript titled *The Urban Unseen,* a historical, theoretical, and design exploration of interstitial spaces in San Francisco's historic urban fabric.

Lisa D. Schrenk is an associate professor of architectural history at the University of Arizona. She received a bachelor of arts from Macalester College, a master's in architectural history from the University of Virginia, and a PhD in art history from the University of Texas at Austin. She has published and lectured widely on international expositions. Her book *Building a Century of Progress: The Architecture of Chicago's 1933–34 World's Fair* (University of Minnesota Press, 2007) was named to Choice Review's 2008 List of Outstanding Academic Titles. A former education director of the Frank Lloyd Wright Home and Studio Foundation, she is currently completing the book *An Architectural Laboratory: The Oak Park Studio of Frank Lloyd Wright* (University of Chicago Press). Dr. Schrenk has served on various professional committees, including as president of the Chicago Society of Architectural Historians, and on the board of directors of the Society of Architectural Historians. Her academic research was featured in a full-page article in the *Chronicle for Higher Education*.

Andrew M. Shanken is a professor in the Department of Architecture at the University of California, Berkeley, where he teaches courses in architectural and urban history, and American studies. His book *194X: Architecture, Planning, and Consumer Culture on the American Homefront* (2009) examines anticipatory designs created on the American homefront. *Into the Void Pacific: Building the 1939 San Francisco World's Fair* was published in 2015. He has published widely on the topic of architecture and memory. His wider academic interests include the unbuilt and paper architecture, visionary architecture and expositions, themed landscapes, heritage and conservation planning, traditions of representation in twentieth-century architecture and planning, keywords in architecture and American culture, and consumer culture and architecture.

John Stehlin is a broadly trained urban geographer with a PhD from the University of California, Berkeley. He teaches geography at the University of California, Berkeley, and urban studies at the University of San Francisco. His research interrogates the relationship between sustainability planning and economic growth in American cities in the context of regional fragmentation and pervasive race and class inequality, with a particular focus on mobility.

Richard A. Walker is a professor emeritus of geography at the University of California, Berkeley, where he taught from 1975 to 2012 and served as chair of Geography, Global Metropolitan Studies, and California Studies. He has written on a diverse range of topics in economic, urban, and environmental geography and is co-author of *The Capitalist Imperative* (1989) and *The New Social Economy* (1992). He has written extensively on California, including *The Conquest of Bread* (2004), *The Country in the City* (2007), and *The Atlas of California* (2013). His awards include Fulbright and Guggenheim Fellowships, a Distinguished Scholarship Award of the Association of American Geographers, the Carey McWilliams Award from California Studies Association, and the Hal Rothman prize from the Western History Association.

Index

Page numbers in **boldface** refer to illustrations.